The

Fourth Labour

Government

The

Fourth Labour
Government

Radical Politics in New Zealand

Edited by
Jonathan Boston and Martin Holland

Auckland
OXFORD UNIVERSITY PRESS
Melbourne   Oxford   New York

Oxford University Press

OXFORD   NEW YORK   TORONTO
DELHI   BOMBAY   CALCUTTA   MADRAS   KARACHI
PETALING JAYA   SINGAPORE   HONG KONG   TOKYO
NAIROBI   DAR ES SALAAM   CAPE TOWN
MELBOURNE   AUCKLAND
and associated companies in
BEIRUT   BERLIN   IBADAN   NICOSIA

Oxford is a trade mark of Oxford University Press

First published 1987
©Oxford University Press 1987

ISBN 0 19 558161 X

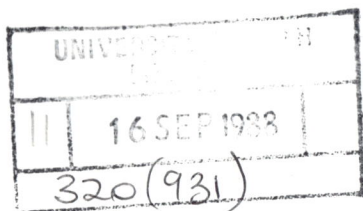

Cover designed by John McNulty
Photoset in Bembo from supplied electronic media
by Jacobsons, Auckland
and printed in Hong Kong
Published by Oxford University Press
5 Ramsgate Street, Auckland, New Zealand

Contents

Acknowledgements

We would like to thank the *New Zealand Political Studies Association* for providing the initial inspiration for this book: the theme of the 1986 conference was "New Zealand Under Labour" and unrevised versions of five chapters were originally presented as conference papers. We would also like to acknowledge the assistance provided by the Department of Political Science at the University of Canterbury, in particular, the excellent word-processing work undertaken by Liz Dobson, Janice Storer and Jill Dolby.

The editors are indebted to numerous individuals who have commented on earlier drafts of specific chapters. We would like to offer our special thanks to Keith Jackson, Chris Laidlaw, Peter Brosnan, Tom Berthold, Stuart McMillan, Charles Crothers, Philip Joseph, Graeme Dunstall, Chris Eastgate, Michael Mintrom, Simon Orme, Ewan McCann and Luke Trainor. We would also like to extend our special thanks to Rob Lay for compiling Appendix II and Mark Laffey, Ann Morrison, and Christine Moore for proof-reading the final manuscript.

Lastly, the editors would like to thank the contributors without whose hard work and co-operation it would not have been possible to produce this book.

J.B. and M.H.
October, 1986

Abbreviations

ALP Australian Labor Party
ANZAC Australia New Zealand Army Corps
ANZUS Australia New Zealand United States
ASEAN Association of South-East Asian Nations
CANWAR Campaign Against Nuclear War
CER Closer Economic Relations
EEC European Economic Community
GDP Gross Domestic Product
GNP Gross National Product
GSP Generalised System of Preferences
GST Goods and Services Tax
IPPNW International Physicians for the Prevention of Nuclear War
LDCs Less Developed Countries
MP Member of Parliament
NZBC New Zealand Broadcasting Corporation
OECD Organization for Economic Co-operation and Development
PERT Programme Evaluation Review Technique
POSDCORB Planning, Organizing, Staffing, Directing, Co-ordinating, Reporting, Budgeting
PPBS Planning, Programming, Budgeting Systems
Qango Quasi Autonomous Non-governmental Organization
SADCC Southern African Development Coordination Conference
SMP Supplementary Minimum Price
SPARTECA South Pacific Regional Trade and Economic Cooperation Agreement
UDI Unilateral Declaration of Independence
UN United Nations

Foreword

Just three decades ago New Zealand was in the top five of the world's wealthiest nations. Today we rank twenty-fifth. The choice New Zealanders face at the General Election of 1987 is to continue the process of change begun by this Government and enter the twenty-first century the envy of others, or return to the policies that preceded this Government and see New Zealand fall into the bottom half of the ranking of nations by wealth. That is why the 1987 election is the most important for the future of New Zealand since the election of the first Labour Government in 1935.

The politics of change, which is the theme of this book, is about turning around this serious decline in New Zealand's economic circumstances and regaining our former position. The ultimate objective is not wealth as such, but having the economic means to attain social goals.

The objective of this book is to help illuminate the key issues that face New Zealanders and assess the consequences of the solutions adopted by the fourth Labour Government. But of even greater importance is the consequences of *not* proceeding with this process of change. It is always easier to do nothing. To initiate change involves risks and creates uncertainties which upset people.

It is here that political scientists and commentators have an important part to play. As I observed in my 1986 address to the New Zealand Political Studies Association, interpreting the politics of change poses a real challenge to the student and analyst of politics. Because change by its very nature involves all the difficulties and uncertainties of a period of transition it is very easy to be negative, and focus on the problems and 'pain' that always accompany change. Naturally the Government's political opponents will seek to exploit the fears created by these uncertainties, but the role of the political scientist is surely to step back from the heat of the political battle and provide an objective analysis which puts events into their proper perspective.

This book provides both a useful record of some of the major changes initiated by this Government, and some telling insights into the current state of New Zealand political science. With a few notable exceptions the essays are more in the nature of political commentaries than 'scientific' analysis. This is not a criticism, as it makes for a much more readable book which seeks to reach an audience far beyond the academic community. There is a real need for more in-depth political analysis of this type. But, as with all political commentary, the reader should be made aware of the writer's own preconceptions and motivations. Scientific objectivity can be tested by having several scientists examining the same evidence and seeing if they reach the same conclusion. Political commentators rarely agree. Such objectivity cannot be achieved in political analysis because politics is a very fluid process in which we are all involved.

What is required at a time of great change is information which will enable the people to understand the process of change, and to make their own judgement. This book assists that process.

David Lange

1

The Fourth Labour Government
Transforming the Political Agenda

Jonathan Boston and Martin Holland

The election of New Zealand's fourth Labour Government in July 1984 brought more than simply a change in political leadership and a reshuffling of the seating arrangements in Parliament; it marked a crucial turning point in the style, character and content of the politics of the post-war era. In virtually every field of public policy long-standing assumptions have been questioned, vested interests challenged, and existing approaches and solutions re-evaluated and often abandoned. In the economic realm, for example, the Labour Government has set in motion a revolution that has affected, to varying degrees, all aspects of New Zealand society: wage and price controls have been removed; the finance sector has been liberalized; the New Zealand dollar has been floated; import controls have been progressively removed and tariffs reduced; agricultural subsidies have been terminated; the tax system has been radically altered; public expenditure in various areas has been substantially reduced and a major restructuring of the State sector has been inaugurated. The aim of all these reforms has been to create a more open, competitive, market-led economy and hence establish — or so it is argued — the necessary conditions for faster economic growth, a higher level of employment, and ultimately a more secure and equitable social welfare system.

In the field of defence policy and diplomacy the Government's approach has been no less radical. Here Labour's anti-nuclear stance has brought the virtual demise of the long-standing ANZUS Treaty and has necessitated a complete reappraisal of New Zealand's identity and role in the Western alliance.

Apart from these abrupt changes in economic and foreign policy, there also have been important reforms in many other policy areas. A Ministry of Women's Affairs has been established. The operation and organization of Parliament have been overhauled. Significant changes have been made to the examination system and curriculum in secondary schools. Prescription charges have been introduced. There has been a move away from the principle of universality in the provision of welfare benefits and a concomitant emphasis on targeting assistance to those considered to be most in need. Moreover, further important changes are planned. A Royal Commission to review social policy is due to report in 1988 and a major restructuring of pay fixing in the public and private sectors is scheduled for 1987. There is the prospect of significant changes in electoral arrangements arising out of the report of the Royal Commission on the Electoral System. And the report of the Royal

Commission on Broadcasting, published on 30 October 1986, recommended reform of public radio and television services.

In terms of the scope and magnitude of the reforms introduced to date, the fourth Labour Government undoubtedly rivals the Liberal Government of the 1890s and the first Labour Government of the 1930s. In terms of the speed with which policies have been amended, it is without peer, certainly in peacetime. Even more remarkable, however, has been Labour's abandonment of many of its traditional commitments and concerns. As Vowles highlights in Chapter 2 of this volume, many of the decisions of the fourth Labour Government, particularly in the economic sphere, constitute a complete reversal of the policies ushered in by the first Labour Government. Whereas the Labour Government of the 1930s introduced a regime of agricultural subsidies and guaranteed commodity prices, the Lange Government has abandoned such policies. Likewise, the first Labour Government embarked upon various protectionist measures, nationalized the Bank of New Zealand, and maintained that the State had a major role to play in directing investment flows and influencing the level of economic activity. By contrast, the fourth Labour Government has reduced the level of border protection enjoyed by New Zealand industry, authorized the sale of shares in the Bank of New Zealand, and cast doubt on the wisdom of State-led investment and an active fiscal policy.

Hence, the initiatives undertaken by the fourth Labour Government amount to far more than mere tinkering with existing policy settings; they represent a decisive break with the past. As Colin James has put it: "This is by any standards a radical government — but radical in directions not at all expected of Labour parties" (*National Business Review*, 15 July 1985, p.49).

Yet if Labour's programme of economic liberalization and institutional reform is unprecedented in New Zealand history, it is by no means unique in the Western world. During the past decade or so many governments of both a social-democratic and conservative orientation have re-evaluated the question of how best to achieve their objectives and as a result have chosen, almost universally, to rely more heavily on market mechanisms (within an appropriate legislative framework) and less heavily on detailed State intervention. For example, such developments have been apparent in Australia, Britain, France and West Germany. What is perhaps unusual about the New Zealand experience, therefore, is not so much the direction of the recent policy changes, but the scope of the reforms and the determination and speed with which they have been instituted.

From the Old Order ...

The extent to which the fourth Labour Government has "broken the mould" of post-war politics in New Zealand and transformed the political agenda can be gauged by contrasting the main features of the politico-economic order before, and after, July 1984. The hallmarks of the old order, which took root in the late nineteenth century and became more firmly entrenched as a result of the actions of the first Labour Government, can be summarized as follows.

To begin with, it was assumed that the State had an active and major role to play in the nation's economic affairs, in the promotion of social justice and in the betterment of the human condition. Not merely did this include measures for correcting market failures, it also involved State provision of goods and services, the detailed regulation of economic activity (including decisions on production and pricing), the redistribution of income, and the supply of welfare benefits for those in need. Correspondingly, the role of the market as an allocative mechanism was diminished and the legitimacy of market outcomes called into question. Such a state of affairs was accepted with only limited demur by both National and Labour and led, almost inevitably, to a highly interventionist mode of economic management – what might be termed "heavily regulated capitalism". This reached its zenith during the pragmatic, populist Muldoon Administration in the form of huge State-backed and funded development projects – the so-called "Think Big" strategy – and the implementation of comprehensive, mandatory controls on prices, wages and interest rates (Muldoon, 1985, pp.87-144).

Coupled with this advocacy of an activist State was the quest for economic stability, security and certainty. At the macroeconomic level this found practical expression in the vigorous pursuit of Keynesian-type demand-management strategies and the maintenance of a fixed exchange rate – at least until 1979 when a crawling-peg exchange-rate regime was introduced. Such policies were supported with guaranteed prices for agricultural commodities, various kinds of subsidies and incentives to the export sector, the maintenance of a substantial level of border protection for domestic manufacturing, the tight control of capital markets, strict limits on foreign ownership, and a highly regulated labour market. In all this the primary aim was to ensure that economic change was planned and gradual, that the economy was shielded as much as possible from the negative consequences of destabilizing events abroad, that the costs of economic adjustment were evenly spread throughout the community, and that full employment was maintained – even at the price of substantial foreign borrowing.

The emphasis on stability and security in the economic realm was mirrored by a similar quest in other policy arenas. Thus in its foreign policy New Zealand, as a "small state", gladly stood in the protective shadow of a major power, at first Great Britain and latterly the United States. In keeping with this it avoided independent policy initiatives which might destabilize or undermine its alliance relationship. A similar stress on stability can be found elsewhere, be it with respect to social policy, the organization and administration of the public sector, or the maintenance of existing political institutions and conventions. To be sure, changes happened from time to time as necessity or expediency dictated; policy settings were not completely rigid or static; but most of the adjustments which did occur tended to be incremental and *ad hoc*, rather than part of a comprehensive and internally consistent package. Above all, there was little rigorous questioning of the basic philosophical principles and ideological assumptions underpinning the existing policy framework.

One of the reasons for this was the sensitivity of the governing party, be it National or Labour, to the demands of the powerful, highly organized, sectional interest groups which dominated the political landscape. As the post-war era unfolded these groups, such as Federated Farmers, the Producer Boards, the Manufacturers Federation and the Federation of Labour, became more and more entrenched in the political system and were increasingly drawn into the process of decision-making. While such corporatist arrangements had the advantage of helping to ensure a degree of consensus on major policy issues, and thus strengthened the forces of cohesion and stability, they also had certain deleterious consequences. For example, there was a tendency for the major sector groups to acquire an expanding range of governmental concessions and privileges. These not merely imposed a cost upon the State, but they often altered the operation of the market, thwarted entrepreneurial initiative and reduced the flexibility and adaptability of the economy. Almost inevitably this process resulted in a large political constituency with a vested interest in resisting change: manufacturers sought to maintain existing levels of protection; unions strove to preserve, if not improve, the real wages of their members; and farmers demanded Government action to defend their incomes in the face of rising input costs and falling export prices. Confronted with such pressures there was a natural reluctance on the part of the major political parties to advocate, let alone implement, sweeping reforms. After all, the consequences of a political backlash were well known — electoral defeat. Instead, governments comforted themselves with the false hope that structural problems and conflicts of interest could either be wished away through increased public expenditure or else regulated out of existence.

The net result of this process was the growth of a pernicious form of institutional sclerosis, a complex web of administrative controls, a relatively low-growth economy (by international standards) and a massive increase in the nation's foreign debt. Interestingly, the New Zealand example seems to provide some support for Olson's thesis (1982) concerning the harmful economic consequences of democratic stability. According to Olson the longer an advanced industrialized democracy remains stable and avoids the upheavals caused by wars and economic crises, the greater the political power of organized interests, the more extensive the range of economic controls and regulations, and the slower the pace of economic growth.

In New Zealand's case these problems were compounded by the three year parliamentary term. In such a short electoral cycle, the political risks associated with bold policy initiatives likely to cause economic pain or spark concerted opposition were intensified; consequently, most governments were cautious and conservative.

Furthermore, in the absence of any significant constraints on the executive, and spurred on by the demands of adversary politics, there was an incentive for governments to manipulate economic activity for electoral gain. Such tactics were particularly evident during the 1970s and early 1980s, the leading and arguably most successful exponent being Sir Robert Muldoon.

The normal pattern was for a government to spend its first year in office implementing its manifesto commitments and making such unpopular decisions as were deemed absolutely necessary. The second year would see the Government attempting to consolidate its position and resolve such policy conflicts and inconsistencies which arose. The third year would witness the proliferation of election bribes and promises. Invariably, this would result in higher State expenditure and a larger fiscal deficit; if the Government were fortunate it would also produce a temporary increase in output, higher real disposable incomes and lower unemployment. Needless to say, there were costs associated with this manipulation of the economy for narrow political ends. It tended to exaggerate, rather than moderate, the effects of the business cycle. It reduced long-term investment and hence slowed the pace of economic growth, and led to progressively larger Budget deficits and a rapidly expanding public debt.

These were some of the hallmarks of the politico-economic order which dominated modern New Zealand politics until mid-1984. A colourful, albeit exaggerated, account of this period was furnished by David Lange in his 1986 Mackintosh Memorial Lecture:

> The government ruled through the corporate state. Vested interests prevailed. Farming, our largest export industry, was heavily subsidized to keep producing more and more of what the world wanted less and less. Farmers farmed for capital gain. The exchange rate was manipulated to support farm incomes. Farmers could accurately have been described as New Zealand's highest paid wage earners. The export sector of manufacturing was subsidised so that when innovation did appear, and it certainly did, it could immediately be swamped by subsidised competition. Monopolies improved their position. Trade unions were regulated out of work. Regulation and control proliferated, culminating in an attempt to legislate inflation out of existence (1986a, pp.17-18).

By the early 1980s the cumulative effects of the post-war legacy of *ad ho* economic interventionism by both major parties, political manipulation of the business cycle, and the dominance of organized, sectional interests were becoming abundantly plain. The results could be seen in the country's relative economic decline, slow rate of growth, poor adjustment to external supply shocks and adverse terms of trade, high levels of inflation, an increasing level of distribution dissent, the growth of structural unemployment, and mounting international indebtedness (Gould, 1982, pp.186-221; Treasury, 1984, pp.103-121). In the field of social policy the results were no less obvious: a massively expensive superannuation scheme (introduced as an electoral bribe); numerous anomalies and inconsistencies in the system of income maintenance; longer hospital waiting lists; increasingly unequal access to medical services; growing racial inequalities; and significant poverty, particularly among low, single-income families (Easton, 1986). Likewise, major problems in the State sector were apparent: the rate of return on public investments was low; many energy-related development projects experienced huge cost overruns; pricing decisions were influenced as much by political considerations as by sound economic criteria; State trading enterprises had imprecise and sometimes conflicting objectives; and there was inadequate parliamentary control and scrutiny of departmental activities. It would be wrong, of course, to place the blame for all these problems solely on poor management by the nation's political leadership. Undoubtedly many of New Zealand's difficulties can be traced to factors beyond the immediate control of the Government: its structural position in the world economy as an exporter of primary products, British entry into the European Community in 1973, and problems of access to overseas markets. Nevertheless, it was evident that whichever political party won the 1984 General Election some important policy changes would be essential.

... to the New Order

In the event the reforms introduced by the fourth Labour Government have been more substantial and far-reaching than anticipated. They have effectively ended the old politico-economic order.

At the heart of Labour's economic strategy is a fundamental questioning of an activist role for the State and an attempt to shift the mix of market and non-market activities in a "more-market" direction. In ideological terms this amounts to a move away from the eclectic combination of corporatist, paternalistic and socialist tendencies which characterized the post-war era, towards a form of market or economic liberalism. (Other labels sometimes used to describe roughly the same phenomena include the "new laissez-faire", "neoconservatism", and "monetarism".) In short, this means a greater acceptance of the allocative role of the market and a recognition that, with certain notable exceptions, it provides a relatively efficient mechanism for identifying, transmitting and satisfying human needs and wants (Harris, 1980). It also implies acceptance of the liberal view that market exchanges extend the domain of human choice, thereby reducing the level of coercion and promoting liberty. On the basis of such assumptions, the Labour Government has sought to disengage the State from those areas of the economy where this is possible and apply market-based criteria where, for one reason or another, complete disengagement is not feasible or desirable.

The magnitude of Labour's philosophical shift must not be exaggerated. The Government has not embraced the more extreme versions of a pro-market philosophy as advocated for example by Hayek or Nozick. It still remains committed to tempering market outcomes in the interests of equality of opportunity, social justice and the public good. As Lange has explained, the aim is to "reduce as much as possible the socially-damaging and disruptive effects of an economy which depends on self-interest without intervening to the point where the economy loses its motive force" (1986a, p.27). In this sense Labour remains a broadly social-democratic party, rather than a party of the "new right".

At the macroeconomic level the new approach has been highlighted by the rejection of Keynesian-type demand management policies, the floating of the New Zealand dollar, and the abandonment of formal incomes policies. Instead, as outlined by Easton (Chapter 8) and Boston (Chapter 9), the Government has committed itself to the pursuit of stable, consistent, and firm monetary and fiscal policies, and has stated repeatedly that it will not accommodate excessive wage and price increases. Despite the problems which have been experienced in fulfilling these objectives, there can be no doubt that Labour's present course represents a departure from the economic strategies of previous post-war governments. What is more, it is clear that the Government has little intention of adjusting its macroeconomic policy settings to suit the short-term interests of the electoral calendar. In any case, given the floating of the dollar, such an approach is now more risky, and less likely to succeed.

At the micro level, too, there has been a shift away from the pattern of detailed, often *ad hoc*, State regulation which characterized the post-war era. It has been replaced by various supply-side measures designed to improve efficiency, enhance the incentive structure and increase the flexibility of the economy. Such moves have been particularly evident in the finance sector, the labour market (as noted in Chapter 9), and in the management of the public sector (as discussed in Chapters 6 and 7). This has certainly not meant complete deregulation or the total withdrawal of the State; nor has it meant the large-scale privatization of public assets as has occurred, for example, in Britain under the Thatcher Government. Nevertheless, Labour's corporatization and commercialization policies in the public sector have brought sweeping changes, and, as indicated by Roberts and Gregory in this volume, rank as the most radical reforms since 1912. The changes in tax policy, discussed by Scott in Chapter 10, have been no less dramatic. The Government has altered the mix of tax revenues by placing a greater reliance on indirect taxes; overhauled the complicated system of sales tax and introduced a comprehensive single-rate Goods and Services Tax; and reduced substantially both marginal and average income tax rates. At the same time, it has made a number of significant changes in the area of income maintenance, including the introduction of a guaranteed minimum family income for those in employment.

It is not clear yet to what extent the principles of market liberalism will be applied to the production and distribution of such goods and services as education, health care, housing and social welfare. To date, most of the changes in this area have been modest and incremental, at least when compared with the reforms introduced in other areas. The Government's approach has been to address the strategic economic issues first and to leave the fundamental questions concerning social policy — the appropriate role of the State, the most efficient mode of intervention, and the level of assistance to be provided, to whom and by what means — until after the report of the Royal Commission. As Easton notes, this is a somewhat strange ordering of priorities for a Labour Government, but then this is no ordinary Labour Government.

Another central feature of the new order has been the willingness of the Government to tackle vested interests and challenge sacred cows. Nowhere has this been more apparent than in its imposition of a surtax on National Superannuation (although subsequently the rate was reduced), the removal of State assistance to the agricultural sector, the planned changes to pay fixing in the public and private sectors, and the phasing out of protectionist measures. Moreover, the Government has firmly resisted attempts by various groups to alter its strategy in the interests of minimizing social, industrial and economic disruption. There have been no major U-turns, and none appear likely. This is not to suggest that the Government has been absolutely consistent or completely immune from political pressures. There are undoubtedly instances when short-term expediency has prevailed over longer-term objectives and where electoral considerations have affected expenditure decisions. For example, the amount of drought relief received by South Canterbury farmers in mid-1985 seems to have been linked, if indirectly, to the Timaru by-election. Similarly, the decision to subsidize the movement of West Coast coal via the railway network was plainly influenced by the desire to assist an economically depressed region and avoid the loss of a potentially marginal seat. But arguably such "extravagances" have not been common.

Policy innovations in the economic arena have been coupled with equally important initiatives in the area of constitutional and parliamentary reform. For example, the Government has announced its intention of enacting a Bill of Rights. As Elkind explains in Chapter 4 this proposal raises major constitutional issues and, if implemented, would significantly alter existing conventions. It would place limits on the sovereignty of the legislature and constraints on the power of the executive. Correspondingly, the role of the Judiciary in the political process would be greatly enhanced. It remains to be seen whether the Government will actively pursue this initiative and, if it does so, how much support, if any, it receives from the Opposition and the public at large. In the meantime the Government has overhauled the operations of Parliament. This has included the reorganization and revamping of select committees, the establishment of a Parliamentary Service Commission to administer Parliament and various changes to the Standing Orders of the House. As explained by Skene in Chapter 5 the aim here has been to ensure that Parliament acts more effectively as a check on the executive and has the resources necessary for reviewing and scrutinizing the activities of the bureaucracy.

The new order inaugurated by the fourth Labour Government has not been confined to the domestic policy arena. Many observers considered the foreign policy of the third Labour Government innovative. Amongst other things it recognized the People's Republic of China, withdrew military personnel from Vietnam, protested against French nuclear testing in the South Pacific, and promoted the concept of a nuclear weapons free zone. However, as Kennaway notes, the Kirk-Rowling Administration was generally non-controversial, bipartisan and predisposed to continuity rather than radical change: in particular, it "continued to believe that the best way to ensure New Zealand's basic security interests [was] by maintaining the alliance relationship with a superpower" (Kennaway, 1975, p.163). By contrast, the fourth Labour Government, in pursuit of its anti-nuclear objectives, has been prepared to countenance the most dramatic foreign policy departure of the modern era, namely the rupture of the ANZUS alliance with the United States. The origins of Labour's anti-nuclear policy, the seemingly inflexible negotiating strategies adopted during 1985 by the respective governments, and the resultant impasse in 1986 are examined by Alley in Chapter 11.

With the breakdown of its long-standing defence links with America the Lange Government has been forced to rethink its whole defence strategy. In this process it embarked upon another remarkable innovation by establishing a Defence Committee of Enquiry to elicit the preferences and opinions of ordinary New Zealanders on security issues. Such a procedure for determining defence policy is unique among nations in the Western world where security issues have normally been the exclusive province of military personnel, defence analysts and senior politicians. The work of this Committee of Enquiry, together with its findings and political impact, is discussed by one of its members, Kevin Clements, in Chapter 12.

Yet another diplomatic initiative, the re-opening of the Delhi High Commission and the establishment of a new High Commission in Harare, also constitutes a notable departure from the foreign policy of the Muldoon Administration and has breached the traditional bipartisan approach to international diplomacy. As explained by Holland in Chapter 13, the Harare post was established in response to a variety of pressures: the Prime Minister's personal interest in the Third World; the desire to improve New Zealand's image among black African nations; and, not least, as an anti-apartheid gesture.

In summary, then, New Zealand has witnessed many notable policy switches under the fourth Labour Government. In the economic sphere the dominant theoretical paradigm has changed from Keynesianism to monetarism. Detailed regulation of the economy has given way to a greater reliance on the market. The quest for stability has been replaced with a drive for flexibility, efficiency and growth. And the influence of certain economic interest groups has been reduced, albeit for the time being. In the public sector there has been a shift away from the service ethic in favour of the "user-pays" principle. Government agencies are now expected to make money, rather than simply spend it. In addition, equally profound changes have occurred in many other fields. Cumulatively, there can be little doubt that this amounts to a turning point in the style and substance of politics in the post-war era. Just as it is claimed that the Thatcher Government has altered the "rules of the game" in Britain, much the same can be said of the Labour Government in New Zealand.

Explanations

The scope and magnitude of Labour's reforms certainly call for an explanation. Various theories are considered in this volume. Vowles, for example, examines the influence of the changing composition and electoral base of the Labour Party. He also notes the importance of Lange's election to the leadership of the party in 1983 and his selection of Douglas as finance spokesperson. Easton points to the impact of the Muldoon Administration on the views of Labour's leadership and stresses the critical importance of the economic advice tendered by the Treasury both during and after the devaluation crisis in July 1984. John Roberts, too, emphasizes the role played by the devaluation crisis, but also notes the generational shift associated with Labour's election victory and the remarkable youth of the Lange Cabinet, particularly among the senior Ministers. In addition, both Roberts and Skene allude to some of the other factors which have facilitated the process of radical change in New Zealand: a unicameral Parliament, a powerful executive, and a competent, non-partisan public service.

Another explanation worthy of mention arises out of Olson's analysis of the rise and fall of nations. The central point here relates to the potential returns to a political entrepreneur who is willing, in the face of a faltering economy and institutional rigidities, to tackle vested interests and challenge outmoded ideas. Brittan provides a useful summary of this argument:

> As the output gap widens between a slowly growing country held back by restrictive interest groups and other countries employing best-practice techniques, the incentive to catch-up also becomes larger. The more atrophied become a country's techniques and habits, the greater becomes the return to innovation. The gains can be so great that it may be possible to make agreements to share them with restrictive interest groups. Moreover, restrictive practices are never of the same severity across the economy; and if innovation is blocked in traditional or well-organized sectors, talent and capital will drift to newer areas, where groups loyalties have not yet "solved" the free-rider problem. In the last resort, too, the returns to political entrepreneurship from trying to change the institutional and political rules in favour of better economic performance may become so great that the changes are made (Brittan, 1983, p.238).

How well such an argument applies in New Zealand is open to debate. There can be little doubt concerning Labour's attempt to improve the country's economic performance. What remains uncertain is how successful this will prove and whether the "returns to political entrepreneurship" will be sufficiently great to ensure the party's re-election in 1987.

The Politics of Change

One is reminded here of Machiavelli's oft-quoted dictum:

> ... there is nothing more difficult to arrange, more doubtful of success, and more dangerous to carry through than initiating changes in a State's constitution. The innovator makes enemies of all those who prospered under the old order, and only lukewarm support is forthcoming from those who would prosper under the new (Machiavelli, 1973, p.51).

The fourth Labour Government has certainly made plenty of enemies as a result of its policy innovations. It has alienated much of the farming community. It has angered manufacturers and national superannuitants. It has caused a great deal of anxiety amongst public servants and those dispossessed by the process of economic restructuring. Perhaps most importantly, it has alienated many its traditional supporters within the wider labour movement.

Two main types of criticism have been levelled at the Government's overall strategy. First, some have attacked the Government for abandoning many of the party's previous commitments and pursuing so-called "orthodox" economic policies. Those arguing along these lines – primarily, but by no means exclusively, those on the left of the political spectrum – have highlighted the risks associated with a floating exchange rate, the problems of relying solely on monetary and fiscal policies to control inflation, the enormous social costs of rapid economic restructuring, the dubious wisdom of making public agencies act as if they were privately owned, and the Government's failure to give greater priority to the areas of health, education, employment and social welfare. Another particular bone of contention relates to the potent influence which the Treasury appears to have exerted on policy making and to its apparently dogmatic adherence to the narrow theoretical assumptions of neoclassical economics. Some of these concerns are reflected in the chapters by Boston, Easton and Gregory.

Against this, the Government has also been criticized by those on the right for not going far enough. For example, it is claimed that Labour should have privatized, rather than corporatized, the main State trading enterprises. It is argued further that the Government has failed to cut the Budget deficit sufficiently, that its management of monetary policy has been poor, that its income maintenance schemes, such as Family Support, are too generous, and that the proposed labour market reforms are inadequate. Some have even suggested that Labour has implemented its reforms too slowly! The Government's anti-nuclear policy has also sparked a good deal of opposition from those favouring nuclear deterrence and a strong ANZUS alliance.

Despite such criticisms and the obvious disenchantment felt by many traditional Labour supporters, the Government's popularity has remained high. As Nigel Roberts points out in Chapter 3, public opinion polls since the 1984 election have revealed strong support for both the party and its leadership, and on only a few occasions has support for National exceeded that for Labour. There are doubtless many reasons for Labour's good showing in the polls. As Roberts argues, part of the explanation is to be found in the leadership squabbles and policy conflicts experienced by National since the 1984 election. Other factors would include: the disintegration of the third parties; the strength of anti-nuclear sentiment in the country, magnified no doubt by the ANZUS row with the United States and the *Rainbow Warrior* affair with France; the relative solidarity and unity of Labour's Cabinet; the presentational skills of the Prime Minister; the improvement in real disposable incomes experienced during 1985/86; the support of big business for the Government's economic strategy; the personality and policy divisions within the union movement; and the fact that urban areas were little affected by the major economic downturn in the rural sector during 1985/86.

At a deeper level, it may well be that the Labour Government has achieved a significant political realignment in New Zealand. Obviously until suitable polling data is available one can but speculate. However, there are good reasons for supposing that Labour, by virtue of its new policy stance, is now attracting a much higher proportion of urban, liberal, middle class voters than has hitherto been the case. At the same time, it appears to be retaining most of its traditional working class support. Conversely, the National Party seems to be losing ground in urban areas and amongst the business community, and increasingly has acquired the image of a country party. This does not mean of course that Labour is guaranteed re-election in 1987. New Zealand's electoral geography is such that Labour could retain all its urban seats and yet still lose an election as a result of a pro-National swing in rural and semi-rural electorates. Much will depend on the outcome of the contests in the key marginal seats which Labour currently holds in the provinces, such as East Cape, Gisborne, Hamilton East and West, Hawke's Bay, Horowhenua, Tasman, Wairarapa, and Waitaki.

Regardless of whether the "returns to political entrepreneurship" prove to be positive in 1987, the Labour Party will face many political, ideological and practical challenges in the years ahead. One question relates to the future of its traditional alliance with the union movement. Given the disaffection towards the Government in union ranks and the virtual exclusion of the Federation of Labour from the corridors of power, it must be wondered how much longer the old relationship can continue. While a complete rupture is unlikely, it is certainly possible that over time a greater number of unions will sever their formal association with the party. In due course Labour could become a social-democratic party in the British mould dominated by market liberals with a commitment to equality of opportunity, but with virtually no formal relationship with sectional interest groups.

At the ideological level a whole series of questions need to be resolved by the party in the coming years. When and in what manner should the State intervene in the market place? Should the State be in the business of providing education and health services and, if so, by what means? In what circumstances, if any, is public ownership justified? What content is to be given to concepts like social justice, equity and fairness? Is equality of opportunity the primary objective of social policy and, if so, how is this to be achieved? Where is the line to be drawn in the harsh trade-offs between equity and efficiency and between liberty and social justice? How much income redistribution is possible in the context of a society which places a premium on home ownership and in which house prices and interest rates are comparatively high? What State encouragement, if any, should be given to co-operative enterprise, industrial democracy and profit sharing? And what stance should New Zealand adopt in the international community – allied to the West, neutral or non-aligned? These and other themes will be at the heart of the political debate in New Zealand for the remainder of the 1980s and beyond. It may well be that in the periods of difficulty which doubtless lie ahead, many will wish the fourth Labour Government had not so drastically transformed the political agenda.

Conclusion

Reflecting on the new course being charted by the fourth Labour Government, the Prime Minister, in a speech to the New Zealand Political Studies Association Conference in 1986, made the following observations:

> This government presents a real challenge to the political analyst. The complexities of a period of rapid change call for a new level of sophistication in political commentary. While some parts of our news media are rising to the challenge, I regret that there is a lack of good in-depth political analysis, and too much attention to trivia and an over-eager willingness to see conflict and division (Lange, 1986b, p.4).

The Prime Minister is correct in his judgement that the policies of his Government provide political analysts with a serious challenge. It is hoped that this collection of essays goes some way towards supplying the kind of rigorous, in-depth analysis that is needed, and which the public deserve. It must be recognized at the outset, however, that this volume does not cover all of the Government's policy initiatives and reforms. Many important areas of public policy, such as education, employment, health, housing, social welfare, energy and transport, have not been addressed in detail. Likewise, readers will find virtually nothing here on questions relating to gender, race, violence, and environmental protection. This is regrettable, but unavoidable given the constraints of time and space. Further, even in the areas covered, such as wages policy, the reorganization of the State sector and defence policy, the analysis is sometimes limited and incomplete. This is partly because the precise nature or full details of the Government's approach had yet to be announced at the time of writing. For all these reasons, therefore, this volume must be regarded as a provisional survey. In due course a new, revised and more complete account of the fourth Labour Government will be necessary. In the meantime it is hoped that the chapters which follow will help illuminate the issues which face New Zealanders in the mid-to-late 1980s and assist readers in assessing the merits and consequences of the solutions adopted by the fourth Labour Government.

References

Brittan, S. (1983) *The Role and Limits of Government: Essays in Political Economy* Hounslow, Maurice Temple Smith.

Easton, B. (1986) *Wages and the Poor* Wellington, Allen & Unwin.

Gould, J. (1982) *The Rake's Progress? New Zealand's Economy Since 1945* Auckland, Hodder and Stoughton.

Harris, D.C. (1980) The State of Social Democracy. Paper prepared for the Politics Policy Seminar, Nuffield College, Oxford.

Kennaway, R. (1975) Foreign Policy. In R. Goldstein (Ed.) *Labour in Power: Promise and Performance* Wellington, Price Milburn.

Lange, D. (1986a) The New Welfare State Prestonpans, Mackintosh Memorial Lecture.

Lange, D. (1986b) New Zealand Under Labour: Interpreting the Politics of Change. *POLS* 11-2: 3-9.

Machiavelli, N. (1973) *The Prince* Harmondsworth, Penguin Books.

Muldoon, R.D. (1985) *The New Zealand Economy: A Personal View* Auckland, Endeavour Press.

Olson, M. (1982) *The Rise and Decline of Nations: Economic Growth, Stagflation and Social Rigidities* New Haven, Yale.

The Treasury (1984) *Economic Management* Wellington, Government Printer.

2

The Fourth Labour Government
Ends, Means, and for Whom?

Jack Vowles

In November 1985, at a gathering celebrating the fiftieth anniversary of the election of the first Labour Government, Labour Members of Parliament present and past viewed a 1938 Labour propaganda film. Certain historical ironies did not escape the audience, many of whom were directly engaged in undoing much of the legacy of the very Government they honoured (*New Zealand Listener*, 21 December 1985, p.7). Yet senior Ministers have denied that Labour has changed its principles, claiming that the *ends* of Government policy remain constant; it is merely the *means* that have changed. As the Prime Minister, David Lange, has put it: "The principles remain the same, but the methods of the 1930s are clearly not appropriate to the problems of the 1980s and beyond" (1986c, p.5). While there can be no dispute about the obvious policy discontinuities between the fourth Labour Government and its forerunners, the ideological implications are less clear. The first part of this chapter explores whether a break from Labour's traditional principles has occurred since July 1984. To those well versed in the history of social democracy, the following account will be a familiar one. For the changes in Labour's objectives which can be identified are comparable to the dilution, if not abandonment, of socialist objectives by many other contemporary Western social-democratic parties.

Some commentators argue that the discrepancies they identify between Labour's traditional principles and policies, and those of the fourth Labour Government, can be traced to a transformation in Labour's social and electoral foundations. The second part of the chapter scrutinizes this explanation. No longer predominantly a working class or proletarian party, Labour has sought widely for its members and voters, and recently has been relatively successful among the expanding professional "salariat", or salaried class. Yet if its social foundations are now more widely dispersed, Labour's present reign is also less firmly rooted than that of any previous Labour Government, based as it is on the support of just 43 per cent of the voters in July 1984. Indeed, the Government's future could be jeopardized for at least three reasons: first, the possible refusal of Labour supporters and voters to accept the radical reversal of many previous Labour policies; second, the relatively low level of electoral support on which it came to power combined with the tendency of governments to lose support from election to election; and third, the fact that only a relatively small percentage of Labour's electoral coalition are party identifiers. Thus after brief attention to the social composition of the party, the chapter concludes with an examination of Labour's electoral support, using data drawn from a postal survey of three Auckland marginal electorates in July 1984. While Labour's choice of new directions may have been assisted by a broader social base (see Gold, 1985, p.330), certain claims about the nature of this electoral base need qualification.

Labour's Principles: Their Origins

It is easy in political debate to call upon Labour's traditional principles; it is more difficult to define and analyse them. Unlike its forerunner, the Social Democratic Party, the Labour Party did not include an explicit statement of principles in its original constitution of 1916; it merely stated as its material objective "the socialization of the means of production, distribution, and exchange".[1] The absence of a statement of principles was noted at the time by one of the members of the first Labour Party Executive, Arthur McCarthy, who wrote cynically that the party had "no principles, but a platform merely. It stands, as all political parties must stand, for opportunism only" (Vowles, 1982, p.49). This paucity of clearly stated principles is compounded by New Zealand politicians, who only rarely provide comprehensive statements of their political philosophy. Consequently, various accounts identify the ideological roots of the Labour Party in "Gladstonian liberalism, Marxism, and Fabianism" (Kirk, 1969, p.7), radical liberalism and Christian Socialism (Gustafson, 1985, pp.146-147), and American and British theories of industrial democracy (Vowles, 1982, pp.49-53). Within this complex mixture one can isolate, with difficulty, three main strands: socialism, radical liberalism, and a more modest humanitarian social liberalism. Scrutiny of early Labour Party programmes and rhetoric provides some indication of a philosophical framework drawing upon these main strands. Within this framework, it is possible to distinguish between means and ends, although the boundary between the two is often blurred. Further, one can identify two variants of Labour's most fundamental ends, which may be seen as stronger and weaker versions of the same reformist impulse.

The radical liberals of the late nineteenth and early twentieth centuries, in common with many socialists, had as their fundamental goal the self-fulfilment of all, or "self-realization" as it is often called. The Social Democratic Party, part of the Labour Party until the early 1920s, contained such principles in its constitution. The end it pursued was "national greatness", founded upon individual development — physical, mental, and moral — and equality of opportunity (especially in the area of education) achieved by means of "the economic independence of the average individual".[2] With the exception of "national greatness", such principles have been prominent in the rhetoric of the Labour Party throughout its history; indeed, they have been in evidence since the origins of social democracy in New Zealand in the 1890s. Arising out of them has been a theory of "positive" freedom; put crudely, this emphasizes "freedom to" more than "freedom from" (Berlin, 1969, pp.141-166).

On the basis of these principles interventionist Labour Governments have sought to maximize opportunities and personal choice for all citizens.

While sharing the fundamental end of self-realization, the radical liberals and socialists who influenced Labour's early policy platform were able to compromise on the question of means. To the socialists, the weapon was democratic class struggle — both political and industrial — and the means socialization of much of the economy; to the radical liberals the extension of political democracy through constitutional and electoral reform was emphasized in conjunction with proposals for the extensive modification of capitalism. The aim here was to prevent any monopoly, to improve access to land, and to attack the power of financial capital, thereby increasing and promoting the interests of small independent producers.[3] Both strategies were reflected in Labour's earliest policy platforms (see New Zealand Labour Party, 1918).

From its origins, however, the Labour Party included many whose ends were more modest, and whose voices were initially more muted. Their goals were derived from a more moderate liberalism, Fabian socialism, and Christian social concern. For example, in 1918 prominent Labour politician J.T. Paul believed that all the Labour Party wanted was to eliminate poverty (Oliver, 1981, p.57), and summed up Labour's first thirty years as "humanism in politics" (Gustafson, 1980; Paul, 1946, p.147). This humanitarian and utilitarian strand was restated more broadly in 1962 when a party committee declared that the party's aims had always been "the brotherhood of man and the greatest good of the greatest number" and "fair shares for all" (Gustafson, 1976, p.38).

These variants of the ends to be pursued are far from being mutually exclusive. Reforms based on moderate liberalism may promote self-realization; on the other hand they may not. For example, some initiatives to alleviate poverty may be inconsistent with the pursuit of self-realization if the nature of the assistance given creates "poverty traps", such as high effective marginal tax rates, and thus encourages passivity, lowers self-confidence and pride, and promotes a psychology of dependence.[4] This conflict over ends, and the means to achieve them, is central to an understanding of the history and evolution of the Labour Party. Also central is an appreciation of changes in the broader philosophical context of Labour's avowed ends, and in the rhetoric and concepts used to give them meaning and resonance. From the beginning Labour has used words such as fairness, justice, equity, brotherhood, and caring. But such concepts on their own lack specificity and hence can be taken to mean almost as much or as little as one likes. Within a particular philosophical context they take on a distinctive meaning. If this context changes, then so do the meaning and implications of the concepts. For these reasons a simple distinction between ends and means is inadequate for an understanding of Labour's philosophical evolution. More fundamentally, ends and means are sometimes hard to distinguish from each other, and even when distinguishable often remain mutally dependent. A political philosophy focusing only on ends would be inadequate without some attention to their practical application and achievement. A new choice of means can also alter the nature of the ends pursued, sometimes in only small ways, sometimes significantly.

Over the decades Labour's basic philosophy has been progressively modified and redefined. Whereas initially radical liberal and socialist principles were in the ascendency, today the policies of the party are largely the product of moderate liberal and humanitarian impulses. This does not mean that the concern for self-realization has been entirely forgotten, but rather that it has been confined primarily to the area of social policy, and has been neglected in other fields, such as industrial democracy. For example, Norman Kirk, the leader of the party from 1965 to 1974, defended the welfare state on the grounds that it set people free and established rights for all (Kirk, 1975, pp.145-146). Similarly, in a general statement on social policy in March 1986 Lange put forward Labour's traditional view that all should be encouraged to "achieve their full potential in whatever sphere they choose". Social policy should "encourage individuals in autonomy and independence", "enhance freedom by giving individuals more chance to choose how their lives will be led" and promote individual dignity (Lange, 1986a, p.4; 1986c, p.5).

Labour's much chronicled "retreat from socialism" is well illustrated in its changing stance on property ownership. While Sinclair's description of Labour's 1919 programme as "a red-hot blueprint for a socialist society" (1959, p.237) is more colourful than precise, the platform did aim to further public ownership of land, food production, banking, insurance, shipping, and "national utilities". It did not indicate, however, that private ownership would be completely displaced in these areas. Where public ownership was established the trade unions in the industry would appoint half the Governing Board and would entirely control the hiring and firing of labour. The basis of this approach was the view that those who worked should have the first title to control of that work (see Sinclair, 1976, pp.57-58). The commitment to State ownership plus workers' control remained in the party platform until 1933, when the entire section on State ownership was pared to the bone although not entirely excised. After its defeat in 1949, Labour drew up a short statement of principles which were endorsed by the 1952 conference (New Zealand Labour Party, 1952). While still identifying Labour as a socialist party, the principles stressed its commitment to democracy and a mixed economy. Defeat in 1960 produced a further and more lengthy statement of principles which were approved in 1962 (New Zealand Labour Party, 1962, pp.18-20). While building on the 1952 statement, key aspects were withdrawn. Hedged with qualifications, identifying and yet not identifying with socialism, it argued in favour of nationalization and planning, but failed to promote or advocate such policies.

Labour's early tax policies called for a capital gains tax, a more sharply graduated income tax scale, and correspondingly lower indirect taxation. In government

Labour was never to implement comprehensive and thoroughgoing capital gains taxes, but at least until the 1970s Labour politicians strongly defended progressive taxation and opposed extending indirect taxation and the related concept of "user pays" (Shorter, 1974, pp.301-303). This policy stance has altered considerably during the 1980s, as will be shown shortly.

Labour's initial demands in the area of social welfare included the extension and increase of pensions, particularly for the "incapacitated", the nationalization of medical services and free medical care (New Zealand Labour Party, 1918, p.4). During the 1920s and 1930s social policy became the focus of the party's programme and an important element in its electoral appeal. The Marxist class war rhetoric of the Social Democratic Party gave way to language expressing principles summed up by Michael Joseph Savage's description of social security as "applied Christianity". Likewise, Walter Nash, in terms parallel to those of R.H. Tawney's Christian Socialism, stressed the principle of "social service" as the only title to wealth (Tawney, 1920, pp.51-52). He also declared that Labour's most fundamental principle was that "a first charge on all wealth created shall be the care of the aged, the ailing, the young ..." (Sinclair, 1976, p.65), to which the 1922 manifesto added "and all those engaged in the production of essential utilities" (Brown, 1962, p.72). Here the influence of a labour theory of value probably derived from Marx is apparent: those who worked created wealth and so served society; to them should be given the fruits of their labour. The only qualification to this principle was the requirement that the first to be assisted should be those who, through no fault of their own, were in need.

For a long period Labour's constitution stated that the political role of the party was to promote a "just distribution" of the products of natural resources among "those who render social service". This phrasing had significant philosophical implications: those who served the community through their labour should receive their just entitlement; by contrast, those owning capital were the object of scepticism concerning their right to wealth. A distaste for unrestrained profiteering survived among Labour politicians, at least into the 1960s, on the grounds that this did not enhance the development of all and thus was against the public interest (Oliver, 1981, pp.387-390; Shorter, 1974 p.297). In short, Labour's rhetoric in its early years, while employing concepts such as justice and equity, was part of an ideological framework which gave these words a specific meaning rooted in entitlement. As late as the 1960s, Labour's principles could be identified as based upon "a largely socialist ethic" (Shorter, 1974, p.160).

The welfare state created by the first Labour Government was strongly based on this notion of entitlement. While failing to fulfil it entirely, Labour fought hard to implement its commitment to a universally free medical service. Receipt of a State pension by the aged was also declared a "right of citizenship" in Labour's revised platform of 1927, and universal provision was promised in the 1935 manifesto. This was to become a focus of struggle between the Labour Cabinet and Caucus in 1938, when Caucus pressure preserved the principle of universality for pensions, albeit in attenuated form (Castles, 1985, p.27; Hanson, 1938, pp.74-80). The first Labour Government went on to make child allowances, later renamed the family benefit, universally payable in 1946. Thus while the first Labour Government was obliged for economic reasons to limit the scope of universal benefits, it at least maintained the principle of universality. Indeed, the classic argument for universal provision acknowledges its philosophical and practical limits (Tawney, 1964, p.148).

Some thirty years later, however, the third Labour Government re-assessed Labour's pensions policy. It introduced an income-related, contributory superannuation scheme in 1974. Ironically, this led the National Party to advocate a generous, universal, non-contributory superannuation scheme during the 1975 election campaign, thereby appropriating Labour's hopes of the 1930s. Labour's humiliating defeat in 1975 forced the party not merely to continue its long-standing debate over the nature and relevance of socialism but also to re-examine its whole approach to social policy.

A New Philosophy

In 1976 Labour finally adopted a set of explicit principles as part of its constitution. These reaffirmed previous ideals put forward either explicitly or implicitly, such as equality of opportunity and preference for co-operation over competition in economic relations. Yet in other important respects these principles failed to articulate positions long defended by the party. Freedom and liberties were referred to extensively, but were not defined so as to assert Labour's long-held view of positive freedom as the means to self-realization. Until the 1970s, Labour politicians had argued that wealth was a community creation (Shorter, 1974, p.33), with the implication that ownership of property was not an absolute right but one subject to the needs of the community (Tawney, 1920, pp.52-83). However, Labour's principles of 1976 failed to affirm this explicitly, asserting only that New Zealand's natural resources belonged to all, and acknowledging a right to individual ownership of wealth and property subject to the requirement of justice (New Zealand Labour Party, 1979, p.1). While the principles called for a just distribution of wealth, production, and services for the benefit of all, Labour's new and attenuated concept of social justice was based essentially on liberal and humanitarian principles and lacked the power and resonance of earlier conceptions based on entitlement.[5]

The philosophical debate continued during the latter half of the 1970s. One of the major contributors was Geoffrey Palmer, who sought to define and strengthen Labour's concept of social justice. In doing so he moved it further from an entitlement basis and instead advocated the position of the American liberal philosopher, John Rawls, who defined social justice as fairness (Palmer, 1977, p.33). Palmer endorsed the principle of equality of opportunity and sought its realization through affirmative action in favour of the most underprivileged. He argued that people should have equal access to material and cultural resources and that the Government should control community resources for that purpose. This meant that the distribution of wealth and resources ought to be socially determined rather than left to unrestrained market forces.[6] However, Palmer qualified this approach in line with Rawls's so-called "difference principle". According to this, liberty, wealth, income and opportunity ought to be distributed equally unless it can be clearly demonstrated that unequal distribution will benefit the least advantaged (Rawls, 1971, p.78). The major purpose of this qualification is to ensure that individuals and groups have the necessary material incentives to create wealth and thereby generate economic growth. This approach has subsequently been endorsed by the fourth Labour Government with the Prime Minister arguing that, while inequality is unattractive, it is "the engine which drives the economy" (Lange, 1986b, p.26).

Palmer's notion of equal access also involved citizens as consumers rather than as producers or initiators. Certainly, Palmer called for "participatory democracy", but this implied greater access to information rather than the power to initiate, except at the local level. In addition, Palmer's notion of freedom was negative in the sense of "freedom from" rather than positive in the wider sense of "freedom to". As he put it, the essence of freedom is the protection of "the individual against both public and private power" (Palmer, 1977, p.34). Hence, Labour's evolution away from socialism has gone hand in hand with a change from a radical to a more moderate version of liberalism.[7] For many in the party of the 1980s, a modest redistribution of wealth has become an end in itself, rather than a means for expanding the positive freedom of ordinary people. Moreover, modest redistribution is thought to be contingent upon the realization of another goal, economic efficiency, which has become the major objective of economic policy (Aitken, 1985). Efficiency is a means to increase prosperity. Prosperity will mean that the redistribution of wealth can take place in accordance with the principles of equity and fairness without requiring a major transfer of resources from the rich to the poor, a transfer that Labour has never seriously attempted. Moreover, Labour's new diagnosis of the means by which to encourage efficiency has led to the abandonment of many traditional Labour policies. For example, the fourth Labour Government has adopted the "user pays" principle; it now encourages profiteering as the engine of economic growth; it has challenged the universal provision of benefits for both pensions and child support; it has reduced the progressivity of direct taxation and introduced indirect taxation on all goods and services (see Chapter 10);[8] and it has rejected planning and State-directed investment for a market-based private sector growth strategy, which includes both corporatization and partial privatization of some public sector institutions (see Chapter 7).

Some supporters of the Government's policies have claimed that they are authentically radical. In the abstract sense of going "to the root" of an issue, such a case can certainly be made. Yet this notion of radicalism is quite different to that usually associated with the radical tradition in politics, certainly the tradition of radical liberalism. For example, radical liberals have generally defended the rights of working people and small independent producers against the State, financiers, and other concentrations of privilege and private economic power. While a reliance on the market, as opposed to State intervention and direction, is consistent with some forms of radicalism — as is the Government's removal of subsidies, licensing, and the protection of capitalist enterprise — it cannot escape notice that the strongest and most consistent support for the fourth Labour Government during its first few years of office came from the financial and corporate sectors of the economy. Compounding such paradoxes, Roger Douglas has described the Government's economic policies as radical only in appearance; rather he identifies them as "conventional" and "orthodox".[9]

A different interpretation claims that any redistribution of wealth through the State is socialist. Redistributive policies with a "more market" economic strategy thus add up to "market socialism" (Butcher, 1985). Yet in recent years the most widely debated exposition of market socialism assumes a key role for some central planning and implies fairly extensive socialization and democratization of production, albeit in varied forms within a mixed market economy (see Nove, 1983). In terms of either socialization or economic democracy, there is little or no socialism in the main thrust of the Government's policies, and extension of the term to cover mildly egalitarian liberalism confuses rather than clarifies the debate.

To summarize, Labour has progressively abandoned its early Marxist-influenced Christian socialism. During the 1970s the party explicitly adopted a policy programme based largely on moderate social liberalism. In this sense the principles underpinning the policies of the fourth Labour Government do not constitute a sharp break with the immediate past. The principles behind its current policies were apparently accepted by the party, consciously or unconsciously, during the late 1970s. Nevertheless, the economic and social strategy pursued since July 1984 is certainly very different from that of the first Labour Government and involves a major departure from many of the party's early principles. Most significantly, concepts like equity, justice and fairness have taken on different, more limited meanings in a new philosophical context. Over a number of decades the socialist theory of entitlement has given way to liberal humanitarianism. How can this transformation be accounted for? Is it possible to account for the philosophical and policy shifts which have taken place by reference to the evolving character of Labour's membership and electoral coalition?

Party Composition

Demographic changes in New Zealand have led to the transformation of the social composition of the Labour Party, particularly between 1945 and the early 1970s (Gustafson, 1976, p.15). Yet, as Gustafson has noted, this transformation has not been due primarily to the reduction in the relative size of Labour's traditional support base among the workers in mining, manufacturing, and transport, as it appears that this reduction has been slight. According to one estimate, for example, the working class in New Zealand comprised 57 per cent of the labour force in 1911, 58 per cent in 1936, and 49 per cent in 1976 (Crothers, 1985, p.31). Rather, the major demographic changes have been the decline of employment in rural based primary production (from 29 per cent of the labour force in 1916 to 10.9 per cent in 1981); the relative decline of the "old middle class" of higher professionals, businessmen, and farmers (from 21 per cent in 1911 to 9 per cent in 1976); and, the relative increase of the "new middle class" of lower professionals, sales, managerial and clerical workers (from 19 per cent to 41 per cent). Meanwhile, employers and the self-employed shrank from 25 per cent of the labour force in 1911 to 12 per cent in 1976, while the proportion of trade unionists rose from around 16 per cent to about 50 per cent in the same period. Other things being equal, such social changes might have been expected to benefit Labour; over the party's seventy years, the proportion of manual workers has shrunk only slightly, that of wage and salary earners has increased, and the percentage of trade unionists in the labour force has risen three-fold.

Labour came into being as a workers' party with close ties to trade unionism. Over half its first executive were (or had been) manual workers, active unionists, or union officials. By 1984 five out of the eight elected to the party executive were trade union officials, indicating continued ties to the wider labour movement (Vowles, 1985, p.8). Against this, there has been a decline in trade union affiliation to the party since the high point reached in the 1940s (Brown, 1962, p.52; Vowles, 1983, p.42), and also a fall in the proportion of trade unionists belonging to affiliated unions since about 1950. However, these trends probably reflect Labour's failure to recruit newer white-collar unions as affiliates, rather than wholesale rejection of Labour by traditional blue-collar unionists.

But if white-collar unions failed to affiliate to the party, since the 1940s white-collar unionists and professionals from the new middle class have formed an increasing proportion of Labour's branch membership. Whereas in 1949 manual workers made up 45 per cent of Labour's members, by 1969 this had declined to 30 per cent. By contrast, the proportion of professionals and white-collar workers had risen from 8.5 per cent to 21.6 per cent during this period. Moreover, these changes took place against a background of an absolute decline in party membership. It was not that there was an influx of new white-collar members up to the mid 1970s;

rather, Labour lost disproportionately more of its blue-collar members, while white-collar membership ebbed away more slowly. When party membership revived from 1976 onwards, the occupational structure of party membership of the early 1970s was replicated in the influx of new members. A study of the 1983 Labour conference indicated that just over 70 per cent of delegates were members of associations or unions of wage and salary earners (Vowles, 1985, pp.7-8, 12-13). Thus, Labour's traditional basis as a party of organised employees remains intact at the membership level, and has diversified into areas of the economy which have expanded since its foundation — public employment and the salariat. While failing to persuade white-collar unions to affiliate, Labour has at least attracted some of their most politically conscious members as individuals.

If the social basis of party membership has changed, that of the Labour Caucus has altered even more dramatically. Five of the eight Labour Members of Parliament elected in 1919 were manual wage earners and unionists, and the other three had been involved in trade unionism at various times. By 1935 manual workers and trade union officials constituted only about a third of the Labour Caucus and by 1984 the comparative figure was nine per cent with nearly three-quarters of the Caucus drawn from professional occupations (Gustafson, 1985, p.151).

It has been widely assumed that Labour's changing social composition, in particular the growing prominence of middle class members at the parliamentary level, has had political consequences. In the context of arguments about a retreat from socialism, such beliefs lack support as the effective abandonment of the socialization objective took place when the party was still led mainly by former manual workers (Vowles, 1985, p.2.). However, although members of the salariat share some of the interests of the traditional working class in that they are usually employees, their jobs are of a higher status and usually provide greater autonomy and reward. A declining proportion of those with personal experience of economic and social deprivation in Labour's membership and Caucus could be linked to the party's gradual abandonment of its entitlement theories.

Another explanation of Labour's ideological transformation in the 1970s focuses primarily on the impact of specific political events, the role of particular individuals at the leadership level and the ebb and flow of intellectual tides in the wider international context, and only secondarily on social class (Lange, 1986b, pp.23-24). For example, in 1975 the National Party was elected to power after a campaign based in part on right-wing populism. Subsequently some middle class liberals formerly associated with the National Party began to gravitate towards Labour, while working class voters began supporting National in greater numbers than hitherto. In this sense it could be argued that Labour's ideological transformation has been the consequence and mirror-image of an ideological and strategic shift in the policies of its main opponent, the National Party. Also of importance in the evolution of the party's economic policies was the election of Lange to the party leadership in early 1983 and his appointment of Roger Douglas as the party's finance spokesperson. During the late 1970s Douglas and a number of the party's intellectuals were in search of an economic policy to restore growth. Unable to find one on the left, they turned to the rising economic orthodoxy of neoliberalism or neoconservatism which was taking hold among economists – most notably in the Treasury. This inevitably meant a turn away from collective and co-operative values toward those of competition and individualism. Considering leaving politics at a time when his economic views were still unacceptable to most of the Labour Party, in 1981 Douglas was privately promised the Finance portfolio if Lange became Prime Minister (*National Business Review*, July 11 1986, p.17).

The Electorate

Data on electoral support for parties in New Zealand before the 1960s is fragmentary, and subsequent survey research is sparse by standards set elsewhere.[10] In the early 1920s Labour had the support of about 75 per cent of manual workers in its core city seats (Chapman, 1969, p.16; Fairburn, 1985, p.107). By the 1930s Labour had amassed the support of a broadly based electoral coalition similar to that of the Liberals in the 1890s (Chapman, 1961, p.24; 1981, pp.335-337). Analysis of voting behaviour between the 1963 and 1981 elections supports the contention that the distinction between manual and service occupations on the one side, and non-manual occupations on the other, has become less central to voting choice. The Alford index of class voting – calculated from the Labour percentage of the manual vote minus the Labour percentage of the non-manual vote – has declined among urban voters from 30 in 1963 to 16 in 1981 (Bean, 1984, p.292). New Zealand class voting, so defined, is declining in accordance with patterns evident in other advanced capitalist democracies. Furthermore, as table 2.1 shows, since 1938 there has been a slow but fairly consistent long-term decline in Labour voting.

Survey data on the 1984 election is relatively limited, but some is available from a postal survey of three Auckland marginal electorates, each of which changed hands from National to Labour in 1984.[11] In this sample the Alford class voting index showed a small decline from the 1981 figure, down one point to 15. Of course, such a purely manual/non-manual definition of class voting is open to serious question. While itself criticized, a study of the 1983 British election found no evidence of class dealignment when employing a more sophisticated classification which distinguished between the salariat, clerical workers, the self-employed, supervisory and technical staff, and the manual working class (Heath, Jowell, and Curtice, 1985, p.16). There are at least two dimensions to class other than the manual/non-manual dichotomy which has been the main approach in New Zealand (Kelley and McAlister, 1985).[12] Recent work using aggregate data on an electorate basis has

Table 2.1
Votes, seats and swings at New Zealand general elections, 1935-1984

	Labour			National			Social Credit			Others			2 party
Year	Votes %	Seats No	%	Votes %	Seats No	%	Votes %	Seats No	%	Votes %	Seats No	%	swing to Govt.
1935	47.0ᵃ	55	68.8	31.8ᵇ	19	23.8				21.2	6	7.5	—
1938	55.8	53	66.3	39.9	25	31.3				4.3	2	2.5	-1.3
1943	48.4	45	56.3	42.3	34	42.5				9.2	1	1.3	-5.0
1946	51.3	42	52.5	48.4	38	47.5				0.3	—	—	-1.9
1949	47.2	34	42.5	51.9	46	57.5				0.9	—	—	-3.8
1951	45.8	30	37.5	54.0	50	62.5				0.2	—	—	1.7
1954	44.1	35	43.8	44.3	45	56.3	11.1	—	—	0.5	—	—	-4.0
1957	48.3	41	51.3	44.2	39	48.8	7.2	—	—	0.3	—	—	-2.3
1960	43.4	34	42.5	47.6	46	57.5	8.6	—	—	0.4	—	—	-4.5
1963	43.7	35	43.8	47.1	45	56.3	7.9	—	—	1.3	—	—	-0.4
1966	41.4	35	43.8	43.6	44	55.0	14.5	1	1.3	0.4	—	—	-0.6
1969	44.2	39	46.4	45.2	45	53.6	9.1	—	—	1.5	—	—	-0.7
1972	48.4	55	63.2	41.5	32	36.8	6.7	—	—	3.5	—	—	-4.4
1975	39.6	32	36.8	47.6	55	63.2	7.4	—	—	5.4	—	-	-8.4
1978	40.4	40	43.5	39.8	51	55.4	16.1	1	1.1	3.7	—	—	-5.0
1981	39.0	43	46.7	38.8	47	51.1	20.7	2	2.2	1.6	—	—	0.2
1984	43.0	56	58.9	35.9	37	38.9	7.6	2	2.1	13.5	—	—	-4.2

Source: Clive Bean, "From Confusion to Confusion: The 1981 General Election in New Zealand", *Politics* 17 (1982): 109.

Notes: a The figures for Labour in 1935 include votes and seats won by Ratana in the Maori electorates. Labour, having formed an alliance with Ratana, did not contest the Maori seats and after the election the successful Ratana candidates submitted to the Labour whip (Jackson and Wood, 1964: 393).

b The "National " Party in the 1935 election was an electoral alliance of the United and Reform Parties.

shown that over the three elections since 1978, Labour majorities correlated negatively and very strongly with the percentage of self-employed and the percentage engaged in administrative occupations, indicating a class basis to the electoral map founded on property and control over work rather than occupation as such.[13] As table 2.2 shows, there are somewhat sharper differences exposed when respondents in the labour force are divided into manual wage earners, non-manual wage and salary earners, and the self-employed, the latter group being the least likely to vote Labour in 1984. The table also shows low support for Labour among the retired and higher support (although statistically insignificant) among women not in the labour force.[14] As expected trade union members were also more likely to vote Labour. Yet the relationship was again weak (at 55.6 per cent compared to the overall Labour vote of 46.4 per cent).[15]

Table 2.2
1984 Labour voting among occupational/social groups

	Labour %	n
Manual wage earners	56.9[a]	109
Non-manual wage and salary earners	39.7[b]	141
Self-employed	33.9[a]	84
Retired	35.4[b]	59
Women not retired outside labour force	51.7	129
All groups	46.4	563

Notes: a Significant at p=.05 or better
b Significant between p=.05 and .10

Another way of measuring the influence of class on voting is by multivariate analysis. Reducing the sample to only those in the labour force who voted Labour or National in 1984, a regression model was constructed and tested against a dichotomized variable of Labour *versus* National voters. The model contained a class scale, union membership, education and income variables. It failed to account for more than five per cent of the variation between Labour and National voting among members of the labour force. By comparison, a similar regression model constructed from attitude, leadership, and ideological variables accounted for 73 per cent of the variation between all Labour and all National voters (see table 2.3).[16] Of course, such variables are themselves influenced by more general impressions of and identifications with parties, so the greater explanatory power of the model is not unexpected. More significantly, the model indicates that perceptions of political leadership and the issue of nuclear ship visits were more powerful factors in July 1984 than ideological, economic or social issues, although these clearly registered as well.

To extend the analysis somewhat further, respondents were classified into three groups on the basis of their voting record since the 1978 election.

(a) *Core Voters*: those who voted Labour in 1978, 1981, and 1984;

(b) *Changers*: those who had voted Labour in 1984 but not in 1981 (thus

(c) *Non-Labour*: those who had not voted Labour at any of the 1978, 1981 and 1984 elections.

(c) *Non-Labour* : those who had not voted Labour at any of the 1978, 1981 and 1984 elections.

On the basis of this classification, it is possible to identify a greater concentration of trade unionists among Labour's core voters. Trade unionists made up 24 per cent of the entire sample, 28.6 per cent of 1984 Labour voters, and 34.4 per cent of Labour's core voters.[17] Meanwhile, 22.5 per cent of the changers were trade unionists. This indicates a modest union ripple toward Labour in 1984, but one not statistically significant in comparison with movement in the rest of the sample.

Table 2.3
1984 Labour voting: attitudes, ideology, leadership

	R	BETA
Attitudes		
Intervention excessive	.21	.13
Intervention misdirected	.45	.11
Social welfare	.21	.05
Nuclear ship visits	-.61	-.19
Ideology		
Private enterprise	-.33	-.06
Socialism	.50	.10
Leadership		
Sir Robert Muldoon	-.77	-.28
David Lange	.71	.32
R 2 = .73		

Notes:

1 The model is the result of a stepwise regression procedure which deleted variables which did not meet a .15 statistical significance level. All variables except those indicated are significant at 0.01 or better.

2 With two exceptions, all items in the model are attitude measurements on a scale of one to seven, with four in the middle registering neutrality. All appreared in the questionnaire in the form of the key words or phrases shown in the table.

3 The two intervention variables were based on the following question: "In your opinion, has government intervention in the New Zealand economy under National been about right, excessive, misdirected, or too little?" "Too little" was chosen by only a handful of respondents. They were combined with those choosing "about right" to provide the residual category: intervention excessive and intervention misdirected are therefore dummy variables.

Trade unionists made up about a quarter of those who, not having voted Labour in 1981, voted Labour in 1984.

Table 2.4 shows the level of Labour voting among wage and salary earners, manual and non-manual, and unionists and non-unionists: all percentages are calculated on a base of the entire sample. The right-hand column indicates the degree to which each occupational/union category contributes more or less than average to Labour core voting; the second column describes those who were changers to Labour in 1984; the third column all those voting Labour in 1984; and the fourth column refers to those who had not voted Labour in either 1978, 1981, or 1984. The table shows that union membership has a positive association with various forms of Labour voting within the two broad occupational categories.

The traditional class basis of Labour voting remains, but in much attenuated form, with limited support drawn from Labour's core voting base. Almost 36 per cent of manual wage-earning trade unionists had not voted Labour for three

Table 2.4

Profile of 'core voters', 'changers', and overall Labour voting in 1984 by trade unionism and manual/non-manual wage and salary earners

	Core support 1978-84	Changers 1984	All Labour 1984	Not Labour 1978-84	Whole sample (%)
Manual union	18.7[a]	16.5[b]	14.8[a]	8.1[b]	11.2
Manual non-union	11.6[a]	5.0	7.1	6.8	6.7
Non-manual union	7.7	7.5	7.0	7.3	7.2
Non-manual non-union	9.0[b]	15.0	12.9[c]	18.5	16.0
n	90	113	261	279	563

Notes: a Significant at .01
       b Significant between .01 and .05
       c Significant between .05 and .10

consecutive elections. Although this represents a smaller proportion than those among the entire sample who had not voted Labour over the period (49.5 per cent), Labour has failed to attract overwhelming support from its traditional base. Class still counts, but increasingly so at the margins and less as a foundation of Labour support. The present strength of Labour's overall core support in the social structure appears small. While this may be due to some bias in the sample, table 2.5 shows the total number of consistent Labour voters over three elections was only 16 per cent of the entire sample.[18] Manual wage earners provided between one-fifth and one-quarter of Labour voters in these electorates. Moreover, only 30.5 per cent of the sample and 61.5 per cent of 1984 Labour voters identified as Labour supporters. By contrast, 35.7 per cent of the sample identified as National supporters. Thus, despite the fact that National voting was down to bedrock, its foundations remained relatively solid, for over 90 per cent of National identifiers in the survey voted National.

Table 2.5 shows the relative contribution of the various groups in the social structure to Labour's core voters, to the changers, and to all those who voted Labour in 1984. It also shows the contribution of each occupational group to those who had not voted for Labour at least since 1975. The table indicates that the disposition to vote Labour is still strongest among manual wage earners and weakest among the self-employed. While Labour has come to rely heavily on the professional salariat for Members of Parliament and members, there is no statistically significant evidence that electoral support for Labour from professional salary earners is any different from the general level of support in the sample. Labour's strength in the three electorates surveyed was in the two largest groups in the table: manual wage earners and women not in the officially-defined labour force, although again in the latter case the differences were not statistically significant. Both groups also contributed relatively strongly to the changers. Also, respondents in the clerical/sales category, while significantly more against Labour, were possibly as disposed as the rest of the sample to change to Labour in 1984. Overall, Labour's attraction to white-collar unionists as individual members does not appear to spill over into a propensity for a broader group of white-collar workers to vote Labour.

Table 2.5
Profile of Labour core support, changers, and overall voting by social structure

	Core support 1978-84	Changers 1984	All Labour 1984	Not Labour 1978-84	Whole sample (%)
Manual wage	30.3[b]	21.5[d]	21.9	14.9[c]	17.9
Women at home	23.4	25.2	23.9	19.8	21.2
Professional/salaried	9.0	6.3	7.9	7.9	8.1
Retired	15.2[d]	4.9[c]	7.7[d]	11.8	9.9
Clerk/sales	5.5[c]	12.5	9.5[d]	14.1[d]	12.0
Administration/management	2.1	3.7	2.5	3.9	3.1
Self-employed	4.8[b]	5.5[b]	9.5[c]	14.4	13.1
n	90[a]	113[a]	261	279	563
Whole sample (%)	16.0	20.0	46.4	49.5	100.0

Notes:
a   The remaining 58 respondents who changed to Labour in 1981 and remained Labour in 1984 were considered too few to be included here. However, a relatively high 24.7 per cent were self-employed (p=.01, cc=.12) and a relatively low 9.8 per cent were manual wage-earners (p=.09, cc=.08), intriguing retrospective hints of possible movements to Labour in 1981.
b   Significant at .01
c   Significant between .01 and .05
d   Significant between .05 and .10
1   Percentages do not always add up to 100 due to a few respondents not classifiable into the above categories.
2   23 other respondents had voted Labour in 1978 or 1981, or both, but had not done so in 1984; but their numbers were too small for fruitful analysis.

The apparent tendency for women who were not in the labour force to vote Labour is consistent with analysis of the national post-election poll conducted by the Heylen Research Centre. This showed women were slightly over-represented as Labour voters compared with the voting population: 53 per cent to 51 per cent respectively (Julian, 1985, pp.269-270). This contrasts with all previous election studies which have indicated that women were marginally more prone to vote National. But like all these earlier findings, the 1984 Heylen data showed a difference unlikely to be statistically significant in a sample of its size. The 1984 postal survey found no gender difference in relation to voting Labour. Nevertheless, it remains possible that a shift in the voting behaviour of some sections of women assisted Labour's victory; certainly the party's election strategy worked toward that goal. Labour's electoral research identified women aged 25 to 40 in clerical and semi-skilled occupations as potential new supporters, whereas higher income women in the same age group were less likely to vote Labour (*National Business Review*, July 30 1984, p.39). The postal survey also found evidence of such a tendency, albeit inconclusively. The sample size and response rate were insufficient to do more than hint at strong non-Labour tendencies among women members of the professional salariat as compared with a slightly more than average tendency towards Labour among their male counterparts. Women between twenty-five and forty in manual, service, clerical, and sales positions produced a high 61.9 per cent 1984 Labour majority, a figure of moderate statistical significance.[19] However, there were hints that such Labour strength was of core support, while new Labour voters in the group were only slightly above the average in the entire sample. The group as a whole made up 5.9 per cent of the sample, and new voters recruited from it may have contributed at most between one and two points to Labour's total vote. This is much less than that contributed by increased support among Labour's core social groups: manual wage earners and trade unionists.

The survey evidence considered in this chapter also contains hints that Labour's new economic policies could disillusion those with radical and socialist aspirations among its membership and voters. About one-third of 1984 Labour voters in the sample expressed positive feelings about socialism, for example, and 56.5 per cent chose "misdirected" rather than "excessive" as a description of the previous National Government's policies of economic interventionism. While few imagine that old-fashioned socialist rhetoric still has wide appeal, it is open to doubt whether free-market purity can spark the same response as Labour's powerful moral arguments of the 1920s and 1930s.

Conclusion

With respect to the party's future electoral prospects, the survey shows that despite the erosion of Labour's working class support and, to a lesser extent, the decline of the traditional working class itself, manual wage-earners remain Labour's most reliable foundation of support and also the largest occupational group within New Zealand society. Second, at the time of the last election it was apparent that Labour's declining electoral base among manual wage-earners had not been offset fully by increased support elsewhere in the social structure. This is of particular significance given that the proportion of Labour identifiers remains low compared with that of the National Party. On the other hand, it could be contended that a consequence of the fourth Labour Government's political and economic strategy has been to broaden substantially the party's electoral base. For example, during the first two years of its term opinion polls have at times shown Labour's support running at more than 50 per cent (see figure 3.1). Yet much of this support may be transitory, particularly given the very low level of core support in 1984 and increasing numbers of uncommitted voters who are not included in the polling figures reported on party support. Strong evidence of a further lessening of support for the Government from Labour's core occupational groups came to light in polls in mid-1986, combined with evidence of new support from higher status occupational groups (*National Business Review*, 29 August 1986, p.13). It is hard to escape the conclusion that a Government breaking with many traditions, and with much of its weight still resting on traditional foundations, should be careful not to cut the ground out from under its feet.

Notes

1 For recent supplementary accounts of the policies and organization of the New Zealand Labour Party see Vowles (1983) and Gustafson (1985).
2 See *The Maoriland Worker*, 2 December 1914, p.16. For their persistence among Labour politicians into the 1960s, see Shorter (1974. pp.31- 32, 38). In 1970 about 70 per cent of Labour conference delegates identified with a "freedom/self-fulfilment" definition of socialism (Gustafson, 1976, p.38).
3 On New Zealand liberalism in the nineteenth century, see Lyon (1982). The New Zealand Labour Party owed much of its early economic theory to radical liberals such as Henry George and J.A. Hobson (Gustafson, 1985, pp.146-147).
4 For criticisms of the fourth Labour Government's early social policy initiatives on these grounds see C. Perrings (1985); H. Dubb (1985, pp.9-10); and M. Slater (1985, p.5).
5 David Lange has described the party's present principles as "social democratic" rather than "democratic socialist" (Lange, 1986b, p.21, p.39). They are referred to here as "liberal" because, firstly, they are hard to distinguish from liberalism; and secondly because the term "social democracy" has traditionally been used to include a tradition of social reform which spans a broad political spectrum including progressive liberalism and democratic socialism. Lange's distinction reflects the special circumstances of the formation of the British Social Democratic Party, which is of course a close ally of the Liberal Party. On the equally problematic difficulty of agreeing on a definition in an Australian context, see Rawson (1986, pp.1-2).
6 Palmer's resistance to absolute principles of property rights is hinted at in his unwillingness to include them in his proposed Bill of Rights.
7 For a brief sketch of the differences between redistributive principles based on Tawney and Rawls, see Wright (1984, p.88).
8 The regressive nature of such a step has been reduced somewhat by tax cuts and benefit increases to low income earners.
9 See *New Zealand Herald*, 2 February 1986, p.5.
10 Academically analysed national samples include one mail survey (Levine and Robinson, 1976); a telephone survey (Gold, 1985); and dissection of 1975 Heylen Research Centre data (Chapman, 1976). There were two relatively large multiple electorate-based studies in 1963 and 1981 — see Robinson (1967) and Bean (1984, pp.506, 516-517).
11 Eden and the new electorate Glenfield were National-held on the basis of the 1981 election; with changed boundaries, West Auckland was theoretically Labour-held but was defended by an incumbent National Member of Parliament. The sample size of the post-election survey was 563, and a response rate of 37.7 per cent achieved. Weighting

within the same number of cases was used to adjust the ratios of occupational groups to those reported in the 1981 census for the three electorates to correct over-representation of professionals and under-representation of manual workers. While improving the overall fit to census characteristics, and particularly bringing weighted sample voting into close proximity to the 1984 distribution of votes in each electorate, the weighting only partially compensates for the problems of a mail survey with a relatively low response rate; in particular, the self-employed are still over-represented.

12 A study of party support in 1981 does, however, include the self-employed in a higher level category (Gold, 1985), and Mitchell (1969, p.213) appears to have classified the self-employed along with professional and managerial groups, thus making his calculations of class voting on a basis of wage earners only, unlike those of Bean (1984). Also see Wilkes, Davis, Tait, and Chrisp (1985), and Chrisp (1986).

13 Multivariate analysis of census data broken down by electorate indicates these two variables were associated with about 70 per cent of the variance between Labour and National support by electorate in the 1978, 1981, and 1984 elections: for a preliminary analysis see Vowles, Crothers, and Nunweek (1985).

14 Statistical significance in all cases except where otherwise stated has been calculated using the chi-squared test (indicated by p-), isolating the figure quoted in a 2 x 2 table on the basis of the entire sample.

15 Significant at p-.01.

16 For a further alternative model using a wider range of data, and for frequency breakdowns of individual variables by voting see Vowles (1985b, pp.10-15). In particular, the addition of feelings about the two main parties and of dichotomized variables representing party identification added another ten per cent to the overall explanatory power of the model, and dropped all attitude and ideological variables except for social welfare and nuclear ship visits.

17 The latter figure is significant at p-.01.

18 The sample weighted or unweighted appears to under-represent Labour voters of 1981 and 1978, and therefore probably also over-represents changers to Labour in 1984.

19 At p-.06.

References

Aitken, J. (1985) New Priorities, New Structures: Treasury and Expenditure Policies in the 1980s. In Gold, H. (Ed.) *New Zealand Politics in Perspective* Auckland, Longman Paul, 112-118.

Bean, C.S. (1984) A Comparative Study of Electoral Behaviour in Australia and New Zealand, unpublished PhD thesis, Australian National University.

Berlin, I. (1969) *Two Concepts of Liberty* London, Oxford.

Brown, B. (1962) *The Rise of New Zealand Labour* Wellington, Price Milburn.

Butcher, D. (1985) Can the Left Cope with Market Socialism? *National Business Review*, 15 July 1985, 7.

Castles, F.G. (1985) *Working Class and Welfare* Wellington, Allen and Unwin.

Chapman, R.M. (1961) *Ends and Means in New Zealand Politics* Auckland, Auckland University Press.

Chapman, R.M. (1969) *The Political Scene 1919-1931* Auckland, Heinemann.

Chapman, R.M. (1976) The Politics of Change. In *National Business Review* 4 August - 13 October 1976.

Chapman, R.M. (1981) From Labour to National. In Oliver, W.H. (Ed.) *The Oxford History of New Zealand* Wellington, Oxford, 333-368.

Chrisp, P. (1986) Labour Sympathies and Social Class *Labour Network* 4: 8-9.

Crothers, C. (1985) Pearson and Thorns: A Methodological Critique. In Crothers, C. (Ed.) *Eclipse of Equality: An Auckland Critique* Auckland, University of Auckland Sociology Department, 28-39.

Dubb, H. (1985) Doing it the Treasury Way *Labour Network* 3: 9-10.

Fairburn, M. (1985) Why Did the New Zealand Labour Party Fail to Win Office Until 1935? *Political Science* 37: 101-124.

Gold, H. (1985) The Social Bases of Party Choice. In Gold, H. (Ed.) *New Zealand Politics in Perspective* Auckland, Longman Paul, 320-333.

Gustafson, B.S. (1976) *Social Change and Party Reorganisation: The New Zealand Labour Party Since 1945* London, Sage.

Gustafson, B.S. (1980) *Labour's Path to Political Independence* Auckland, Auckland University Press/Oxford.

Gustafson, B.S. (1985) The Labour Party. In Gold, H. (Ed.) *New Zealand Politics in Perspective* Auckland, Longman Paul, 141-158.

Hanson, E. (1980) *The Politics of Social Security* Auckland, Auckland University Press/Oxford.

Heath, A., Jowell, R. and Curtice, J. (1985) *How Britain Votes* Oxford, Pergamon.

Julian, R. (1985) Women: How Significant A Force? In Gold, H. (Ed.) *New Zealand Politics in Perspective* Auckland, Longman Paul, 266-272.

Kirk, N.E. (1969) *Towards Nationhood* Palmerston North, New Zealand Books.

Kirk, N.E. (1975) The Philosophy of the Labour Party. In Levine, S. (Ed.) *New Zealand Politics: A Reader* Melbourne, Cheshire, 142-146.

Kelley, J. and McAllister, I. (1985) Class and Party in Australia: Comparison with Britain and the USA *British Journal of Sociology* 34: 383-419.

Lange, D. (1986a) Royal Commission on Social Policy Wellington, Prime Minister's Department.

Lange, D. (1986b) The New Welfare State Prestonpans, Mackintosh Memorial Lecture.

Lange, D. (1986c) New Zealand Under Labour: Interpreting the Politics of Change *POLS* 11: 3-9.

Levine, S. and Robinson, A.D. (1976) *The New Zealand Voter* Wellington, Price Milburn.

Lyon, R. (1982) The Principles of New Zealand Liberal Political Thinking in the Late Nineteenth Century, unpublished PhD thesis, University of Auckland.

Mitchell, A.V. (1969) *Politics and People in New Zealand* Christchurch, Whitcombe and Tombes.

New Zealand Labour Party (1918) *Constitution and Platform* Wellington, New Zealand Labour Party.

New Zealand Labour Party (1922) *Manifesto of the New Zealand Labour Party: 1922 Election* Wellington, New Zealand Labour Party.

New Zealand Labour Party (1934) *Labour Has a Plan* Wellington, New Zealand Labour Party.

New Zealand Labour Party (1952) The Principles of Labour. In New Zealand Labour Party Executive Minutes.

New Zealand Labour Party (1962) Draft Statement on Aims and Objectives. In *Report of the 46th Annual Conference* Wellington, New Zealand Labour Party, 18-20.

New Zealand Labour Party (1979) *Constitution and Rules* Wellington, New Zealand Labour Party.

Nove, A. (1983) *The Economics of Feasible Socialism* London, Allen and Unwin.

Oliver, R.B. (1981) A Study of the Ideology of the New Zealand Labour Party in the 1930s, unpublished MA thesis, Auckland.

Palmer, G. (1977) Winning is the Name of the Game. In *It's Time to Think* Wellington, New Zealand Labour Party, 31-40.

Paul, J.T. (1946) *Humanism In Politics* Wellington, New Zealand Worker.

Perrings, C. (1985) Speenhamland Revisited *Labour Network* 3: 8-10.

Rawson, D. (Ed.) (1986) *Blast, Budge, or Bypass: Towards a Social Democratic Australia* Canberra, Academy of the Social Sciences in Australia.

Rawls, J. (1971) *A Theory of Justice* Cambridge, Mass., Harvard University Press.

Robinson, A.D. (1967) Class Voting in New Zealand. In Lipset, S.M. and Rokkan, S. (Eds) *Party Systems and Voter Alignments* New York, Free Press, 95-114.

Sinclair, K. (1959) *A History of New Zealand* Harmondsworth, Penguin.

Sinclair, K. (1976) *Walter Nash* Auckland, Auckland University Press/Oxford.

Shorter, C.B. (1974) Political Thought in New Zealand, unpublished MA thesis, Auckland.

Slater, M. (1985) Should Benefits be Targetted? *New Nation* 5 March.

Tawney, R.H. (1920) *The Acquisitive Society* New York, Harvest.

Tawney, R.H. (1964) *Equality* London, Unwin.

Vowles, J. (1982) Ideology and the Formation of the New Zealand Labour Party: Some New Evidence *New Zealand Journal of History* 16: 39-55.

Vowles, J. (1983) New Zealand: Social Democracy in the Balance. In Davis, P. (Ed.) *New Zealand Labour Perspectives II: Social Democracy in the Pacific* Auckland, Davis, 28-47.

Vowles, J. (1985a) Delegates Compared: A Sociology of the National, Labour, and Social Credit Party Conferences, 1983 *Political Science* 37: 1-17.

Vowles, J. (1985b) Social Structure, Political Attitudes, and Trade Unionism: An Analysis of Aspects of the Fourth Labour Government's Electoral Coalition. *New Zealand Political Studies Association Conference Paper*, Auckland.

Vowles, J. Crothers, C. and Nunweek, B. (1985) Social Class and the Electoral Landscape: Towards a Revival of New Zealand Political Ecology. New Zealand Political Studies Association Conference Paper, Auckland.

Wilkes, C. Davis, P. Tait, P. and Chrisp, P. (1985) The Jobs and Attitudes Survey: the New Zealand Class Structure. *Report for the Social Sciences Research Fund Committee*, Massey University, Palmerston North.

Wright, A.W. (1984) Tawneyism Revisited: Equality, Welfare, and Socialism. In Pimlott, B. (Ed.) *Fabian Essays in Socialist Thought* London, Heinemann, 81-100.

3

Nats, Fat Cats, and Democrats
The Opposition Parties Under Labour

Nigel S. Roberts

The first two years of the life of the fourth Labour Government were charmed. The Government was very much in the ascendancy. Opinion poll statistics reproduced in Figure 3.1 show that during the period from July 1984 until September 1986, Labour was only twice ranked below National as the preferred party of government — and on each occasion it quickly regained the lead.

Conversely, the opposition parties were confused, divided, and demoralized. National changed leaders twice; the New Zealand Party twice tried to dissolve itself (losing a leader on each occasion); and Social Credit lost not only its name, deputy-leader, and leader (in that order), but also its credibility. Many of these events had a strong sense of *deja vu* about them. The replacement of Jim McLay by Jim Bolger as leader of the National Party in late March 1986 (in all probability 18 months prior to the next General Election in September 1987) paralleled the overthrow of Jack Marshall by Robert Muldoon in July 1974. Similarly, the decline by the Social Credit/Democratic Party in the opinion polls and the subsequent intra-party feuding were reminiscent of the traumatic period faced by the party after its electoral support fell sharply in 1969 and the party's leader, Vernon Cracknell, had lost his seat in Parliament. Looking ahead to the next General Election a former President of the National Party, Sir George Chapman, has argued that "history looks like repeating itself in 1987" (*National Business Review*, 5 September 1986, p.11). Whether this will be so, time alone can tell; but the experiences of the opposition parties during the first two years or so of the fourth Labour Government are similar enough to those of previous periods in the electoral and parliamentary history of both New Zealand and other countries to demand careful examination. Hence, while the rest of this book concentrates on the actions of the Labour Government, this chapter analyses and assesses the behaviour of New Zealand's main opposition parties — the National Party, the New Zealand Party and the Democratic Party — since July 1984.

Of course, these are not the only political parties opposed to the fourth Labour Government. The 1984 snap-election was contested by a myriad of minor parties, the most notable being Mana Motuhake and Values. Both underline the problems faced by tiny parties in a predominantly two-party parliamentary system with first-past-the-post elections: they get virtually no publicity on a day-to-day basis; they have few members and even fewer active ones; they are starved for funds; and

Figure 3.1
Public opinion poll results 1984 to 1986

Election

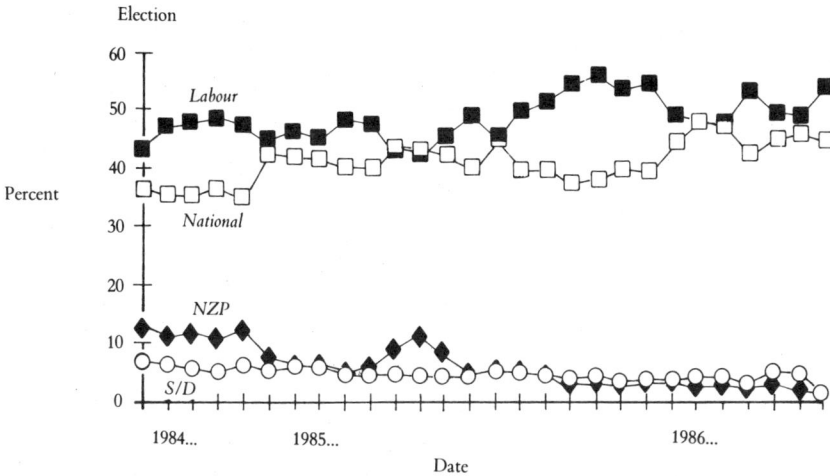

Date

Responses to the question: If a general election were held today, which political party would you vote for?

Source: Heylen Research Centre, 1986, p. 6.

their leadership is dispersed and fragmented. Indeed, parties this small are really only election-time phenomena. They barely exist during inter-election periods (although Values was alive and reasonably well during 1972 to 1975). In the words of Maurice Duverger, they are "not ... capable of playing an important part either in the government or *in the opposition*" (Duverger, 1954, p.290; author's emphasis). Consequently, for the purposes of this chapter they can reasonably be ignored.

National's Heritage

When the National Party was founded in 1936, the new organization included among its objectives the pursuit of "progressive and humanitarian legislation". Proposals that the party should pledge to "combat Communism and Socialism" and to "oppose interference by the State in business" were defeated, because as Gustafson has argued, "it was essential that the party officially stand for positive objects rather than exist simply as a negative reaction to Labour" (1986, p.9). Nevertheless, from its earliest days the National Party's publicity stressed that it stood "for the liberty and security of the individual, and opposes Socialism and Communism" (to quote a 1936 party pamphlet), and that it believed "the right of free enterprise to be essential to the prosperity and vitality of our country" (to quote a 1943 party leaflet: see Gustafson, 1986, pp.10 and 182).

Consequently, like most political parties the National Party has always had conflicting objectives. On the one hand, both the former party President, Sir Alex McKenzie, and party critic, Professor John Roberts, are in agreement that National has not been dedicated to the principle of non-intervention in the economy. In his 1959 presidential address to the party, for example, McKenzie argued that in matters "of vital concern to the great mass of the people" a National Government had an "over-riding responsibility to intervene", and he championed "the benefit of co-ordination and guarantee by a central authority" (see Gustafson, 1986, p.183). Twenty-four years later Roberts noted baldly that National has:

> ... never been a party of non-intervention, a party ... encouraging private enterprise. They have been, from their very first period of office in 1949, interventionist manipulators ... They've been a social welfare minded, middle of the road, state centrist party (*Truth*, 31 August 1983).

On the other hand, however, the current objectives of the party are, *inter alia*, "to emphasise in all policies the freedom and independence of the individual and the promotion of individual effort, initiative and opportunity coupled with responsibility" and "to encourage sound economic growth through competition and the promotion of individual ownership and private enterprise" (New Zealand National Party, 1986, pp.3-4). Yet, paradoxically, policies based on these principles have tended to be stressed only when the party has found itself in Opposition. For example, it is instructive to consider some of the policies espoused by National when it was last in Opposition, during the term of the third Labour Government.

National reacted adversely to the establishment of the New Zealand Superannuation Corporation by the third Labour Government. The large pool of investment funds that would have been available to the Superannuation Corporation was of particular concern to the Opposition (Roberts, 1975, pp.114-115), and as a result the National Party's manifesto for the 1975 General Election promised that "the *trend towards State ownership and control will be reversed* and the vast superannuation fund which is designed to provide State ownership of industry will be abolished". Furthermore, the party pledged that a National Government would "work with Commercial bodies and Trade associations *to develop competitive enterprise and maintain a vigorous private sector* "; but at the same time it also warned that "a prices-incomes policy will be essential", entailing "a continuation of price control" (Muldoon, 1975, pp.20/2 and 21/2; author's emphasis).

National's sweeping victory in the 1975 General Election meant that the third National Government was able to start implementing its policies with determination and speed and, initially, without even summoning Parliament (Levine, 1977, p.100). The new National Administration followed its stated policies closely, and lowered or removed subsidies (and thus raised prices) on a wide range of products within weeks of taking office (Roberts, 1976, p.112). It also reduced public expenditure significantly and cut the Budget deficit. By the end of 1976, the Prime Minister, Robert Muldoon, was claiming that his Government had "implemented more of its election policy in its first year than any other government" *(New Zealand Parliamentary Debates,* 1976, p.4754).

But governments are often pulled in different directions, and the National Administration of Muldoon was no exception. In March 1978, in a policy reversal reminiscent of Edward Heath's famous 1972 U-turn in Britain (Butler and Kavanagh, 1974, pp.23-24), the Muldoon Government, far from fulfilling its campaign promise to give "workers in every industry the choice of voluntary or compulsory unionism" (Muldoon, 1975, p.7/1), went so far as to settle a pay dispute by offering freezing workers NZ$3 million in public funds. Expressions of "extreme concern" and "horror" by the executive director of the Freezing Companies Association underlined both the degree to which the Government had departed from its expected course of action, and the degree to which the National Party was prepared to intervene in the running of the economy. After this the standing of the party never recovered; although it won the 1978 and 1981 elections it did so on each occasion with fewer votes than Labour.

Two of the most important influences on the life of the National Government — as well as on the debates that racked National once it was in Opposition — occurred within days of each other in June 1982. On 7 June, Derek Quigley, the Minister of Works and Development, criticized the "Think Big" energy projects undertaken by the Government, and argued that "our main problem as a governing party is ... one of identity. We haven't as yet decided whether we should continue to attempt to dominate the economy, or adopt a more passive role" (*The Dominion,* 11 June 1982, p.6). Not only was Quigley dismissed from the Cabinet for raising such questions, but his views were also directly countered by other members of the Government. Aussie Malcolm, the Minister of Health, for example, gave one of the clearest expositions of the pragmatic basis of the Muldoon Government's economic policies when he said they were:

> ... not pure, calculated, precise, right-wing free-market politics as espoused by those who are born to privilege or who have gained it. It is, however, human politics. There should be no confusion about the Government's role in this. It is a participant — an active and vigorous participant (*Evening Post,* 19 June 1982).

Then, little more than a week after Derek Quigley was forced to leave the Cabinet, Muldoon showed just how active and vigorous a participant his Government was in the management of the economy by announcing the introduction of a comprehensive year-long prices and wages freeze. The significance of the introduction of the freeze on mid-winter's day was not lost on many National MPs, who were "stunned by the extent of the measures. One MP ... pointed out that what Mr

Muldoon had done was more to the left than anything the Labour Party would have contemplated" (*Evening Post*, 23 June 1982).

These two events defined the ideological split in National more clearly than any other actions of the Muldoon Government. On the one hand, the free marketeers in the party had a spokesman (if not a martyr); on the other hand, the Prime Minister was clearly prepared to use regulations under the *Economic Stabilisation Act 1948* to an extent and for a period of time virtually unknown outside wartime conditions in any Western country (see Chapter 9). The fact that these two events also contributed to National's downfall two years later meant that they were to have serious reverberations within, and repercussions for, the National Party once it was in Opposition.

The circumstances surrounding the 1984 General Election also contributed to the difficulties faced by National in Opposition. The unnecessary and ill-judged snap-election was opposed by the party's administrative hierarchy. For example, Sue Wood, the then President of the party, had warned that "an early election would be disastrous", and even Muldoon later conceded that "the party organization was not ready for an election" (*The Dominion*, 10 March 1986). As a result, both Wood and Barrie Leay, the General Director of the party, later found themselves aligned against Muldoon in a battle that raged within the party for more than two years.

Internecine Warfare

Losing the election did not start the battle. As has already been shown, there were clear philosophical rifts within the National Party when it held the reins of government. But defeat for a political party is always hard to bear, the more so when the party is the incumbent Government and seen, by itself at least, as the natural party of government. In this respect, there are obvious parallels between the New Zealand National Party, on the one hand, and the Australian Liberal Party and the British Conservative Party, on the other. All three have dominated post-war politics in their respective countries, and National's shock of losing office in 1984 bore many resemblances to the pain the Tories experienced when they lost the snap-elections in Britain in February and October 1974 (Butler and Kavanagh, 1974, pp.268-269; Butler and Kavanagh, 1980, p.60), and to the distress visited upon the Australian Liberal Party when it lost the snap-election called by Malcolm Fraser in 1983 (Penniman, 1983, pp.248-320).

The altercations, bitterness, and confusion that dominated the behaviour of the National Party during the period from July 1984 to March 1986 were thus hardly surprising. Whereas Fraser resigned the leadership of the Liberal Party immediately after the defeat of the Government he had led for more than seven years (Hughes, 1983, pp.304-305), Muldoon, like Heath in Britain ten years earlier (Butler and Kavanagh, 1980, pp.61-63), clung to power as leader of a party that generally judged him to be the architect of its defeat. In late July 1984, the National Caucus agreed to let Sir Robert stay on as leader until early 1985, while Muldoon announced that "it is unlikely I will be a candidate" (*Evening Post*, 20 July 1984). Four months later, however, he said that he would contest the leadership because "I am not yet satisfied that one of the declared candidates is capable of turning this government out as I am" (*The Dominion*, 23 November 1984). In response, the National Caucus hurriedly brought the date for considering the issue forward — first to late December, then forward again a few days later to 29 November 1984, when Muldoon was finally toppled from the leadership. At the time, few people recollected that it was exactly nine years to the day since Muldoon's triumphant sweep to power in the 1975 General Election. If an outsider such as Margaret Thatcher could beat Edward Heath (Butler and Kavanagh, 1980, p.62), then Muldoon's defeat by his own deputy-leader, Jim McLay, was wholly predictable. However, Andrew Peacock's rough road in Australia was an equally good indicator of the perilous path that the new leader of the National Party in New Zealand would have to follow. Just as Peacock lacked the support of his deputy, John Howard, so too was McLay denied the loyalty and support of his former leader, who spent 1985 openly campaigning to remove his successor.

Less than a week after he had been elected leader, McLay was complaining that Muldoon's attacks on him could not be tolerated, and early in 1985 matters became far more serious when groups of National Party supporters established the Sunday Club dedicated to restoring Muldoon as party leader and displacing Wood and Leay from their positions at the top of the party's administrative structure. "The party wolves are baying", Richard Long concluded correctly in early 1985 (*The Dominion*, 9 April 1985). The wonder of it really is not how short McLay's leadership of the party was, but how he managed to retain his position for another 11 months. Throughout 1985 the National Party fought internally with a fervour that astonished observers and delighted its opponents. The one bright spot for the party was the Timaru by-election in June, where National won the seat previously held by Labour for 57 years. But National failed to capitalize on this victory: what could have been a turning point was instead a diversion, as the party's annual conference held a short while later saw Muldoon supporters raise embarrassing questions about loans to party officials and National Members of Parliament.

After a public dispute in October about whether Sir Robert would be elevated to National's front-bench McLay demoted Muldoon to 38th position, the lowest possible, in the Opposition's rankings. "He's broken [our] deal and yet again he's demonstrated that he's not prepared to work within the commonly accepted standards of the Caucus", complained McLay (*The Dominion*, 19 October 1985). Muldoon countered that the party's leadership contained "some political pygmies" (*Evening Post*, 21 October 1985).

In one sense, Muldoon was undoubtedly correct. Immediately after the 1984 election, McLay's personal standing in the opinion polls had risen sharply, while Muldoon's had declined. As Figure 3.2 shows, four per cent of Heylen's July 1984 sample chose McLay as the politician they preferred to be Prime Minister. By early December, the figure was 11 per cent. Muldoon, by way of contrast, fell from being the preferred choice of 24 per cent to less than ten per cent by October 1984. Thereafter, however, support for McLay fell back to an average of only four per cent throughout 1985, while Muldoon climbed to an average of 20 per cent. Significantly, even McLay's deputy-leader, Jim Bolger, had surpassed McLay in the polls by October 1985. The writing, if not on the wall, was in the polls for McLay.

Figure 3.2
Preferred Prime Minister 1984 to 1986

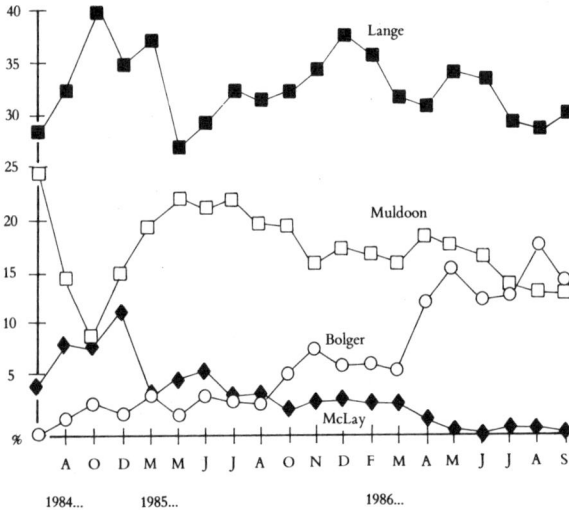

Responses to the question: Of all the politicians in New Zealand of any party, which one would you personally prefer to be Prime Minister right now?

Source: Heylen Research Centre, 1986, p. 17.

The ferocity of Muldoon's battle and the siege faced by McLay are without precedent in New Zealand. Although Sir John Marshall had shown a lack of loyalty towards Muldoon after being deposed by him in July 1974, it must be borne in mind that Marshall was never supported by an extra-parliamentary ginger group like the Sunday Club, and that by the time of the 1975 General Election he had retired from Parliament wearing the mantle of an elder statesman (Roberts, 1976, pp.100-101). The undermining of McLay by Muldoon was not without irony. As *The Dominion* pointed out in a trenchant editorial:

Sir Robert sacked Mr. Quigley from Cabinet and, according to Mr. Minogue, demanded the Hamilton West MP's resignation when he criticised the Security Intelligence Service Amendment Bill in 1977. Sir Robert, in short, demanded unquestioning loyalty from his colleagues, but he is not prepared to give it himself (*The Dominion*, 25 October 1985).

To some extent, Muldoon's stance could be equated with the lack of loyalty that Heath has had for Thatcher ever since she deposed him as leader of the British Conservative Party. Unlike Thatcher, however, McLay and his allies within the ranks of the party's organization made several crucial errors. The attempt to expel critics of McLay (such as the deputy chairperson of the party's Methven branch, Margaret Quin, and former Cabinet Minister, Ian Shearer) from the party was inept. This merely resulted in a loss of both face and money as a result of an out of Court settlement. Similarly, McLay's shadow-Cabinet reshuffle on 10 February 1986 was constructed without finesse or forethought. The demotion of senior Caucus colleagues like George Gair (dropped from fourth place to eleventh in Caucus seniority), Bill Birch (dropped from third place to twelfth place), and John Falloon (from seventh to tenth place) provoked antagonism.

This provocation was answered on 26 March 1986, when McLay was deposed even more easily than Andrew Peacock had been as Australian Liberal Party Leader in September 1985. Significantly, the leaders of the group that deposed McLay included George Gair and Bill Birch. As was mentioned in the introduction to this chapter, the coup within the National Party was very similar to the coup that had deposed Marshall and installed Muldoon as leader of the National Party in July 1974 (Jackson, 1975, pp.8-20; Muldoon, 1977, pp.82-96).

Indeed, there are further parallels with the situation in 1974. Three weeks before McLay was deposed, Wood had announced that she would not stand for re-election as the President of the party. From the perspective of Sir Robert and his Sunday Club supporters, it was a case of one down, two to go. McLay's defeat made it two down with only one — Barrie Leay — to go. Less than three months later, Leay announced that he too would "declare his innings" (*Evening Post*, 18 June 1986). As a result, the National Party found itself in a position it had not faced for more than a decade: it had a new parliamentary leader; a new President (Neville Young, who was elected in August 1986); and the opportunity to appoint a new General Director. In 1975 National used its newly installed team to great effect: it had a new leader (Muldoon), a new General Director (Leay, chosen in 1973), a new President (George Chapman, elected in 1973), and a new director of research (David Lloyd, appointed in 1974). In 1986/87, National has a similar opportunity to use its new leadership team to construct a campaign that will capture the imagination of New Zealand's voters and the reins of government. That Bolger and his colleagues have made a start in that direction cannot be doubted. The opinion poll results reproduced in Figure 3.1 and the new leader's own standing in the polls (Figure 3.2) are encouraging for the party and a clear contrast with McLay's dismal showing in the polls.

Enterprise and Intervention

However, one major difficulty for the party is its inability to agree on a common philosophy and, consequently but even more importantly, its failure to unite its supporters behind an agreed set of policies. The ideological divisions within the Muldoon Government still confront the party in Opposition.

Immediately after the 1984 General Election, Sir George Chapman blamed "socialist-type interventionist economic policies" for National's defeat. He criticized the Muldoon Government's policies of attempting to control interest rates and inflation, and said that they had badly hurt the image of National's private enterprise philosophy. Not surprisingly, Derek Quigley, who had stepped down as an MP prior to the election, agreed: "We did not adhere to what so many of the National Party believed we were all about" (*The Dominion*, 16 July 1984). Ironically, the policies adopted by the Labour Government made finding new directions for the National Party even more difficult than they would normally have been. In one of the most remarkable developments in New Zealand's political history, the Lange Administration — guided by the strongly-held views of its Minister of Finance, Roger Douglas, and urged on by a delighted Treasury — began to implement free-market economic policies and to deregulate many aspects of the country's commercial life. Other chapters in this book consider these moves in more detail. Suffice it to say here, that the new directions taken by Labour have had profound implications for National. One of the reasons why Labour was sufficiently emboldened to strike out on a new economic course was that the old ways of managing the New Zealand economy had been thoroughly discredited by Muldoon and his colleagues. But where did this leave the National Party? It could hardly advocate a return to the old policies it had recently implemented but which had been so decisively rejected by the electorate.

Within two weeks of the 1984 election, McLay tried to shift his party's thinking. Economic intervention "cost us votes", he argued. "What we need now are the strategies that remove the need for further government intervention" (*The Dominion*, 31 July 1984). When he formally announced his candidacy for the leadership of the party, McLay elaborated on his ideas, propounding:

> ... a belief in free enterprise [and] the effectiveness of a competitive marketplace ... Give a trader competition and he or she will respond. Make railways and road transport compete. They respond and costs drop dramatically. Competition provides people with more jobs and raises their standard of living (*The Dominion*, 30 October 1984).

Once he became leader of the party, McLay tried to promote and expand these views, but he was dogged by three difficulties. For a start, he had an important role in the formation of the policies pursued by the Muldoon Administration: he had been Muldoon's Deputy Prime Minister. Second, his continuing fight with Muldoon distracted him, and the attention of the public, from policy formation; and third, as Labour's policies began to bite and pain began to be felt particularly in the farming sector, there was a natural temptation for some members of the National Caucus to call for palliatives. Not only was McLay unable to control Muldoon, but he was also unable to prevent disagreements within Caucus on economic strategy from being aired in public. Just one month before his accession to the leadership of the party, Jim Bolger, McLay's deputy-leader, signalled the fact that he was an important source of dissent within the party. He argued strongly against "articulating some ultra-right policy which would appear to value wealth and the creation of wealth over the needs of people ... Even worse would be to try and join the new failing economic bandwagon pushed by the Minister of Finance, Mr Douglas, and the technocrats in the Labour Party" (*Evening Post*, 25 February 1986).

Bolger's implicit criticisms of the policy directions of the National Party under McLay's leadership were followed by dissenting statements from other MPs such as Tony Friedlander and Winston Peters. Friedlander said he did not join the National Party for the dream of a virtually unfettered free market, and:

> At a time when uncharacteristic Labour Party policies of freeing up the market-place are doing immense harm to the people we represent, our spokesmen have curiously concentrated on emphasising the free-market mechanisms National will use to rectify it. Unfortunately, in some cases there is even a hint of support for the very policies which are currently doing so much damage. Governments must govern. Every National Party conference over the past 20 years has called on National's government to influence market forces in one form or another (*The Dominion*, 14 March 1986).

Similarly, Peters advocated that National reject the Labour Government's "doctrinaire experimentation" in favour of "tried and true principles that had worked in the past and, if reshaped and remodelled, would work in the future".

These views took on a great deal of significance when Bolger became leader of the party. His first speech after winning power was widely interpreted as debunking free-market theory, and he quickly hinted at the need for a National Government to return to a more interventionist style. Taken together with his promotion of Muldoon (raised from 38th place to eighth in Caucus rankings), his promotion of the previous Government's main advocate and architect of "Think Big" policies, Bill Birch (up from 12th to third place), and his promotion of both Tony Friedlander and Winston Peters (from 18th and 20th positions in the Caucus to the ninth and 15th slots respectively), the changes from the days of McLay were profound.

McLay's decision to retire altogether from politics, at the time of the next election, underlined the significance of the philosophical shift in the National Party's perspective.

Double Dissolution

One of the factors that contributed to the defeat of the Muldoon Government was the New Zealand Party. The party was formed in late 1983 with millionaire property investor Bob Jones as its mentor and leader. Even though it had been in existence for only a short while, the party played a crucial role in the 1984 General Election, when it won 12.3 per cent of the votes (a remarkable achievement by any standards, but especially so in a first-past-the-post electoral system). Despite the fact that the New Zealand Party won no seats, the overall result — the defeat of the Muldoon Administration — was wholly in accord with Jones' reasons for founding the new party.

After the election, however, the New Zealand Party was in a quandary. The fourth Labour Government instituted many of the New Zealand Party's policies. Financial markets were freed from constraints and restrictions; controls on interest rates, prices and wages were abolished; and by early March 1985 Labour had floated the New Zealand dollar. In addition, Labour's foreign affairs and defence initiatives led to a nuclear-free New Zealand — yet another policy strongly advocated by the New Zealand Party (see Chapters 11 and 12). Taken together with the fact that the New Zealand Party had not won a parliamentary seat, there was little to justify their continued existence, and the leader's enthusiasm waned markedly.

Nevertheless, Jones' announcement in mid-1985 that his party would be going into recess caught many observers by surprise — including the party's executive! Jones resigned as party leader, but the party refused to dissolve itself. Instead, John Galvin was elected in Jones' place, and the executive resolved to continue in existence. Beset with the twin problems that face all minor parties (especially those with no parliamentary base from which to maintain even a minimum profile), namely a lack of publicity and a lack of money, the party soldiered on for eight more months until March 1986 when the executive decided (this time by a narrow 4 to 3 majority) to disband and urge its members to join the National Party. In an ironic twist of timing, the so-called "merger" was decided on 26 March, the very day that the National Party Caucus deposed McLay in favour of Bolger as its leader. As a rural interventionist, Bolger is the personification of many of the forces and ideas that had originally led to the formation of the New Zealand Party — so much so that in December 1985 Bob Jones threatened to re-enter politics if Bolger were ever to become leader of the National Party. Although he has not acted on that threat, the chances of Jones being persuaded either to campaign directly for the National Party, or less directly, simply to urge former New Zealand Party voters to cast their votes for National candidates are extremely remote. Jones' "annointment" or "blessing" would be a considerable advantage for a political party in 1987, and "Rogernomics" means that Labour is more likely to benefit from it than National. In more ways than one, Bob Jones was the "joker" of the electoral pack in 1984. He may yet perform the same role, but in a somewhat different style, at the time of the next General Election.

Not everyone accepted the proposal to dissolve the New Zealand Party in late March 1986. The party's deputy leader, Janie Pearce, and others have tried to resurrect the party from the grave of its merger, but there seems little likelihood that they will be able to achieve this miracle. Even Pearce has admitted that those within the party opposed to its dissolution may now have to regroup and, possibly, fight the next election under a new name.

There are parallels between the New Zealand Party and the Progress parties in Denmark and Norway (Aimer, 1985, p.201; Aimer, 1986, pp.1-13). For example, the three parties were all founded by ebullient, charismatic men who attracted publicity in their own right. The Danish Progress Party was founded by tax lawyer, Mogens Glistrup. When his fortunes declined (true to his anti-tax principles, he was convicted of tax evasion and sent to prison), his party's fortunes also declined markedly. Likewise, after the death of its founder, Anders Lange, the Norwegian Progress Party lost its representation in the Norwegian Parliament for a term, and is now the smallest party in the Storting with just two seats. In a similar way, the rise and fall of the New Zealand Party are inextricably linked with the role played by Bob Jones: he attracted a great deal of publicity both before and during the 1984 election campaign, his public appearances drew large audiences, and the news media could always rely on him for pungent, controversial copy. Once he left, in somewhat predictable style given his previous involvement with a diverse range of organizations ranging from ballet companies to women's refuge centres, the party's fortunes inevitably never recovered.

... But Names Will Never Hurt Me?

Social Credit's political fortunes were on the wane long before the 1984 General Election. Despite having fought its best two elections ever in 1978 (winning 16 per cent of the poll and one seat) and 1981 (with 21 per cent of votes cast and two seats), the party suffered a major loss of support in mid-1982 when its two MPs voted to save the National Government's plans for a high dam on the Clutha River. To arrest the decline, the party sought a new image and at its 1982 conference voted to alter its name from the Social Credit Political League to the Social Credit Party. The public wasn't deceived by such timidity and, faced with a strong challenge for third party status by the New Zealand Party in 1984, Social Credit's vote was reduced by more than 13 per cent in the snap-election. What is more, Social Credit's long-time-leader, Bruce Beetham, lost his Rangitikei seat in the election to National, although the party managed to retain its overall complement of two seats by holding East Coast Bays and winning Pakuranga from National.

A decline in the party's support and an accompanying loss of the leader's parliamentary seat had occurred in 1969. On that occasion "recriminations and wrangling followed on a gargantuan — and Gilbertian — scale" (Roberts, 1975, p.102). After the 1984 General Election, similar squabbles broke out amongst Social Credit supporters. In May 1985 Social Credit decided to complete the process it had tentatively started nearly three years previously, and the party's annual conference voted to change its name to the New Zealand Democratic Party. This cosmetic change altered nothing with respect to the party's standing in the public opinion polls and, as Figure 3.1 indicates, by mid-1986 the party's support hovered around only four per cent in the Heylen polls. In early 1986 the party's deputy-leader (and the senior of its two MPs), Garry Knapp, tried to persuade Beetham to stand aside as party leader. Knapp failed to achieve this goal, and as a result announced that he was resigning as deputy-leader and that he would retire from politics at the end of the parliamentary term. Beetham, however, remained increasingly isolated as leader of the Democrats, a point that was initially underlined when the party chose Neil Morrison — a trenchant critic of Beetham — as its new deputy-leader to replace Knapp. Only four months later the party's annual conference rejected Beetham as leader (after he had held the position for 14 years) and elected Morrison in his stead. Beetham's view that Morrison had been installed as a "puppet leader" by a "clique who had hijacked the party" was reminiscent of rhetoric from Albania rather than New Zealand, and only served to isolate Beetham still further from the party he had previously served so well and for so long.

Some Theoretical Considerations

The surprising aspect of an examination of the behaviour of opposition parties under the fourth Labour Government is the paucity of theory to aid that examination. For example, the seminal work edited by Robert Dahl, *Political Oppositions in Western Democracies*, is basically concerned with how opposition parties come to be accepted as a legitimate and integral part of Western political systems, not about how opposition parties can be expected to behave, or why (Dahl, 1966).

Furthermore, at first sight there appears to be a case for saying that the policies espoused since July 1984 by New Zealand's two main political parties actually damage an important theory that has won a significant degree of acceptance in New Zealand with regard to the behaviour of political parties. Anthony Downs' *Economic Theory of Democracy* constructs a scale based on the following argument:

> If we assume that the left end of the scale represents full government control, and the right end means a completely free market, we can rank parties by their views on

this issue in a way that might be nearly universally recognised as accurate (Downs, 1957, p.116).

Then, says Downs, political parties like "two grocery stores ... will converge on the same ocation until practically all voters are indifferent between them", especially if the electorate is composed of "voters whose preferences cause them to be normally distributed" (Downs, 1957, pp.117-118).

Provided that the New Zealand electorate can be assumed to have a normal attitudinal and partisan distribution, and as long as the Labour Party is generally judged to be middle-of-the-road/left and National centrist/right, New Zealand politics fits the Downs model with exceptional accuracy. However, what is now to be made of a Labour Party pursuing free market goals (placed at "the right end" of Downs' spectrum), while National's leader, as we have seen, rejects an "ultra-right policy which would appear to value wealth ... over the needs of people"? Is this the downfall of Downs' theory?

On three accounts, the answer is no. Firstly, National's economic policies are far from clear. While Bolger is generally seen as something of a traditionalist in economic terms, he is neither National's finance spokesperson, nor has he ever held Cabinet portfolios in this field. It is significant that two of the party's three spokesmen on finance were publicly at odds with Bolger as late as mid-October 1986. Taxation spokesman Doug Graham dissented from the view that National would automatically repeal Labour's Goods and Services Tax (GST). "Whether we do," he said, "will depend on how the country reacts to it. If everyone loves it, then we will reconsider" (*The Dominion*, 7 October 1986). Although Bolger was, in the words of one journalist, "quick to jump on this indication of open-mindedness" (*The Dominion*, 10 October 1986) a few days later George Gair muddied the waters by arguing that the National Party was "not interested in change for the sake of change" (*The Dominion*, 16 October 1986). When National's economic policies for the next election are announced, they will probably be close to Labour's free market orientation. Details will differ, but the agenda for political action has been rewritten, not so much by Labour as by overseas trends which Labour has accepted, and National will not find itself outflanked to any significant degree on "the right end" — the free market end — of Anthony Downs' scale. As has been the case for many decades in New Zealand, Labour and National will vie for a place near the centre of the scale, but it is a scale that has, in effect, been reconstructed as their respective policy agenda have been rewritten. Certainly, National is not planning simply to change places with Labour on the old scale.

Secondly, Downs' *An Economic Theory of Democracy* also posits the view that:

> ... parties in a two-party system converge ideologically upon the centre ... [and], therefore, in the middle of the scale where most voters are massed, each party scatters its policies on both sides of the mid-point. It attempts to make each voter in this area

feel that it is centred right at his position. Naturally, this causes an enormous
overlapping of moderate policies (pp.140 and 135).

New Zealand's politics have long exhibited these tendencies. Two examples will
suffice. In the mid-1970s, New Zealand was treated to the ironic spectacle of a
supposedly egalitarian Labour Party promoting the "earnings-related contributory
funded" New Zealand Superannuation Scheme while reputedly elitist National, on
the other hand, favoured a "generous ... simple ... flat-rate pay-as-you-go scheme"
(Easton, 1979, pp.73-74; see also Chapter 2). Second, before the Muldoon Administration was even one term old, Bob Jones put forward the view that "Muldoon's
personal belligerency draws a considerable working-class support just as Rowling's
more genteel facade attracts a white collar erosion, notably from women" (Jones,
1978, p.23). Jones then produced a classic, if unwitting, summary of the Downs'
thesis:

> ... by his leftward actions Muldoon is stealing Labour's sizable vote-base while
> Rowling moves in his utterances more and more to the right for only marginal gains
> numerically. Party political philosophy appears to have gone down the drain as the
> two leaders battle for the middle ground (p.24).

Consequently, there is no need for surprise at finding either that the Muldoon
Government adopted a strongly interventionist set of economic policies or that the
fourth Labour Government is currently promoting policies that, arguably at least,
could be expected to be more suited to the promulgated philosophy of the National
Party. These facets of New Zealand politics simply reinforce Downs' argument that
"in two-party systems there is a large area of overlapping policies near the middle of
the scale, so that parties closely resemble each other" (1957, p.141).

Finally, there is an even more compelling reason for rejecting the view that *An
Economic Theory of Democracy* fails to account for changes such as those that have
occurred in New Zealand since mid-1984. Downs himself argues against "the
assumption that each party's platform contains only its stand on the proper degree of
government intervention in the economy. ... Each party takes stands on many issues
..." (p.132); he elaborates on this argument by adding that:

> ... each citizen may apply different weights to the individual policies, since each policy
> affects some citizens more than others. Therefore the party has no unique, universally
> recognised net position. Some voters may feel it is more right-wing than others, and
> no one can be proved correct. However, there will be some consensus as to the range in
> which the parties' net position lies; so we can still distinguish right-wing parties from
> centre and left-wing ones (p.133).

Thus, it may still be valid to distinguish in broad terms between National as a
centre-right party and Labour as centre-left. There are many issues where the
traditional left-right distinctions between Labour and National still apply. For

example, the National Party has criticized the fourth Labour Government for refusing to deregulate the labour market in New Zealand. Labour's industrial relations policies have not won widespread favour amongst private or public sector unions, but neither have they been strongly supported by employers. National's pledge to reintroduce voluntary unionism is in no danger of being interpreted as a left-wing policy. Furthermore, support for income redistribution, the role of the State in providing basic social services as well as the public ownership and control of resources and utilities (even if through corporatization) all locate Labour firmly on the left of any unidimensional policy continuum. The National Party's opposition to the New Zealand Nuclear Free Zone, Disarmament and Arms Control Bill is implacable, and a wide gulf exists between Labour's non-nuclear policies and National's stance on ANZUS and plans to restore the *status quo ante*. Similarly, far more National parliamentarians than Labour took a conservative stand with respect to the Homosexual Law Reform Bill. Although opposition to the Bill was spear-headed by a Labour MP (Geoffrey Braybrooke) as well as a National MP (Graeme Lee), the Bill was promoted by Fran Wilde, a Labour MP and Junior Whip. The overwhelming bulk of the Bill's supporters were Labour. Of the 49 MPs who voted for the Bill on its third reading, only three were National: George Gair, Ian McLean and Katherine O'Regan. As Downs has argued, "voters choose policy vectors rather than policy scalars, and each vector is really a weighted frequency distribution of policies on the left-right scale" (p.133). Despite the unexpected upheaval for New Zealand politics that "Rogernomics" represents, Labour and National's policy vectors are still left- and right-oriented respectively.

It is necessary to turn briefly to another theoretical perspective on the behaviour of political parties. Maurice Duverger's *Political Parties* is helpful with its distinction between "parties with a majority bent" and others. Duverger argues that "a party with a majority bent knows that it is likely at some date to have to shoulder alone the responsibilities of government", and that it is therefore "necessarily realistic" (Duverger, 1954, pp.283-284). This helps account for the behaviour of the New Zealand and Democratic parties. They are undoubtedly "personality" and "permanent minority" parties respectively (Duverger, 1954, p.290); and to be blunt, there is no need for and little likelihood of "necessarily realistic" behaviour on their part.

Duverger's distinctions also give an indication of underlying reasons for the ruthlessness with which opposition parties with a majority bent (especially those on the right of the political spectrum) in Australia, Britain, and New Zealand discard failed leaders and search for electorally acceptable substitutes. But not even Duverger is much help in explaining the relationship between the behaviour of government and the leading parties opposed to it. There appears to be a symbiotic relationship between government and opposition which is not accounted for by Duverger. When the fortunes of a government are riding high, those of an opposition will be low, and vice versa. Naturally this will be borne out by opinion polls (see Figure 3.1) where the trends for the Government and the Opposition appear to be mirror-images; but this is, it must be admitted, partly a reflection of the fact that in a two-party situation the tally for the Government and Opposition together will always be 100 per cent. When events are treating the Government kindly and when the Government is perceived to be treating the electorate well, then — almost by definition — it will be impossible for an opposition party, especially one with a majority bent, to behave in a strong, decisive, and convincing manner. The Government has already captured the high ground. Furthermore, an Opposition in such a predicament will search for solutions to the problem; it will criticize the party's leader, argue about new policy directions, and indulge in faction-fighting, all of which will, more often than not, simply compound its difficulties. As a result of reasoning like this, Francis Castles has "explained ... the dominance of the Scandinavian Social Democratic Parties" by arguing that the Scandinavian Right is "so much weaker than ... elsewhere in Europe" (Castles, 1978, p.132).

The Labour Government's stance on the question of admitting nuclear weapons into New Zealand's ports and its consequent differences with the United States Administration, let alone the Greenpeace affair, gave New Zealand a higher profile internationally than it has had during the past 40 years. As a result, the Prime Minister received massive publicity, and it was nigh on impossible for an Opposition voice to be heard through the clamour. The National Party, in turn, reacted adversely to both its defeat and its continued eclipse by the Government, and compounded the situation by spending almost 21 months engaged in vicious intra-party feuding of a kind not witnessed in New Zealand since the establishment of the modern two-party parliamentary system more than half a century ago.

No wonder, then, that the Government rode through the bulk of the first two years of its term on a charger with a charmed life. It remains to be seen whether the regrouping by the opposition parties that occurred in March 1986 can dismount the Government from its steed, but at the very least the main Opposition, the National Party, appears to have stopped flogging its own dead horse.

References

Aimer, P. (1985) The New Zealand Party. In Gold, H. (Ed.) *New Zealand Politics in Perspective* Auckland, Longman Paul.

Aimer, P. (1986) The New Right in New Zealand and Scandinavia. New Zealand Political Studies Association Conference paper.

Butler, D. and Kavanagh, D. (1974) *The British General Election of February 1974* London, Macmillan.

Butler, D. and Kavanagh, D. (1975) *The British General Election of October 1974* London, Macmillan.

Butler, D. and Kavanagh, D. (1980) *The British General Election of 1979* London, Macmillan.

Castles, F.G. (1978) *The Social Democratic Image of Society* London, Routledge and Kegan Paul.

Dahl, R.A.(Ed.) (1966) *Political Oppositions in Western Democracies* New Haven, Yale University Press.

Downs, A. (1957) *An Economic Theory of Democracy* New York, Harper and Row.

Duverger, M. (1954) *Political Parties* London, Methuen and Co.

Easton, B. (1979) *Social Policy and the Welfare State in New Zealand* Auckland, George Allen and Unwin.

Gustafson, B. (1986) *The First 50 Years: A History of the New Zealand National Party* Auckland, Reed Methuen.

Heylen Research Centre (1986) *Eye Witness News Heylen Political Poll: 13 September 1986* Auckland, Heylen Centre of Marketing, Social and Opinion Research (Auckland) Ltd.

Hughes, C.A. (1983) An Election About Perceptions. In Penniman, H.R. (Ed.) *Australia at the Polls: The National Elections of 1980 and 1983* Washington D.C., American Enterprise Institute.

Jackson, K. (1975) Political Leadership and Succession in the New Zealand National Party *Political Science* 27: 1-24.

Jones, B. (1978) *New Zealand The Way I Want It* Christchurch, Whitcoulls.

Levine, S. (1977) New Zealand Politics: Annual Review *Australian Quarterly* 49: 99-117.

Muldoon, R.D. (1975) *National Party 1975 General Election Policy* Wellington, New Zealand National Party.

Muldoon, R.D. (1977) *Muldoon* Wellington, AH & AW Reed.

New Zealand National Party (1986) *Constitution and Rules of the New Zealand National Party* Wellington, New Zealand National Party.

New Zealand Parliamentary Debates (1976) Vol. 408, Wellington, Government Printer.

Penniman, H.R. (Ed.) (1983) *Australia at the Polls: The National Elections of 1980 and 1983* Washington, D.C., American Enterprise Institute.

Roberts, N.S. (1975) The New Zealand General Election of 1972. In Levine, S. (Ed.) *New Zealand Politics: A Reader* Melbourne, Cheshire.

Roberts, N.S. (1976) The New Zealand General Election of 1975 *Australian Quarterly* 48: 97-114.

4

The Bill of Rights

Jerome B. Elkind

The fourth Labour Government has pledged to introduce a Bill of Rights for New Zealand. There would seem to be no clear political motive for doing so and, to the extent that it will limit the Government's powers in a number of areas, it appears to be a rare act of political self-denial based on moral principle. The chief proponent and advocate of the Bill of Rights is the Attorney-General and Minister of Justice, the Rt Hon. Geoffrey Palmer. The Bill of Rights is currently before a travelling Select Committee and, while no specific timetable has been established, the aim seems to be to modify the Bill based on the Select Committee's hearings and to resubmit the modifications to another round of hearings before the Bill is passed. It is doubtful that the Bill will be passed during this term of the Labour Government: its ultimate passage is therefore dependent upon the re-election of the Labour Government.

This chapter examines the Bill of Rights as a political phenomenon and the impact it will have on New Zealand society. How will it affect the practice of the lawyer, the function of the Judge and, eventually, the lives of the ordinary citizen? The question of the need for a Bill of Rights has dominated discussion of the present draft: to date, the debate has not moved very much beyond this point.

One area which eludes many people, but which is essential to any informed commentary on the Bill of Rights, is an understanding of the international context of the Bill of Rights. The Bill of Rights is, in part, a response to treaty obligations in the area of human rights undertaken by the New Zealand Government. These are legal obligations undertaken towards the community of nations. Therefore, one of the fundamental grounds for analysis and criticism of the draft Bill of Rights is the extent to which it adheres to these obligations. Response to treaty obligations also concerns the Treaty of Waitangi and its relation to the Bill of Rights.

The Nature of the Change

The Bill of Rights, if enacted, will launch a legal revolution in New Zealand. It has the potential to shift power from the legislature, which is controlled by the executive, to the judiciary. It is this shift which worries the legal profession. Under our current system of Government, Parliament is "sovereign" or supreme.[1] The doctrine of parliamentary sovereignty is quite unambiguous. It means: (a) that the Courts and all other organs of Government are bound to follow Acts of Parliament;

(b) that Parliament can pass any law it wishes on any subject; (c) that Courts cannot declare Acts of Parliament invalid; and (d) that Parliament cannot bind its successors.

This doctrine has not always been an axiom in English constitutional law. It is the result of an evolutionary development: the working out of a struggle which raged most intensely in Stuart times between the Crown, Parliament and the Courts. It was Parliament which put William and Mary on the English throne in 1689 and, in doing so, was able to exact significant conditions about the relationship between Parliament and the Monarchy. That result was handed to New Zealand as part of its heritage. Today, both in the United Kingdom and New Zealand, the executive (the Queen's Ministers) rule by virtue of their majority in Parliament.

Courts sit to interpret the will of Parliament and, in the event of a conflict between an earlier and a later statute, the Courts will apply the later statute as the most recently expressed will of the sovereign legislature. In theory there are no limitations on the power of Parliament to pass legislation. Any bill, no matter how odious it may be from a human rights standpoint, which is passed by the House of Representatives and receives the assent of the Governor-General becomes law and the Courts are bound by it. Parliament could, if it so desired, pass a law requiring that all persons who wear spectacles shall be summarily shot and that Judges shall ensure that this occurs. By the time of the next election, the sentences, one assumes, will have been carried out and the Government may well have geared up its propaganda machinery to convince everyone else that it was a measure necessary for national security and political stability or for the purity of New Zealand stock. The best a Judge would be able to do with such a law would be to try to mitigate its effects through interpretation. No one is suggesting that this Government or any foreseeable New Zealand Government would do such a thing. But theoretically it is possible and, it is submitted, there is something fundamentally wrong with an allocation of power where that is even a theoretical possibility. The Bill of Rights attempts to alter this. Article 1 says:

> This Bill of Rights is the supreme law of New Zealand, and accordingly any law (including existing law) inconsistent with this Bill shall, to the extent of the inconsistency, be of no effect.

Article 28 says that the Bill of Rights may only be altered by a 75 per cent majority of the whole House of Representatives or by referendum. Thus, when a statute is not passed in accordance with Article 28, Courts will be able to review that statute and, if it is inconsistent with the Bill of Rights, declare it to be of no effect. This power is called "judicial review".[2]

The Bill of Rights will create a new phenomenon called "fundamental law". This means that some law will be higher than other law. This notion is not completely alien to New Zealand: for example, Administrative Regulations and

Municipal by-laws must give way to an Act of Parliament if they conflict with it. However, this will be the first time that Acts of Parliament will have to give way to any other form of law.

In addition to creating a shift in power between the legislature and the judiciary, the Bill of Rights will also result in a significant change in the work of the legal profession. The following scenario illustrates these changes. Faced with a client's specific legal problem, in addition to considering how common law and statute law bear upon the problem, the lawyer may conclude that the Bill of Rights is also involved. If the client feels threatened by a proposed law, it may be possible to obtain a declaratory judgment under the *Declaratory Judgments Act 1908* if the proposed law can be shown to actually affect the client. The law cannot be challenged on grounds of principle alone: rules of standing require that a party must have some actual interest in a dispute before he or she can go to Court. If a declaratory judgment is not feasible, the best the lawyer in question will be able to do is to discuss with the client the advantages and disadvantages of testing the proposed law when it eventually comes into force.

If the client is aggrieved by an existing law, then there will be the possibility of challenging the law in court. But in the current draft of the Bill of Rights there appears to be one obstacle to invocation of the Bill of Rights. Article 23 says:

> The interpretation of an enactment that will result in the meaning of the enactment being consistent with this Bill of Rights shall be preferred to any other interpretation.

Before challenging the statute, Counsel will have to consider all possible interpretations of the statute to determine whether any of them could be viewed as rendering the statute consistent with the Bill of Rights. It might be that a consistent interpretation will aid the client and a challenge to the statute will not be necessary. Counsel will then argue in court for the favoured interpretation on the ground that the interpretation makes it consistent with the Bill of Rights. Only when the Court finds that there is no way that the statute can be interpreted consistently with the Bill of Rights, will it be able to strike down a statute for repugnancy to the Bill of Rights.

It is arguable that Article 23 is redundant. It is almost universal practice in countries with bills of rights that courts will first attempt to find an interpretation which allows a statute to be upheld. But this Bill of Rights contains a provision known as the general limitations clause, Article 3, which says:

> The rights and freedoms contained in this Bill of Rights may be subject only to such reasonable limits prescribed by law as can be demonstrably justified in a free and democratic society.

The words "as can be demonstrably justified" would seem to indicate that the onus of proving that such limitations are justified is on those seeking to justify them (usually the Government). Does Article 23 mean that the obligation of the Courts will be to hold that a statute is reasonable and justifiable in a democratic society, in effect reversing the apparent onus of proof in Article 3? What weight should be given the general limitations clause? Should it be read in conjuction with Article 3? This possible internal inconsistency in the Bill of Rights needs to be resolved.

Another question which is of interest is how the Bill of Rights will alter the citizen's perception of his or her relationship with the State. Currently, a person who feels aggrieved by a proposed law has only a limited range of responses. One of them is to appear before the select committee considering the Bill and recommend changes. But, if the Bill is a matter of official policy, any such testimony is likely to prove ineffectual. Another response is to demonstrate against the Bill which places the individual in the invidious position of being seen as a "protester" whom Parliament may freely ignore. Yet another possibility is to join a pressure group. But the success of the pressure group will depend upon how favoured it is and how much bargaining power it has.

Under our current system, once a Bill passes, the State has spoken and its action must be accepted. The individual citizen is helpless even though the new law may have an enormous and adverse impact on him or her. A Bill of Rights will give the individual some opportunity to take direct action in the Courts to invalidate legislation which offends human rights. This will not happen immediately; but the ultimate result will be to modify or remove the average New Zealander's perception of self as a victim of the State.

Written Constitutions *versus* Bills of Rights

Some confusion exists between a bill of rights and a written constitution. The terms are sometimes used interchangeably although such usage is imprecise and misleading.

A constitution is the basic design or organization of the State. It defines and establishes the organs of government; the legislative, the executive and the judiciary and, more importantly, dictates their relationship with each other. A written constitution is a blueprint for this organization. Much of New Zealand's Constitution is not written down. It exists in the form of "constitutional conventions" which are unwritten rules adhered to on the conviction that they are binding. Officials conform to these conventions because of a general feeling that it is right and proper to do so. However, because these conventions are not formally written down they are, at times, difficult to identify with precision.

The chief drawback to the establishment of a written constitution is the magnitude of the task. If we wanted to adopt a written constitution, we would either have to restructure our entire system of government or we would have to identify and codify many of the unwritten conventions that comprise our present Constitution.[3] This might be viewed as a healthy exercise in some respects. It might also be seen as a stultifying constitutional development.

In contrast to a written constitution, a bill of rights deals with a more limited part of the constitutional framework. Its primary function is to set certain limits on the executive and legislative branches of Government by prohibiting them from passing certain laws and by setting boundaries on executive and administrative practices. It is quite possible to have a written constitution without a bill of rights. Australia provides a current example although a draft Bill of Rights has been introduced into the Australian House of Representatives.

The important question for New Zealand is whether an entrenched Bill of Rights can exist in conjunction with an unwritten Constitution. It is at least open to argument that, by enacting a Bill of Rights, we will be grafting on to the New Zealand Constitution something which is alien to it. This question involves a rather complex analysis of constitutional theory. In essence, the issue is whether it is consistent with parliamentary sovereignty to provide that a statute cannot be repealed except by using a special manner and form, in this case a 75 per cent majority of the House of Representatives or a referendum.

There are a number of English cases which hold that this is not possible.[4] The authors of the White Paper on the Bill of Rights are aware of this constitutional problem, but they profess to perceive a change of judicial attitude over the past 35 years[5] evidenced by judicial decisions involving the Constitutions of New South Wales, South Africa and Ceylon (now Sri Lanka).[6] However, the New South Wales case involved a legislature which was subordinate to a higher legislature, the United Kingdom Parliament, and it is at least arguable that the legislatures of South Africa and Ceylon were not supreme in the sense that limitations had been imposed upon them in their original Constitutions.

The problem of grafting a Bill of Rights onto an unwritten Constitution is very tricky and may not succeed although the attitude of a number of senior Judges is encouraging. Arguably, it would not be necessary to produce an entire written Constitution in order to entrench a Bill of Rights into our law, but some more clearly signalled break with the present system would be desirable (Elkind and Shaw, 1985, pp.148-150; 188-189).

Types of Bills of Rights

There are many types of bills of rights of varying degrees of effectiveness. Probably the weakest type of bill of rights is the non-justiciable bill of rights – one which is simply not enforceable in the Courts. A bill of rights may be a declaration carrying no legal force. One example of this sort of declaration is the French Declaration of the Rights of Man of 1789. A more modern example is the United Nations General Assembly resolution 217 passed on 10 December 1948, creating the Universal Declaration of Human Rights. Another type of non-justiciable bill of rights is one which proclaims a set of human rights' standards and actually creates a body to review legislation in the light of those standards but gives that body no binding authority. It has been contended that section 6 of the *New Zealand Human Rights Commission Act 1977* creates such a bill of rights (Elkind, 1984, p.198). Section 6 gives the New Zealand Human Rights Commission the power to recommend to the Prime Minister "... the desirability of legislative, administrative or other action to give better protection to human rights and to ensure better compliance with standards laid down in international instruments on human rights ...". Since the recommendations of the Commission are neither binding on the Prime Minister or Parliament nor enforceable in the Courts, the standards laid down in the international instruments are non-justiciable.

Another non-justiciable bill of rights is found in the Soviet Constitution. Some groups appear to be attempting to spread the notion that the White Paper Bill of Rights is based on the Soviet Constitution. This claim is actually a misunderstanding of a slightly more sophisticated argument to the effect that the Charter of Rights in the Soviet Constitution has been ineffective in protecting the rights of the Soviet people. This is offered as evidence that such bills and charters lack value. The Soviet Constitution, in fact, does contain a charter purporting to enshrine certain rights. Few people would disagree that the protection of human rights in New Zealand is far superior to the protection of human rights in the Soviet Union. But that is not the point. The Soviet Union has a Bill of Rights which is not subject to judicial review and which, therefore, cannot be used by the Courts to strike down repugnant laws. An individual may enforce rights under the Soviet Constitution only through resort to the relevant Communist Party machinery. It is not a justiciable charter. It is therefore fundamentally different from the proposed New Zealand Bill of Rights.

Another type of bill of rights is one which is justiciable but which is ordinary law and can be expressly or impliedly repealed, altered or amended by any subsequent legislation. Such a bill of rights can be enforced in the Courts but it represents no check on the powers of the legislature. A good example of that type of bill of rights is the Canadian Bill of Rights 1960. Another example is the current Australian draft Bill of Rights. The White Paper Draft Bill of Rights is the most effective type of bill of rights. If it passes it will be an "entrenched" Bill of Rights. This means that it can only be repealed, altered or amended in accordance with a special manner and form which is more stringent than the manner and form required for passage of ordinary legislation. This type of bill of rights is both justiciable and an effective check on legislative power.

The Bill of Rights and the Judges

The Bill of Rights will allow Judges to invalidate laws passed by Parliament. The fetters which it will place on legislative policy have proved to be a source of concern to politicians and some lawyers. Since it will allow Judges to thwart political aims, the fear has been expressed that Judges will be making political decisions and that this will lead to the selection of Judges on political grounds.

The question of the political appointment of Judges can be disposed of fairly easily. Firstly, the assumption that political considerations do not currently enter into the appointment of Judges in New Zealand requires examination. Political figures do have a say in the appointment of Judges in New Zealand as elsewhere. The Chief Justice of New Zealand is appointed by the Governor-General on the advice of the Prime Minister. Other Judges are appointed on the advice of the Attorney-General. A politician charged with such a power may be tempted to seek a candidate for appointment whose judicial philosophy is consistent with his or her political aims.[7] According to Sir Robert Muldoon the political appointment of Judges is absolutely impossible under the New Zealand constitutional system. Further, Sir Robin Cooke, the President of the Court of Appeal, has commented:

> Last, the matter of political appointments to the bench. If the Bill added significantly to the risk, of course one could have no part of it. The question is not easy, but on balance I think that the New Zealand tradition against political appointments and the consultations that occur in practice should be an effective restraint, if restraint were needed. So the point does not prevent a welcome to the idea of the Bill, and this I now give (*Bill of Rights Seminar*, 1985, pp.57-58).

But if we accept that the political appointment of Judges is impossible under the parliamentary system then it becomes necessary to ask why the Bill of Rights should make any difference?

The question whether Judges would be making "political decisions" is more complex and requires an understanding of the role that Judges play in the political system. Legislation is an outcome of the political process. Laws are passed by Parliament and the Members of Parliament are politicians. Laws passed by Parliament are therefore an expression of their political will. In our system, the function of Judges is to interpret and apply the will of Parliament expressed in legislation. Insofar as they uphold the policy and values of the social system, Judges inevitably play a political role. Policy choices must enter into the process of judicial decision-making. But that does not make a judicial decision "political". What makes a decision "judicial" is not the subject-matter of the decision but the intellectual and juridical process by which the decision is arrived at.

A politician is by nature partisan. This is almost a tautology except to the extent that it indicates that impartiality is not central to a politician's makeup. A politician is likely to base a decision on political criteria such as whether a particular policy will lead a desired political objective. Or the decision may be based on policy criteria and the notion of the general good of society. There are no other intellectual constraints on political decision-making. There are, however, additional intellectual constraints on judicial decision-making, constraints which have developed from the nature of the judicial function.

An essential characteristic of justice is impartiality. This is accepted as axiomatic in our system of justice and some of the constraints on the process of judicial decision-making grow out of the demands of impartiality. The term "impartiality" can be used either in a narrow sense or in a broad sense. In the narrow sense it means "no [person] may be a judge in his [or her] own cause" and a Judge with a personal interest in a case must be prepared to accept disqualification from that case.[8] In the broader sense, "impartiality" means that Judges should be isolated from politics and that they should attempt to disregard biases and prejudices and decide fully and fairly according to the law.

Another axiom in the New Zealand legal system is that like cases should be treated alike. This can be regarded as a corollary of impartiality. It means that two persons who go to the law with substantially similar cases should be treated equally. Our judicial system meets this criterion by its devotion to precedent. A case in which the facts are substantially similar to a case decided previously should be decided in the same way. Therefore that previous case is binding authority for the present case. In addition, there are distinct canons of statutory interpretation which are intended to ensure that Judges attempt to ascertain and apply the will of the legislature rather than their own biases and prejudices.

Therefore, the intellectual constraints imposed on judicial decision-makers involve the demands of impartiality, the rules of precedent and the canons of statutory interpretation. A Judge is not allowed to ask whether a particular law is good or bad. A Judge may modify the effects of a bad law by interpretation, but the judicial task is to apply the law to the situation at hand. The fact that a case has political subject-matter does not, by itself, place it beyond the judicial process. Nor do Judges abdicate their judicial function when they address such questions in the judicial process.[9] For the most part, we can expect Judges to bring the same judicial skills to the task of interpreting a Bill of Rights that they employ in all other areas of judicial activity. This does not mean that the judicial function will not change. In some ways it will change profoundly.

The Bill of Rights will be "fundamental law", superior to ordinary law. Some have argued that such a Bill of Rights will lock 1986 notions of human rights into New Zealand law and bind future generations to what may well become outmoded concepts. It must be conceded that conceptions of human rights do change. In times of public hysteria concern for human rights may well fade into the background in the face of public demand to solve some immediate problem by disposing of certain rights. These are precisely the times when a bill of rights is needed. No bill of rights or constitution can survive an enraged and determined majority over a long period of time. But a bill of rights, because it is more difficult than ordinary legislation to repeal or amend, can at least slow the process down and protect these rights until passions have had time to cool and people have had time to think again. Setting these times of crisis aside, two questions remain to be answered. Firstly, are there core conceptions of human rights which will remain universally valid? And secondly, is the law capable of evolving with the changes that do occur?

Resolving the dispute between cultural relativists and proponents of universal law is outside the scope of this chapter. However, the rights which are or should be included in the New Zealand Bill of Rights would be recognized by most members of society. They form an integral part of New Zealand's multicultural heritage. They include rights such as the protection of life, freedom from torture and inhuman treatment, freedom from slavery, the right to liberty and security of the person, the right to vote, the right of petition, the right to *habeas corpus* (the right of a detained or imprisoned person to have a Court determine the legality of the detention and order the person released if it is unlawful), the right to bail, the right to a fair trial, the right to trial by jury, the right to privacy, freedom of the press, of religion, of expression, of movement and of assembly, the rights of the Maori people under the Treaty of Waitangi, and the rights of the child, among others.

It is fair to say that there is a consensus in New Zealand that these rights ought to be protected by the legal system even among those who do not favour protecting them through a Bill of Rights. Recognition of many such rights forms an unbroken chain from the writings of John Locke, through the French Declaration of the Rights of Man, the United States Bill of Rights to the Universal Declaration of Human Rights and many other national and international bills of rights. This consensus will not disappear in twenty-five or even a hundred years' time. It can do so only if society succumbs to dictatorship. Certainly it will not do so if an attachment to liberty is maintained.

The second question involves the role of the Judges and some change in the discipline of judicial decision-making. Where human rights principles have been set out in treaties, state constitutions and/or bills of rights, Judges may differ in the liberality or narrowness of their construction. But they have shown an awareness that the interpretation of these documents must evolve with the times. For example, in *McCulloch v. State of Maryland*, Chief Justice Marshall of the United States Supreme Court expressed the principle that "a constitution [is] intended to endure for ages to come, and consequently, to be adapted to the various crises of human affairs".[10] The Judicial Committee of the Privy Council has employed the metaphor "a living tree capable of growth and expansion" to describe the living and vibrant character of constitutional instruments.[11] More recently, in *Minister of Home Affairs v. Fisher*, Lord Wilberforce stated with reference to the Bill of Rights incorporated

in the Constitution of Bermuda that what was called for was "a generous interpretation avoiding what has been called the austerity of tabulated legalism suitable
to give individuals the full measure of the fundamental rights and freedoms referred
to".[12] Furthermore Freund expressed this idea aptly when he admonished the
American Courts "not to read the provisions of the Constitution like a last will and
testament lest it become one".[13]

Another problem which a bill of rights poses is that claims to rights clash. For
example, to what extent is a free press to be allowed to influence a fair trial? In New
Zealand, newspapers are prevented from printing comments which might influence
imminent or pending litigation on peril of being in contempt of court under the *sub
judice* rule. This rule is a very clear limitation on freedom of expression and freedom
of the press. Another limitation on freedom of expression, the tort of defamation, is
seen as necessary to uphold the right of individuals to protection of their honour and
reputation. Does freedom of expression include the right to incite racial hatred? The
rights of arrested and detained persons and people charged with criminal offences are
often seen to come into conflict with the need to protect the public against criminal
activity.

A balance must be struck between conflicting claims of right. This can either be
done in the Bill of Rights itself or left to the Judges. Overly controversial issues
should not become the subject of a bill of rights. An example of this is the abortion
issue. There is a heavily organized "pro-life" group which has urged the select
committee considering the Bill of Rights to ensure that the rights of "the unborn
child" are specifically protected. An equally vociferous group has urged the select
committee to ensure that the Bill of Rights protects the right of a woman to do as
she sees fit with her own body. The point is that people are so polarized on this issue
that it must be left to be worked out through the political process. If the Bill of
Rights were to take either side of this issue, this would arouse the unremitting
opposition of the other side and would probably doom the Bill of Rights.

The White Paper Draft Bill of Rights deals with the balance of conflicting claims
of right through the mechanism of Article 3. This Article appears to allow the Judges
to arrive at a balance at least between the claims of the Government and the claims
of the individual. By extension, it will allow the Courts to uphold claims of right if
it agrees with the Government that these claims are superior to other claims. As it is
presently drafted this provision appears to give the Judges enormous power: more
power than Judges have in the United States. The question whether a law is
reasonable and can be justified in a democratic society would seem to be highly
subjective. A Judge who is well-disposed to the Bill of Rights or a provision in it
could demand relatively strict proof that the potentially conflicting law is reasonable
and can be justified in a democratic society. A more hostile Judge could accept such
evidence all too readily.

In the end, a balance must be struck and this will involve policy choices. English and New Zealand Courts have, for many years, been prone to the illusion that legal problems can somehow be freed from policy choices. But the fact is that such choices are inevitable and that they are made by English Judges and New Zealand Judges as well as by American Judges. When policy choices are not faced and articulated within the framework of some conscious working principle it is very difficult to avoid injecting beliefs and prejudices in place of reasoned judicial decision. The conscious working principle is that the basis for policy choice must be the interests which the law protects and not merely the social philosophy of the Judge.

A bill of rights is a code of political morality. It states explicitly the interests that are to be protected and the policy values that are to be chosen in protecting them. If this will have any effect on the role of the Judges, it will be in assisting them to face the necessity of such choices more directly and in a clear and consistent manner.

The International Environment

New Zealand has important legal obligations in the field of human rights. It is a party to the 1976 United Nations International Covenant on Civil and Political Rights. This means that New Zealand has a legal duty to extend the rights and freedoms granted in the Covenant to every person in New Zealand. But the New Zealand Law Society seems completely unaware of the relationship between the Covenant and the Bill of Rights. Otherwise it could not have said of the rights in the Bill of Rights:

> There is a need to be wary of confusing rights in the strict sense with those broad statements of desirable ends which the White Paper sees fit to describe as fundamental rights (New Zealand Law Society, pp.10-11).

The rights set out in the White Paper Draft Bill of Rights are drawn from the new international consensus on the rights that ought to be protected. For New Zealand, as for many other nations, this is represented by the Covenant on Civil and Political Rights. This crucial point was eloquently stressed by the late Quentin-Baxter. He strongly emphasized that New Zealand needed to see its constitutional development in the wider context of the international environment and international legal obligations. He said:

> It has not, however, yet been fully realized that the massive changes in our international environment render constitutional development both more necessary and more difficult to achieve. No country can arrange its international environment to suit its own preferences; and no country can prosper if it fails to meet the challenge of that environment (1984, p.206).

Referring to the Bill of Rights debate in the United Kingdom he noted:

In the continuing British debate regarding a new Bill of Rights, the constitutional and international aspects are never separated. It is generally agreed that such a Bill should follow the standards established by the European Convention on Human Rights, which also meets the requirements of the corresponding United Nations treaty — the International Covenant on Civil and Political Rights. This is, of course, partly a matter of convenience, so that compliance with the international obligation is more easily established, but it is also a recognition that the content and drafting of a domestic Bill of Rights could be an extremely contentious matter, if there were not an international standard to invoke (p.206).

The same guiding principles, he said, are apposite to the New Zealand debate:

It is because New Zealand is a sovereign state that the question of constitutional development assumes special importance. Membership of the international community creates a tension which can be invigorating or totally destructive. We have, in principle, no need to be defensive: in most respects, our record will stand up to international inspection. But when we do become defensive, inquiring endlessly why our case should be examined when others have more of which to be ashamed, we put ourselves at risk. It is then only one further step to the point at which people appeal to organized international opinion against conditions in their own country, and those who believe that they are upholding United Nations principles are denounced for disloyalty in doing so. Ignorance, rather than bad intention, is the root cause of these situations. The best cure may be to import relevant international standards into our own laws and procedures, so that they do not have the character of an unexplained, foreign interference in our domestic affairs (pp.206-207).

An example of the Law Society's apparent ignorance in this area may be drawn from the Article in the Bill of Rights which it singles out for criticism. Article 7 says:

Everyone has the right to freedom of expression, including the freedom to seek, receive and impart information and opinions of any kind in any form.

This, it says, has the potential to throw large parts of our law into a state of chaos:

So presumably the whole of our law on defamation, on censorship, on official information, become *tabula rasa* to be laboriously rebuilt (New Zealand Law Society, p.12).

The Law Society seems unaware of the similarity of Article 7 to Paragraph 2 of Article 9 of the Covenant. That paragraph reads:

Everyone shall have the right to freedom of expression; this right shall include freedom to seek, receive and impart information and ideas of all kinds, regardless of frontiers, either orally, in writing or in print, in the form of art, or through any media of his choice.

The point is that, under Article 19(2) of the Covenant, New Zealand is already under a legal duty to protect freedom of expression. So, if our laws on defamation, on censorship and on official information offend the Covenant, then they must be rebuilt. We have a legal duty to do it. Either the Law Society is unaware of this legal duty or they are urging us to ignore it.

A question frequently asked is whether we need a Bill of Rights in order to conform to the Covenant. It has been suggested that New Zealand law is already in broad conformity with the Covenant and that adoption of the Bill of Rights will do little more than confirm rights which New Zealanders already possess. A second question that is sometimes asked is whether the draft Bill of Rights already substantially conforms to the Covenant. This question has been addressed elsewhere (Elkind and Shaw, 1986). As to whether a Bill of Rights is needed for compliance with the Covenant, Article 2(3) of the Covenant provides that each Party to the Covenant undertakes:

> (a) To ensure that any person whose rights or freedoms as herein recognized are violated shall have an effective remedy, notwithstanding that the violation has been committed by a person acting in an official capacity;
>
> (b) To ensure that any person claiming such a remedy shall have his right thereto determined by competent judicial, administrative or legislative authorities or by other competent authority provided for by the legal system of the State, and to develop the possibilities of a judicial remedy.

At present, the New Zealand legal system does provide for remedies against officials who act unlawfully, unreasonably or in excess of authority. What it manifestly does not have are remedies against Parliament when it passes a statute denying the rights and freedoms contained in the Covenant. The Covenant clearly requires that there must be some means by which these statutes can be reviewed on the application of those claiming to be injured by them; it suggests that a judicial remedy is the best form of remedy. There is a clear contractual obligation to do this.

As to the notion that New Zealand law is already in broad conformity with the Covenant, it must be conceded that New Zealand's record of compliance with the Covenant is superior to that of most other signatories. But that does not mean that New Zealand is in full compliance with the Covenant. It is submitted that this view is born of an over sanguine confidence that New Zealand law is consistent with the Covenant. The source of this confidence seems to be a statement made by Chris Beeby when he introduced New Zealand's Initial Report to the United Nations Human Rights Committee. He was reported as saying that:

> ... before his country had ratified the covenant, it had found it necessary to undertake an extensive review of domestic law and practice. The review had been lengthy owing to his country's wish to ensure scrupulous compliance with the obligations which it had been about to accept (Ministry of Foreign Affairs, 1984, p.1).

In April 1984, the present author requested, under the *Official Information Act 1982*, a copy of the study that had allegedly been done at the time of ratification to determine whether New Zealand law complied with the Covenant along with any other material concerning New Zealand's compliance with the Covenant. Extensive documentation was received on New Zealand's compliance with the Covenant but there appears to have been no specific and systematic study of New Zealand law in relation to the Covenant.

The claim that New Zealand law is already in broad compliance with the Covenant does not mean very much at all. If New Zealand accepts the Optional Protocol to the Covenant, individuals will be able to complain to the United Nations Human Rights Committee in New York when they feel aggrieved by alleged violations of the Covenant. If the Committee finds that there is a specific violation of the Covenant, "broad compliance" will not even be a plea in mitigation. New Zealand will be under a legal duty to remove the violation and provide the injured party with a remedy.

A rather similar confidence was expressed in the United Kingdom when it ratified the European Convention on Human Rights. Yet the European Court and European Commission of Human Rights have ruled against the United Kingdom in quite a few cases, particularly in the *Sunday Times* case, the treatment of Irish detainees and birching.[14] The Bill of Rights should ensure that New Zealand is in compliance with the Covenant.

The Treaty of Waitangi and the Bill of Rights

Quentin-Baxter also spoke of the special importance in the New Zealand context of the Treaty of Waitangi and the need on the part of non-Maoris to recognize the views of the Maori people as to its proper implementation:

> The characteristic New Zealand demand, now taken up by the Maori, was always for fairness and equality of opportunity — an affirmation of the intrinsic worth of every human being, found also in the Universal Declaration of Human Rights (p.208).

This wisdom is a beacon to our future constitutional development and maturity. Questions concerning the Treaty of Waitangi assume extreme importance with the introduction of the proposed Bill of Rights. There is a pressing need to accord full constitutional status to the Treaty and, at the same time, to recognize the views of the Maori people as to its proper implementation. It is difficult to conceive of a New Zealand Bill of Rights which does not make a genuine and conscientious attempt to restore the mana of the Treaty. For his part, the Minister of Justice, Mr Palmer, has stated that the Treaty issue has become both "central and essential" in any discussion on the Bill of Rights (1985).

By now, considerable evidence has been collected which fully exposes the repeated injustices that have occurred in relation to the Treaty. In suggesting that the Treaty must be accorded full constitutional recognition in the Bill of Rights, there is at least some prospect that this may rekindle and restore the expectations of the parties to the Treaty in the widest possible way. The Chief Judge of the Maori Land Court and Chairman of the Waitangi Tribunal, E.T.J. Durie, has developed this theme:

> I do not think it is too late to reinstate the original expectations of the Imperial Government. I think it is timely that we should. We have moved from the kinder-garten of our colonial past and from the Land Wars fought in our youth. We have since experimented successfully with idealism. It is proper that in now proposing a national Bill of Rights, we should declare not just those rights that are thought fundamental to our ways, but should revive those that are meant to be fundamental to our nation's birth, but which subsequently fell by the wayside.
>
> Our history indicates that Maori people need some form of proper recognition for their rights. I believe they have suffered more than any people should, for the lack of it. We can no longer ignore Maori demands in the hope that they will simply go away or maintain an ignorance of world-wide recognition of the rights of an indigenous people. Those who say we do not need a Bill of Rights can say so from the standpoint of a people whose rights have never been seriously threatened. That is not an experience that Maori people have enjoyed (1985, p.171 and p.174).

Chief Judge Durie also refers to the scepticism in some quarters, not confined to Maoridom, concerning the incorporation of the Treaty in an Act of Parliament. Chief Judge Durie does not himself share this scepticism. It is said that this is inconsistent with the mana of the Treaty; that this would allow Parliament to alter or repeal the Treaty; and that the Courts, which will have jurisdiction under the proposed Bill of Rights, will emasculate the Treaty. With respect to those views, the incorporation of the Treaty in a statute which is constitutionally entrenched as supreme law does not, by itself, infringe or harm the mana of the Treaty. The *lack* of incorporation of the Treaty in New Zealand law has been a major stumbling block to the enforcement of the Treaty. The possibility that the inclusion of the Treaty in a Bill of Rights could allow Parliament to alter or repeal the Treaty is one that can easily be excluded simply by stating in the Bill of Rights that Parliament shall not have that power.

It is necessary to consider two other major criticisms that have been voiced concerning the Bill of Rights and its relation to the Treaty of Waitangi. The first is the claim made by some Maori activists that individual rights of the sort protected in the Bill of Rights are irrelevant to the Maori people for whom the protection of "group rights" are more important. The second objection is related. It is simply that the protection of the group rights recognized in the Treaty of Waitangi sits uncomfortably in a Bill of Rights and is in fact not justiciable in a Court of Law. The first claim seeks implementation of the Treaty of Waitangi without "the baggage of a Bill of Rights" (Jones, 1985, p.216). The second objection is an argument for excluding the Treaty of Waitangi from the Bill of Rights. To answer the first, one need only point to the Universal Declaration of Human Rights. This Declaration was promulgated as a universal standard for all people to observe. To the extent that the Bill of Rights is based on the Universal Declaration it is rooted in a universal standard.

The second argument proceeds from a monocultural view of New Zealand. Inclusion of the Treaty of Waitangi in the Bill of Rights may be seen as coming to terms with our bicultural heritage. If the Treaty of Waitangi appears to sit uncomfortably in a Bill of Rights, it is because the Treaty makes the Bill a bicultural document and this is bound to look odd to lawyers versed in English Common Law. Courts may not be the fora most suited to enforcement of the Treaty of Waitangi. Indeed, arguably it would be more appropriate to vest enforcement entirely with the Waitangi Tribunal (Elkind and Shaw, 1986, pp.45-46). However, we must begin to incorporate Maori values into our law and the Bill of Rights is the best place to start.

Conclusion

The Bill of Rights will effect a legal revolution in New Zealand. It will affect not only the duties of Judges and lawyers but also the lives of ordinary citizens. Indeed, it will even affect the rights of persons only temporarily in New Zealand. It will do so by taking power away from Parliament and from those who govern by virtue of their control over Parliament, the executive branch of the Government. It is this shift in power from the legislature to the judiciary which is the most controversial aspect of the Bill of Rights. It is also its chief virtue. As has been argued here, the allocation of virtually unlimited power to the legislature which is characteristic of the present system, is both dangerous and wrong in principle. Palmer has campaigned for years against "unbridled power" and although at one time opposed to a Bill of Rights, he has come to see it as an essential curb on such power.[15]

In evaluating the Bill of Rights two eminent legal authorities offer guidance. One, the late Professor Quentin-Baxter of Victoria University, understood better than anyone in New Zealand the importance of New Zealand's international legal obligations and the necessity of complying with them. The other, Sir Robin Cooke, was the first to articulate the need for a Bill of Rights that would grip the imagination, that would reflect New Zealand's unique national character and establish a fundamental constitutional identity for New Zealand. These two beacons represent the challenge and vision that the Bill of Rights must address.

Notes

1   "Parliament" is the colloquial expression for the House of Representatives. Section 32 of the *Constitution Act 1852* says, "There shall be in New Zealand a General Assembly, to consist of the Governor-General ... and House of Representatives". The Constitution

Bill renames the General Assembly. Under Clause 17, it will henceforth be called "Parliament" and it will consist of "the sovereign in the right of New Zealand and the House of Representatives".

2   This is distinct from judicial review of administrative action which currently occurs in New Zealand.

3   A written constitution is not completely free of constitutional conventions. For example, the two-term Presidency was considered to be a constitutional convention in the United States until the convention was broken by President Franklin D. Roosevelt in 1940. It was subsequently codified as the 22nd Amendment to the United States Constitution.

4   *Vauxhall Estates Ltd v. Liverpool Corporation* [1932] 1 King's Bench Reports (KB) 733 (Divisional Court (Div. Ct.)); *Ellen Street Estates Ltd v. Minister of Health* [1934] 1 KB 590 (Court of Appeal (C.A.)).

5   *A Bill of Rights for New Zealand: A White Paper* (1985), paras 7.11.-7.18.

6   *Attorney-General for New South Wales v. Trethowan* [1932] Appeal Cases (AC) 526 (Judicial Committee of the Privy Council (J.C.)); *Harris v. Donges* [1952] 1 The Times Law Reports 1245 (Supreme Court of South Africa, Appellate Division); *The Bribery Commission v. Ranasinghe* [1965] AC 173 (J.C.).

7   There have been cases, however, in which a politician, after being instrumental in the appointment of a Judge, has been surprised to find that the Judge's decisions did not conform to political expectations.

8   *Dimes v. Grand Junction Canal* (1852) 3 House of Lords Reports (HLR) 759, 10 English Reports 301.

9   This point is emphatically made by Madame Justice Wilson of the Supreme Court of Canada in *Operation Dismantle Inc. v. R.*, unreported decision of the Supreme Court of Canada of 9 May 1985, File No. 18154, pp.22-24. The case concerns the decision of the Canadian Federal Cabinet to allow the United States of America to test cruise missiles in Canada. This decision was challenged on the basis of section 7 of the Canadian Charter of Rights and Freedoms which reads:

> Everyone has the right to life, liberty and security of the person and the right not to be deprived thereof except in accordance with the principles of fundamental justice.

Wilson observed:

> If the Court were simply being asked to express its opinion on the wisdom of the executive's exercise of its defence powers in this case, the Court would have to decline. It cannot substitute its opinion for that of the executive to whom decision-making power is given by the Constitution. Because the *effect* of the appellants' action is to challenge the wisdom of the government's defence policy, it is tempting to say that the Court should in the same way refuse to involve itself. However, I think this would be to miss the point, to fail to focus on the question which is before us. The question before us is not whether the government's defence policy is sound but whether or not it violates the appellants' rights under s.7 of the *Charter of Rights and Freedoms*. I do not think there can be any doubt that this is a question for the courts (pp.22-23).

The challenge under section 7 failed on other grounds and the statement of claim was accordingly struck out. The same view was strongly affirmed by Lord Scarman in an address to the New Zealand Law Conference: see Scarman (1984) Britain and the Protection of Human Rights, *New Zealand Law Journal* 175, 176.

10 17 United States Reports (US) (4 Wheat.) 316, 415 (1819). See also Cardozo, B.N. (1921) *The Nature of the Judicial Process* pp.82–85.

11 *Edwards v. Attorney General for Canada* [1930] Appeal Cases (AC) 124, 136 (per Viscount Sankey).

12 [1980] AC 319, 328. See also the decision of the Privy Council in *Attorney General of The Gambia v. Momodou Jobe* [1984] AC 689, 700 where Lord Diplock observed:

> A constitution, and in particular that part of it which protects and entrenches fundamental rights and freedoms to which all persons in the state are to be entitled, is to be given a generous and purposive construction.

13 *Hunter v. Southam Inc.* (1985) 11 Dominion Law Reports (DLR) (4th) 641, p.649.

14 *Sunday Times v. The United Kingdom* (1979) 58 International Law Reports (ILR) 491; *Ireland v. The United Kingdom* (1978) ILR 188; *Tyrer v. The United Kingdom* (1978) 58 ILR 339.

15 See, Palmer, G. (1979) *Unbridled Power?* Auckland, Oxford.

References

A Bill of Rights for New Zealand: A White Paper (1985) Wellington, Government Printer.

Bill of Rights: The Pros and Cons Seminar Held Under the Auspices of the New Zealand Section of the International Commission of Jurists (1985) Wellington.

Cardozo, B.N. (1921) *The Nature of the Judicial Process* New Haven, Yale.

Durie, E.T.J. (1985) "Part II and Clause 26 of the Draft New Zealand Bill of Rights", in Legal Research Foundation Inc. *A Bill of Rights for New Zealand* Seminar, University of Auckland.

Elkind, J.B. and Shaw, A. (1986) *A Standard for Justice: A Critical Commentary on the Proposed Bill of Rights for New Zealand* Auckland, Oxford.

Elkind, J.B. (1984) The Human Rights Commission as a Law Determining Agency *New Zealand Law Journal* 198–202.

Jones, S. (1985) "The Bill of Rights and Te Tiriti o Waitangi", in Legal Research Foundation Inc. *A Bill of Rights for New Zealand* Seminar, University of Auckland.

New Zealand Law Society (1986) The NZ Law Society's Stance *Law Talk* March 10–12.

Ministry of Foreign Affairs (1984) Human Rights in New Zealand. *Information Bulletin No. 6* Wellington, Government Printer.

Palmer, G. (1985) Speech to the New Zealand Society for Legal Philosophy, Auckland Branch, 19 November.

Quentin-Baxter, R.Q. (1984) Themes of Constitutional Development: the need for a favourable climate of discussion *New Zealand Law Journal* 203–208.

Scarman, Lord (1984) Britain and the Protection of Human Rights *New Zealand Law Journal* 175–177.

United Nations Document CCPR/C/SR 481.

5

Parliamentary Reform

Geoff Skene

Wholesale change in the institution of Parliament is uncommon in New Zealand. The changes made by the Lange Government in 1985 were the first attempt to improve the parliamentary process since the procedural modifications adopted in 1979. Since the abolition of the Legislative Council in 1950, committees to review the standing orders of the House of Representatives have been convened on average every five years. Individually, each of these reviews only resulted in minor changes. In a nation of legislative meddlers, it is hardly surprising that the Constitution has evolved in such a piecemeal fashion. The *Electoral Act 1956*, for instance, has been amended no less than 15 times and has been the subject of inquiry by several committees and commissions. Palmer's claim, therefore, that the current changes are "the most dramatic and the most important ... this century" *(New Zealand Parliamentary Debates,* 1985, p.5599) deserves some scrutiny. Do they amount to a revolution in the manner in which Parliament conducts itself or are they another phase in an evolutionary trend?

The second uncommon characteristic of these changes is that they are the work of a Labour Government. By and large it has been the National Party which has had the closer association with constitutional and parliamentary change, be it the abolition of the upper house in 1950, the passage of the *Electoral Act* in 1956, the establishment of the Office of Ombudsman in 1962, or the convening of the Standing Orders Committee. Yet in 1984 it was the Labour Party which went into the election with the most comprehensive package of parliamentary and constitutional reforms. It promised to strengthen the powers of select committees, control Government by regulation, make parliamentary sittings more regular and debates more effective, enhance the accountability of the public service, increase public participation in government and review the electoral law. It argued for reform of the privacy laws, greater freedom of information, better law-making and less red tape. It saw virtue in greater separation between the branches of government and defended the independence of the judiciary and the rule of law.

It is tempting to ascribe the Labour Government's commitment to parliamentary reform to the influence of one man, Geoffrey Palmer, deputy leader of the party and former Professor of Law at Victoria University. There can be little doubt that Palmer's influence and persuasive advocacy was of outstanding importance, but it was not the only factor involved. The origins of the 1985 reforms can be traced to the mid 1960s when Labour's basic constitutional and parliamentary policies included, *inter alia*, a planned parliamentary term with breaks for committee work, reform of standing orders, committees with the power to make on the spot investigations, a referendum on a four year parliamentary term, and a general review of existing legislation. Most of these proposals found their way into the party's "open government" policy in 1981.

Palmer's achievement was to elevate these policies to a position of electoral significance and to tie their implementation into the party's broader demands for consensus and reform. This occurred for at least four reasons. First, it was easy to justify a reform programme of this nature in political cost-benefit terms: that is to say, there were votes to be won at very little cost. Second, the manner in which Labour took power in mid-1984 highlighted the need for greater certainty in the working of the Constitution, particularly with respect to the rules for governmental succession (see Chapter 6). Third, Palmer brought to this reform package enthusiasm, expertise and his status as deputy leader of the party. In addition, as a supporter of former leader, Sir Wallace Rowling, he had an important symbolic and practical significance in uniting two formerly disputing groups within the party. Fourth, and most important, the open government policy went hand-in-glove with Labour's commitment to a new style of government, one that would replace Muldoon's interventionist and confrontational approach with less State interference in economic matters and a greater emphasis on consensus. Such a policy implied that the *style* of the Muldoon Administration was as much a cause of the country's woes as its *policies* and that a radical change in style held the promise of better government. Indeed, three months prior to the snap election, Palmer was selling his proposals in terms of their potential contribution to the management of the economy (Palmer, 1985). In this respect his ideas were in complete accord with the movement within the parliamentary party for more streamlined and efficient government.

Palmer and the Constitution

New Zealand has been described as having a system of "responsible government". Traditionally, this means that government has "to be responsive to public opinion, to pursue policies which are prudent and mutually consistent and to be accountable to the representatives of the electors" (Birch, p.20), or more precisely, that Ministers are responsible to Parliament for their departments' conduct; they have the last word in relations with officials; and officials are accountable to the public only through the accountability of Ministers and Cabinet to Parliament (Parker, 1978).

Much of the criticism of New Zealand's political system over the past 20 years has centred on the defects in the application of this theory of responsible government: Ministers sit in Parliament, but are rarely held responsible for their actions; the distinction in status between Ministers and public servants is evaporating as the latter become more politicized; big government and the power of officials means Ministers have much less control over the bureaucracy than they should; and Parliament has failed to ensure that the line of accountability runs unimpeded from officials to Ministers to Parliament and, thereby, to the electorate. Parliament's failings and proposals for reform have been cited with increasing frequency as the size and complexity of government has grown (Jackson, 1973; Marshall, 1978; Thomas, 1976). Palmer's criticisms form a significant part of this critique. He has emphasized, amongst other things, that government has excessive power, is too centralized, overly intrusive, and cloaks its business in secrecy; that many of the important policy decisions are made by bureaucrats in Wellington who cannot be controlled adequately or called to account; and that, because of the high level of party discipline, Parliament has too little power and simply goes along with the wishes of the executive (Palmer, 1979).

In short, the balance between the executive, legislative, and judicial branches of government has tipped more and more in favour of the executive, in particular the Cabinet and the Prime Minister. Although there are some limits on the executive (e.g. public opinion, pressure groups, parliamentary scrutiny, and the rule of law) these are insufficient to ensure "careful, measured decisions" and have caused a "lack of faith in the process by which decisions are reached" (Palmer, 1979, p.16).

Faced with the current dominance of the executive, there are, broadly speaking, two options for the reformer: either to abandon the theory of responsible government and fashion a new system of government on the basis of an alternative constitutional theory; or to try and revitalize the theory of responsible government by counterbalancing the power of the executive in some way. If the former strategy is adopted, namely the path of radical reform, one option would be to reconstruct New Zealand's Constitution in accordance with a presidential model, perhaps along the lines of the American system of government. This would involve the separation of powers with various checks and balances on the power of the executive. Clearly, such a move would have enormous implications for New Zealand's political institutions: Members of Parliament (MPs) would have an enhanced role in the decision-making process through temporary coalitions built around separate legislative issues. This would change Parliament from an arena-type legislature to a transformative-type legislature (Greenstein and Polsby, 1975); Cabinet Ministers would no longer be members of the legislature; and neutrality, anonymity and security of tenure would cease to be the dominant bureaucratic norms, and instead recruitment — certainly at the senior levels — would be largely on the basis of political compatibility.

While Palmer believed executive power to be oppressive, unresponsive, overbearing, concentrated and arrogant, he has not advocated axiomatic change in the system along such lines. To be sure, he has suggested greater separation of powers and lamented the lack of checks and balances in the Constitution. However, he has not advocated a radical attack on responsible government as the correct theory of how power should be exercised. Responsible government of the Westminster kind is accepted as the best mechanism available to forge the necessary connection between the imperiousness of power and the democracy of popular representation, thereby making the exercise of that power legitimate and acceptable. Once the prerogative powers of government are forced through the parliamentary filter the trick is to balance the Opposition's demands for responsiveness with the needs of the Government for effectiveness. According to Palmer, the executive is not sufficiently accountable because the parliamentary filter has become ineffectual.

Thus the remedy is not to radically weaken the executive, but to balance the scales by enhancing the status and role of the legislature and the judiciary. Consequently, the degree of change Palmer seeks is measured. Cabinet should be altered, but not so as to preclude Ministers from answering in Parliament or to cause "uncertainty and delay in making decisions" (Palmer, 1979, p.31). The recruitment of outsiders, i.e. people from the private sector, into the upper echelons of the public service should be made easier, but not in a manner which undermines the political neutrality of the career service. There should be a new system of accountability in accordance with which officials would be directly accountable to parliamentary committees for "administrative performance", but Ministers should remain responsible for basic policy choices. In addition, Parliament itself should be reformed: it should sit more regularly; its committees should be granted wider powers and improved resources; MPs should be provided with additional parliamentary and electorate staff; standing orders should be amended to avoid unnecessary procedural wrangles and improve the standard of debate; there should be less secrecy; the Speaker should be given greater independence; and there should be more MPs, thereby reducing existing workloads and providing more people to service select committees. Absent from this agenda are changes which would fundamentally alter the Constitution, such as the separation of the executive from the legislature or the replacement of the Monarchy with republican political structures. The proposed Bill of Rights, of course, will place certain limits on the sovereignty of Parliament and the power of the executive, but it remains to be seen whether the Bill will actually become part of New Zealand's constitutional arrangements (see Chapter 4).

The New Zealand system of Government has three cardinal rules which have not been challenged by any of the reforms of Parliament this century: the Government is entitled to support and legitimacy from Parliament once it has received the imprimatur of the voters; it is entitled to have its policies put into effect by the public service; and most important of the three, it should be allowed to get on with the business of governing. This means that Parliament's role is subsidiary to that of the Government and it is not its task to operate as a governing body. Labour's reforms increase the vulnerability of the Government to the criticism of Parliament but they do not impede the Government's capacity to implement its programme.

It is within these broad parameters that Labour has responded to the growing concern over the last few decades about the conduct of politics and the desire for a better balance between participation and effective decision-making. As Butt has observed, the fundamental function of Parliament is to "ensure that this dialectic of politics never ceases; [to] channel into broad and manageable streams the ultimate choices available to the community; and, above all, to bring the Government into constant consultation with the elected representatives of a community which is governed by consent" (1967, p.415).

With that in mind, there are two criteria by which to judge the latest parliamentary reforms. First, by how much more do they channel the activities of Government through the parliamentary filter; and second, to what extent do they alter the balance between the executive and the legislature or, to put it differently, between power and participation?

The 1985 Reforms

Select Committees

Labour believes the key to ensuring better parliamentary scrutiny of public sector spending, management and administration lies in the reform of the select committees. The shape of the new committee system owes much to the committees set up in the British House of Commons in 1979 (Englefield, 1984). These are known as departmental committees because their areas of scrutiny and investigation mirror the major departments of the civil service. When the issue of how parliamentary committees should be structured was last debated in New Zealand the Clerk's Office put forward a proposal embodying departmental committees. However, this was rejected by the then Prime Minister, Sir Robert Muldoon, although the referral of legislation to committees after the first reading debate was accepted as a compromise. This time Parliament's Standing Orders Committee accepted the concept of departmental committees influenced, no doubt, by Palmer's favourable impressions of the Westminster experience.

Thirteen new committees functionally related to Government departments came into being in August 1985. These are: Commerce and Marketing; Communications and Road Safety; Education and Science; Finance and Expenditure; Foreign Affairs and Defence; Government Administration; Internal Affairs and Local Government; Justice and Law Reform; Labour; Maori Affairs; Planning and Development; Primary Production; and Social Services. In addition, there is a Business Committee (principally, though not exclusively, to arbitrate disputes between committees), a Standing Orders Committee, a Privileges Committee, an Electoral Law Committee, and a Regulations Review Committee. Of the committees that existed prior to the 1985 reforms only the Privileges Committee remains intact. The Petitions Committee was abolished, largely because most petitions were automatically referred to the relevant subject committee under the old system. Local and private bills are now dealt with by the Internal Affairs and Justice committees respectively. The committees formerly concerned with House matters have been superseded by a new body, the Parliamentary Service Commission.

Another major change was the abolition of the Public Expenditure Committee. This was by far the most important of the old committees, not only because of its substantial formal powers, but also because it was usually the haunt of ambitious and capable backbenchers. The committee had the right to initiate its own inquiries, it could scrutinize the Estimates of Expenditure before their consideration by the House, it could conduct post-expenditure reviews of public service efficiency, and its members could question Government officials (McRobie, 1978). It was the Public Expenditure Committee's successful review of the efficiency of various public sector operations that established its status and reputation. In the new structure the Finance and Expenditure Committee has responsibility for monitoring and overseeing financial management in the public sector whilst the Government Administration Committee deals with overall public sector management and machinery of Government issues. The departmental committees now undertake the bulk of the Estimates work.

It was the intention of the Standing Orders Committee to pass the Public Expenditure Committee's mantle to the Finance and Expenditure Committee, but this has not occurred so far as that committee has devoted itself largely to legislative work (such as the Goods and Services Tax legislation). Perhaps the Office of the Auditor-General, on whose resources the Public Expenditure Committee relied and which now assists Government Administration, will enable this latter committee to assume the Public Expenditure Committee's investigative and audit roles. However, the drawback remains that there is now no single, powerful committee to which the ambitious and bright might gravitate and thus there is less likelihood of there being a vigorous, ongoing challenge to the Government's financial policies and man-agement of the State sector.

Another major change has been the creation of a committee to review statutory regulations. The use of delegated legislation or regulations is a powerful tool for Government, enabling it to avoid governing through Parliament. Every year hundreds of regulations are passed dealing with all kinds of matters — industrial relations, safety, transport, customs, immigration and so forth. Prior to 1985 the Statutes Revision Committee was empowered to review any regulations which were referred to it by Parliament, but this very rarely happened (Smith, 1978, pp.137-40). Hence, a huge body of legislation effectively went unexamined by Parliament. In some other Commonwealth countries parliamentary committees have existed for many years with a specific mandate to review delegated legislation. As a result of the 1985 reforms this now applies in New Zealand: under the new procedures all regulations are automatically referred to the Regulations Review Committee. Moreover, to enhance the independence of this committee the Government has appointed a senior Opposition MP, Doug Kidd, as chairperson. Such a procedure is rare in the New Zealand Parliament and currently this is the only committee chaired by a member of the Opposition.

Despite the committee's wide powers, it suffers from many of the afflictions of its predecessor: the nature of its work has few visible political rewards; its members are busy and cannot always be present at meetings; the quantity of work is considerable — on average about five regulations are introduced every week, some of them very detailed and complex; and its research capacity is limited — it is serviced by one full-time member of the parliamentary staff and is assisted by a part-time legal adviser. Moreover, notwithstanding Labour's "open government" policy and its commitment to reducing reliance on regulations, the number of regulations issued in 1984 and 1985 was 20 per cent higher than in the previous two years. On the other hand, the existence of the committee represents a vast improvement on the previous arrangements for scrutinizing regulations.

The new departmental committees are now as powerful as any in the Westminster model. In addition to their principal legislative review role, each committee has the power to examine the "policy, administration and expenditure" of the departments and quangos (quasi-autonomous non-governmental organizations) for which they are directly responsible. They can meet anywhere in the country, may summon witnesses, hear evidence in public, and make minority judgements (Standing Orders of the House of Representatives, Part XXXIII). They also have the power to begin inquiries without formal reference from the House of Representatives, although they are not empowered to conduct detailed reviews such as a Commission of Inquiry. Finally, if Parliament is in recess, their reports may be presented by giving a copy to the Clerk. They will then be regarded as having been tabled. Once such reports have been presented the Government is obliged to provide a written response to Parliament within 90 days. This procedure ensures that controversial or critical reports cannot easily be ignored or brushed under the carpet.

How have the committees performed in their first year? While it is difficult to measure the effects of committee activity or compare the old with the new, an interim assessment can be made and some of the likely consequences of the reforms considered.

The legitimacy and effectiveness of the old committee system had been threatened by a high level of membership substitution. This procedure was necessitated by the desire of each party to ensure that it had its full representation of MPs at committee meetings in case of divisions being called. In 1980, for example, there were 306 meetings of Parliamentary Select Committees. At these some 485 substitutions occurred; altogether 17 per cent of those present at committee meetings attended as replacements. Another feature of the old system was the tendency for

MPs to turn up for only part of a meeting. Hence, meetings were generally well attended, but rarely by the same members. As might be expected this proved injurious to effective deliberations — meetings were disrupted, specialization impeded, and decisions thrown into doubt as MPs heard only fragmented accounts of the evidence being presented.

In an effort to minimize such problems and make the system more effective, the reforms in 1985 reduced both the size and the number of committees. For example, the size of most committees was cut from between seven to 12 members to just five. In 1970 there were 20 committees and 200 positions to fill (an average 2.4 assignments per member); in 1980 there were 18 committees and 151 places (1.7 assignments per member, although in reality some MPs were on as many as four committees). As a result of the 1985 reforms the number of assignments has dropped to 0.9 per member; however, a comparison with the 1980 figure is distorted by the current procedure of excluding Ministers from committee membership.

Smaller committees, however, have caused several problems. First, although they now have fewer assignments, MPs probably have to work just as hard because the quality of that work must be higher. Whereas a committee of ten could count on perhaps half that number committing themselves to an issue, now the same workload is likely to be shared by only two or three. Second, chairpersons report that it is much more difficult to maintain a Government majority and, surprisingly, membership substitutions continue at a high level. This problem will only be solved when the proliferation of Caucus committees is controlled as their quantity makes scheduling and attendance difficult.

A number of other difficulties have also emerged since the reforms were introduced. As noted above, Ministers no longer serve as committee members (with the exception of the Standing Orders Committee, Maori Affairs Committee and the Privileges Committee). Although this obviously reduces the dominance of the executive, it also restricts the opportunities for scrutinizing ministerial decisions. The major problem, however, is that the existing function of scrutinizing legislation has swamped the new investigative function, there being insufficient members to perform both tasks simultaneously. If this situation is to be rectified it may be that the committees' staff resources will have to be enhanced (Davies, 1986, pp.10-11).

As noted, the main reason for the restructuring of the committee system was to enhance the accountability of the executive to the legislature and to give Parliament improved oversight of the administration of government. Although the committees have the power to consider policy issues, their principal role, in the words of the 1985 Standing Orders Report, is to scrutinize "policy implementation, administration and expenditure" and investigate "specific issues [such as] ... the level of performance in the execution of a particular departmental responsibility" (1985, p.34). The implication of this is that officials have a responsibility to Parliament for the soundness of their work separate from their responsibility to their Minister for the substance of that work. If public servants are to be directly accountable to Parliament, then this is one aspect of the reform package which is not consistent with Palmer's overall acceptance of responsible government. In fact, there is a clear contradiction between responsible government and this particular reform.

The notion that officials should be answerable directly to Parliament closely follows the trend towards managerialism in public administration (see Chapter 7). This idea, which has found widespread acceptance amongst officials, is that they should be freed from the restraints of ministerial responsibility and is summed up in the phrase "let the managers manage" (Skene, 1985b). That is to say, they resent ministerial intervention, which frequently occurs for political reasons, because it undermines good management.

Managerialism is posited on the assumption that a distinction, however rough, can be drawn between policy and administration. It claims the Minister's task is to make the policy; that having occurred, officials should be left alone to get on with the job. Accountability for the administration of policy, according to this theory, comes about not via the Minister in Parliament as responsible government would suggest, but through bureaucratic reporting procedures such as annual reports, internal auditing within public sector organizations, the external audit of the Auditor-General, and bureaucratic answerability to parliamentary committees. In essence, managerialism is nothing more than an attempt to exercise power without popular, democratic control. The distinction between policy and administration is suspect, to say the least (Aberbach, 1981; Lindblom, 1980; Parker, 1960; Smith, 1974), yet it appeals to officials because it allows them to avoid answering for policy, even though they are involved with Ministers in most policy decisions (McGee, 1985, p.208). It also appeals to Ministers because it enables them to push back the limits of parliamentary criticism by disclaiming responsibility for administration.

If the committees accept their terms of reference as a guide to their activities, they will tend to focus on administration and let Ministers off the policy hook. They must not lose sight of the tenets of responsible government which require that Ministers provide answers to Parliament on how policies deal with particular problems, and why those policies were chosen over others. If this is done, responsible government will be enhanced in two ways. First, it is likely the wider coverage of the activities of the Government will give Parliament better information about what Ministers and their departments are doing than was the case under the old committee system. And second, the existence of the departmental committees will provide an additional avenue through which Ministers can control their departments and related quangos.

It is to be hoped that departments will act responsibly in the knowledge that a committee exists with the power to examine their activities. This will only happen, however, if the committees establish their credentials with the departments at an early stage. This depends to a large extent, as indeed does the overall effectiveness of the committees, on the recruitment of sufficient and able staff. When the new committees came into operation they were serviced by a secretary and could also seek additional assistance from the Clerk's Office. While each committee now has the services of an advisory officer they remain understaffed.

Despite the new powers granted to parliamentary committees, it is unlikely that they will become deeply involved in policy initiation or in proposing solutions to policy problems. Rather, their role is likely to remain confined to scrutinizing the legislative proposals of the Government and from time to time conducting investigations of existing programmes. Moreover, their challenge to the executive will continue to be constrained by the fact that the Government maintains a majority on all the committees, and that with only one exception the committees are chaired by members of the governing party. This does not mean they will be unable to make a significant contribution to governance, but that within the intimacy of a small Parliament and the pervasiveness of party control, they will not become autonomous centres of political power.

It is one thing to provide the machinery for greater scrutiny, it is another to make it work. For example, consider the problem of membership substitutions: it is not so much that there are insufficient people to undertake all the necessary parliamentary jobs (although a larger number of MPs would certainly help), it is rather that too many MPs choose to do other jobs. By and large, they manage to attend the meetings they wish to, particularly where there are political pay-offs for the effort involved. Hence the new committees will only work satisfactorily if parliamentarians are convinced that participation will result in adequate political rewards. In the past the dividends of committee service have not been great because so much of the work occurred behind the scenes. It is to be hoped that the reforms introduced by the Labour Government will change this state of affairs.

The Parliamentary Service Commission

Labour's approach to the administration of Parliament is based on the principle that it is Parliament's business, not that of the executive, to determine its staffing and resources. In the past, Parliament's day-to-day affairs were managed by the Legislative Department. This Department had a hierarchical structure and a permanent head. It generally complied with the directions of the Treasury and the State Services Commission — although it was not obliged to — and had a Minister answerable in Parliament. Despite its unusual functions, the department sat comfortably, if nervously, within an executive-centred system of government and the convention of ministerial responsibility. Change and growth in the facilities for MPs was minimal because few Ministers wanted to increase the resources of their adversaries, either in their own party or in the Opposition.

As a result of the *Parliamentary Service Act 1985* the Legislative Department was replaced by the Parliamentary Service Commission. The Commission is comprised of the Speaker, the Leader of the House, a nominee of the Leader of the Opposition, and three other members. The Speaker heads the Commission and has day-to-day control of the Service. Although the Minister (and thus ministerial responsibility) has gone, responsibility is not equally shared among the commissioners. The political system demands that one individual be "responsible" and that person is now the Speaker.

Complete control of parliamentary resources has not been handed over to MPs, but there is greater room for bargaining between the parties and for MPs to be involved in the internal affairs of Parliament. The new arrangements have several advantages over the previous system of ministerial control: first, the procedures for dealing with backbenchers' demands have been institutionalized; second, the power of the executive, in particular the Prime Minister, to thwart desirable changes has been reduced; and third, through the obligation of the Parliamentary Service Commission to report to Parliament, accountability has been enhanced.

The Parliamentary Service Commission has control over nearly all the funds it needs. The estimates for the Service are prepared by the Commission and sent by the Speaker to the Minister of Finance for inclusion in the Appropriation Bill. The Government could, if it so wished, set limits for the Commission, but in the first year of operation it did not try to do so. Nevertheless, the Speaker attends the relevant Cabinet committee when the estimates of Parliament are being considered and he can be required to justify them. Moreover, there is no guarantee that future governments will allow the estimates to go to the House unchallenged. To give the Parliamentary Service Commission effective independence, it would be better if its budget was passed by Parliament in the form of a private member's bill. Any interference would then be immediately obvious, as indeed would any profligacy by the Commission.

Although the provision for financing is dealt with satisfactorily, if not perfectly, by the *Parliamentary Service Act*, it fails to find an acceptable solution to Parliament's personnel problem. Over the years the number of employees working in political jobs for MPs has increased alongside those of line bureaucrats in the old Legislative Department. Thus many staff were only nominally responsible to the Clerk of the House and took effective instruction from a political party. Labour tackled this problem by introducing contracts of service for political staff and giving the Clerk's administrative tasks to a new permanent head and general manager. This position was filled in June 1986 by Peter Brooks, the Deputy General Manager of the Tourist and Publicity Department and a former Commissioner for the Environment.

The implications of these changes have been considered elsewhere (Skene, 1985c), but two points should be made. The first is that although the Legislative Department was often said to be inefficient and its administration a quaint reflection of an earlier era — and thus a prime example of the administrative practices the new Labour Government wanted to remove — the main obstacle to efficiency was always the unusual nature of the job it was required to do. Each of its 95 clients was a representative of a constituency, and justifiably expected equitable and fair service. But for a variety of political and pragmatic reasons this was rarely acheived. Such constraints are unlikely to disappear under the new administrative arrangements.

The second point is more serious. Prior to the latest changes the Legislative Department, while a part of the public sector, was not subject to the *State Services Act*. Consequently, it was free — in theory at least — from the control of the Treasury and the State Services Commission. Now this semi-independent status has been given away in order to encourage mobility between the public and parliamentary services. This means that the Parliamentary Services Commission has lost the power to decide promotions, transfers, appointments and salaries to the State Services Commission. This permits a degree of control over Parliament's constitutional functions which is undesirable.

Standing Orders

Standing orders are the rules which determine the balance between the Government's desire to pass legislation and the Opposition's desire to frustrate its passage. Generally speaking, the Opposition opposes only a small proportion of legislation introduced into the House, so when the rules are modified it is usually disposed to accept them as long as they don't reduce the opportunities for criticizing the Government and communicating its concerns to the electorate. As noted earlier, Labour's reforms of the select committee system have not undermined the convention of a strong executive or the view that a government has the right to implement its programme. The same is true of the changes which Labour has made to the timetable and procedures of Parliament and the process by which bills become law.

A trade-off has been made in the new standing orders: while private members have been granted greater opportunity to criticize and rebuke the Government, in return the Government has been granted greater efficiency in debate. Parliament now sits for three days per week (instead of four), three weeks on and one week off (to give select committees time to meet), and over a greater proportion of the year (formerly it usually sat only between June and December). Its hours of sitting have also been extended slightly: the House now meets from 2.00 to 5.30pm and from 7.30 to 11.00pm. While the total number of sitting days remains about the same, there is now a greater likelihood of the Government being challenged on its performance. When Parliament is sitting it acts to amplify the Opposition's discontent. The Opposition also benefits from the fact that most of Wednesday is now devoted to private members' business. For example, there is a new provision for a two-hour debate that day, the subject of which is chosen by the Opposition. Notices of motion, which enabled MPs to make critical comments on topical issues, have given way to questions of the day in which Ministers have little prior notice of the matters to be raised. Further, under new urgency rules it is no longer possible for the Opposition to demand all-night sittings, although it can still force long sittings to demonstrate its discontent with Government policy (e.g. during the National Party conference in mid-1986 a small band of Opposition MPs kept the House sitting during much of the weekend).

In return the Government has reduced what it considered to be time-wasting procedures. For example, it has halved the time given to speeches in committee and speeches on the short title, reduced the Budget debate by one-third, and erased debate on some procedural motions and the reading of notices of motion. It appears from Hansard that Government demands for the Budget debate, Address-In-Reply, and committee stage to be subject to a guillotine (in which overall time limits are set prior to the debate) were not successful *(New Zealand Parliamentary Debates,* 1985, p.5599). Debate on the Estimates has reverted to the pre-1972 position which excludes discussion of policy matters. The reduction in the quorum for the chamber from 20 to 15 MPs was supported by both major parties, granting busy Ministers, in particular, greater opportunities to attend to other business. This is further evidence of the slow decline of the chamber as the prime focus for the business of Parliament.

Despite these new rules, to date there has not been a marked improvement in the management of the legislative programme. There are a number of reasons for this: the nature of the 1984-85 sitting (former Ministers now in the Opposition were able to clog the Order Paper with their bills, introduced as private members' bills), the considerable time devoted to the Homosexual Law Reform Bill during 1985/86, and the overly generous gesture of private members' Wednesdays. All these things delayed Labour's legislative programme and caused the Government to take urgency 13 times between August and December 1985. Nevertheless, there was still the usual end-of-session rush in 1985 which the changes to standing orders were meant to avoid. The House took urgency in the second-to-last week of the session and passed 20 bills. Thirteen bills were introduced in the last week and 64 were held over for the 1986 session. The criticism of legislation by exhaustion — too many bills being passed too quickly — is thus no less valid under Labour than any previous administration.

In general, most of the important legislative work of Parliament takes place in select committees. The role of the chamber is to communicate to the nation each party's political programme. Yet the general belief persists that what transpires in the chamber is paramount: the parties are aware that it is the most visible testament to Parliament's work and thus guard it jealously. Because of this, committees are not permitted to sit coterminously with the chamber and there are complaints when proceedings are not broadcast. The new standing orders have reduced the dominance of the chamber and have altered its role within the scope of Parliament's functions. Committee work is now more important, so much so that the Standing Orders Committee expressed its annoyance with the media for not covering this aspect (1985, p.13). But because Parliament has yet to determine which of its roles is the more important, it persists with a programme which satisfies neither. The result is long and unusual hours and hasty legislation, of which the public are justifiably critical. In fact, nobody wins: the end-of-session rush steamrolls the Opposition and reduces its ability to communicate its discontent to the electorate, while the pressure of work reduces the legitimacy of the Government and the level of public support for, and understanding of, its policies.

It is because of the chamber's broadcasting function that New Zealand's politicians have dabbled occasionally with the idea of televising Parliament. Labour extended radio coverage to all parliamentary proceedings and experimented with television in June 1986 when TV New Zealand broadcast Parliament for three days. Of the many arguments against televised broadcasts, perhaps the most common is that MPs will play to the cameras. The real reasons, however, are more fundamental. First, because of its role in the continuous election campaign waged between the parties, the House more often has the appearance of a sweaty, bellicose talk-shop, than a place where high-minded individuals rationally deliberate on important matters of public policy. There is nothing unusual or necessarily wrong with this, but the politicians fear the public's awakening to this realization. Second, television reduces the political parties' control over the images they wish to present and the process of projecting them. Where it is not possible to televise Parliament continuously, there is a need for editorial licence for which the broadcasters alone are responsible.

The greatest benefit of television would be to force Ministers to communicate with the electorate through the House. In recent times the press conference and the public address have replaced parliamentary speeches as the preferred method of communication, a trend believed by many to be in conflict with the constitutional principles of responsible government. The knowledge that a speech would get broad dissemination via television might increase Ministers' regard for the chamber as well as the amount of time they are prepared to spend there.

Minor Reforms

This chapter has concentrated on the major parliamentary reforms of the Labour Government, but there have been a number of other changes which deserve mention. In addition to a more effective voice in the allocation of their resources, MPs now have paid electorate workers (half-time), a full-time secretary in Wellington, and improvements are promised in their office accommodation. This reflects the experiences of the young professional Labour MPs elected in 1978 and 1981: they resented, quite rightly, the unseemly triennial squabbles for office furniture and equipment, and were critical of the poor level of staff support.

In mid-1986 Labour had a number of additional measures under way designed to expose the executive more critically to the parliamentary filter. The Public Finance Amendment Bill requires the Crown to inform Parliament of some of the larger guarantees it gives. The Official Information Amendment Bill will provide for judicial review of the controversial ministerial veto aspects of the 1982 Act. Maori has become an official language of Parliament. The Government is considering the possibility of providing MPs with research staff and requiring them to declare their private interests. Also, the findings of the Royal Commission on the Electoral System established in 1985 may have substantial implications for Parliament. In accordance with its terms of reference it is required, amongst other things, to consider the size of Parliament, the merits of the first-past-the-post method of electing MPs, the public funding of political parties, the procedures for revising electoral boundaries, and the question of Maori representation. Finally, the Constitution Bill should prevent the kind of confusion that arose after the 1984 election as to when a person becomes or ceases to be an MP (see Chapter 6).

Conclusion

The changes introduced by the Labour Government in 1985 have undoubtedly altered both the organization and operation of Parliament. Collectively they overcome many of the weaknesses which have afflicted New Zealand's legislature during the 1970s and 1980s. But the changes certainly do not amount to a radical redistribution of political power from the executive to the legislature. Thus, although they represent the most significant reform of Parliament this century, they are best regarded as an evolutionary rather than revolutionary step in the development of New Zealand's political institutions. The select committees have been restructured and granted wider powers, but they remain under the control of the governing party. The staff resources available to MPs have been improved, but they do not compare favourably with the levels available in many legislatures around the world. The trend away from the chamber as the focus of parliamentary activity has been continued, but not to the extent that it has become irrelevant. In fact, the changes to standing orders will do much to ensure that the chamber remains important.

Labour's parliamentary reforms, therefore, should not be regarded as having brought about axiomatic changes to the system of New Zealand's government. The legislature remains a unicameral one. The theory of responsible government has been retained. The concept of ministerial responsibility has been preserved, and possibly enhanced. Further, although the changes have tipped the balance between the legislature and the executive slightly back in the direction of the legislature, the dominance of the executive remains. By virtue of its control of Caucus, the Cabinet can continue to exercise influence over the legislative process, the work of select committees and the character of parliamentary debate.

If the dominance of the executive is to be reduced, and the independence of the legislature enhanced, further reforms will be needed. One possibility here – and something which might well be recommended by the Royal Commission on Electoral Reform – would be to substantially increase the number of MPs. Those who favour such a change point to several desirable effects. It is said a larger Parliament would reduce party discipline, provide a larger pool from which to select talent for the Cabinet, and assist in committee work by reducing workloads (Cleveland, 1979; Jackson, 1973). Such views, however, require qualification as they ignore the underlying political forces at work in Parliament.

While more MPs would produce a larger pool from which to choose the Cabinet, it must be remembered that ministerial selection and ranking does not depend on ability alone. The recent history of both major parties shows that ministerial rankings depend as much on personal loyalty to the leader as talent. One solution to this problem of inadequate talent might be to enhance the status of politics as a vocation, thereby attracting better parliamentary candidates.

Party discipline is undoubtedly the single strongest variable in explaining the behaviour of MPs and, irrespective of the size of Parliament, is liable to bind politicians together so long as parties remain the dominant vehicle for political recruitment and advancement. Parliament would need to be a great deal larger to create any real possibility for dissension from the party whip. A better approach, therefore, might be to enhance the status and rewards of committee chairpersons. This could create an alternative career structure within Parliament, separate from ministerial office, where promotion would be based as much on an individual's contribution to Parliament as on party loyalty. It is worth noting that the success of the committees of the House of Commons is in no small part due to the fact that the Government has little influence over the selection of the committees' chairpersons.

The desirability of the current influence of party and Caucus on Parliament is open to debate (Mulgan, 1984). If parliamentary reform is intended to promote the independence of Parliament and MPs, then the power and solidarity of Caucus needs to be addressed. From this perspective Labour's current reforms must be considered a failure. If, however, Parliament's role is primarily to bring the Government under the close scrutiny of its elected representatives, then the parliamentary changes introduced since 1984 can be viewed less critically.

As with most legislative institutions, New Zealand's Parliament works best when the informal agreements between the parties are honoured and the unwritten rules respected. It is up to the parties to make the new rules work and to show that Parliament is an important and viable institution: the success of the reforms depends on this.

References

Aberbach, J., Putnam, R. and Rockman, B. (1981) *Bureaucrats and Politicians in Western Democracies* Cambridge, Harvard.

Birch, A.H. (1964) *Representative and Responsible Government* London, Allen and Unwin.

Butt, R. (1967) *The Power of Parliament* London, Constable.

Cleveland, L. (1979) *The Politics of Utopia* Wellington, Methuen.

Davies, S. (1986) Parliamentary Accountability of Government-owned Corporations and Companies *Public Sector* 9: 3-15.

Englefield, D. (Ed.)(1984) *Commons Select Committees - Catalysts for Progress* Harlow, Longman.

Greenstein, F. and Polsby, N. (1975) *Governmental Institutions and Processes* Reading, Addison-Wesley.

Jackson, W.K. (1973) *New Zealand: Politics of Change* Wellington, Reed Education.

Jackson, W.K. (1985) Caucus: the Anti-Parliament System? In Gold, H. (Ed.) *New Zealand Politics in Perspective* Auckland, Longman Paul.

Jackson, W.K. (1987) *The Dilemma of Parliament* Sydney, Allen and Unwin (forthcoming).

Judge, D. (1981) *Backbench Specialisation in the House of Commons* London, Heinemann Educational Books.

Lindblom, C. (1980) *The Policy Making Process* 2nd ed. New Jersey, Prentice Hall.

Marshall, J. (Ed.)(1978) *The Reform of Parliament* Wellington, New Zealand Institute of Public Administration.

McGee, D. (1985) *Parliamentary Practice in New Zealand* Wellington, Government Printer.

McRobie, A. (1978) Parliamentary "Control" of Public Expenditure. In Levine, S. (Ed.) *Politics in New Zealand* Auckland, Allen and Unwin.

Mulgan, R. (1980) Palmer, Parliament and the Constitution *Political Science* 32: 171-177.

Mulgan, R. (1984) *Democracy and Power in New Zealand* Melbourne, Oxford.

New Zealand Parliamentary Debates Wellington, Government Printer.

Palmer, G. (1979) *Unbridled Power* Wellington, Oxford University Press.

Palmer, G. (1985) The Contribution of the Open Government Policy to Economic Management. Speech to the New Zealand Labour Party's Central North Island Regional Conference.

Parker, R. (1960) Policy and Administration *Public Administration* 19: 113-120.

Parker, R. (1978) The Public Service Inquiries and Responsible Government. In Smith, R. and Weller, P. (Eds) *Public Service Inquiries in Australia* St Lucia, Queensland University Press.

Sabatier, P. and Mazmanian, D. (1979) The Conditions of Effective Implementation: A Guide to Accomplishing Policy Objectives *Policy Analysis* Fall: 481-503.

Skene, G. (1985a) Parliament: Reassessing its Role. In Gold, H. (Ed.) *New Zealand Politics in Perspective* Auckland, Longman Paul.

Skene, G. (1985b) Auditing, Efficiency and Management in the New Zealand Public Sector *Australian Journal of Public Administration* 44: 270-286.

Skene, G. (1985c) Administering Parliament *Public Sector* 8: 23-28.

Smith, J. (1978) Statutes Revision: The Lawyers' Committee. In Levine, S. (Ed.) *Politics in New Zealand* Auckland, Allen & Unwin.

Smith, T. (1974) *The New Zealand Bureaucrat* Wellington, Cheshire.

Standing Orders of the House of Representatives (1985) Wellington, Government Printer.

Thomas, E. (1976) Parliamentary Control of the Administration of Central Government: Fact or Fiction? *Otago Law Review* 3: 437-457.

6

Ministers, the Cabinet and Public Servants

John Roberts

The fourth Labour Government succeeded an Administration notable for startling constitutional adventures. The Muldoon Government had precipitated an early election with only the second dissolution of the New Zealand Parliament in the twentieth century, compelled, according to the explanation offered by the then Prime Minister, by the threatened defection of at least one Government back-bencher. A Cabinet Minister, Derek Quigley, had been forced to resign following a deliberate breach of collective responsibility involving criticism of Government policy. A Committee of Enquiry had been empowered to investigate allegations of improper interventions in a land deal on behalf of relatives by a senior Minister, Duncan McIntyre. A Minister of Works and Development had, in effect, declined to accept even the shadow of vicarious responsibility for the cost of a complex irrigation scheme which substantially exceeded the estimates made by officers of the Ministry. A fellow Minister had strongly criticized the Ministry's officers in relation to the same project on the grounds that it affected the interests of his constituents. It is reasonable to argue that the initiatives in Government economic policy had been virtually delegated by Cabinet to the Cabinet Economic Committee. Furthermore an *Official Information Act* calling into question some of the fundamental rules of the Westminster constitutional process came on to the Statute Book and in two major cases the Government employed retrospective legislation to reverse the effect of important Court decisions. These were no more than high points in an era of dramatic adjustment to sustained pressure on the economy and society.

It is a measure of the times that this penchant for extraordinary, if sometimes involuntary, constitutional innovation seems now to fade to colourless orthodoxy in the light of the policy changes initiated by the fourth Labour Government. For there is general agreement among those widely experienced in central government administration that the scope of the present constitutional and administrative reforms is without historical precedent; they, naturally, seek to understand why the Labour Party should think that the moment has arrived for an abrupt departure from the historical course of political change in New Zealand. Some tentative explanations may be offered.

The Succession Crisis in Mid 1984

The first and most obvious explanation is the unexpected circumstances in which Labour assumed office. The dissolution precluded the long build-up to election day with its customary compromises on policy commitments. While Labour's leaders were not given a *tabula rasa* upon which they could write such bright inventions as occurred to them following the victory, neither were they burdened with the baggage of an orthodox election campaign. They also reaped the benefit of a notable financial and constitutional crisis immediately after the election (see Chapter 8). In their judgement a substantial devaluation of the currency was required, but it appeared that statutory requirements concerning the return of the electoral writs prevented them from assuming office. Rather inadequate precedent suggested that it was the duty of the outgoing Government to place its constitutional authority at the disposal of the incoming Government. The defeated Prime Minister, however, indicating his disapproval of devaluation, appeared unwilling to assist the new Administration to achieve its purpose.

It was reported on 17 July 1984 that "impeccable sources" had revealed that "... Sir Robert Muldoon had been advised by the Reserve Bank and Treasury to lower the value of the dollar". The advice had been given on the basis that "... authorities had exhausted every other prudent measure that could be taken to meet the foreign exchange crisis sparked by the calling of the snap election" (*Evening Post*, 17 July 1984). Later it was reported that National Cabinet Ministers had confirmed that on 18 June "... the full Cabinet had been advised by Sir Robert Muldoon of his rejection of the devaluation advice" (*Evening Post*, 19 July 1984). The same source stated that "... in a television interview on 16 July Sir Robert had refused to concede the need for a devaluation and had called on Mr Lange to join with him in a statement announcing that there would be no devaluation" (*Evening Post*, 17 July 1984).

Lange quickly accused Muldoon of committing "economic sabotage" (*Evening Post*, 17 July 1984). It was reported that three senior members of the National Cabinet, Jim McLay, the Deputy Prime Minister, Bill Birch, the Minister of Energy, and Jim Bolger, the Minister of Labour, had met to review the situation. According to the same source, the Secretary to the Treasury, Bernard Galvin, and the Governor of the Reserve Bank, Spencer Russell, had considered the need for them to "break the traditional silence of public servants and make public their advice" (*Evening Post*, 17 July 1984). It was reported on 17 July that "... the Deputy Prime Minister met Sir Robert and, in effect told the Prime Minister that if he did not co-operate with the incoming government he could not guarantee the backing of the Muldoon team" (*Evening Post*, 17 July 1984). On 18 July a 20 per cent devaluation was announced following the decision of the Prime Minister to place his powers as Minister of Finance at the disposal of the Labour leaders.

The alarums and excursions associated with these extraordinary events certainly focused attention upon the critical state of the New Zealand economy. The leading group in the new Government were seen to act decisively. This undoubtedly helped to establish an ascendancy which carried over into the so-called Economic Summit Conference later in the year.

The Constitution Bill

In the wake of the crisis, the Labour Government introduced a Bill to regulate governmental succession. At the time of writing (October 1986) this had yet to be debated by Parliament. The Bill reiterates a rule embodied in the *Civil List Act 1979*. Under section 6(1) a "person may be appointed as a member of the Executive Council or as a Minister of the Crown only if that person is a member of Parliament". To this there is one exception designed to meet the succession crisis of 1984. In that case a new Administration could not be formed owing to uncertainty concerning the "time when a person actually becomes and when a person actually ceases to be a member of Parliament". Under Section 6(2) a person:

> ... who is not a member of Parliament may be appointed and hold office as a member of the Executive Council or as a Minister of the Crown if that person was a candidate for election at the General Election of members of the House of Representatives held immediately preceding that person's appointment as a member of the Executive Council or as a Minister of the Crown but shall vacate office at the expiration of the period of 40 days beginning with the date of the appointment unless, within that period, that person becomes a member of Parliament.

Thus, the problems of special votes and electoral deficiencies which delay the return of the writs are overcome and a Government may assume office immediately the results of a General Election are known and the Governor-General calls on the Leader of the ostensibly victorious party to form a Government. The Bill goes on to provide for problems of transition by permitting Ministers who cease to be a Members of Parliament to continue in office for 28 days after their defeat.

Problems have not previously arisen from the delay in succession caused by the electoral process. Scott says simply that: "If an opposition party wins a clear majority in a General Election the ministry must resign very soon" (1962, p.102). In a discussion of practice in previous elections, he says that each "... defeated ministry resigned within a week or two". But behind such an informal and flexible process lies the fact that, since the passage of the *Triennial Act 1879*, all Parliaments, bar five, have lasted their expected electoral period and the return of the writs in this century has, in every case except three, occurred in November or December.[1] The exceptions are the election of 1946 when the sitting Government was returned; 1951 following an early dissolution when the sitting Government was returned; and 1984 when the Government was defeated. Usually, then, elections have been foreseen. Parliamentary and Government business has been completed in anticipation, and an orderly transition provided for those new Governments coming to office as a result of an election victory. The case of 1984 is unprecedented in our parliamentary history.

It is true that in 1890 — a crucial moment of political transition — the Atkinson Ministry held on to office for seven weeks after defeat by the Liberal Party. But Scott records that this delay in resigning "... was widely regarded as improper" (p.102). If the Constitution Bill is duly passed it seems that the Governor-General will be expected to call upon the Leader of the winning party to form a Government if any obstruction to their legitimate requirement appears. It is not clear, however, that the Bill assumes an immediate transfer will normally occur once an Opposition election victory is revealed. Nor is it clear that this would be advantageous.

The long tradition of orderly transfer of power had several advantages. In the first place, an incoming Government can go about the business of forming an administration in deliberate fashion with time for sensible consultation and, in the case of the Labour Party, the organization of a Caucus election for the new group of Ministers. The outgoing administration has reasonable time to wind up business and make arrangements for the disposition of confidential papers. The individual Ministers, outgoing and incoming, can deal with the upheaval in their personal lives as they vacate homes and re-establish their families. The breathing space also gives time for departmental officers to complete the briefing documents for incoming Ministers in the light of the political developments arising from the election and to prepare themselves for the arrival of the new Minister. In comparison with the confusion of 1984, previous procedures seem like a model of civilized politics. It is true that an immediate transition occurs in England but there seems to be no outstanding advantage and, on the basis of experience, it appears best to leave the powers in the Constitution Bill for use only in cases of political emergency.

The Public Expenditure Committee's Investigation of the Currency Crisis

An interesting constitutional imbroglio arising from the succession crisis might have tripped the new Government at the start when the former Prime Minister attempted to justify his post-election tactics and to refute the criticism of his attempts to maintain a stable exchange rate. In the event, a promised passage of high political drama fizzled out in a prudent exercise of executive power.

Parliament's Public Expenditure Committee had made some attempt to conduct objective and bipartisan enquiries into the management of public assets (see Chapter 5). It was not, however, a forum for the debate of major policy. The new Labour Government injudiciously agreed to a proposal that the controversial decision to devalue the New Zealand dollar in July 1984 be referred to a sub-committee of the Public Expenditure Committee. This would be chaired by a leading Labour dissident, Jim Anderton, clearly antagonistic to the inflationary effect of the devaluation. The sub-committee also included among its members the redoubtable Sir Robert Muldoon who had provoked the post-election constitutional crisis by his obdurate opposition to devaluation.

According to a statement in the House of Representatives on 3 October 1984 by the acting chairperson of the Public Expenditure Committee, Fran Wilde, the Committee decided on 22 August 1984 to establish a sub-committee to:

(1) enquire into events, acts and omissions leading up to and following the decision to devalue the New Zealand dollar on 18 July 1984;

(2) establish the impact of these moves on the public finances;

(3) examine the management and level of foreign exchange holdings in that period and the extent and nature of foreign exchange transactions;

(4) investigate measures taken to protect the New Zealand currency in that period;

(5) review measures that could be used in the future to protect the New Zealand currency and public finance from the effects of currency speculation (*New Zealand Parliamentary Debates*, Vol.457, p.777).

The members of the sub-committee were, on the Government side, Jim Anderton as Chairman, Peter Neilson and Peter Dunne, and for the Opposition, Sir Robert Muldoon and John Falloon. Jim Anderton stated in the House on 3 October that "the devaluation sub-committee was not set up to investigate whether the decision was necessarily good or bad but to investigate the circumstances surrounding the devaluation". In the same speech he acknowledged that he was among those who had doubts about the wisdom of devaluation as an instrument of economic policy (p.781).

In practice, the decision sparked off a notable constitutional crisis. The Committee met once on 22 September 1984 and heard evidence from Dr Deane, then of the Reserve Bank. It was later announced that a challenge to the legal status of the inquiry had been received and that the matter had been referred to the Speaker. It was reported on 27 September that further meetings of the Committee had been cancelled. Opposition members accused the Government of abusing the parliamentary process. The chairman of the Public Expenditure Committee, Peter Neilson, alleged that Muldoon had "torpedoed the enquiry" (*Evening Post*, 27 September 1984).

Two factors seem to have been at work in bringing the sub-committee to disaster so quickly. First, the public servants who had been advising Sir Robert on the exchange crisis were concerned that he would use the hearings to justify his refusal to accept their recommendations and in the process would publicly discredit them. Second, the Government realized belatedly that they would be embroiled in a nasty political row at a time when it was of urgent importance to negotiate a consensus on the principles of their economic policy.

It was reported on 26 September 1984 that "... civil servants here told the *Post* that legal opinion was sought because of fears that the State employees could be placed in a position of jeopardy" (*Evening Post*, 26 September 1984). Wilde confirmed on 3 October 1984 that several legal opinions had been prepared (*New Zealand Parliamentary Debates*, Vol.457, p.778). She also alleged that during the actual currency crisis Muldoon "... would not even see or speak to the Officials he tried to crucify during the Public Expenditure Committee sub-committee hearing" (p.778). In effect this part of the debate turned on two issues. The first, in the words of the Chairman of the State Services Commission, Dr Probine, is the question of:

> ... whether public servants should be asked to account for policy decisions or to indicate what advice may or may not have been sought, offered, or taken. But the responsibility for policy has been regarded as that of the Minister and it has been for him or her to answer in respect of it. It is likely to undermine the relationship between Ministers and advisors if a precedent is to be established for public servants to be examined, without the concurrence of the responsible Minister, on what advice was given and the reason for it. That will be particularly so if, for public servants to be usefully examined on policy issues they will have to be permitted to disclose informal discussions and Ministers' responses as well as the content of formal advice (Probine, 1984).

The second issue relates to the fairness of inquisitions of official advisors in conditions of intense political conflict. Dr Probine, speaking of the devaluation inquiry, said:

> It was conveyed to me that officers of the Public Service had a strong feeling that they were being put on trial in this matter and that they were being tried by a Tribunal which by the tests ordinarily applied would not be seen to be disinterested. That is contrary to generally accepted concepts of justice and, in addition to the question of fairness to the individuals involved, is again likely to be detrimental to the future working of the Public Service. Senior public servants in New Zealand try to give, as best as they can, proper advice whilst leaving policy decisions in the hands of the Ministers of the day where they belong. Any procedure which may cause public servants in future difficult situations to look primarily at self protection is, I suggest, damaging to the broader public interest.

Jim Anderton argued an opposing point of view:

> The people expect us to be accountable and we must act as watchdogs of the people for both the Executive and those who advise it. There are those who suggest that those advisors should not be accountable to Parliament; that only Ministers should be answerable. I cannot accept that. It is readily accepted that party politics should not be brought into the Civil Service. Those officials who leaked information to the media to serve their own ends should know the two-edged sword they have grasped. For a department, whether it is Treasury, the Reserve Bank or the Ministry of Works and Development, to deny that a major department of State does sometimes adopt a policy position is to deny reality. To suggest that senior officials of these departments should not be scrutinised by Parliament or made accountable through its Select Committee procedure is to deny that institution has a rightful function as the place where the buck stops and accountability finally rests (*New Zealand Parliamentary Debates*, Vol.457, p.781).

Who is correct? Is it not the case that the public servant expects certain standards of behaviour from his masters, but suffers in silence when the conventions are broken? On this view was it right to raise legal obstacles to the sub-committee hearing? How well will the new Select Committee procedures which the Standing Orders Committee has established work if they cannot call public servants to discuss the implications of policy with them? Have we, despite Probine's defence of the traditional relationship between an anonymous (and unreachable) administration and an accessible (and blameable) political executive, reached a point where institutional distinctions will have to be made and the official required to stand up to his or her critics in appropriate circumstances? If this line of reasoning leads to the involvement of officials who work in close relationship with Ministers to devise, negotiate and introduce policy, the relevant Westminster conventions may as well be abandoned altogether, which necessarily means abandoning the tradition of dedicated confidential administrative service to the politician. But there are many situations where policy initiatives rest in practice with the administrators and the Ministers' political survival is not in question. Ministers should retain the right to instruct their officials on responses to be made to Committees. On the other hand, the members of Select Committees should be able to make public requests for the appearance of administrators, together with supporting evidence, to show that the confidential relationship with the Minister is not threatened.

In the case of the investigation by the Public Expenditure Committee sub-committee the officials had every right to believe that they were to become the scapegoats who would suffer for the frustration felt by Members of Parliament. Perhaps they were justified in believing that this was unfair. Unquestionably the Government was notably foolhardy in allowing the inquiry to take place. But for all this the outcome cannot be seen as a warrant for public servants called to Select Committees to duck behind a spuriously justified anonymity.

The Labour Cabinet

It must be emphasized that the Labour Cabinet elected in July 1984 was no band of experienced colleagues hardened by the fire of office. The Prime Minister, David Lange, had been in Parliament for seven years, and the Deputy Prime Minister, Geoffrey Palmer, for five years. Of the rest, only the Minister of Finance, Roger Douglas, the Minister of Agriculture, Colin Moyle, the Minister of Energy, Bob Tizard, and the Minister of Works and Development, Fraser Colman, had previously held ministerial portfolios. Yet it is reasonable to claim that this lack of experience was a principal reason for the vigour and range of their reforms. The inner group of Prime Minister, Deputy Prime Minister, Minister of Overseas Trade (Mike Moore), Minister of Finance, Minister of Transport (Richard Prebble) and Minister of Trade and Industry (David Caygill) — the last two also Associate

Ministers of Finance — are all relatively young, and most hold professional qualifications. Not being in any sense hostages to the past they embraced the future with equal measures of intelligence and blithe ignorance.

They had, moreover, an enthusiastic guide to the new territory. The Minister of Finance, Roger Douglas, energetic Minister of Broadcasting and Housing in the third Labour Government, had taken up the task of rethinking Labour's economic policy during the Muldoon era (see Chapter 8). His opinions, put forward at times in "alternative budgets", were not greeted with enthusiasm by the party as a whole and at one stage it seemed possible that he might part company with Labour. If any lingering doubt existed in the Caucus it was not sufficient to persuade the members that they should reject Douglas in the election of the group to be nominated for ministerial appointment. It also must have been clear to the Caucus that Douglas would become Minister of Finance. Perhaps the interventionism of the declining Muldoon Administration had inclined Labour MPs to accept the arguments in favour of economic deregulation and liberalization.

The new Government was clearly intent upon improving the quality and coherence of decision making. To this end it has made a number of changes to the operation of the Cabinet system. Firstly, the Cabinet usually takes a short period of about half an hour at each meeting to discuss general political issues and problems of co-ordinating policy before moving on to agenda items. Secondly, as early as 30 July 1984 the Government announced a reorganization of the structure of Cabinet Committees which dismantled the long-standing National arrangements and revived a concept originally introduced by the Kirk Administration. Thus, powerful co-ordinating Cabinet Committees such as Economics, Works and State Services were abolished and the Cabinet Policy Committee created. This Committee includes the Prime Minister, the Deputy Prime Minister, the Minister of Finance and his two Associates. The Ministers of Overseas Trade, Education, Agriculture and Fisheries, and Labour, all chairpersons of the "Sector" Cabinet Committees mentioned below, are also members. The Cabinet Policy Committee is chaired by Lange but, in the nature of things, the claims upon his time are pressing whether in his Prime Ministerial role or as Minister of Foreign Affairs. In the circumstances it is fortunate that Labour has an acceptable and authoritative Deputy Prime Minister to assist Lange in this duty. Indeed, it is obvious in the debate on State owned enterprises that Palmer's influence has extended well beyond the limits that his Justice portfolio would imply.

The Cabinet Policy Committee is concerned with broad policy issues and the achievement of clarity, coherence and integration, rather than the detailed implementation or formulation of policies. It appears that, in intention and in practice, the Cabinet Policy Committee exercises considerable control over policy directions, sets the context of debate on major proposals and defines the overall resource limits for the major areas of the Government's programme.

There are five "Sector" Committees whose broad function is to plan and co-ordinate policies and to improve performance in each sector. They comprise the following:

1. *Development and Marketing*: This covers the portfolios of Agriculture and Fisheries, Forests, Inland Revenue, Lands, Overseas Trade and Marketing, Publicity, Regional Development, Rural Banking and Finance Corporation, Science and Technology, Statistics, Tourism, Trade and Industry, Valuation, and Works and Development (except roading). The substantive policy fields include industrial and commercial development, overseas trade, capital and labour resources, industry assistance, trade relations with Australia, economic regulation and regional development.

2. *Social Equity*: This covers the portfolios of Arts, Education, Health, Housing, Immigration, Internal Affairs, Justice, Labour, Local Government, Maori Affairs, Pacific Island Affairs, Recreation and Sport, Rehabilitation, Social Welfare, War Pensions and Women's Affairs. The substantive policy fields include the promotion of social equity and justice, redressing imbalances in society, and integrating social policies.

3. *Transport, Communications and State Enterprises*: This covers the portfolios of Broadcasting, Civil Aviation and Meteorological Services, Government Life Insurance Corporation, Government Printing Office, Postmaster General, Public Trust Office, Railways, State Insurance Office, Transport, Works and Development (roading) and generally all State owned enterprises. The substantive policy field (probably the most active to date) is inadequately given as the planning and co-ordination of policies relating to transport and communications.

4. *External Relations and Security*: This covers the portfolios of Civil Defence, Earthquake and War Damage Commission, Foreign Affairs, New Zealand Security Intelligence Service and Police. The substantive policy field is defence, organization of armed forces, internal policing, civil defence and disaster relief.

5. *Management and State Employment*: This covers Audit, Attorney General, State Services, Works and Development (control functions). The substantive policy field is State employment policy and in addition the Committee is concerned with the review of matters relating to service-wide Government administration and the system by which agencies account for their actions.

In addition to these "Sector" Committees there are three special purpose Committees as follows:

1. *Legislation*: This consists of six members to determine drafting priority for legislation, to review draft bills and to consider Parliamentary petitions.

2. *Terrorism*: This consists of five members to review reports from officers on contingency plans, co-ordinate plans and determine policy in an emergency.

3. *Honours and Appointments*: This consists of five members to recommend honours and make Government appointments.

Three of the Sector Committees are reasonably logical in structure: Social Equity, Development and Marketing, and Management and State Employment (which is really a conflation of the resource allocating functions of the old Cabinet Works and State Services Committees). However, External Relations and Security contains, as uneasy bedfellows, police and foreign affairs; also, Transport, Communications and State Enterprises appeared, at first blush, to be rather a mish-mash, but with the reorganization of most of the agencies in the field of the Committee's concern into public companies with Government shareholding, it is clear that this Committee could have a significant co-ordinating role in the Labour Government's overall economic strategy.

It is possible to discern an administrative strategy here designed to achieve two aims. The first is to ensure that the Government's policies are consistent and that resources are used wisely. The second is to make Ministers in the Sector Committees think beyond their portfolios to co-ordinate action taken by Government agencies and to allocate resources according to need rather than arbitrary institutional divisions. The fulfilment of these objectives has been assisted by the fact that there are three Finance Ministers in the Cabinet, all of senior status. Moreover, as noted above, all three are members of the Cabinet Policy Committee and there is at least one Finance Minister on each of the Sector Committees. Not only does this overlapping membership ensure a degree of policy co-ordination, it also provides the Treasury with the opportunity to exercise a good deal of influence in the policy making process.

The Cabinet restructuring did away with an important innovation of the Muldoon Government, the Cabinet Committee on Expenditure, which assumed responsibility for reviewing the Budget proposals of each Minister and devised the procedures by which expenditure for new policy proposals had to be found from compensatory savings made in existing departmental programmes. Treasury officials have indicated that the process still continues but, in place of formal procedures involving officials as well as Ministers, discussions now take place between each "spending" Minister and one of the three Treasury Ministers to identify savings and otherwise to restrain expenditure.

This draws attention to an important difference in attitude and procedure between the Muldoon and Lange Administrations. Whereas Cabinet Committees in the Muldoon Government frequently involved officials very closely in the deliberations over the whole field of discussion and up to the point of decision-making, the Lange Government has tended to reduce the influence of officials. Discussions with officials reveal that, while they are frequently called to provide information to Ministers in Committee, they do not normally remain for the deliberative and decision-making stage. It appears that the Labour Government feels that officials had been accorded a role in Cabinet procedures which diminished ministerial control over policy development.

So far the process seems to be operating well enough but every Administration seems to find difficulties in confining itself to the formal structure. Labour, for example, faced with problems associated with the introduction of the State owned enterprises programme has apparently formed, at least temporarily, a "super" committee chaired by the Deputy Prime Minister to get the policy through.

Ministers and Departments

The foundations of constitutional order under the Westminster system of Government lie in the relationship between the Minister and the State servant. As long as confidence in the observance of the conventions by each side remains, the small revolution threatened by each approaching General Election disturbs neither the country nor the members of the executive. It is assumed that existing policies will be maintained until an incoming Government has had a chance to review them and that State agencies, after submitting an assessment of their policy commitments, will devote their skill and experience to devising the programmes required to achieve the new Minister's objectives. There is a promise of continuity and renewal implied in the comprehensive conventional and statutory duties owed to the Minister. Armoured in that belief, so the tradition proposes, a new administration can face incessant public criticism in the knowledge that they have at least one informed and powerful ally bound entirely to their cause.

Of course, the executive structure has never been wholly consistent. Agencies vary in their relationship with Ministers. A limited liability company such as Air New Zealand is not under duty to the Ministers of Transport and Finance as are the Ministry of Transport and the Treasury. Even the directly responsible agencies vary in their duties to the Minister. The Justice Department, for example, has a number of officers performing statutory duties which the Minister may not direct. The Department also has responsibilities to the Judiciary where some delicacy is needed to preserve the independence of the Courts and, at the same time, to serve the Minister's interests. In some Departments the expert nature of the job or the need to serve the clientele impartially and fairly limit the Minister's influence in practical terms. The Valuation Department, for example, must maintain the professional competence and integrity of its operation; the State Fire Office, an ordinary department, must deal in terms of commercial impartiality with its clients; the Maori Affairs Department has modified its administration in a way which hands much of the initiative to the client groups thus compromising ministerial influence in decision making.

The constitutionalist must also keep in mind that the State Services Commission has independent authority to make individual personnel decisions for many of the State agencies subject to ministerial control. The legislative provisions for the Ombudsman and for procedures under the *Official Information Act* have further modified the relationships between Ministers and departments.

These exceptions do not cause great problems to the process of accountability taken singly, but their accumulation over time, together with other factors, has affected attitudes towards the conventions of ministerial responsibility. State servants are no longer seen as mere dependents of the political executive, but as autonomous managers accountable directly for their control of departmental assets. Indeed, it is not too much to say that agencies are now considered as corporate structures subject to the Minister's direction but accountable not to the Minister alone but also to Parliament, the Auditor-General, Treasury, the State Services Commission and, of course, the media. This still leaves, of course, an area of traditional responsibility to cover direct relationships between the Minister and the department — advice on policy, reports on reactions to proposals, budgetary submissions, preparation of speeches and answers to parliamentary and other questions. Even here there have been misgivings about the commitment to the conventions.

An exchange between Lange (then Leader of the Opposition) and the Chairman of the State Services Commission in December 1983 provides a guide to the doubts felt by Labour about senior officials. Lange said it was obvious that some departments were run by their civil servants rather than their Ministers. While he was "not knocking" civil servants it was essential that they should be willing to carry out Labour's policy. In Lange's view:

> ... if heads of departments answered that they would implement Labour policy they would be doing no more than their job. If they answered "no" they would have to go because they would not be able to carry out their duty.

The Opposition Leader went on to report that:

> ... the idea to ask heads of departments where they stood was ... contained in a report being prepared by a committee of Labour MPs and administrators to ease a Labour Opposition into power (*Evening Post*, 27 December 1983).

The Chairman of the State Services Commission understandably shocked at the departure from precedent and procedure proposed by Labour commented that:

> ... Mr Lange's proposed action was undesirable and totally unnecessary. I don't think anybody's got anything to worry about the loyalty of permanent heads. They're all highly selected and completely loyal to any government as they know it's their duty to be.

J.F. Robertson, a former Secretary of Defence and of Justice, also responded to Lange's views claiming that:

> ... in his experience he had never known permanent heads to deliberately not carry out the wishes of a new government. But he remembered problems when the last Labour Government was elected in 1972. The Government had a raft of new policies which had been formed without access to information or knowledge of the problems facing

government. About three months after the election the Prime Minister, Mr Norman Kirk, called all permanent heads together and told them they weren't helping Government. He told them they were telling Ministers what the problem was rather than helping Government get its new policies on the road (*Evening Post*, 27 December 1983).

This probably reflects Labour's view pretty accurately. It is not so much the loyalty of officials which is in doubt as their capacity to encompass the changes Labour wants. Although no test of willingness to serve the new Government was actually applied — it would have been completely meaningless anyway — there seems no doubt that on the whole Labour has kept many officials at arm's length from the final stages of policy making when compared with the practice of the National Party.

Labour's State Sector Strategy

This modification in the role of public servants, however, pales into insignificance when set alongside the implications of Labour's moves to corporatize the major State trading departments and commercialize many of the operations of the non-trading departments. The nature of these reforms is discussed in detail in Chapter 7. The purpose here is two-fold: firstly, to note briefly some of the key features of the State Owned Enterprises Bill and the proposed changes to state sector pay fixing; and secondly, to consider some of the constitutional implications of these reforms.

The State Owned Enterprises Bill introduced to the House on 30 September 1986 by the Deputy Prime Minister provides not only a structure for new agencies and the rules under which they will be held accountable but also a set of exhortations which might be described as an operational philosophy. Section 4 of the Bill reads:

4. *Principal objective to be successful business* — (1) The principal objective of every State enterprise shall be to operate as a successful business and to this end, to be —

(a) As profitable and efficient as comparable businesses that are not owned by the Crown; and

(b) A good employer; and

(c) An organisation that exhibits a sense of social responsibility by having regard to the interests of the community in which it operates and by endeavouring to accommodate or encourage these when able to do so.

(2) For the purposes of this section, a "good employer" is an employer who operates a personnel policy containing provisions generally accepted as necessary for the fair and proper treatment of employees in all aspects of their employment, including provisions requiring —

(a) Good and safe working conditions; and

(b) An equal opportunities employment programme; and

(c) The impartial selection of suitably qualified persons for appointment; and

(d) Opportunities for the enhancement of the abilities of individual employees.

This is an innovative prescription for management, but it is open to the charge that the legal obligation is obscure.

The Bill applies to the 15 agencies set out below. Those which are starred are new agencies carrying out functions at present under the control of the Department shown in brackets.

> Air New Zealand Limited
> Airways Corporation of New Zealand Limited* (Ministry of Transport)
> Bank of New Zealand
> Coal Corporation of New Zealand Limited* (Ministry of Energy)
> Development Finance Corporation of New Zealand Limited
> Electricity Corporation of New Zealand Limited* (Ministry of Energy)
> Forestry Corporation Limited* (New Zealand Forest Service)
> Land Corporation Limited* (Department of Lands and Survey)
> New Zealand Railways Corporation
> Petroleum Corporation of New Zealand Limited
> New Zealand Post Limited* (New Zealand Post Office)
> Post Office Bank Limited* (New Zealand Post Office)
> Post Office Telecom Limited* (New Zealand Post Office)
> Tourist Hotel Corporation of New Zealand
> The Shipping Corporation of New Zealand Limited

In a paper delivered to the 1986 Convention of the Institute of Public Administration, the Deputy Prime Minister expressed the Government's argument for the reforms in these terms:

> The taxpayer has over the last 20 years, poured the equivalent of 10 per cent of New Zealand's income in 1986 into five major state trading organizations. These are the Post Office, the Ministry of Energy, the Forest Service, the airways system and the trading activities of Lands and Survey. The net post-tax return to the Government, and therefore the taxpayer, on that investment in the current year is exactly zero. Such a state of affairs cannot continue. It is simply not on. These are commercial investments made by Government on behalf of taxpayers. The taxpayer is entitled, as of right, to a return on his or her investment (Palmer, 1986, p.7).

Clearly, the Government intends that, in future, State owned enterprises will be required to accept the responsibility of operating at a reasonable profit. To this end, the Bill provides that each State owned enterprise will deliver to the Shareholding Ministers a draft Statement of Intent which, among other matters, will specify the "performance targets and other measures by which the performance of the group may be judged in relation to its objectives" Section 13(2)(e), and an "estimate of the amount or proportion of accumulated profits and capital resources that is intended to be distributed to the Crown" Section 13(2)(f).

It is also provided in Section 12(1)(a) that the "Shareholding Ministers" (who will be the Minister responsible for a given State enterprise and the Minister of Finance) may give written notice directing the Boards of some of the companies to be established to "include in or omit from a statement of corporate intent" any of the matters specified by the Bill. In addition, the Minister of Finance may, under Section 12(1)(b), direct such boards by written notice "... to determine the amount of dividend payable by the company". The agencies to which this Section applies are those which are now being formed from the existing Government departments starred in the list set out above.

The Statement of Corporate Intent will also contain important information on the objectives and capital structure of the companies, the accounting policies, estimates of the commercial value of the Crown's investment and the procedures for acquisition of interests in other organizations.

There is some contradiction here. The Government has vigorously promoted the idea of state sector reorganization in order to give managers the freedom to pursue commercial policies and thus secure an adequate return on publicly owned assets. Yet the Bill provides very considerable powers of ministerial direction. This reveals a number of intractable elements in the process. Many of the goods and services provided by the corporations to be formed are delivered under conditions of monopoly or near monopoly which will not be altered by the legislation. They are also part of an infrastructure in which the citizens' abilities to pursue their private objectives are largely determined. Fixing prices for electricity, telephone and airport services have unavoidable political consequences. Moreover, the ordinary disciplines of the market such as shareholders' confidence, takeover bids and bankruptcy will not compel managerial efficiency. This will not be changed by the provision in Section 11 of the Bill concerning the issue of "State Equity Bonds". These are similar to shares and transferable but do not confer voting rights on the holders. In the end, as with traditional Government departments, the success of the whole system will depend upon the emergence of certain conventions of ministerial and company forbearance. These may establish a climate in which the managers manage while the politicians maintain sufficient oversight to serve the financial interest of the citizen and identify incipient failure early enough to take corrective action.

The Bill uses the *Companies Act 1955* for the basic structure of the new enterprises. The Shareholding Ministers accordingly will appoint the Boards observing the conditions of Section 5 which requires that Directors should be persons who will "assist the State enterprise to achieve its principal objectives". In a rather superfluous clause 6, it is provided that the shareholding Ministers of a State enterprise "... shall be responsible to the House of Representatives for the performance of the functions given to them" under the Bill. The Bill provides for a number of additional accounting procedures and, for all companies other than the Bank of New Zealand, requires the Auditor-General to carry out audits of company accounts.

A concept much employed by the protagonists of commercialization is "competitive neutrality". It is intended to signify that State owned enterprises should be placed in a position which confers neither competitive advantage nor disadvantage on the enterprise in comparison with private organizations. Wherever a true market exists, the object should be to establish the enterprise on a footing that allows a fair judgement on the management's ability to achieve a competitive return on the assets employed. Where this is not possible because of operating conditions or the exigencies of public policy, performance measures should be devised as substitutes for market outcomes. The doctrine of "transparency" should be applied where the Government decides that the enterprise should seek "social" objectives. In that case competitive neutrality demands that the enterprise should be entitled to compensation from Government revenue for the agreed cost of actions not justified by market considerations.

The critics of these doctrines argue that there is no case to justify State trading in a competitive market. National MP, Simon Upton, for example has argued that:

> If government operations are indistinguishable from private sector ones, then they should be in private ownership, paying private dividends to private investors rather than providing the Government of the day with a slush fund for its own political purposes. On the other hand, if the function is one which the private sector won't provide, then it should be done as a matter of public service without pretence of commercialization (1986, p.7).

Upton does not necessarily have a compelling influence on National Party strategy, but his analysis may indicate the lines of future attacks on Labour by National. For example, National may advocate vigorous privatization to outbid Labour's commercialization philosophy. They will scorn "transparency" and allege that the desire for a "return on assets" from State owned enterprises is simply a tactic for raising funds to promote Labour's political interests by means of taxes disguised as trading profits and unsanctioned by Parliament. At the same time we may also witness the unaccustomed spectacle of National offering sympathy to bureaucrats oppressed by hard-hearted Labour paymasters!

State Sector Employment

Staffing the companies to be formed from existing departments presents special difficulties. The staff of the departments are, of course, employed under the provisions of the *State Services Act 1962* and negotiate terms and conditions of employment under the *State Services Conditions of Employment Act 1977*. By long standing conventions, and under rigorous statutory conditions for the review of personnel decisions provided by the *State Services Act*, public servants have enjoyed security of tenure (including officers in the Ministry of Energy, the Ministry of Transport, the State Forest Service and the Department of Lands and Survey). The problem of their future when the State owned enterprises are formed is crucial to the successful commercial operations and, of course, to those staff members who may not wish to transfer to the new companies or may find themselves surplus to requirements. Negotiations between the Combined State Unions and the Government have produced a "Permanent Staff Deployment Package". While this records an historic agreement to give up the principle of security of tenure, it reflects also the difficulty the Government has experienced in reaching a deal which will be seen as reasonably fair to the State servants affected.

More importantly, it is now apparent that the *State Services Conditions of Employment Act* will be greatly amended. A document entitled *Pay Fixing in the State Services* has been issued by the Minister of State Services, Stan Rodger. This study reviews existing principles and procedures in the fixing of pay and associated conditions in the public sector and outlines important reforms. Indeed, taken in conjunction with the redeployment agreement it signals an historic break from the conditions of State sector employment which have applied since the *Public Service Act 1912*.

Among these, the most important was that the Public Service should provide a "universal" employment pool with similar conditions applying to all departments and preference for public servants in relation to any job vacancy in the public service as a whole. While there were always exceptions to this rule, the practice tended to harmonize conditions (though not preferences for appointment) for all agencies in the State Services. The 1977 Act provided a standardized procedure for that practice.

The new proposals go so far as to propose that an "enterprise" (e.g. a public service department or division) might "... operate as an employing authority in its own right" (Rodger, 1986, p.49). This would allow:

> ... managers to provide remuneration packages that offer staff appropriate incentives to perform, permit responsiveness to changing economic conditions, and that encourage staff to invest in skills and experience — and train others accordingly — so that the public sector can perform effectively and in a manner consistent with the objectives set by Government (p.37).

It is recognized that some form of occupational classification would have to be retained and that the State Services Commission would be required to take part in negotiations to set parameters within which the enterprise could determine individual staff progression according to performance and market conditions. Annual General Adjustments, the great occasion for universalizing pay, should be given up. The present role of the State Services Coordinating Committee in "standardizing" State conditions of employment should become one of "liaison, coordination and consultation rather than the exercise of a control function" (p.47).

While the trading enterprises will be required, according to the provisions of the State Owned Enterprises Bill, to consult with the State Services Commission on proposals for pay and conditions, it is anticipated that "... the operation of market forces may provide very real constraints" (p.44). "It is clear that, primarily, these enterprises' managers will be accountable for the 'inputs' (e.g. labour costs) and decisions in the context of their enterprise's overall performance" (p.45). The proposals are extremely complex and, as the Minister acknowledges, have not been accepted by the Combined State Unions. There will be hard bargaining to follow.

The Implications for Ministerial Responsibility

It is not clear what effect all these changes will have on the relationship between Ministers and their departments, particularly with respect to traditional agencies where so much is governed by convention. If a department, or some significant section of a department, is to be judged predominantly on the quality of its asset management and commercial trading success it is difficult to see how the current rules of accountability can be sustained. The traditional purpose of a department is to provide a Minister with the services required to make and carry out his or her policy. The Minister's predominant interest is in survival in office, not commercial success. If the nominal relationship remains as it is, confusion between these two objectives is bound to arise. It is unconvincing to suggest that the Ministers will obey some self-denying ordinance forbidding them to use their power to secure some advantage or to limit political damage.

The question must now be asked how far the separate managerial responsibility of the permanent official is to be brought forward and at what point the conventions of ministerial responsibility — clearly inappropriate in the case of the statutory corporations — become inapplicable also to the reformed, partly self-funding, trading department? This is a most serious constitutional problem. It is necessary to pause for a moment to consider what might be lost by inadvertent or deliberate modification of the departmental concept.

No one disputes the fact that New Zealand public administration is largely free from corruption. What is not perhaps so well recognized is its ready alignment to the wishes of citizens and its remarkable freedom from authoritarian behaviour. This point was clearly established by the Royal Commission in 1962 and has been confirmed by the meagre number of offences revealed by the Ombudsman and the willingness of officials to redress grievances. It is also confirmed by the very limited number of convincing cases where vicarious ministerial responsibility is provoked (that is, where allegations are made that officials deserve blame for actions not expressly authorized by the Minister or flowing clearly from the Minister's directions). Officials are, on the whole, careful of both their own and their Minister's reputations. While it is probably true that vicarious responsibility has lost much of its original political significance, this is largely because Ministers are increasingly unwilling to accept their obligations, not because bureaucrats act in an irresponsible or self-interested manner.

Two points arise from this conclusion. First, the case for reforms which reduces the links between Ministers and officials requires deliberate and careful investigation. In particular, the somewhat unspecific proposals for the savings in revenue available from departmental market operations require clear and unequivocal substantiation before actions are taken that will necessarily impair the operation of traditional constitutional conventions. Second, if the valuable and flexible forms of accountability provided by such conventions are to be diminished by changes in structure and functional obligations, alternative forms of accountability will have to be devised.

The most recent case of vicarious responsibility arose with the decision of the Minister of Finance to offer his resignation to the Acting Prime Minister on 11 August 1986 when it became clear that copies of the Budget released for delivery on 31 July had been delivered to many recipients some hours before the specified time. An investigation carried out by the Permanent Head of the Prime Minister's Department, Gerald Hensley, concluded that misunderstandings had arisen among inexperienced staff but that there was no evidence to suggest that the Minister was involved in the "administrative details of the distribution plan" (1986). Nonetheless, the Minister felt that the matter was sufficiently serious to require him to offer his resignation. The Prime Minister, who was in Fiji at the time, had been informed by the Acting Prime Minister and by Douglas of the circumstances and arranged to return to Wellington earlier than intended. In his statement to Parliament on 12 August announcing that he had decided not to accept the offer to resign, Lange stressed "that the Minister knew nothing of the breaches of security, did not approve of the steps taken which led to those breaches, and on learning of them, immediately informed the Acting Prime Minister" (*New Zealand Parliamentary Debates*, Vol.473, p.3777). Lange also emphasized that "there has been no instance in New Zealand of the resignation of a Minister who has personally done nothing wrong" (p.3777).

This may seem to be an insignificant matter. The Minister stays — a few minor officials are blamed. That interpretation is mistaken. The matter is indelibly on the record. Should it be shown that the Minister of Finance has not correctly stated his position, it is certain that he would have to resign. If it came to light that, however innocent Douglas may have been, some third party derived direct financial benefit from his or her prior knowledge of Budget details, the Government would suffer significant political damage. Douglas and all his successors have had a sharp reminder not just of the care needed in preserving Budget security but the exacting standards of probity and concern for procedure demanded by parliamentary scrutiny.

How then can these standards be maintained if the operation of ministerial responsibility is partially obstructed by corporatization, by major delegation of management accountability or by procedures designed to give administrators commercial flexibility? Public institutions must account to the public at large through the established political process. Thus, corporations and departments report to Parliament annually. The problem is that these reports tend to be ignored in the hurly burly of parliamentary business, or, where they are raised, it is usually in the partisan context of an attack on the Government. While this is legitimate and necessary, the major requirement is a careful, thorough and objective assessment of the way in which the public interest has been served by the administration of each public body. At the moment there is simply no process appropriate to this task. The problem is to achieve a reasonable review in which the public can have confidence, the quality of management can be assessed and the viability of the enterprise established while allowing the managerial freedom and commercial confidentiality to operate successfully in a competitive market.

Several possibilities exist. The reform of the Select Committee structure in 1985 (see Chapter 5) suggests that an allocation might be made among the appropriate Committees of responsibility to review agency reports, call the administrators before the Committee to explain reserved points and initiate particular enquiries as may be deemed necessary. For this to be successful a long overdue provision of adequate investigatory staff to assist Select Committees would be essential. The establishment of a Parliamentary Service Commission to provide support to Parliamentarians is an encouraging start.

Of course, the sticking point here is the willingness of MPs to give up their habitual adversary frame of mind in the pursuit of objective assessments. The Public Expenditure Committee provided some hope that this is not out of the question. It would also be possible to establish an independent review agency to set the standards of commercial performance expected and, perhaps in association with Select Committees, to conduct inspections and assessments of performance for report to Ministers and Parliament. Another possibility is a consumers' committee formed by representatives of appropriate interest groups and experts to comment upon performance and policy in practice. The committee, assisted by a small investigatory staff, would have no directive duties but, in pursuit of transparency, would stimulate public debate and give the Ministers an indication of public concern which might call for policy interventions.

This indicates the appropriate function of the Minister in relation to the commercialized operations. The agency must, of course, have a clear policy direction from the Government and an unambiguous control structure. If neither of these prove adequate the Minister must quickly provide the necessary changes. Where particular requirements of Government policy demand that the agency carry out some policy objective, it is likely that this will be specifically negotiated, costed and charged to the Government's general revenue account. If performance proves, on reliable evidence, to be unsatisfactory it is the Minister's task to recommend appropriate action to Cabinet with the ultimate options of sacking some or all of the Board or closing down the operation in whole or in part.

Conclusion

It will be for historians to judge whether 1986 was an *annus mirabilis* in New Zealand's history or a false start in a process of political and economic adjustment which has been going on since 1968 — the year of the nil wage order and the convening of the National Development Conference. Much will depend on the result of the next election, but at the moment it appears that what is in train is comparable with the reforms of the decades 1890 to 1900 and 1936 to 1946. It is not the author's province to analyze the ideological and instrumental objectives of Labour's policy, but a few concluding remarks about the nature and implications of the reforms are in order.

We can see that the first objective is that of clarity, co-ordination and control in the operation of the political executive. The reorganization of the Cabinet Committee system is designed for this purpose. The second aim is to stimulate a higher sense of personal and institutional responsibility for winning a reasonable return on the assets controlled by Government agencies. Where the assets are normally tradeable a major organizational change has been made to encourage performance and to limit the deviations from rational economic responses caused by political intervention. In the future if intervention is thought to be unavoidable or expedient, the resulting cost is to be funded openly from Government revenue.

In the belief that the long standing "universal" career service prevents adaptation to changing circumstances and to necessary specialization of functions, very substantial changes are proposed in the way State servants are recruited and promoted, and their remuneration fixed. It is probable that each Government agency will have to accept far greater formal responsibility for negotiating with its employees and for securing the talents needed to achieve their new objectives. How this will be dealt with in institutional reform is as yet uncertain. What is clear, however, is that the old order based on the *Public Service Act 1912* will soon pass away.

Notes

1 It should be noted that the life of two wartime Parliaments was increased to five years, and that of the Parliament of the Great Depression to four years.

References

Hensley, G. (1986) Report on Breaches of Budget Security, Wellington.

New Zealand Parliamentary Debates Volumes 457 (1984) & 473 (1986) Wellington, Government Printer.

Palmer, G. (1986) Directions for State Enterprise, Speech to the Convention of the Institute of Public Administration, Wellington.

Probine, M.C. (1984) Submissions to Standing Orders Committee of Parliament.

Rodger, S. (1986) *Pay Fixing in the State Sector* Wellington, Government Printer.
Scott, K.J. (1962) *The New Zealand Constitution* Oxford, Oxford University Press.
Upton, S. (1986) Commercialization or Privatization, Speech to the Convention of the Institute of Public Administration, Wellington.

7

The Reorganization of the Public Sector
The Quest For Efficiency

Robert Gregory

[Those] who think first and foremost of efficiency and conceive of it in narrow terms
are seldom democrats. (Lindsay, 1943, p.140)

Few people would have noted a little reported address given in June 1980 to the
former Civil Service Institute by the then Deputy Leader of the Opposition, David
Lange. In that speech Lange rejected the National Government's three per cent
across-the-board cuts in public service expenditure as "simplistic, superficial, and
futile". Instead, he promised a Labour Government would provide "the most
radical shake out of the whole system since the demise of provincial government".
A stronger and more effective public service would be achieved not by random
cut-backs, but by "substantially strengthening the financial accountability of
government departments and of the government through to Parliament" (Lange,
1980, p.8). Six years later, the fourth Labour Government introduced radical
changes to the public sector, though these were impelled by concerns stretching well
beyond the financial accountability of departments. They had become a major part
of the Government's strategy of market-led economic reform, and could easily have
been paraded under a former National Party election slogan promising "less
government in business and more business in government".

However, no such promise had been offered by the Labour Party in its campaign
before the unscheduled general election in July 1984. During those weeks no detailed
programme of public sector reform was (or could have been?) proposed that might
have enlarged upon the signals made by Lange to the Civil Service Institute. Instead,
a clearer picture of what the new Government might do was provided shortly after
the election by the release of a comprehensive statement entitled *Economic Management* prepared by the Treasury before the election as advice to whichever party
won office (1984b, pp.275-315). In that organization, as in the Reserve Bank, were
economists who regarded Keynesian theories as an inappropriate response to New
Zealand's economic difficulties, and as a result of the election found themselves freed
from the slavery imposed by a now defunct Minister of Finance.[1] Sir Robert
Muldoon's populist and strongly interventionist policies, long since the bane of his
Treasury and Reserve Bank advisors, seemed electorally discredited. The way was
now open for a marriage of convenience between themselves and the new Minister

of Finance, Roger Douglas. An advocate while in Opposition of market-led economic reform, Douglas could give them the political authority they needed for their
advice to be translated into action; similarly, he could be assured that his officials
were likely to offer the type of counsel he preferred to hear. With respect to the State
sector, two principal ideas emerged from this meeting of political and bureaucratic
minds: corporatization and commercialization.

Corporatization and Commercialization of State Enterprises

In *Economic Management* the Treasury observed that resources used by the public
sector (excluding transfers) amounted to about 25 per cent of gross domestic
product, and that just under half of this was accounted for by State owned
enterprises, some of which were much larger than any publicly listed company in
New Zealand.[2] A more precise categorization than that presented by the Treasury
would distinguish at least five types of publicly owned organizations:

(a) State enterprises that were full departments of State (e.g. the Ministries of
Energy, and Works and Development, the Post Office, and the Forest Service);

(b) public corporations within the public service subject to the provisions of the
State Services Act 1962 (e.g. the Housing Corporation, the Rural Bank, the
Government Life Insurance Company);

(c) public corporations within the State services subject to the provisions of the
State Services Conditions of Employment Act 1977 (e.g. New Zealand Railways, the
Broadcasting Corporation of New Zealand);

(d) corporations in the public sector (e.g. the Development Finance Corporation
of New Zealand); and

(e) Government owned limited liability companies, registered under the *Companies Act 1955* (e.g. Air New Zealand, the Bank of New Zealand, the Shipping
Corporation of New Zealand).

In the Treasury's view, State owned enterprises would have a beneficial effect on
the national economy if two "essential efficiency conditions" were met: output must
be worth at least as much as the resources used, and it must be supplied with the least
consumption of resources (Treasury, 1984, p.276). In practice these conditions were
undermined by a lack of clear, non-conflicting objectives to guide managers and by
various political imperatives, such as the need to provide uneconomic social services
(e.g. rural postal delivery), to sustain employment levels (by way of job creation
programmes), or to hold prices below the cost of supply. In pursuing their objectives
State enterprises were afforded commercial advantages — like subsidized finance and
taxation dispensations — which, together with a lack of commercial competition,
made it possible to retain customers while providing poor quality and high cost
services.

The Treasury's prescription for improved economic performance of State
enterprises included: the making transparent of social objectives by the payment of

Government subsidies to cover extra costs, and the separation of policy and regulatory functions from trading activities; the elimination of commercial advantages and disadvantages so that resources used would be commensurate with relative performance; the setting of clear and measurable performance targets based on private sector norms of profitability; the formulation of corporate plans to translate these targets into objectives and performance criteria for lower-level management; and the appointment of boards of directors where none currently existed. This was a reference, made almost *en passant*, to the process which in the ensuing months became known as corporatization.

Conflicting Policy Models

Just what corporatization was to mean in practice, and how far it would be applied across the range of publicly-owned trading activities quickly became a matter of intense bureaucratic debate between the Treasury and the State Services Commission. This divergence of views reflected each agency's perception of its organizational mission and responsibilities, and each mission in turn implied differing attitudes towards the reform of the public sector. The Treasury was committed to the pursuit of an economically rational allocation of resources, in both the private and public sectors, and to a free-market theoretical paradigm as a means of ensuring this. Accordingly it took the view that if public ownership were to be retained, then trading activities within the state sector should be rendered as similar as possible to private business. This led it to favour the limited liability company as the appropriate model for corporatization. Of paramount importance, in the Treasury's view, was the need for the new corporations to have the political freedom to pursue clearly specified commercial objectives on equal terms — wherever possible — with private enterprise.

The State Services Commission, conscious of its own statutory responsibilities for economic and efficient management within the State services, was much less enamoured of the idea that the commercial market place could be the principal arbiter of these values, while at the same time ensuring the political accountability of State enterprises. It was also concerned about the substantial implications for the career service should the new corporations be set up as limited liability companies outside the rubric of State employment legislation. As an alternative the State Services Commission advocated a case by case analysis of each corporatization proposal to determine which corporate model might provide the best financial, regulatory, operating and accountability framework for each organization:

> There is no one best way; there is no automatic linking of characteristics; after all the economic, financial and management advice has been given, the form and its distance from or proximity to central Government, the role it plays in the market,

will be determined politically and will remain within the oversight of Parliament (State Services Commission, 1985, p.9).

The Commission was sceptical of the Treasury's assumption that market discipline would best enhance the performance of State enterprises, since some of them at least would continue to operate as natural or *de facto* monopolies. In its view, the most appropriate way of integrating political and managerial processes was through the formal involvement of Ministers in the planning and monitoring procedures of their own organizations. What was needed, according to the Commission, was the further development of systems of corporate planning, a process already well underway within the State services. Enterprises operating in free competition *could* be established with corporate boards responsible to a Minister, but those not doing so, or with significant non-commercial functions, should remain under a permanent head. As the possibility of using market mechanisms decreased, more detailed corporate plans would be needed, together with a more direct political involvement. These views were consistent with the Commission's proposals for all departments operating within the budget cycle of annual appropriations.

This divergence of opinion between the two main control agencies became apparent to the Cabinet Policy Committee as it sought advice on how corporatization principles might be applied to agencies like the Housing Corporation, the Post Office, and the Electricity Division of the Ministry of Energy. By November 1985, an interdepartmental review of the Electricity Division proposals had highlighted the complexity of the issues involved, while the Controller and Auditor-General had publicly joined the debate in his annual report to Parliament. Reflecting his office's institutional concerns, he advocated the application of Parliamentary authority to all State enterprises, regardless of their form. To this end, he called for a general framework for accountability to be laid down by legislation requiring, among other things, a prescription of the objects of the enterprise, a statement of corporate intent (i.e. specifying goals and targets), together with any non-commercial obligations and their costs. Such statements would need to be approved by the appropriate Ministers, and tabled in Parliament (Controller and Auditor-General, 1985, pp.25-27).

Environmental Administration

Concomitant with, though separate from, this comprehensive examination of corporatization proposals, the Government was proceeding with what the Minister of State Services, Stan Rodger, has called "the biggest machinery of government changes in New Zealand's history" (Radio New Zealand, 1986), involving the reorganization of forestry, environmental, conservation, and land use administration (see table 7.1). In short, this restructuring involved the abolition of the Forest Service, the Department of Lands and Survey and the Commission for the Envi-

Table 7.1
Main structural reorganization, to be effective by 1 April 1987

Agencies abolished	New Agencies			Functions transferred from existing agencies
	State owned enterprises (Corporations)	Government departments	Other	
NZ Forest Service (Govt. department)	Forestry Corporation	Ministry of Forestry		
		Department of Conservation		Historic Places Trust, Dept. of Internal Affairs; Wildlife Div., Dept. of Internal Affairs
Department of Lands and Survey (Govt. department)	Land Corporation	Department of Survey & Land Information	Crown Estate Commission	
Commission for the Environment (non-statutory executive body)		Ministry for the Environment	Parliamentary Commission	
NZ Post Office (Govt. department)	New Zealand Post; Post Office Bank; Post Office Telecom			
	Airways Corp.			Civil Aviation Div. Ministry of Transport
	Electricity Corp.			Electricity Division Ministry of Energy
	Coal Corp.			Mines Division. Ministry of Energy

ronment, and in their place the establishment of a Forestry Corporation, a Land Corporation, a Ministry for the Environment, a Department of Conservation, a Department of Survey and Land Information, and a Ministry of Forestry.

Although impelled in the first instance by the Labour Government's willingness to respond to concerns expressed by conservation and environmental interests, this galaxial reordering also coincided neatly with the Government's thinking regarding State owned enterprises. Thus, the abolition of the Forest Service brings to an end the necessity for conflicting commercial (e.g. timber production, processing and marketing) and non-commercial (e.g. conservation of indigenous forests, and recreation) objectives to be mediated within a single administrative hierarchy, a state of affairs which had been strongly criticized by the Joint Campaign on Native Forests (Gregory, 1984, pp.62-87). The new Forestry Corporation now concentrates exclusively on its commercial objectives, conservation concerns having been transferred to the Department of Conservation, which has also taken over the administration of wildlife and historic places, formerly the responsibility of the Department of Internal Affairs. Its regulatory and advisory duties have been given to the new Ministry of Forestry.

The same philosophy underlay the abolition of the Department of Lands and Survey, whose commercial functions now rest with the Land Corporation. The Department's responsibilities for national parks and reserves have gone to the Department of Conservation. Unlike the other components of this restructuring, the creation of a Ministry for the Environment was promised in the Labour Party's 1984 election manifesto, and results more directly from the Government's commitment to the strengthening of environmental administration.

The Underlying Principles of Reform

By late 1985 there was no doubt that the Government was committed to establishing State owned enterprises as successful business enterprises with clear commercial objectives. According to the Government, billions of dollars of taxpayers' investment had produced little, if any, return, a situation that would be brought to an end.[3] In December, Douglas outlined five principles underlying the drive for successful State enterprises: (a) non-commercial functions would be separated from major State trading organizations; (b) managers would be required to run them "as successful business enterprises"; (c) they would also be responsible for resource use and pricing decisions, within performance objectives set by Ministers — and so would be accountable to the Cabinet and Parliament for their results; (d) State owned enterprises would be required to operate without any competitive or other advantages or disadvantages so that commercial criteria would provide a fair assessment of managerial performance; and (e) they would be reconstituted on a case by case basis under the guidance of boards drawn generally from the private sector (Douglas, 1985, p.12).

That the new organizations would be set up under the guidance of such boards was an acknowledgement of the Government's commitment to commercial efficiency within the new regime. But it also reflected the difficulty the Government had been having in resolving many of the questions placed on the agenda by the commercial logic of its reforms, particularly those represented in the submissions of the State Services Commission and the Controller and Auditor-General. The Treasury's views certainly had the inside running, but wider concerns were equally pressing, in many cases complicating the elegant commercial principles laid out by Douglas.[4] Interim establishment boards would be given the task of examining: the cost structures of the new organizations, how public ownership might best be reconciled with commercial performance, the most appropriate legal form for the new corporations, how public accountability might be exacted, and if and how the staffing policies of these commercially competitive entities would be consistent with the legislation covering the conditions of employment of State servants.

All this was of great concern to the State unions. They called for a moratorium on the reorganization, charging the Government with failing to consult adequately on the proposed changes, particularly on the matter of possible job losses and on the form of union coverage that would be provided for employees of the new corporations. The Labour Party Council (the party's ruling executive) sought an assurance from the Government that there would be no privatization of the State sector; that equal weight would be given to social factors; that the service component would be taken into account; and that staff would continue to be covered by State services industrial legislation. Government backbenchers expressed the same concerns at a caucus meeting, which resolved that corporation employees should remain under the *State Services Conditions of Employment Act 1977*, but that this would however (and ambiguously) be "modified as necessary".

These concerns were highlighted by the Minister of Finance's announcement in May 1986 that the five principles would also be applied to the Electricity Division, State Coal Mines, the Post Office, and the Civil Aviation Division (Douglas, 1986b) (see table 7.1). The Post Office, New Zealand's biggest employer with 39,000 staff, would be divided into three Government owned independent business groups, providing telecommunications, postal, and banking services. These would become corporations legally separate from the Crown, and by 1 April 1987 working under legislation similar to the *Shipping Corporation Act 1973*. This Act establishes the Corporation as a Government owned limited liability company, whose employees are not State servants subject to the *State Services Conditions of Employment Act 1977*.

The new legislation would provide for full commercial objectives, rights and responsibilities for the new organizations, and would also contain monitoring and accountability procedures that would enable the Government and Parliament to assess the performance of the enterprises and their boards. Incentives and sanctions appropriate to trading organizations would replace public service controls, and restrictions imposed by Government fiscal constraints would be lessened. The new corporations would borrow in the marketplace, pay taxes, and would price their goods and services competitively. To this end the Government would review the protection accorded to electricity, telecommunications and postal trading activities. Under the new regime, unprofitable services intended to meet social criteria would be negotiated by means of contracts between the Government and the corporations. In this way the taxpayers' subsidies would be fully transparent, and the managers of the new organizations would remain free to concentrate on meeting their commercial objectives.

Commercialization

The move towards corporatization has been accompanied by a closely related process, namely, the increasing commercialization of departmental activities in general. The Government hopes this will further improve public sector efficiency and reduce the burden on taxpayers. In future, public trading organizations will be required to fund additional spending from private sector loans, instead of subsidized Government ones, and to repay and refinance from the market any cheap Government loans. They will be given strong incentives to raise their own revenue — that is, the Government will contain their net funding so that departmental activities reflect levels of real demand. For example, this policy has been applied in respect to research conducted by a range of Government agencies, including the Department of Scientific and Industrial Research. The organizations will have to recover from users, including other State agencies, the costs of supplying goods and services instead of providing them free or below cost at the taxpayers' expense. According to Douglas, a department's activities will be expanded if its goods and/or services are shown to be in demand, while:

> ... charging the full cost of government services encourages people to think more carefully about whether they really need a particular level of service. It discourages waste and reduces the deficit. The power of such an approach should not be underestimated. It will go on reducing net government expenditure year after year (Douglas, 1986b, p.18).

In addition, overall funding reductions will be used where necessary to improve departmental efficiency; quangos will be reduced or abolished where they are no longer relevant;[5] opportunities for departments to offer their services to the private sector will be progressively opened up, and they will no longer be compelled to obtain goods and services from other Government organizations but will be able to shop around the public and private sectors for the best deal (Douglas, 1986a, 1986b).

Excluded from the Government's 1986 expenditure review, however, were policies "specifically addressed at equity", those administered by the Social Welfare, Health and Education Departments. Here it was acknowledged that considerations of need were uppermost, and that broader principles of expenditure would have to be worked out by independent inquiries, including a Royal Commission on Social Policy.

A Critique of Labour's Approach

The impetus for this major shake-up of the public sector has come from the Labour Government's commitment to market-led reform of the New Zealand economy. It has, however, meshed easily with impulses for governmental reform, felt for a number of years in New Zealand as in other Western democracies, that aim to ensure a more results-rather than process-orientated administrative ethos. In accordance with this there has been a growing emphasis on the need for financial accountability, for "value for money", for organizations to specify their objectives, and for governmental managers to be given the authority to pursue those objectives. Cutt (1978) has conceptualized this as a progressive shift from concerns of "fiscal accountability" to those of "efficiency accountability", and then to those of "effectiveness accountability". Operationally this has been apparent, for example, in the development of more sophisticated managerial information and accounting systems, in the growth of techniques for policy evaluation, and in the writing of corporate plans.[6] In short, while the current reorganization has been shaped externally by the Government's strategy of economic management, it has also coincided with internal changes driven by the bureaucracy's calculation of its best interests in a period of increasing pressure on the economic viability of the welfare state. Peculiar to New Zealand's reforms has been the drive towards corporatization, that is, the move to establish publicly owned enterprises which are expected to act as if they were private ones. How viable is this expectation?

The Problem of Conflicting Values

It is clear that the reorganization promises the most profound and far reaching changes to the character of central government administration in New Zealand since the *Public Service Act 1912* created a unified, permanent career service. In the offing are reforms that will sharpen up practices of financial management that have long been found wanting (Shailes, 1978), and which will generally provide public officials with the freedom both to get on with their jobs and to accept the consequences. The arguments presented by the Government to justify its actions appear compelling, even to many who do not share the popular prejudice against "inefficient" public bureaucracy. The need to specify objectives clearly, to ensure that Government agencies provide a fair return on their capital investments, and to strip away the red tape which inhibits the effectiveness of State servants, all these are irresistibly appealing responses to the perceived need for greater public sector efficiency.

However, as Wilson (1967) has pointed out, there is no single problem of bureaucracy, but several, all of which are interrelated. Thus, a preoccupation with the need to enhance formal accountability might reduce organizational effectiveness: greater responsiveness to individual and group needs tends both to undermine norms of impersonal universality and to threaten systems of control; and a concern for social equity may be bought at the expense of economic efficiency, or vice versa. Public organizations have to satisfy simultaneously a range of often conflicting values — to be "miracle workers", in the words of the Minister of Finance (Radio New Zealand, 1986). They share their authority to set objectives (notably with Parliament and Cabinet); they are expected to play by the rules set by external agencies (particularly the control departments); and they must often proceed with uncertain knowledge as to how to pursue purposes which themselves are highly contentious (for example, controlling or reducing crime, educating children, reducing inflation and/or unemployment, improving or maintaining the "quality of life" and standards of public health). For all these reasons the "problem" of public administration stems as much from the fact of its being *public* as from its tendency to be *bureaucratic*.

The task of the public administrator, therefore, is rarely a technical one in the sense implied by a purely instrumental view of bureaucracy, which postulates rationally ordered action in pursuit of externally defined objectives. Instead, it is a process of seeking room for effective action amidst a range of values and constraints which conflict in differing ways under differing circumstances (see Pressman and Wildavsky, 1984). This task is highly frustrating and enormously challenging; but, however it is experienced, it is not imposed on the public official as a penance for turning his or her back on an allegedly more productive, stimulating, and risky life in private business. Rather, it reflects public concern that authority exercised in its name, and using its resources, should be both efficient and economic, yet socially responsive; that it should enable services to be provided in a fair and impartial way, yet with proper regard to particular differences in need; that it should be concerned to get things done, yet not at the expense of due process and individual rights; that it should promote standards of professional excellence, yet remain responsive to the desires of the laity (that is, mediate a democratic dilemma referred to in acerbic terms by the legendary American journalist H.L. Mencken, who once defined democracy as the form of government which ensures that the public gets what it wants — good and hard). This ethos also requires that administrators exercise initiative and discretion in fulfilling the intentions of their political masters, yet be able to show that they have operated according to proper procedures, and that they remain loyal to the intentions of their Minister even when they consider the Minister a fool.

Determining a course of action in the face of such conflicting demands requires miracle workers, and a major "human resource" problem faced by most Governments is that there are so few about. What emerges, therefore, is an administrative culture in which success or failure tends to be measured not by the achievement of purpose, but by compliance with procedure, so that failing is acceptable providing it is done correctly, succeeding correctly is laudable (but very rare), succeeding incorrectly may be tolerable, but failing incorrectly is to be avoided at all costs. Consider, for example, the Army's preoccupation with discipline. Training is intended to reduce the numbers of potential candidates for those two extreme categories which most threaten the possibility of disciplined collective action, i.e. heroes and cowards. However, what we might call successful heroism is totally laudable if it results from properly disciplined action, but is only just tolerable (a nod and a wink) if it does not. Unsuccessful or would-be heroism is also laudable if it is properly disciplined, but damnable if it is not. Cowardice is by definition unsuccessful action, and may or may not be procedurally improper. If it is not, it is tolerable; if it is then it too is considered damnable. Fortunately, not all public agencies look upon their members as potential heroes or cowards, but the relationships between substantive success and failure, and procedural propriety generally hold true. There is nothing pathological in this: it is not, as some assume, a measure of the incompetence of State servants (though it is a reflection of their general inability to walk on water), but is explicable by the paradoxical character of the public and bureaucratic context in which they work (Gregory, 1982).

It is, however, a state of affairs that greatly offends the sensibilities of reformers whose instincts are rooted in rationalistic assumptions. Such people promise that what they see as the two main problems of public administration — economic efficiency (achieving the same with less or making the same produce more), and accountability (making it clear just what is failing and who is to blame) — can be solved by obedience to the first commandment handed down by the gods of rational action: "thou shalt specify objectives clearly!" In 1984, before the snap election was called, Treasury had made a definitive exhortation along these lines, in the interests of better financial management in Government departments (The Treasury, 1984a). Similar but more grandiose sentiments had been expressed four years earlier by Roger Douglas, who argued that "a businesslike approach" would require that New Zealand set itself "simple, explicit objectives for every area of activity" if it sought to be "a successful nation" (Douglas, 1980, p.55).

Such philosophies render virtually anything that will shift the structure of bureaucratic incentives in favour of a greater preoccupation with purpose (i.e. ends, goals, objectives, targets), as against maintaining internal systems, almost self-justifying. Questions of representativeness and compassion, which have underpinned the growth of welfare bureaucracies in the past (Kaufman, 1977) and which have provided the focus for governmental reform, are shed from the agenda. Instead, massive programmes of public sector reorganization are impelled by an economic logic which has much to say about market-led efficiency drives, and little to say about the political, institutional, social and moral questions that arise out of them. The term "public administration" itself is in danger of expunction from the reformists' lexicon, since it implies all that is sacrilegious to the rationalistic theology. In its place appears the neologism "public management", a sleight of tongue which invites the naïve and the unwary to believe that dilemmas of reconciling public ownership with private management are illusory. The concern for due and proper process, the source of most bureaucratic red tape, is to be overtaken by the demand for results, to be measured against objectives, targets, and performance criteria. Public officials (i.e. managers), freed from the nightmares of miraculous expectations, will be able to get on with their jobs.

However, any answer to the question of whether the changes will work must involve a choice among differing criteria of success or failure, and not simply financial or economic ones. That there are inevitably multiple criteria involved is, perhaps ironically, reflected in the Government's own eagerness to justify the reforms in Panglossian terms – the public service is to be rendered more accountable, responsive, efficient and effective, all at once.

The Minister of Finance promises a better return on taxpayers' investment, and the contributions this will make to the management of the economy as a whole will improve the Government's capacity to pursue its social equity objectives. Net funding and cost-recovery innovations will improve public sector responsiveness and permit the expansion of Government services, where demand exists for them, at their true cost to the taxpayer. Freed from central controls, State servants will not only feel better about themselves, but their newly found autonomy will also make them more publicly accountable.

The "threat of privatization" will be diminished rather than enhanced by reforms that will lead to greater popular satisfaction with a more efficient public sector. Moreover, it is argued that the user-pays principle will not diminish the Government's commitment or capacity to provide services on the basis of need rather than ability to pay, but that a healthy, growing economy is essential to the achievement of a fairer society. Finally, it is claimed that the greater operating efficiency of State enterprises which are natural or *de facto* monopolies will reduce any tendencies towards cost-plus pricing, especially if the scope for competition is increased in areas such as telecommunications, electricity and postal services (Douglas, 1986c). It seems, in short, that just about anything desirable can be made possible in the name of increased efficiency.

Do Clear Objectives Help?

One suspects that any programme of governmental reorganization that simultaneously enhanced all these values would bring an end to the search for the philosopher's stone of administrative reform, but there is good reason to doubt whether corporatization and commercialization will produce such a miraculous result. Above all, objectives, no matter how clearly specified, have no validity other than that they are agreed upon (Lindblom, 1959), an insight that makes the call for explicit objectives look like a recipe for tiger soup: first agree upon the objectives, first catch the tiger. However, while the *collective* character of political and administrative decision-making creates the problem in the eyes of the economic rationalists, in the eyes of those who understand the process as a political exercise the same factor solves it. Objectives are left only vaguely and broadly specified, since it is action that is called for rather than, as Lindblom so neatly pointed out, agreement on what the action is good for. Those with an interest in reaching agreement can decide that for themselves. This is what political coalition-building is all about. For example, people with opposing ideological views and political interests could nevertheless agree that the establishment of a welfare state was desirable, without having to agree on what "objectives" it should "achieve". Delaying action pending agreement on the purposes of that action, or the values to be promoted by it, would in most cases result in political and administrative paralysis. The real question, therefore, is not about why and how objectives should be clarified and ranked, but why this so seldom happens. Intelligent inquiry into the latter issue would enhance awareness of the fact that public administration — indeed politics generally — is much less about reaching the point when objectives have been "achieved", than about setting and maintaining standards over time, ensuring acceptable justification for action that occurs, while all the time seeking room for manoeuvre as fallibility demands or circumstance dictates.[7]

It may be tempting to dismiss this point as a mere semantic difference. However, as in many spheres of human interaction, but especially in the political, the concepts and vocabulary used in everyday discourse do not merely describe action: they shape — even constitute — it. To be hung-up on the perceived importance of "objectives" may be to encourage administration that is insensitive to the problematical nature of collective political endeavour, and which is thought to be legitimate only in so far as it succeeds in "achieving" those goals. There is not the space here to develop further this line of argument, but its significance is far-reaching, particularly where, as in New Zealand, it has hitherto been preferred that governance be legitimated by democratic rather than authoritarian symbolism.

If objectives are to be relentlessly clarified so that they might serve as benchmarks of the administrator's success or failure, then the classical bureaucratic problem of "goal displacement" (means becoming ends in themselves) is reversed: ends become means in themselves, in the sense that administrative action is increasingly determined by the need (pending reward or punishment) to do all that is possible to ensure that the specified objectives *are* achieved.

However, such single-mindedness cannot resolve the antithetical demand for effectiveness (i.e. knowing what to do and how to do it) and accountability (i.e. knowing who to blame, and how much) that is inherent in the call for clarity of objectives. For in practice objectives can serve either one master or the other, rather than both simultaneously. Critical choices present themselves. Do we adhere to the objectives in the interests of accountability, or do we alter them in pursuit of effectiveness in a changing environment? If the former path is taken, then tight systems of organizational control (control being a synonym for accountability) and monitoring are called for. This means that bureaucratic tendencies will be enhanced rather than diminished — a reason why, as some research has suggested, private managers may feel more inhibited by red tape than public ones (Buchanan, 1975). If the latter path is chosen, then objectives must remain flexible and open to reassessment at regular intervals, which means that it becomes increasingly difficult to expect managers to achieve them. And if objectives are to be constantly changing, why set them?

What usually happens is that objective-setting exercises, or corporate planning as it is generally known, become detached from the serious, and infinitely more demanding, business of running the organization on a daily basis. This is not to say that such exercises make no difference. On the contrary, they may greatly assist the organization to reflect upon itself, to answer the critical political question (political, because it entails making an appeal to an often disparate range of values), "what business are we in?" (Drucker, 1955; Selznick, 1957). The answer is formally known as the statement of organizational mission.

These exercises may also help administrators create for themselves enough elbow room to get on with what they want to do — the Programme Evaluation Review Technique (PERT) phenomenon, well illustrated in the development of the United States Navy's Polaris missile system. In that, as Sapolsky (1972) has shown, the effects of PERT were far more political and symbolic than technical. By creating the *appearance* of a rationally organized planning system it helped to secure the operating autonomy that allowed the programme to forge ahead in the face of political and bureaucratic resistance. All this is not about rendering the organization a more "rational", "efficient", or even "accountable" enterprise. It is about the way administrators necessarily exercise political and social judgement while engaging in financial, economic and technical calculation. The shortcomings of rationalist theories of administration and organization, whether public or private, have long since been exposed by classical critiques (Barnard 1938; Cyert and March, 1963; March and Simon 1958). These show why the various nostrums that are derived ultimately from Taylor's (1911) principles of scientific management (e.g. POSD-CORB, PPBS, PERT) have delivered far less than they promised. The current concern for corporate planning and the like suggests that either there is nothing new under the rationalist sun, or that modern management experts, oblivious to the lessons of the past, cling to the belief that these techniques have failed only because they have been neither well understood nor applied.

The Problem of Accountability

The rhetoric that seeks to justify the need to specify objectives characterizes the general movement towards public sector reform through the adoption of so-called private sector means. It is central to New Zealand's particular move towards corporatization. The directors and managers of these organizations will be held accountable for organizational performance, to be measured against targeted returns on investment. They will be given the autonomy necessary to ensure they can get on with the job of meeting commercial objectives, which will no longer be fudged by non-commercial, or social, responsibilities. This elegant model of accountability posits, in effect, that it is better for shareholders — Ministers of the Crown[8] — to know when management has been precisely wrong rather than when it has been roughly right. Managers, in effect, are seen to be agents, or instruments, of the owners and as such their competence is expected to be measurable against clearly prescribed performance criteria set by the owners. Accountability is both clear and direct. (This concept may be contrasted with the proposition that in public administration authority for the performance of broadly specified functions is delegated by Parliament, representing the owning public, to Ministers and their officials, who in turn are held answerable to the legislature for their actions.) Hence, since their careers will depend upon it, managers obviously will have a powerful incentive to act *as if* all that really matters is the need to meet commercial and financial objectives.

For State owned enterprises this is a curious position to be in, because New Zealand's economic and social development can be traced through the histories of a wide range of publicly owned utilities (e.g. railways, broadcasting, works, postal services and telecommunications) which, especially if natural or *de facto* monopolies, have all been required to protect other values alongside those of financial performance. If that philosophy no longer remains compelling — if it is believed that State organizations have no more social responsibilities than a street corner dairy — why is it necessary that they remain publicly owned?

Any supposed ideological objection to privatization on the part of the Labour Government may be less important than the pragmatic reality that such a large body of State owned enterprises, driven by clear commercial imperatives, will also be a handy instrument for Government economic management, particularly in fiscal matters. However, that possibility is likely to have a pernicious effect on the original justification for these corporations: the need to set them up as autonomous trading enterprises driven by the demands of the commercial market place, not by the dictates or whims of politicians. If it so chose, the Government could "give away" shares in the corporations directly to the public, on a non-tradeable basis, a possibility hinted at by the Prime Minister (*National Business Review*, 11 July 1986, p.21). This could serve to diminish the political prospects for any future privatization — or any return to full shareholding by the Crown, for that matter — but would also render the organizations far less useful as Government revenue-raising mechanisms (see Brittan, 1984).

Although it may not have been realized by those advocating these new organizations, there exists a considerable body of literature attesting to the practical problems faced by public corporations as they seek an acceptable balance between political accountability and operating independence (for New Zealand studies see Gregory, 1985; Mascarenhas, 1982; Polaschek, 1957; for overseas literature see Jones, 1977; Peres, 1968; Robson, 1960; Smith, 1972; Webb, 1954). In Westminster-styled parliamentary systems what is at issue is the status of the theory of ministerial responsibility. Not surprisingly, this theory has little to say that would help us secure the accountability of public managers required to act as if they were private ones, and much to say about the responsibilities of officials (both elected and appointed) who know, or should know, that they exercise power in the public's name.

Both practical experience and academic theory indicate that, for a whole host of reasons, Governments often find themselves under political pressures to intervene in the activities of "independent" public corporations. The resulting influence over, or interference in, the activities of corporations might be open or covert, but it will often reflect the discomfort of politicians who have perceived responsibility (especially when the relevant ministerial portfolio remains in existence) but uncertain power.

It is not difficult, particularly in light of New Zealand's intimate social culture, to envisage all sorts of political repercussions being generated over time, not only as the commercialization drive encourages the adoption of a user-pays principle, for example, but also as the impact of these new large trading corporations is felt throughout the economy as a whole. In the former case, despite the Government's assurances that it is not abandoning the principle of providing services according to need rather than ability to pay, and that its reforms do not affect the administration of health, education and welfare services, there is considerable plausibility in claims made by the Public Service Association that, "The costs [to the consumer] of a wide range of services are likely to go up", and when a user-pays approach is adopted "it is difficult to draw the line between services that should be provided without charge as a basic social service (through taxes) and those for which the user should be charged directly (through the wallet)" (*PSA Journal*, "Action Supplement", 18 June-15 July 1986).[9]

As for the new corporations, their strong commercial orientation must have direct economic and social effects. Forestry provides an illustration. Many of its planting, logging, and processing activities have, over the years, been dictated by political and social concerns (particularly job creation and maintenance) rather than purely commercial considerations. It is difficult to see how a new corporation dedicated to commercial success will continue to preserve these and other standards, which directly affect the lives of thousands of people, especially in rural communities.

The point here is not whether such changes are or are not desirable, but that the answer to this question can only be determined politically, a factor which does not appear to be self-evident to those who consider that "objective" economic analysis is the surest means of discovering political truth. Confronted with the certainty of political repercussions, however, Governments may refuse on principle to intervene in the corporations' affairs, or they may seek to intervene to ensure that the public interest is protected. They must accept any electoral consequences of inaction, or try to avoid them through interaction. The corporations, while accounting for their activities to Parliament through statements of corporate intent, and through scrutiny provided by Parliamentary Select Committees,[10] may refuse to respond to political and social influences. In that case their essentially *post hoc* accountability for satisfying prescribed commercial criteria is purchased at the price of social responsiveness, particularly if the main recourse for the Government is only to hire and fire new directors. This conundrum will be intensified if board members (and executives?) are persons selected from the ranks of private business, who pride themselves on their hard-nosed managerial competence, and who are less than enthusiastic about exposing their commercial information to public scrutiny. The worst scenario is a situation where there is little or no political responsibility for the operations of State enterprises which display minimal responsiveness to social and political considerations. In that case a State owned enterprise is effectively privatized, not in a financial but in a political sense: it becomes a public organization exercising power in a private way.

The Labour Government's requirement that social or other non-commercial objectives be negotiated by contract between the Government and the corporations appears to be an ingenious solution to this dilemma, but it is not at all clear how this device will circumvent the difficulties inherent in the desire simultaneously to enhance the contradictory values of political accountability and commercial autonomy. It also seems insensitive to more pragmatic administrative realities. Even when such contracts are negotiated they may be administered less than enthusiastically, since organizations, public or private, are usually reluctant to embrace functions and responsibilities that are inconsistent with, or at worst jeopardize, for practical and political reasons, the pursuit of their central task. For example, traffic officers did not welcome the "car-less days" programme, seeing themselves in the business of traffic law enforcement rather than energy conservation, just as the police disliked their security intelligence function before the establishment of the Security Intelligence Service, because they believed that their job was to catch thieves, not spies. In cases where non-commercial obligations are not being properly fulfilled the Government will have an incentive to act if it is expected to be responsible. If it is not, then no one will.

Commercial Markets and Political Choice

The fourth Labour Government's reforms in the public sector may well provide public officials with the freedom both to get on with their jobs and to accept the consequences. The big question mark that hangs over them, however, is whether they will require the replacement of one set of would-be miracle workers with another. The principles of action that underpin both the corporatization of State trading enterprises and the commercialization drive in the public sector generally, may enhance efficiency measured solely in financial terms, but they seem less consistent with the concept of a public service in which operating values are determined by political and social judgements as well as financial and economic calculations. Can the Minister of Finance and the new breed of accountable State servants part the muddied waters of political, organizational and social complexity so that the golden chariot of untrammeled commercial efficiency may pass safely through? Or will this bold innovation — which would seem to be a uniquely New Zealand response to the budgetary problems facing Western countries generally — sooner or later be compelled to confront the contradictions implicit in the attempt to reconcile public ownership with private management?

Whether for ideological or practical reasons, or both, the Labour Government has eschewed the option of direct privatization of State trading activities, such as that adopted by the Thatcher Administration in Britain. There, where the Government has been selling many or all of its shares in some enterprises, the nationalization *versus* denationalization debate has been informed by the chequered career of public corporate enterprises which have had to grapple in practice with the dilemmas of public ownership and commercial efficiency.[11] In New Zealand, a *sine qua non* of the successful performance of the new corporations (as measured against the expectations of their creators) must be the provision of a genuinely competitive commercial environment for them to operate in, just as the need for "liberalization" of anti-competitive laws and practices may be necessary for Britain if the full benefits of privatization are to be realized. It remains to be seen just how far the Lange Government will be willing and able to go to ensure that the new corporations are subjected to the anticipated discipline of the market rather than actual regulation by the Crown.

The much vaunted notion of "competitive neutrality" will rapidly be seen to be meaningless rhetoric unless, as Lange puts it, the new corporations do remain "on their own", with no Government guarantees for new loans, no lender of last resort facility, and "no thought that the Government would write off debts in 10 years' time" (*National Business Review*, 11 July 1986, p. 21). If they are to remain Government owned with their shares non-tradeable, it is exceedingly difficult to envisage how such a situation might be sustained. The logical alternative, if the imperatives of commercial efficiency are to dominate all others, would seem to be a sort of indirect "privatization", which sees Government enterprises selling off those parts of their activities which no longer seem to be profitable or sound investments for the future, or issuing shares to private investors in order to overcome problems of undercapitalization, a course of action that received official sanction in a Government announcement of June 1986.

However these uncertainties are resolved in practice, it is clear that the policies of corporatization and commercialization set new parameters for debate on administrative reform and place the role and scope of Government squarely on the political agenda. (According to Heald (1985), in Britain it has taken five years for public debate to come to terms with privatization issues that should have been detected much earlier.) Despite New Zealand's traditional commitment to the role of the State in providing public utilities, it seems most likely that future political pressures will shift the corporatization policies in the direction of more orthodox privatization. Significantly, the establishment board of the Forestry Corporation immediately indicated to the Government that it would have preferred to operate with full or partial sharemarket-listed ownership in order to ensure "a more effective and profitable management of the resource" (Report of the Establishment Board, 1986, p.6).

Apart from any other factors which might enhance these pressures, such as possible business dissatisfaction as the commercial advantages enjoyed by the corporations become clear, neither of the main political parties – at least in the foreseeable future – could credibly pin their colours to the mast of increased State ownership and regulation. Some proponents of the Labour Government's corporatization policies would probably claim that, given the party's historical commitment to the principles of public ownership, corporatization and commercialization represent the most feasible compromise between genuine privatization, on the one hand, and State control, on the other. And they are probably correct. The flaw in their argument is to be found in their apparent belief that the establishment of public corporations which are expected to act as if they were private, and of a more general ethos of managerialism in public administration does not embody some major dilemmas, the practical resolution of which – in either direction – must inevitably subvert some of the values (notably accountability and/or commercial efficiency) which the reforms were intended to promote.

As these dilemmas are tested by experience much more will be at stake than questions of privatization, corporatization, and commercialization. The traditional issue of public *versus* private ownership must increasingly be defined as much in terms of social considerations as of efficient resource allocation. State ownership and controls have in the past been seen as desirable, even essential, in moderating the injustices and inequalities of private ownership and market-led exchange. Paradoxically, the public sector reforms of the fourth Labour Government are explicitly designed not to diminish market-led economic forces, but to enhance them. Continued public ownership is to be made compatible with market imperatives, since economic objectives, in particular the need to reduce the Budget deficit, are seen as a necessary condition for the fulfilment of social ones. This is another manifestation of the traditional bind in which Labour Governments find themselves. Either they can try to make a capitalist economic system work more efficiently and equitably by attending to the problems of capital formation (J.K. Galbraith's "horse and sparrow theory" of economic management: feed the horses enough oats and sooner or later the sparrows too will benefit), or they can seek to protect those disadvantaged in the market economy by instituting policies that may ultimately threaten the imperatives of capital formation. Hence the rise, and uncertain future, of the welfare state. Under the first alternative — the one being followed by the current Government — all beneficiaries (that is, all the horses and all the sparrows) are regarded as either producers and/or consumers, whereas this is not necessarily so under the second paradigm.

In other words, there are two distinct intellectual traditions that underpin the rise of the welfare state: the dominant view sees it as the mechanism for providing social goods and services, and regards individuals solely as consumers, be they in the public or private realm; the less dominant view sees the provision of social goods and services not simply as a means of satisfying consumer demands, but also as a process of civic enlargement. As Lilla (1985) points out, all modern welfare states have in rhetoric and in practice mixed both traditions.

The significance of the word "public", when considered within this conceptual framework, lies not just in the question of ownership *per se*, but also in what public ownership is to be valued *for*. While the question of public or private ownership may become increasingly contentious, and while the dilemmas of political responsibility and commercial efficiency may be mediated in practice, a more subtle change in consciousness will be occurring if the debate is dominated by the metaphoric vocabulary of the market place (Ramos, 1981). Not only might this diminish the intrinsic importance of public activities by regarding their components as commodities to be bought, sold and otherwise disposed of, but as Buchanan has put it (in making a point similar to that raised earlier in regard to "objectives"):

> ... to the extent that we come to view our interactions as market transactions they may actually come more closely to approximate the model by which we seek to explain them (Buchanan, 1985, p.103).

In these times when virtually all politicians are scurrying to carry the banner of market-led efficiency for both public and private enterprise, where can a people turn when, sooner or later, it becomes apparent that much more is at stake than a narrow economic logic might suggest?

Notes

1   "Practical men, who believe themselves to be exempt from any intellectual influences, are usually the slaves of some defunct economist" (Keynes, 1936, p.383).

2   For a general summary review of the State services in New Zealand see Thynne (1986).

3   According to Douglas, over the previous 20 years successive Governments had spent a total of NZ$5 billion (in 1986 dollars) of taxpayers' money on the Post Office, the Electricity Division of the Ministry of Energy, the Forest Service, the State Coal Mines, the Lands and Survey Department, and the airways system, which taken together have assets valued at more than NZ$20 billion, and employ about 60,000 staff. The corporatization and commercialization proposals would reduce the financing requirements of net Government expenditure by NZ$900 million in 1986/87, NZ$1200 million in 1987/88, and NZ$1400 million in 1988/89 (Douglas, 1985b, pp.11, 23). The Minister has conceded, however, that NZ$500 million of the NZ$900 million is "saved" in 1986/87 merely by transferring borrowing requirements from the public accounts to the open market.

4   The appointment of Reserve Bank economist, Dr R.S. Deane, to the chairmanship of the State Services Commission, to replace the retiring Dr M.C. Probine, from 1 April 1986, was widely thought to reflect the Government's desire to find a suitable appointee who was in sympathy with its preference for market-led reforms in the State services.

5   In May 1986, the Deputy Prime Minister, Geoffrey Palmer, announced that after only three months of his "great quango hunt" he had been able to abolish 56, had his sights set on another 60, and would then consider the 127 administrative tribunals in existence.

6   For an examination of these developments in New Zealand see, for example, Morris (1985); Shailes (1978); Skene (1985); Vaughan-Jones (1986).

7   "In any case, goals and threats are not ultimate governors of behaviour; on the contrary, they are the most superficial of all. Much of the confusion which surrounds the discussion of ends and means comes from the fact that a 'goal' or 'end', if it is attainable once for all, is never more than a 'means' to maintaining some relationship which must always be sought anew ... The specific goals we pursue – I will call them objectives – are always means to attain or preserve some relationship, internal or external, which we need or think we need ... These continuing relationships I will call norms" (Vickers, 1984, p.125). Vickers' conceptualizations in public policy contrast sharply with those found in more orthodox, economically rational, models. See, for example, Vickers (1965, 1968).

8   According to the Deputy Prime Minister (*New Zealand Times*, 25 May 1986, p.1), the Minister of Finance would be one of two shareholders for each of the corporations to be operating by April 1987. The other would be the relevant portfolio Minister. The board of directors of each corporation would be responsible to the two Ministers.

9   In the "Supplement", the Association predicted, *inter alia*, rising electricity charges; the closure of up to one half of all district post offices; a reduction in search and rescue, and civil emergency services; and "widening inequalities", especially if the user-pays principle is extended to health and education services. It also mentioned the possibility of coin slots on toilet doors in national parks.

10 For a critical examination of the actual and prospective Parliamentary accountability of State owned enterprises in New Zealand, see Davies (1986).

11 Strictly speaking, privatization means transferring full ownership and control of a State asset to the private sector. This has largely been the policy followed in Britain; but the

term has more generally come to mean the selling off of all *or part* of the State's interests in an enterprise. In many instances the State may continue to hold a majority or a minority share (See *The Economist*, 21 December 1985, pp.71-86).

References

Barnard, C. (1938) *The Functions of the Executive* Cambridge, Mass., Harvard.

Brittan, S. (1984) The Politics and Economics of Privatization *Political Quarterly* 55: 109-128.

Buchanan, A. (1985) *Ethics, Efficiency and the Market* Oxford, Clarendon Press.

Buchanan, B. (1975) Red Tape and the Service Ethic: Some Unexpected Differences Between Public and Private Managers *Administration and Society* 6: 423-444.

Controller and Auditor-General (1985) *Annual Report to the House of Representatives* Wellington, Government Printer.

Cutt, J. (1978) Accountability and Efficiency In Smith, R. and Weller, P. (Eds) *Public Service Inquiries in Australia* St Lucia, University of Queensland Press.

Cyert, R. and March, J. (1963) *A Behavioral Theory of the Firm* Englewood Cliffs, Prentice-Hall.

Davies, S. (1986) Parliamentary Accountability of Government-owned Corporations and Companies *Public Sector* 9: 3-13.

Douglas, R. (1980) *There's Got to be a Better Way* Wellington, Fourth Estate Books.

Douglas, R. (1985) *Economic Statement* 12 December, Wellington, Government Printer.

Douglas, R. (1986a) *Press Statement: Cabinet Approves Major Programme to Cut Spending* 27 March, Wellington, Office of Minister of Finance.

Douglas, R. (1986b) *Statement on Government Expenditure Reform 1986* Wellington, Government Printer.

Douglas, R. (1986c) *Government Expenditure Reform: A More Efficient Public Sector for a Better New Zealand* 19 May, Wellington, Office of the Minister of Finance.

Drucker, P. (1955) *The Practice of Management* London, Mercury Books.

Gregory, R. (1982) Understanding Public Bureaucracy *Public Sector* 4: 3-12.

Gregory, R. (Ed.) (1984) *The Official Information Act: A Beginning* Wellington, New Zealand Institute of Public Administration.

Gregory, R. (1985) *Politics and Broadcasting: Before and Beyond the NZBC* Palmerston North, The Dunmore Press.

Heald, D. (1985) Will the Privatization of Public Enterprises Solve the Problem of Control? *Public Administration* (London) 63: 7-22.

Jones, G. (1977) *Responsibility and Government* London, London School of Economics and Political Science.

Kaufman H. (1977) *Red Tape: Its Origins, Uses and Abuses* Washington D.C., The Brookings Institution.

Keynes, J. (1936) *The General Theory of Employment, Interest and Money* London, Macmillan.

Lange, D. (1980) Labour's View *Public Sector* 3: 7-9.

Lilla, M. (1985) What is the Civic Interest? *The Public Interest* 81: 64-81.

Lindblom, C. (1959) The Science of Muddling Through *Public Administration Review* 19: 79-88.

Lindsay, A. (1943) *The Modern Democratic State* Vol. 1, London, Oxford.

March, J. and Simon, H. (1958) *Organizations* New York, John Wiley.

Mascarenhas, R. (1982) *Public Enterprise in New Zealand* Wellington, New Zealand Institute of Public Administration.

Morris, B. (1985) *Departmental Planning in Government* Wellington, State Services Commission.

Peres, L. (1968) The Resurrection of Autonomy: Organization Theory and the Statutory Corporation *Public Administration* (Sydney) 27: 360-370.

Polaschek, R. (1958) *Government Administration in New Zealand* Wellington, New Zealand Institute of Public Administration.

Pressman, J. and Wildavsky, A. (1984) *Implementation* Berkeley, University of California Press, 3rd Ed.

Radio New Zealand (16 March 1986) *Insight* .

Ramos, A. (1981) *The New Science of Organizations: A Reconceptualization of the Wealth of Nations* Toronto, University of Toronto Press.

Report of the Establishment Board of the Proposed New Forestry Corporation 15 May 1986, Wellington, Government Printer.

Robson, W. (1960) *Nationalised Industry and Public Ownership* London, Allen and Unwin.

Sapolsky, H. (1972) *The Polaris System Development: Bureaucratic and Programmatic Success in Government* Cambridge, Mass, Harvard.

Selznick, P. (1957) *Leadership in Administration* New York, Harper and Row.

Shailes, A. (1978) *Report of the Controller and Auditor-General on Financial Management and Control in Administrative Government Departments* Wellington, Government Printer.

Skene, G. (1985) Auditing, Efficiency and Management in the New Zealand Public Sector *Australian Journal of Public Administration* 44: 270-286.

Smith, T. (1972) *Anti-Politics* London, Charles Knight.

State Services Commission (1985) *The Government in the Market: A Basic Guide to State Owned Enterprises* Wellington, Government Printer.

Taylor, F. (1911) *The Principles of Scientific Management* New York, Harper.

Thynne, I. (1986) New Zealand In Rowat, D. (Ed.) *Public Administration in the Developed Democracies* Westport, Greenwood Press.

The Treasury (1984a) *Financial Management Guidelines* Wellington, Government Printer.

The Treasury (1984b) *Economic Management* Wellington, Government Printer.

Vaughan-Jones, G. (1986) *Management and Policy Making Techniques in Government* MPP Research Paper, Wellington, Victoria University of Wellington.

Vickers, G. (1965) *The Art of Judgment: A Study of Policy Making* London, Chapman and Hall.

Vickers, G. (1968) *Value Systems and Social Process* London, Tavistock Publications.

Vickers, G. (1984) What Sets the Goals of Public Health? In Open Systems Group (Ed.) *The Vickers Papers* London, Harper and Row.

Webb, L. (1954) Freedom and the Public Corporation *Public Administration* (Sydney) 13: 101-109.

Wilson, J. (1967) The Bureaucracy Problem *The Public Interest* 6: 3-9.

8

Labour's Economic Strategy

Brian Easton

Since taking office in mid-July 1984 the fourth Labour Government has embarked upon wide-ranging economic reforms. These have included the floating of the New Zealand dollar; the liberalization of the financial sector; the commercialization and corporatization of the State sector (see Chapters 6 and 7); the liberalization of product markets both internally and externally; major reform of taxation (see Chapter 10); and some important changes to the labour market (see Chapter 9) and in the social policy field. As noted elsewhere in this volume, such reforms mark a decisive break from traditional Labour policies. Indeed, ironically many of the current Government's policies are almost exactly the opposite of those of the first Labour Government of the 1930s; in many respects they are more similar to the policies of Britain's Conservative Government under Thatcher. The main purpose of this chapter is to explore the nature and origins of the present Government's economic strategy.

Precursors for the Strategy

Some have claimed that the Labour Government's economic strategy can be found in Roger Douglas's *There's Got To Be A Better Way!* (1980), written long before Douglas was Minister of Finance, and indeed even before he was shadow Minister of Finance. Those who created this myth have obviously not read the book. In summary, it is a collection of policy points and ideas, which are neither comprehensive nor consistent. Inevitably some positions coincide with current thinking – for instance, the relatively low priority given to equity issues, and the scepticism of the efficacy of State intervention in the market. Other policy positions, however, are quite contradictory to current policy. Douglas wanted to reduce interest rates by "compelling" financial institutions to lend a proportion of their deposits to the Government at a modest interest rate (1980, p.38). Then he was *dirigist* and an enthusiast for priority industries, Government subsidized savings schemes, and a savings corporation.

Thus, while one can identify sections of the book which foreshadow the Labour Government's economic policies, it is equally possible to find sections which criticize it. One conclusion to be drawn from this, therefore, is that some time between 1980 and the floating of the dollar in March 1985, Douglas underwent a major development in his thinking on economic policy. It appears that most of this change had occurred by mid-1983 although, as will be noted shortly, the majority of the Labour Caucus shifted its policy stance only much later. What changed Douglas's views can only be conjectured. Clearly, experiences such as Muldoon's wage and price freeze of 1982-84 would have reinforced his antagonism to State regulations and perhaps reversed his previous stand on monetary and exchange rate policies. The "Think Big" debate in the early 1980s over the establishment of the major energy projects could well have discouraged his *dirigist* bent. Overseas trends probably reinforced these developments: the Australian Labor Government's economic policies may have been particularly influential.

The Election Manifesto

The second precursor was the Labour Party's 1984 *Policy Document*. Although a substantial document of 103 pages, only five pages are on "Economic Policy", (though about a third of the document covers topics which are an integral part of economic policy). The relevance of the document for subsequent policy choices was limited. Because of the snap election, it was not complete. Moreover, whereas conflicting views can be resolved by careful wording in a party manifesto, this is not possible when actual policy decisions have to be made.

There was no reference in the document to exchange rate policy, presumably for two reasons. First, any mention of a more flexible regime than the fixed-rate system which Muldoon had pursued could have prompted currency speculation on the expectation of the election of a Labour Government. Second, it seems likely that no compromise on this issue had been reached by party strategists. Probably there was a group, including Douglas, who were committed to floating the currency. Others, however, would have favoured some sort of managed exchange rate.

Judging by the *Policy Document*, Labour's approach to economic management had two central features:

> The first is recognition of the need for a clear set of objectives and priorities which economic policies must satisfy. These will guide the next Labour Government through all the changes of circumstances which arise in the day to day management of the economy. The policies will deal consistently with a range of economic problems.
> The second is the fuller involvement of all sections of our society in setting the objectives, in defining the priorities and in charting the way ahead. We must mobilise the skills throughout the community, reconcile our differences and move forward as people (Labour Party, 1984, p.14).

Apparently the "clear set of objectives and priorities" are a reference to paragraphs 7 to 9 of the Document, although this is slightly inconsistent with "the fuller involvement of all sections of our society in setting the objectives, in defining the priorities ...". In so far as there is content in the statement, it is the notion of policy

consistency — in contrast to Muldoon's regime which was seen to be inconsistent —
and community involvement in the setting of the parameters of economic
management.

The aims of Labour's policy in order of priority were: "full employment,
economic growth, fairness and social justice, maximum possible stability in prices, a
more democratic approach to economic management, [and] greater control by
New Zealanders over their own economy" (p.14). The apparent priority of employment over social justice represents the judgement that full employment
(suitably defined) is the foundation of social justice in a modern economy. The
degree to which these are the current Government's priorities is disputable. It could
be argued that price stability or, in New Zealand's case, reducing the high rate of
inflation has been given a higher, perhaps top, priority at least as an immediate
objective of economic policy. The 1986 Budget remarks "controlling inflation is one
of the most urgent tasks, and is central to our programme" (p.3).

The *Policy Document* then gives eight main foundations for rebuilding the
economy, most of which are dealt with in detail in subsequent sections:

> ... consensus on the programme of economic and social reconstruction; a fair prices and
> incomes policy; an investment strategy to help restore full employment and reduce the
> external deficit; reform of industry assistance; a fair tax system; monetary policy that
> underpins a balanced growth strategy; fiscal policy that tackles the problems caused by
> the internal deficit; and the re-targetting of public resources to ensure a more effective
> delivery of services to those in greater need (p.14).

Much of this is like motherhood and apple pie, but with hints. For instance, in
paragraph 10 there is the remark that "the policies will be applied *gradually*"
(author's emphasis) (p.14). Presumably the document was written to permit any of
a number of exchange rate policies. Nevertheless, even allowing for the elasticity of
such manifestos, it is difficult to interpret it as consistent with a floating regime. Its
emphasis on an incomes policy with a supporting monetary policy cannot readily be
reconciled with a floating exchange rate regime regulated through strong monetary
control, and certainly not with the economic policy stance that emerged during
1985 in which the Government says it takes no view on the level of the exchange
rate. The bargain in an incomes policy needs some guarantee that other prices, such
as that for foreign exchange, will move in an acceptable way.

Economic Management

It is sometimes said, only half humorously, that five parties fought the election, and
that the Treasury Party had the largest and most unreadable manifesto. The
Treasury's post-election briefing papers which were published under the title
Economic Management (1984a) were written in the four weeks between the calling of

the election and the election itself and ran to 325 pages plus supplements. Approximately the first 100 pages dealt with the "Economic Situation and Outlook", which was the "Current Economic Situation" report prepared for the Minister of Finance at the time. The remaining 15 chapters addressed a wide range of economic issues including monetary policy, fiscal policy, exchange rate policy, labour market policy, social policy, structural adjustment and the State sector.

A post-election briefing, particularly one as comprehensive as the Treasury's, provides a considerable, perhaps unique, insight into the attitudes and policy preferences of departmental advisers. It also simplifies subsequent analysis, because *Economic Management* indicates to a very substantial degree the sort of policy advice the Treasury gave to its Ministers in the first few months after the election. That advice can be contrasted with the eight foundations of the *Policy Document*.

(a) The discussion on consultation and consensus in *Economic Management* is probably more "top down" than implied in the manifesto. For instance, the two subheadings in the relevant section are "balancing influences on the decision-making process", which focuses on an institution to help make Government intervention more transparent to the public, and "improving the communication of Government policy", which focuses on how to improve community understanding and acceptance of Government policy (Treasury, 1984, pp.130-33). The issue of how to make policy more responsive to the desires of the public, particularly those who are not readily or properly involved in the current structure, is obviously not a priority for a Government department.

(b) As will be discussed later in detail, basically the Treasury was, and remains, far from enthusiastic about a prices and incomes policy.

(c) The investment strategy outlined in the manifesto was quite different from that advocated by the Treasury. The Treasury's view was that investment decisions should be determined by private market decisions rather than by a public agency.

(d) The manifesto and the briefing papers have much in common concerning industry assistance policy, with the latter perhaps a little more enthusiastic for removing import controls and erratic assistance to industry. This section is a very strong confirmation of a "more-market" stance by the Government. The phrase "more market", introduced by Ian McLean (1979), refers to the use of the market to regulate the decisions of individuals and firms rather than by the use of direct Government controls. In principle, the National Government was also "more market" and, in fact, while in office it had liberalized numerous markets and negotiated the Closer Economic Relations (CER) trade agreement with Australia which reduced border protection. However, such liberalization had been slow and after 1982 the policy thrust of the Government was dominated by the "anti-market" wage and price freeze. A reasonable inference from the *Policy Document* was that Labour would be more determinedly "more market" than the National Government — as it has proved to be.

(e) The manifesto section on taxation is basically very platitudinous. The Treasury, and for that matter any political party, would agree with its sentiments except, perhaps, the view that the lower and middle income households need to be made better off relative to the rest.

(f) Similarly, the re-targetting of public resources advocated in the *Policy Document* is fairly platitudinous, except for its commitment to "help those on low and middle incomes". It is likely that the writers of the Treasury briefing would be happy with the sentiments, but they might well interpret them differently. For instance, "urgently addressing" the areas of health, housing, and education could involve either increased social intervention or increased privatization.

(g) The inflation and monetary policy section has to be viewed in conjunction with the section on a price and incomes policy. Essentially, the manifesto saw the role of monetary policy as buttressing the main anti-inflationary device — a wages accord with the union movement. By contrast, the Treasury argued that inflation should be controlled primarily by means of monetary policy. Both the *Policy Document* and *Economic Management* supported the abolition of the existing financial regimes and controls.

(h) The fiscal policy section in the manifesto is also platitudinous. Perhaps the only interesting content is when the manifesto says that Labour "will gradually reduce the level of the government deficit in real [sic] terms" (Labour Party, 1984, p.18). It is unclear to what extent *Economic Management* is gradualist.

One assumes that when the Secretary of the Treasury looked over the newly elected Government's economic policy as described in the manifesto he gulped over the investment policy, pondered over the prices and incomes policy, decided that the consultative proposals were not his responsibility, and thought he could live with the rest of it although he would have doubted some of the other parts of the manifesto. His real problem would have been what Labour's exchange rate policy was: a different real or nominal rate; a fixed, managed or floating regime?

The Birth of the Labour Government's Economic Policies

The transition to power for the fourth Labour Government was unusually traumatic. Within days of the election result it faced a currency crisis, a run on the New Zealand dollar, and a constitutional crisis — the difficulties in the transfer of authority (see Chapter 6). It was also confronted with difficulties over its anti-nuclear and South African policies (see Chapters 11 and 13).

The roots of the currency crisis have been described elsewhere (Easton, 1985). Following the calling of the election, foreign exchange dealers took forward positions because of the possibility of a post-election devaluation. This led to a run on the dollar in that the Reserve Bank had to supply foreign exchange on the spot market and, later, the forward market. Despite advice from Reserve Bank and

Treasury officials, Muldoon did nothing of substance to resolve the currency problems, presumably for electoral reasons. By election day, the country had virtually no foreign exchange reserves, and foreign exchange trading was suspended the next day. With the exception of the outgoing Minister of Finance, the almost unanimous verdict of economic commentators was that the New Zealand dollar would have to be devalued. By the night of Sunday 15 July senior members of the newly elected Government were being briefed by Treasury and Reserve Bank officials. The Labour Party's *Policy Document* would have been of little use during the crisis, for it made no reference to exchange rate policy. On the other hand, not only did the Treasury and Reserve Bank briefings discuss exchange rate policy, but the officials were present to elaborate and apply the remarks to the particular circumstances. If there were divisions within Cabinet on exchange rate policy, reflecting ideological divisions within the party, the experience of the currency crisis would have shifted the weight behind the Treasury and Douglas view.

Labour's Economic Strategy

Phase One
The 20 per cent devaluation on 18 July 1984, together with the abandonment of most of the controls on interest rates and a three-month price freeze, marked the beginning of a phase of economic strategy which lasted until the floating of the New Zealand dollar in early March 1985. There are two interpretations of this period. It could be argued that the strategy during these seven and a half months was to implement the party's election manifesto with no suggestion of a preordained shift in economic policy at some subsequent juncture. Alternatively, it could be argued that it was a deliberately planned transition period between the old regime of financial (and other) controls, which were largely terminated at the time of the devaluation, and the new monetary regime which began with the float.

The validity of the first proposition can be established by considering each of the eight foundations mentioned in the *Policy Document*.

1. Consensus — Publicly there was the Economic Summit Conference in September 1984 and other minisummits, with sector groups being called in earlier than in the past for consultation. However, several caveats should be noted. First, a lot more consultation had gone on during the Muldoon Administration than is generally recognized. For instance, the agreements with the manufacturers, the farmers, and the labour market organizations which were settled at about the time of the Economic Summit Conference, were the result of negotiations which had begun well before July 1984.

Second, as some sector group representatives have remarked, although there was the appearance of consultation it seemed as if the Government was listening no more carefully than had its predecessor. Indeed, it is hard to think of a decision where the Government was diverted from a major policy stance as a result of consultation.

Third, on the most important economic issue, the floating of the exchange rate, there seems to have been no consultation with anyone outside Government. It could be argued that the issue was too delicate for outsiders to be involved – just as it could have been argued that it was too important for them not to be consulted. On balance, it would seem that discussion outside the bureaucracy and the Cabinet could have been fostered, had there been the necessary political will.

Finally, it is interesting to note that after less than two years in office the Prime Minister, David Lange, stated on 9 June 1986 in the Mackintosh Memorial Lecture in Scotland: "It was inevitable in that context, but perhaps unfortunate, that the Labour Party had chosen to present itself as a party of consensus" (Lange, 1986, p.44).

Perhaps the most important development was that much more Treasury material was released than under the Muldoon Administration, as was proposed by both the *Policy Document* and *Economic Management*.

2. As will be noted shortly, the 1984 wage round was successful and could well have led one to believe that the hopes Labour had for a workable price and incomes policy were being fulfilled (see Chapter 9).

3. No measures of significance were undertaken during this period to implement the party's investment strategy – the one apparent omission from the manifesto commitment.

4. The incoming Government continued the negotiation, perhaps more determinedly than its predecessor, with the manufacturers and farmers to phase out import controls and other forms of industry assistance.

5. The November 1984 Budget included a number of taxation measures which could have indicated that the manifesto commitments were being introduced (see Chapter 10).

6. It could also be argued that the Budget included some re-targetting of public resources. However, the sort of comprehensive review that was implicit in the manifesto did not occur. One might conclude that good intentions remained evident.

7. During the Government's first seven months major and courageous measures were taken to liberalize monetary control in a manner consistent with the manifesto commitment, but arguably more vigorous.

8. With regard to fiscal policy, the 1984 Budget introduced a package of measures designed to reduce the Budget deficit by NZ$1,075 million in 1985/86 and NZ$1,761 million in 1986/87. The way the information was presented suggests that the Government was aware that there were other unmentioned factors, perhaps debt servicing, which would increase the Budget deficit, so the net effect was much smaller.

This brief review suggests that during its first seven months in office the Labour Government pursued its election manifesto commitments honourably, with diligence, and even with courage given the difficulties it faced as an incoming Government.

There is, however, an alternative interpretation. Suppose there was another policy agenda. At the minimum it might consist of as little Government intervention and economic direction as possible, with a floating exchange rate and a carefully controlled money supply. It would have been imprudent to have instituted this policy immediately: the Muldoon Government could best be described as having left the monetary and fiscal situation in chaos. Given this, the immediate introduction of a floating exchange rate regime could well have led to the unleashing of explosive inflationary forces. That there was still the unravelling of the freeze would have compounded the process. Thus, this second agenda would have required a transition phase where, together with liberalization of markets and reduced Government intervention, there would have to be measures taken to reduce the Budget deficit and to rein the monetary situation by market interest rates. The liberalization of foreign capital account transactions which took place just before Christmas 1984, was a further such measure.

It is not being postulated that the entire Labour Cabinet secretly held this "free market" policy agenda from the outset. Nevertheless, from a reading of the post-election briefing papers it is evident that some official advisors must have. The point is that Labour's economic policies during the first phase were, on the whole, consistent with the transition to this alternative policy stance. Perhaps the main criticism is that, the transition took place too slowly; but other than that, its supporters would have been well pleased with the first phase of the Government's strategy, particularly when it switched fully over to the second phase in early March 1985 with the introduction of the floating exchange rate.

Phase Two

As mentioned, the switch from a fixed to a floating exchange rate represents a turning point in Labour's economic strategy although, of course, the effect of such a change was not immediately apparent. The change can be characterized in a number of ways. One is to see a switch from a competitive exchange rate as introduced at the time of devaluation which promised the tradeable sector profitable opportunities for production, to a strategy where the Government would take no responsibility for the level of the exchange rate, and where in the short run the effects of the capital account would dominate (Officials' Paper, 1986).

While this transition was a decisive one, it was not at all evident that the new policy regime would necessarily be better than the old. In particular, given the success of the 1984 wage round, one might have thought that the Government would have persevered with its manifesto commitment to a prices and incomes policy, plus the implicit managed exchange rate. It is this contrast between a prices and incomes policy with a fixed or managed exchange rate and the floating exchange rate with regulation of the economy via control of money stock which is at the heart of the macro-policy debate.

To simplify this debate, which might loosely be described as one between Keynesians and monetarists, it is necessary to focus on the anchors which are intended to hold the economic ship in place (Buckle and Pope, 1985). Keynesians claim that two anchors are needed: the exchange rate and the wage level. One is not enough. If wages are not controlled, the exchange rate anchor will be dragged along by the motion of the ship. If there is no exchange rate anchor, there is a danger of accelerating wage inflation. It is also important that the two are co-ordinated. If each is trying to anchor the ship to a different place, neither will hold, as was shown by Muldoon's economic regime. Moreover, the Keynesian stance implies that in securing trade union agreement on a wage path other policies may be required, such as price controls and more active fiscal management. Keynesians recognize that a firm monetary policy is needed (i.e. monetary aggregates should not grow too far out of line with the growth of incomes) but in the short run they would allow some flexibility.

Monetarists do not believe these anchors will hold. On the contrary, they believe using them wastes effort and interferes with the true stabilizers of the economy. The analogy would be that the ship should float upon the sea, but there exist automatic stabilizers, rather like for some oil rigs, if monetary policy is correctly applied. (In desperately oversimplified terms, if the money stock is kept constant, then the ship will be stabilized, at least in the medium term.) Floating the exchange rate is important for such a monetary policy because it removes one of the major sources of monetary variation — injections and withdrawals through the foreign exchange market. (The other major source of injections is the Government's fiscal deficit.)

The protagonists of the two views justly criticize each other. The monetarist is sceptical of the ability to maintain an effective incomes policy. There is a general as well as a specific point here. Generally prices and incomes policies involve interfering with the market. The committed monetarist is likely to claim that this will result in a marked loss of efficiency. More specifically, there are serious doubts as to whether incomes policies work except in exceptional circumstances (Blyth, 1985). It would seem that in 1985 some of the more pragmatic officials were particularly sceptical as to the ability of the Federation of Labour (FOL) and the Employers Federation to "deliver" on any central agreement. Neither peak organization has the political power to enforce an agreement on its constituents, and there are important agents who are not members of the FOL (e.g. the Electricians Union). It could be argued that one reason why the union movement has withdrawn from such potential agreements as the 1981 wage-tax trade-off was because they knew that they could not deliver.

However, Keynesians may equally claim that monetary control will not deliver wage and price restraint. Since the events of 1985 have provided a test of these contentions, they are reviewed below (see also Chapter 9). The Government chose not to intervene directly in the 1985/86 wage round. Its policy was stated by the Minister of Finance in August 1985:

> We will not step in to accommodate a high wage round through relaxing our financial policies. If a settlement is out of line with the realities of a particular industry then the industry and its jobs will be in trouble, there will be no easy money around to accommodate it ... In a sense, we do already have a guideline for the wage round, it is just that it is not a wage guideline. There is an important difference between the two and it reflects the fundamental shift in thinking, between a control approach and the sort of approach where the right economic environment is established and the parties are then given more freedom to get on with the job. What we have set out is a "guideline" for total nominal incomes — the dollar value of all incomes in the economy, whether in the form of wages, profits, interest or dividends. This is a guideline rather than a target. In the government briefing paper distributed at the Tripartite Conference ... we indicated that the government's policy approach was consistent with nominal income growth of the order of 10 to 13 per cent in the year April 1985 to March 1986, and 7 to 9 per cent next year. This nominal income growth will be split between inflation on the one hand and real growth in output on the other. A higher rate of inflation would mean less output growth. Conversely, if inflation is reduced faster, the prospects for real output growth during the next two years will be better (Douglas, 1985, p.6).

The actual gross domestic product growth for the 1985/86 year was 13.2 per cent, near enough to the Government forecast. However, forecasts for the 1986/87 year are closer to 11 per cent, out of line with the Finance Minister's statement. This is not surprising, given that the wage round outcome was 16 per cent for the private sector and close to 25 per cent for the public sector. Obviously the wage round settled well outside any range which the Minister envisaged, a level which has been described as "disastrous".

A Keynesian would say "I told you so", quoting overseas experience. However, there has been a tendency by some Labour politicians to blame the determination by the Higher Salaries Commission just before the wage round, which gave exceptionally high increases — 38 per cent was a commonly mentioned figure — to prominent persons such as Cabinet Ministers. This effect has been over-rated but if it were not, it gives some credibility to the case for an incomes policy which would aim to limit this sort of damage by controlling such increases.

Even a pragmatic monetarist might consider the attempt to control wages via monetary policy foolhardy in the circumstances. Given the state of the money market when the Government took over, and the massive changes that were taking place under the liberalization programme, it was reasonable to suppose that the relation between the money aggregates and the rest of the economy had changed radically. In such circumstances monetary control would be virtually impossible.

There is no reason to have any confidence in the Government being able to attain the nominal targets its monetary policy aimed for, except by accident, and so those involved in wage bargaining are quite likely to ignore monetary policy announcements.

The above analysis is not with the benefit of hindsight; numerous economists made similar points before the event (see *Quarterly Predictions*, September 1985). Why then did the Labour Government abandon its apparently successful economic strategy of 1984, based on its election manifesto and its apparently special relationship with unions? Two conjectures can be offered.

The first is the "trauma" theory, which is that the Labour Government had been bruised by the difficulties of the July 1984 devaluation and the December 1984 wage round. On 17 May 1986 Lange spoke to a Labour Regional Conference of the stress during the currency crisis, while the 1984 wage round involved intense behind the doors lobbying which, so the story goes, left Douglas muttering in the corridors that "there's got to be a better way". Arguably, by switching over to a float and an unmanaged wage round, the Government avoided similar bruisings from these sources.

The second conjecture is that Cabinet had the wrong analysis of the situation. One can think of at least two reasons for this. It is possible that the official briefings were wrong, inadequate, or misleading. This would be surprising but can be readily checked by reviewing the relevant Cabinet papers when they become available. Alternatively, the politicians may have had a wrong and unshakeable perception of the effects of floating. For instance, there was an unsatisfactory debate on its merits just before the election, associated with the New Zealand Party and Federated Farmers, which seemed to suggest that floating would eliminate the current account deficit on the balance of payments. It does not; all floating does is ensure that a private capital inflow will cover the current account deficit if there is no public borrowing. A float could increase the current account deficit rather than eliminate it. Suppose, for whatever reason, the Cabinet had a faulty perception of the effects of the float, perhaps despite official briefings; then it could have committed the country to a floating exchange rate regime without understanding the implications.

Structural Adjustment

Thus far we have focused upon the incomes policy/monetary control facet of the exchange rate regime. There is a second consequence which needs to be explored. In its manifesto, as well as in practice, the Labour Government was committed to a "more market" strategy, which included the phasing out of import controls, reduction in tariffs, abolition of export incentives and supplementary minimum prices to farmers, and the withdrawal of other subsidies. Such a change involves a major alteration in the industry environment with considerable adjustment.

Resources will move from some activities to others which is likely to result in the expansion and contraction of firms, including labour redundancies and business closures. There is also likely to be some political backlash against the measures.

Economists have one firm conclusion about the conditions for such liberalization to succeed: the exchange rate needs to be competitive, so that those industries which should be expanding in the liberalized regime have strong signals and rewards to do so. In the first phase of the Labour Government the exchange rate following the 20 per cent devaluation, only mild inflation, and partial withdrawal of industry assistance, was favourable. No doubt this, and the belief that the Government would continue such a strategy, was a major factor in getting agreements for the liberalization, and the favourable wage round. The implicit assumption by the manufacturers, the farmers, and possibly the unions, must have been that the Government would continue to manage the exchange rate in this manner.

The introduction of the float represented a major break because the Government no longer managed the exchange rate towards any particular level of competitiveness. Subsequently there was a currency appreciation, and by mid-1985 the exchange rate was less competitive than it had been before the July 1984 devaluation. This outcome is not surprising; certainly some of the critics of floating predicted "exchange rate overshooting" well before the new policy was implemented (Buckle and Pope, 1985; Pope, 1984). This serious loss of competitiveness for over a year is likely to inhibit the process of market liberalization (Easton, 1986).

The most evident example of this inhibition is in the farming sector. Its dependence upon subsidies in the past had left an industry which would have to go through a major adjustment, not only in terms of the pattern of production, but also because farm land was overvalued and its debt ratios too high. Adjustment was further complicated by a weak world demand for the farmers' main exports of meat, wool, and dairy products. An unfavourable exchange rate in addition to this resulted in a farm industry going through considerable trauma by early 1986 (Easton, 1986). While there were other factors compounding the difficulties of farmers, the overvalued exchange rate complicated the adjustment process as some economists predicted it would.

Towards the end of 1986 similar difficulties were beginning to confront manufacturing. The *Quarterly Survey of Business Opinion* shows that manufactured exporting became difficult in late 1985 (i.e. shortly after the loss of competitiveness of the exchange rate). Investment also started reducing about then compounding the business cycle downswing in 1986.

One also wonders to what extent Cabinet was fully aware of the policy agenda which followed floating, much of which is foreshadowed in *Economic Management*, when they made the decision. Among the political hurdles Ministers had to face were: (a) high real interest rates, (b) stern measures to reduce the fiscal deficit, (c) the corporatization of State owned enterprises, and (d) the reorganization of the labour market. Some people see further down that agenda: (e) the reduction in the public provision of welfare services, (f) the privatization of Government corporations, and (g) greater income and wealth inequality.

The Origins of Labour's Economic Strategy

What has thus far been posed is a contradiction between the economic strategy of the Labour Party in Opposition before July 1984 and the strategy of the Labour Government at least since the float in March 1985. It would be easy to explain this by arguing that the Labour Cabinet was captured by the Treasury. However, while it is difficult to document it appears that some Labour Ministers, notably Douglas, had already adopted independently much of the analysis and policy directions while in Opposition. This is unlikely to be true for the whole Cabinet, so if there was a Cabinet capture the agents were the Minster of Finance and his like-thinking colleagues supported by Treasury. Such an explanation raises the question of how the Treasury post-election briefing so well foreshadows Labour's eventual economic strategy. Biology suggests either parallel evolution or miscegenation, or both.

The theory of parallel evolution, that Treasury and some of the Labour Opposition came to broadly similar policy conclusions must take account of the fact that other policy options were possible. In particular, the *Policy Document's* direction of a managed exchange rate and greater use of incomes policy has been advocated by economists outside the Labour Party. It seems likely that the assessments of the potential deliverability of an agreement with the unions and employers was crucial here, and could well have been arrived at independently. The parallel evolution theory is supported by the common experiences of the two groups. They are of similar age (born between 1930 and 1950), of similar family backgrounds (typically middle class and often urban), and have been through similar university education, the economic content of which would have been much the same (1960s neoclassical economics updated to the 1970s). Moreover, the two groups went through rather similar political experiences. In a sense both were in "opposition" to the previous Prime Minster and Minster of Finance, Sir Robert Muldoon; and both on occasions had to negotiate with the union movement. (This is, of course, not to argue that social position and experience are the sole determinants of individual ideology.)

While plausible, the parallel evolution scenario is not quite convincing. Some miscegenation, that is dialogue between the two groups, seems likely to have occurred resulting in a convergence of approaches. Inevitably such miscegenation occurs between Ministers and their official advisers. The question is whether it occurred to some degree before the election. If it did, it need not have been improper, in that there are mechanisms by which a dialogue could take place between official advisers and the Opposition without compromising New Zealand's constitutional or public service procedures. There is even the tantalizing possibility that the post-election briefings were written with the requirements of an incoming Labour Government in mind. After all, if the National Government had been returned the document could have been quickly consigned to an appropriate file.

The Social Content of the Economic Strategy

This picture of parallel evolution, together with some miscegenation, may throw some light upon perhaps the most significant omission in the Government's economic strategy: how it was to relate to social policy. This omission was publicly acknowledged in early 1986 when the Government announced it would establish a Royal Commission on Social Policy.

Those who developed and supported the Government's economic strategy in Opposition were probably a minority. Among the reasons for the majority being opposed to that strategy was that its social implications were unclear. "More market" means labour redeployment and probably some additional unemployment. Regions (and marginal seats) are particularly vulnerable. (In principle unemployment should be transitory, but in practice the long-run outcome is less clear.) Floating the currency involves an interest rate regime that is likely to be (and has been) onerous to the poor young home owner and farmer.

How then was the proposed strategy to integrate with the priorities of Labour's policies: full employment, economic growth, and social justice? It has already been remarked that in practice price stability appears to have been given greater priority in the Government's economic strategy than was envisaged in the *Policy Document*. Further along this path are issues concerning the reform of health, education, and welfare. For instance, it could be argued that the corporatization and user-pays approach applied to State trading enterprises will inevitably have to be applied to schools, hospitals and social security (via an insurance scheme).

This is probably not the Labour Government's intention. Less clear is what it does intend. Indeed, the establishment of a Royal Commission on Social Policy may indicate that the Government is itself unsure. If so, there is an irony in a situation of a Labour Government with a clear economic strategy, and an uncertain social one, a situation more commonly associated with Governments of the right.

It is extremely difficult to assess the distributional consequences of Labour's economic strategy, even though support for "those in need" and "those on low and middle incomes" are promised in the manifesto. In order to analyze this systematically there is a need for a framework which monitors changes in the household income and spending distribution. No such framework existed in the Muldoon era, and the new Government took no initiatives to establish one. Interestingly, in July 1986 Lange thought that "you are seeing a certain amount of redistribution now, but it is perverse. It is a negative redistribution" (*National Business Review*, 14 July 1986). He looked forward to the October 1986 tax package, but an independent observer might be more sceptical about its effect. Much of the tax cuts for the lower paid are the return of fiscal drag, while the greatest beneficiaries of the cuts are the higher income recipients through the reduction of the top marginal income tax rate from 66 per cent to 48 per cent.

The problem becomes apparent once the various statements by Labour politicians are brought together. They claim to have assisted those in need and on low and middle incomes. Moreover, they have cut income tax rates dramatically for the rich during a period of a share boom and high real interest rates. Which groups, then, with the possible exception of richer national superannuitants, are worse off? The cynic might suggest it is the farmer who is bearing the redistributional load, but more likely there are many low and middle income people who are worse off than they were in July 1984.

An indication of the difficulty that Labour is in comes from Lange's address to the 1986 Labour Party Conference. It rambles through some of the major social issues which confront the Government but offers little inspiration or direction except the promise of the Royal Commission on Social Policy (which is due to report in 1988).

While the extent to which the *Policy Document's* commitment to re-targetting of public resources may be disputed (given that much was platitudinous anyway) undoubtedly the Labour Government has made numerous minor improvements in this area. The test will be to the extent to which the Royal Commission on Social Policy tackles the challenge and the fourth Labour Government implements its recommendations — if the electorate gives it a second chance.

Will the Strategy Work?

The ultimate test is whether the strategy will produce better economic performance. This is by no means an easy question to answer, particularly given the short period since the strategy was initiated. At the time of the election the economy was in a strong cyclical upswing which was prolonged by the stimulus to the export sector, and the import competing sector, from the favourable exchange rate consequent on the devaluation, and by a consumption boom funded by the consumer credit released by the financial liberalization measures. By late 1985 the economy had entered the cyclical downswing which was compounded by a deterioration in terms of trade and by the rise in the exchange rate which followed floating. The inflation cycle was not dissimilar with rising inflation in the early stage of the Labour Government as the Muldoon freeze came off, and the price increases from the devaluation and the measures to reduce the Government deficit flowed through. As these effects ended, and in the case of import prices reversed with the rise in the exchange rate, the rate of inflation fell. However, it remained above ten per cent per annum before the introduction of GST kicked the rate up again in October 1986.

The implication of all this is that at the time of writing there exists sufficient data for anyone to select a plausible subset to justify any particular prejudice – a popular form of economic commentary in New Zealand. One approach to cutting this Gordian knot is to focus on the health of the tradeable sector, which is dependent upon a profitable exchange rate (Easton, 1986). On the available evidence the immediate post-float exchange rate was too high (Philpott, 1986) and this is likely to result in a contracting tradeable sector while overseas debt accumulates. This combination of higher debt and reduced ability to service it, not unfamiliar in Latin America, is potentially disastrous. If the exchange rate continues at an unrealistically high rate then Labour's economic strategy will inevitably fail. That the main forecasting agencies thought at the time of writing (September 1986) that the economy would stagnate through 1986 and much of 1987 suggests this writer is not alone in his pessimism.

The alternative view is that there have been major supply-side shifts (Officials' Paper, 1986). If there has, then the mid-1986 exchange rate could well be sustainable. However, little evidence for these shifts has been presented, and the experience of other countries (e.g. the response to Reagan's tax cuts) is that supply-side responses are not significant in the short run.

Conclusion

This chapter has focused on broad themes and neglected details. It has considered only briefly whether the Labour Government's economic strategy will work. It has not asked when the second policy phase will end, although it would not be surprising if subtle shifts were occurring in mid-1986 with the politics of decisive and dogmatic economics policy being replaced by a more gradualist and pragmatic approach – in line with the manifesto commitments.

What this chapter indicates is that it is not obvious why the Government adopted a floating exchange rate and all that this implied. There is no Labour Party documented precursor – only that of the Treasury and Reserve Bank post-election briefings. The first seven months of policy were broadly consistent with its manifesto. And the advantage of a floating exchange rate was not so decisive as to justify the major policy stance in an obvious way. Lange's claim that the floating of the dollar was an "inexorable" outcome of the July 1984 devaluation (*National Business Review*, 14 July 1986) is nonsense. The policy is by no means accepted by all professional economists, and very few countries "free" float their currency; indeed the New Zealand strategy may be the most extreme example of free floating in the world.

In the end the answer may only be known by reading the various confidential policy papers and memoirs of Cabinet Ministers. In the interim a rule of thumb can be offered. Labour's economic strategy was to do exactly the opposite to what

Muldoon would have done. The experience of the Muldoon freeze dominated the
thinking of Labour's strategists, and their response was contrawise. From one
extreme, economic policy lurched to another. We can but wait for the time when
the ghost of the Muldoon economic "miracle" is exorcized from the political
agenda.

References

Blyth, C.A. (1985) Incomes Policy: The Record *Quarterly Predictions* September.
Buckle, R.A. and Pope, M.J. (1985) Issues in Exchange Rate Policy *Quarterly Predictions*
    March.
Douglas, R. (1980) *There's Got to be a Better Way* Wellington, Fourth Estate Books.
Douglas, R. (1985) Speech to Manufacturers. Reported in *Quarterly Predictions* September.
Douglas, R. (1986) *Financial Statement* Wellington, Government Printer.
Easton, B.H. (1985) Devaluation *The Listener* 27 July, p.30.
Easton, B.H. (1986) *The Exchange Rate Since 1981: Performance and Policy* Wellington,
    NZIER Discussion Paper No. 30.
Labour Party (1984) *1984 Policy Document* Wellington.
Lange, D. (1986) The New Welfare State Prestonpans, Mackintosh Memorial Lecture.
McLean, I. (1979) *The Future of New Zealand Agriculture: Economic Strategies for the 1980s*
    Wellington, Fourth Estate Books Ltd and New Zealand Planning Council.
Officials' Paper (1986) *Memorandum for Exporters' Representatives: Exchange Rate Issues*
    Wellington, Reserve Bank.
Philpott, B.P. (1986) *Management of the Floating Exchange Rate* Paper prepared for New
    Zealand Dairy Board, Wellington.
Pope, M.J. (1984) *Floating the Exchange Rate* Wellington, Victoria University Economics
    Department Discussion Paper No. 28.
Reserve Bank (1984) *Post-Election Paper to the Minister of Finance on the Areas of Responsibility
    of the Reserve Bank* Wellington.
Treasury (1984a) *Economic Management* Wellington, Government Printer.
Treasury (1984b) *Economic Management: Land Use Issues* Wellington, Government Printer.

9

Wages Policy and Industrial Relations Reform

Jonathan Boston

Like the Australian Labor Party in 1983, the New Zealand Labour Party centred its 1984 election campaign around the need for a consensus approach to policy making (in contrast to the alleged divisiveness of the Muldoon years) and the desirability of creating a broadly based "economic and social understanding concerning the direction of economic management" (New Zealand Labour Party, 1984, p.15). At the heart of this programme was the promise to end the wage freeze imposed in June 1982 by the National Government and replace it with a negotiated, voluntary incomes policy or wage accord. Such an approach, it was contended, offered the most satisfactory solution to the problems of inflation and unemployment which had plagued New Zealand for many years. In practice, however, the Labour Government has pursued a quite different economic strategy (see Chapter 8). Although Muldoon's comprehensive wage and price controls were removed, they were not replaced with a voluntary incomes policy. Instead, since late 1984 wages have been determined by means of direct union-employer bargaining with only limited State interference, and the Government has relied primarily on monetary and fiscal policies to control inflation. Hence, by mid-1986 the Prime Minister was able to comment accurately, and it seems approvingly, that "there is no prices and incomes policy in New Zealand" (Lange, 1986, p.50).

Such developments stand in sharp contrast to the situation in Australia. Here the Australian Labor Party has, since its election in early 1983, pursued a macroeconomic strategy based on a wage accord with the union movement (Burch, 1985; Gerritsen, 1986; Mulvey, 1984; Plowman, 1984; Rawson, 1986, pp.65-74). Under this policy there has been a return to a system of centralized wage determination governed by certain agreed principles and operated through the Australian Conciliation and Arbitration Commission. More specifically, it has involved biannual national wage adjustments based in the main on movements in the Consumer Price Index with strict limitations on additional negotiations at the industry or workplace level over pay and conditions of employment. In exchange for its co-operation on the wages front, the Australian Confederation of Trade Unions has obtained various concessions from the Government: the establishment of consultative organizations such as the Economic Planning Advisory Council and the Advisory Committee on Prices and Incomes; the creation of a Price Surveillance Authority; the strengthening of anti-monopoly legislation; and significant changes in the social policy arena — Medicare, improved child care facilities, higher housing expenditure and improved benefit levels.

Equally important are the differences in the approaches of the two Governments to the question of industrial relations reform. In New Zealand the Labour Government has embarked upon one of the most important changes to the industrial relations system in the private sector since 1894. It has also announced an even more radical overhauling of the system of wage determination in the public sector. These reforms, which are in line with the Government's strategy of economic liberalization, are designed to increase the flexibility of the labour market, thereby enhancing the efficiency of the economy, improving productivity, increasing real wages and lowering unemployment. By contrast, the Australian Labor Government has adopted a more cautious industrial relations strategy and, in keeping with the recommendations of the Hancock Commission, has proposed only modest adjustments to the long-established system of conciliation and arbitration (Report of the Committee of Review, 1985).

This chapter seeks to explain why the New Zealand Labour Government has pursued a labour market strategy so different from that foreshadowed in its 1984 *Policy Document*, and what impact this has had on the trade union movement and its relations with the Government. Three particular matters require investigation: the controversy over the merits of incomes policies; the political and economic context at the change of Government; and the events surrounding the wage rounds in 1984/85, 1985/86 and 1986/87. The chapter concludes with a brief outline of the nature and likely implications of the proposed changes to the system of industrial relations in the private sector. The proposed reforms to State pay fixing are considered in Chapter 6.

Incomes Policy: Pros and Cons

One of the central, unavoidable dilemmas confronting policy makers in virtually all advanced industrialized democracies during the post-war period has been the question of how to control wage inflation, or more precisely, how to combine high levels of employment with an acceptable degree of wage and price stability. This dilemma became particularly acute in the aftermath of the wage explosion of the late 1960s and early 1970s and the first oil shock in 1973.

By the mid 1970s many analysts had concluded that free collective bargaining was incompatible with full employment and price stability. Certainly this seemed to be the case where the economy was characterized by decentralized wage fixing, a high level of unionization, a low level of employee deference, strongly held notions of comparative wage justice (or interdependent preferences) and vigorous conflict over income shares. In fact, such a setting seemed to have the features of a market failure or a prisoner's dilemma: self-interested, maximizing behaviour by individual bargaining groups, instead of securing collective benefits, brought collective ruin — i.e. low economic growth, inflation, and high unemployment (Boston, 1985b;

Maital and Benjamini, 1980; Sutcliffe, 1982). Another way of putting this might be to suggest that the institutional and sociological characteristics outlined above tend to push up what Tobin has called the "inflation-safe unemployment rate" (1986, p.6). This means, in short, that if a Government tries to maintain a low rate of unemployment – or at least a rate below what is thought to be "inflation safe" – it runs the risk of accelerating inflation.

The broad strategic options available to policy makers faced with this predicament are as follows:

(a) the retention of the existing politico-economic structures and the acceptance of relatively high unemployment;

(b) the abolition of collective bargaining and free trade unions, and the restructuring of the economy along Marxist lines;

(c) the adoption of a co-operative economic strategy based on labour-owned and managed enterprises, perhaps along Yugoslav lines;

(d) a neoconservative strategy involving orthodox monetary and fiscal policies and radical changes to the operation of the labour market, including a major assault on the monopoly power of trade unions; and

(e) a post-Keynesian approach employing restraints on the bargaining process, either by means of direct governmental controls or corporatist arrangements (Boston, 1986; Crouch, 1977; Crouch, 1985; Grant, 1985; Schmitter and Lehmbruch, 1979).

In the West the last two strategies have received the most powerful advocacy; at the heart of the debate has been the merits and utility of incomes policies.

Put simply, neoconservative writers have argued that incomes policies, be they voluntary or statutory, are politically undesirable, economically inefficient and ultimately self-defeating (Brittan and Lilley, 1977; Hayek, 1980; Minford, 1980). They do not reduce the rate of unemployment (or the presumed inflation-safe unemployment rate), nor do they enhance the performance of the economy. Rather, they make things worse. Hence, if a market failure is occurring the solution lies not in collective action (i.e. central co-ordination of wage determination), but in measures to restructure the labour market in order to prevent deleterious outcomes. Amongst the measures usually proposed are the removal of minimum wage laws, the cutting of unemployment benefits and the weakening of the power of trade unions.

By contrast, post-Keynesians maintain that incomes policies can be made to work and are not necessarily harmful politically and economically (Layard, 1982; Meade, 1982; Okun, 1981). Austria and Sweden are often cited as countries which have operated corporatist incomes policies with reasonable success for several decades (see Flanagan, Soskice and Ulman, 1983). Further, it is contended that labour markets have certain distinctive features: transaction and information costs are usually high; wage setting is significantly influenced by relativity considerations and the organizational strength of the bargaining parties; and the flexibility of wages is reduced, not merely by the existence of negotiated contracts, but also by implicit contracts and "invisible handshakes" (Okun, 1981). For these reasons labour markets adjust relatively slowly and wage rates tend to be "sticky", especially in a downwards direction. It is argued that this state of affairs is unlikely to be altered greatly by attempts to remove or weaken so-called "rigidities" in the labour market, such as the bargaining power of organized labour. In any case, an attack on the legal rights and privileges of trade unions, as proposed by many neoconservative scholars, could well present a Government with major political difficulties, certainly in democratic countries with strong union traditions. From this perspective, an incomes policy, while not perhaps the optimal approach, might well be a second-best strategy.

Until the late 1970s such a rationale for an incomes policy was widely accepted in most OECD countries, particularly by Governments of a social democratic orientation (see Marks, 1986). New Zealand was no exception. In fact, few countries have witnessed such extensive State regulation of wages and prices as New Zealand. As table 9.1 shows, between March 1971 and October 1986 statutory wage controls of a selective or comprehensive variety were in force for more than nine years; and during the remainder of this period Governments employed a wide range of non-statutory devices — political pressure, moral persuasion, sanctions against "soft" employers, and threats to re-impose regulations — in an effort to reduce the pace of wage inflation (Boston, 1984; Hawke, 1982). Notable for its absence during this period was any formal bilateral or tripartite wages deal (Brosnan, 1983, pp.135-169; Walsh, 1982). To be sure, there were a number of informal understandings between Ministers and the trade union movement on the desirability of wage moderation. Such was the case, for example, in early 1973, August 1977 and August 1980; but at no stage was there a comprehensive wage agreement similar to those negotiated in Britain, Belgium, Finland, Ireland, Norway and Sweden during the 1970s (Marks, 1986, pp. 270-273). There were four main reasons for this.

First, during most of the period the majority of union leaders and activists — including the current President of the Federation of Labour (FOL), Jim Knox — favoured free collective bargaining and were ill-disposed to the idea of wage restraint, however it be enforced. Second, and equally important, the union movement had little desire to co-operate with conservative administrations. Since the National Party held the Treasury benches for most of the post-war era, and since it sometimes adopted a stridently anti-union stance, a negotiated wages and prices policy was virtually out of the question. Third, policy makers doubted whether a voluntary pay deal could be adequately enforced. This assessment was based on the fact that the principal peak organizations of labour and capital — the FOL and the Employers Federation — lacked an associational monopoly in their respective sectors and possessed few effective sanctions to deter free riders. Moreover, the FOL's

Table 9.1
Incomes policy in New Zealand

Year	Acts and Regulations	Controlling authority	Coverage	Bargaining restrictions
1968–Mar. 1971	General Wage Orders Act (1969)	Arbitration Court		Free collective bargaining. Provision for general wage orders.
Mar. 1971–Mar. 1972	Stabilisation of Remuneration Act	Remuneration Authority	Universal	Free bargaining up to 7% max.; 12 month rule. Provision for anomalies and cost of living orders.
Mar. 1972–Dec. 1972	Stabilisation of Remuneration Regulations	Remuneration Authority	Universal	Zero wage norm; 12 month rule. Provision for anomalies and cost of living orders.
Dec. 1972–Aug. 1973				Free collective bargaining. Vague 12 month rule. Moral suasion by Government for restraint.
Aug. 1973–June 1974	Economic Stabilisation Regulations	Wages Tribunal	Universal	Pay freeze. Provision for anomalies and cost of living orders.
July 1974–May 1976	Wage Adjustment Regulations	Industrial Commission	Universal	Free bargaining up to 2.25% plus negotiable addition of up to 2.25% max.; 12 month rule. Provision for anomalies and cost of living orders.
May 1976–Aug. 1977	Wage Adjustment Regulations	Industrial Commission; Wage Hearing Tribunal (early 1977)	Universal	Pay freeze for 12 months, later extended for 3 months in May 1977. No exceptions initially; later provision for exceptional circumstances. Provision for a general wage order.
Aug. 1977–Aug. 1979	General Wage Orders Act (1977)	Arbitration Court re-established		Restricted collective bargaining. 12 month rule. Governmental threats and coercion. General wage orders available via Arbitration Court.
Aug. 1979–Aug. 1980	Remuneration Act (10.8.79–4.11.80) General Wage Orders Act repealed		Selective	As above, except that general wage orders issued by Government decree.

Aug. 1980–June 1982				As above, except that one general wage order was available from the Arbitration Court.
June 1982–Dec. 1984	Wage Freeze Regulations	Wage Freeze Authority	Universal	Pay freeze, initially 12 months but extended twice. Certain exceptions for: (a) new employment situations, and (b) workers who did not receive increases in the 1981–82 wage round. One general wage order authorised by the Government in April 1984.
Dec. 1984–Sept. 1985				'Managed' wage round; 10 month rule.
Sept. 1985–?				Free collective bargaining; 12 month rule. No provision for general wage orders. Threats and moral suasion by Government.

Source: Boston, J. (1984) *Incomes Policy in New Zealand* Wellington, Victoria University Press, pp. 19–20.

position had been weakened since the 1960s as a result of the growth of second-tier bargaining and shop-floor autonomy; it suffered a further decline in 1984 when the electricians, a key bargaining group, withdrew from the Federation and subsequently helped form the Coalition of Non-Aligned Associations and Unions (a grouping of about 20 unions representing some 60,000 workers).[1] Finally, on the basis of overseas experience the prospects of a corporatist incomes policy succeeding in the medium-to-long term in a country with New Zealand's kind of industrial relations system were not good (Boston, 1986). This judgement appears to have had a bearing on the policy choices of the Labour Government.

It would be wrong to give the impression, however, that attitudes in New Zealand towards incomes policies have remained static. In fact, significant changes have taken place since the late 1970s. For example, within the union movement a number of influential figures, such as Ken Douglas, the Secretary of the FOL, Rob Campbell, at one stage Secretary of the Distribution Workers Federation, and Alf Kirk, the FOL's economic adviser during the late 1970s and early 1980s, became convinced by 1980 that some form of incomes policy was almost inevitable, whichever of the major parties attained office. Given this situation, if the union movement wished to influence the Government's economic strategy, it would have to adopt a more conciliatory approach and be willing to make concessions on wage-related issues in return for policy gains elsewhere (see Campbell and Kirk, 1983). From a union standpoint the logic of the case for "bargained corporatism" became all the more compelling as the events of the early 1980s unfolded. For instance, when the National Government imposed a lengthy, mandatory wage and price freeze in June 1982, the FOL found itself powerless to do anything about it. Although a concerted campaign of industrial action was mounted, the Government and employers stood firm and the wage controls remained intact (Harbridge and Edwards, 1985). In the end, therefore, the union movement was forced to accept a substantial cut in real wages (see table 9.2) and the suspension of wage bargaining for almost three years. The humiliation of this defeat was compounded in late 1983 when the National Government, despite vigorous union opposition, enacted legislation making union membership voluntary. This substantially reduced the level of unionization during 1984, most notably in the service sector. Such experiences made the concept of a wage accord or Social Contract — perhaps along the lines of that negotiated across the Tasman in 1983 or in Britain in the mid 1970s — a much more attractive proposition than might otherwise have been the case.

Table 9.2
New Zealand: Prices, wages and unemployment, 1981-85

Calendar year	Consumers Price Index	Nominal weekly wage rates[a]	Average ordinary time weekly earnings	Real weekly earnings[b]	Unemployment rate[c]
	Annual change (%)	Annual change (%)	Annual change (%)	Annual change (%)	(%)
1981	15.7	19.4	20.1	3.8	3.6
1982	15.3	11.8	11.0	-3.7	3.5
1983	3.6	0.3	2.4	-1.2	5.4
1984	9.4	2.3	4.0	-4.9	5.0
1985	15.3	9.2	12.2	-2.6	3.7

Notes: a Rates within the jurisdiction of all determining authorities.
           b This measures changes in average ordinary time weekly earnings deflated by the Consumers Price Index.
           c Registered unemployment as a percentage of the total workforce, March year.
Sources: Monthly Abstract of Statistics (various issues); and *Labour and Employment Gazette* (various issues).

Paradoxically, at the very time when the union movement was becoming more favourably disposed to the idea of a negotiated incomes policy, the opposite trend was apparent amongst employers and the Government's economic advisers, particularly those in the Treasury. During the 1970s both the Employers Federation and the Treasury strongly advocated direct governmental intervention to restrain nominal wage growth (Boston, 1984, pp.80-84). By the early-to-mid 1980s, however, attitudes had changed significantly. In part, the growing challenge to the wisdom and efficacy of incomes policies merely reflected the rise of neoconservative political and economic doctrines in the West, and the related shift in thinking on the major questions of economic management. But it was also a direct response to the economic policy failures in New Zealand during the 1970s and early 1980s. In particular, it was evident that, notwithstanding repeated State intervention in the process of wage and price fixing, inflation had remained stubbornly high (in excess of ten per cent since 1973) and unemployment has risen substantially (from less than one per cent of the workforce in 1975 to more than five per cent in 1983). Moreover, some of the incomes policies implemented during this period appeared to have compounded the problems of economic management: the "stickiness" of relative wages (especially award rates) seemed to have been intensified; the costly side payments which had sometimes been granted to placate organized interests had exacerbated the fiscal deficit; and on occasions the wage controls had sparked considerable industrial unrest (Boston, 1984, pp.282-302). Such considerations led the Treasury to oppose the National Government's wage and price freeze in 1982 and to adopt a cautious, if not negative, attitude towards the various proposals for wage guidelines and voluntary incomes policies which were advanced during the mid 1980s (Treasury, 1984, pp.242-243). For various reasons the Employers Federation supported the wage freeze. Since the election, however, it has argued strongly for a major overhaul of the industrial relations framework and an end to State intervention in wage fixing (New Zealand Employers Federation, 1986).

The Labour Party, Incomes Policy and the Economic Context in 1984

Prior to 1973 the Labour Party consistently opposed the idea of statutory wage controls and instead favoured free collective bargaining within the then established framework of State-funded and sanctioned conciliation and arbitration. Hence, the party leadership attacked the wage controls introduced by the National Government in 1971 (see table 9.1) and vowed to abolish them if elected. This commitment was fulfilled when the party attained office in December 1972, and for the first seven months of 1973 the country reverted to a relatively free wage fixing regime. However, by early August 1973 there was evidence of a wage explosion occurring and, having failed to secure the co-operation of the FOL, the new Government reluctantly broke its election promise and reimposed statutory controls. From this juncture the party leadership remained in favour of an incomes policy, preferably of a voluntary rather than statutory variety, until the mid 1980s. In this respect Labour's policy stance was broadly in keeping with that of social democratic movements elsewhere in the West, such as Australia, Austria, Britain, Scandinavia and West Germany.

Of course not all members of the party endorsed such a position. On the contrary, a large section of the rank-and-file membership, especially those with trade union connections, opposed the idea of an incomes policy, whatever its shape or character. Similarly, as the 1980s advanced, certain elements within the parliamentary party began to question both the economic rationale for, and actual feasibility of, a wages deal with the union movement. This scepticism did not, however, become a major factor in the policy equation until after the 1984 election. Instead, the Labour Party centred its election campaign around the need for a consensus approach to decision making and the desirability of a comprehensive, negotiated incomes policy. According to the 1984 *Policy Document* such a policy would:

(a) Establish permanent and formal machinery for income determination, including major participation from trade unions, employers and government. Full economic information would be provided to all parties.

(b) Provide for annual wage adjustments aimed at maintaining real disposable incomes – taking into account changes in taxation, increases in productivity and the social wage provided by way of government assistance for such matters as health benefits.

(c) Allow for collective bargaining, within guidelines between employers and trade unions (New Zealand Labour Party, 1984, p.15).

Despite the centrality of an incomes policy to Labour's economic strategy it was obvious from the *Policy Document* that few of the details had been worked out in advance. For example, it was unclear whether the provision for "annual wage adjustments" meant merely that wage bargaining would occur on an annual basis, subject to certain agreed constraints, or that there would be a return to a two-tier system of wage determination as had operated between 1977 and 1981 involving general wage orders *and* collective bargaining. If the latter method was envisaged, then it was uncertain whether the general wage orders would be determined by the Government or by an independent tribunal such as the Arbitration Court. Furthermore, some of the stated policy objectives were not altogether consistent. It would be difficult, for example, to strengthen the protection offered by the national award system while at the same time encouraging bargaining flexibility. Interestingly, this vagueness on policy specifics was in marked contrast to the position in Australia where the ALP had negotiated a comprehensive and very detailed economic accord with the Australian Confederation of Trade Unions *prior* to the general election in early 1983.

The lack of clarity and specificity was all the more surprising given the economic circumstances of 1984. To start with, there was the problem of making a transition from the wage freeze to a less rigidly controlled wage fixing environment. By the time of the election the freeze had been in force for more than two years and many awards had not been renegotiated since late 1981. This represented the most protracted freeze on wages in New Zealand's history, indeed one of the longest anywhere in the Western world in peace time. Since mid-1982 the only pay increase received by wage and salary earners (i.e. excluding pay rises as a result of promotions, breaches of the Wage Freeze Regulations, and the few exceptions granted by the Wage Freeze Authority) occurred in early April 1984 when the Government issued a general wage order of NZ$8 a week (an increase in ordinary time weekly earnings of 2.9 per cent on average). The absence of any significant wage increases for more than two years, coupled with comprehensive price controls, led to a dramatic fall in the rate of wage and price inflation. As table 9.2 shows, average ordinary time weekly earnings, which had been rising at an annual rate in excess of 20 per cent in 1981, rose by only 2.4 per cent in the year to December 1983. Likewise, whereas prices had risen by 17 per cent in the year to June 1982, a year later the annual rate was 8.3 per cent, and by March 1984 a mere 3.4 per cent — one of the lowest rates in the OECD. The fact that wage inflation declined more rapidly than price inflation, especially during the first year of the freeze, brought a substantial fall in real wages. For example, real average ordinary time weekly earnings fell by 4.8 per cent in the two years to December 1983.

As table 9.3 indicates the path of real disposable incomes was somewhat different. Most groups maintained their position during the first two years of the freeze, largely as a result of the substantial tax cuts introduced in October 1982. By late 1984, however, real disposable incomes were failing rapidly. This was due primarily to the 20 per cent currency devaluation in July and the lifting of the price freeze. In these circumstances it was only a matter of time before the union movement demanded large, compensatory pay increases.

This was not the only problem generated by the freeze. the lengthy suspension of wage bargaining meant that most groups had accumulated long bargaining agendas which would have to be addressed once negotiations were permitted again (e.g. the resolution of pay anomalies, the restructuring of awards to accommodate changes in technology and job content, improvements in working conditions, and new or improved fringe benefits). Added to this, by mid-1984 there were growing shortages of skilled labour in both the public and private sectors. This was due partly to the strong upturn in economic activity which had commenced in mid-1983 and partly to the loss of skilled workers overseas, most notably to Australia.[2] No doubt a contributing factor to the net migration loss was the decline in real wages resulting from the freeze. If skill shortages were to be reduced, substantial pay increases would be necessary. Yet if particular groups were granted large rises there was a danger that increases of an equivalent magnitude would flow on to the remainder of the labour force by means of historic relativity relationships and union pressure.

Table 9.3
Real disposable income, 1982-86[a]

Calendar year	Quintile fraction of full-time wage and salary earners[b] First (lowest 20%)	Second	Third	Fourth	Fifth (highest 20%)	All full-time wage and salary earners	Households of full-time wage and salary earners
			Percentage change from previous quarter				
1982 Mar.	0.4	0.2	0.0	-0.2	-0.3	0.0	0.0
June	-0.7	-0.4	-1.2	-1.1	-1.0	-1.0	-1.1
Sept.	-3.8	-4.3	-4.0	-4.1	-4.1	-4.0	-3.7
Dec.	-0.6	0.7	2.0	5.8	13.8	6.1	5.4
1983 Mar.	0.7	1.0	0.7	1.0	0.7	0.9	0.9
June	-0.7	-0.9	-0.8	-0.8	-0.6	-0.8	-0.8
Sept.	-1.7	-1.9	-1.6	-1.7	-1.6	-1.7	-1.6
Dec.	0.9	1.0	1.2	0.4	-0.1	0.5	0.4
1984 Mar.	0.9	1.7	1.0	1.5	1.3	1.3	1.2
June	0.7	-0.1	-0.3	-0.8	-1.3	-0.6	-0.6
Sept.	-3.2	-3.4	-3.2	-3.3	-3.4	-3.3	-3.1
Dec.	-1.9	-1.9	-2.0	-1.7	-1.7	-1.9	-1.8
1985 Mar.	2.4	-0.3	-1.4	-1.4	-1.5	-0.8	0.3
June	-1.7	-2.2	-1.6	-1.7	-2.3	-2.0	-2.0
Sept.	-2.6	-2.4	-2.2	-2.2	-2.4	-2.3	-2.1
Dec.	0.4	0.2	0.6	0.9	0.4	0.4	0.4
1986 Mar.	3.3	3.2	4.2	4.6	3.2	3.7	3.6
June	2.7(P)	2.6(P)	2.9(P)	3.0(P)	1.7(P)	2.4(P)	2.3(P)
			Percentage change from same quarter of the previous year				
1982 Mar.	-1.2	-1.8	-2.3	-3.3	-3.8	-2.8	-2.8
June	-2.1	-2.5	-3.7	-4.1	-4.3	-3.7	-3.7
Sept.	-5.5	-6.0	-6.7	-6.9	-7.1	-6.7	-6.4
Dec.	-4.6	-3.8	-3.3	0.2	7.8	0.8	0.3
1983 Mar.	-4.3	-3.0	-2.6	1.4	8.9	1.7	1.2
June	-4.4	-3.5	-2.2	1.7	9.3	1.9	1.5
Sept.	-2.3	-1.0	0.2	4.2	12.1	4.4	3.8
Dec.	-0.7	-0.7	-0.6	-1.1	-1.6	-1.1	-1.1
1984 Mar.	-0.5	0.1	-0.3	-0.6	-1.0	-0.7	-0.8
June	0.9	0.7	0.2	-0.6	-1.7	-0.5	-0.6
Sept.	-0.6	-0.8	-1.4	-2.2	-3.5	-2.1	-2.1
Dec.	-3.4	-3.7	-4.4	-4.3	-5.0	-4.4	-4.2
1985 Mar.	-2.1	-5.6	-6.8	-7.0	-7.7	-6.4	-5.1
June	-4.4	-7.6	-8.0	-7.8	-8.7	-7.8	-6.4
Sept.	-3.8	-6.7	-7.1	-6.8	-7.7	-6.8	-5.5
Dec.	-1.5	-4.6	-4.7	-4.3	-5.7	-4.6	-3.4
1986 Mar.	-0.6	-1.3	0.8	1.5	-1.2	-0.2	-0.2
June	3.8(P)	3.5(P)	5.5(P)	6.3(P)	2.9(P)	4.3(P)	4.2(P)

Source: Department of Statistics
Notes: a After-tax income from all sources in dollars of constant (1980-81) purchasing
            power with respect to the regimen of the Consumers Price Index. Indexes relate to
            midpoint of the quarter.
         b Persons working 30 or more hours per week for wages and/or salary, and whose
            principal source of income is wages and salaries.
         P = Provisional estimate.

In Search of an Accord

It was clear, then, on the eve of the snap election that the avoidance of a post-freeze
wage explosion would represent a major challenge for the incoming Government. In
the event, the magnitude of the task proved even greater than expected. The newly
elected Administration discovered within hours of the polls closing that it had
inherited a currency crisis and that a large devaluation was unavoidable. If the
benefits of this devaluation – in terms of improved international competitiveness –
were to be preserved it would be necessary for the vast bulk of the workforce to
accept a further period of real-wage restraint. Inevitably this meant that the task of
securing an agreement with the union movement would be all the harder, and the
dangers of failure all the greater.

   One of the first decisions of the new Government was to extend the wage freeze
for about four months to give it time to fashion a mutually acceptable policy.
During this period extensive consultations were held with the FOL and the Employers Federation and an Economic Summit Conference was organized to explore
the policy options and secure the support of various sector groups for the
Government's post-devaluation economic strategy.

   The reaction of the trade union movement to the new political environment was
mixed. On the one hand, union leaders having worked hard for a change of
Government were eager to co-operate with the new Prime Minister and his
Cabinet. They welcomed the opportunity to participate more fully in the process of
policy formulation. They looked forward to the lifting of the wage freeze. And they
keenly awaited legislation to repeal the *Industrial Relations Amendment Act 1983*
under which the National Government had introduced voluntary unionism. Such
legislation was duly enacted in 1985: the *Industrial Relations Amendment Act 1985
No.1* (see Hodge, 1985b, pp.157-161). On the other hand, union leaders resented the
lack of consultation during the currency crisis and were worried by the economic
direction being charted by the new Minister of Finance, Roger Douglas, and his
Associate Ministers, David Caygill and Richard Prebble: the commitment to
orthodox monetary and fiscal policies; the emphasis on efficiency and market forces;
the proposed changes in tax policy (see Chapter 10); and the apparent lack of
importance being attached to questions of equity and social justice. These tensions
between the political and industrial wings of the labour movement intensified

during 1985/86 as the nature and magnitude of the Government's economic reforms became clear. Of particular concern was the Government's decision in early March 1985 to float the New Zealand dollar (see Chapter 8), the commercialization and corporatization of the the public sector (see Chapters 6 and 7) and the proposals to reform public and private sector wage fixing announced in late 1986. More will be said about this last matter later in this chapter.

It was against this background that negotiations over a post-freeze wages policy took place. From the outset it was evident that there were two major issues to address: firstly, what should be the shape of the wage fixing system in the medium-to-long term; and secondly, how could a smooth transition to such a system be effected and a post-freeze wage blow-out avoided.

The Wage Fixing Framework

With respect to the long-term issues, the Government was assisted by the work already undertaken by the Long-Term Reform Committee, a tripartite body established by the National Government in early 1983. By March 1984 the Committee had hammered out a tentative, compromise agreement on the basic structure of a post-freeze system of wage determination (Long-Term Reform Committee, 1984a). However, no final agreement had been reached prior to the change of Government partly because of the FOL's unwillingness to be seen co-operating publicly with the Muldoon Administration during an election year. Following the election, the new Government reconvened the Committee, and after about a month of debate, a "Statement of Understanding" was agreed upon. This was announced publicly during the Economic Summit in mid-September. The basic elements of the agreed package were as follows:

(a) A return to collective bargaining and annual wage rounds under a system of arbitration and conciliation;

(b) The establishment of a Tripartite Wage Conference. This would meet prior to each wage round to consider the economic context, examine the position of the lower paid, and explore the desirability of negotiating a wage guideline. It would include representatives of the Employers Federation, the FOL/Combined State Unions, and the Government;

(c) Changes to the operation of the Arbitration Court including a new system of voluntary arbitration and the introduction of market-oriented criteria to guide the Court's deliberations; and

(d) The retention of the national award system, but the encouragement of greater wage flexibility through the development of industry and enterprise-based bargaining (Hodge, 1985a, pp.31-32; Long-Term Reform Committee, 1984b).

Legislation giving effect to the proposed changes (the Industrial Relations Amendment Bill) was introduced in Parliament in early November 1984, and was passed through all its stages before the end of the year, thereby enabling bargaining to begin under the revised ground rules.

The new wage fixing system combined elements of both corporatist and neoconservative thinking. In keeping with the Government's emphasis on flexibility and market forces, there was encouragement for more decentralized (i.e. plant and enterprise-based) wage bargaining and a move away from the relativity-driven national award system. This desire for greater wage flexibility was highlighted further by the various modifications to the Arbitration Court and the absence of any provision for the Court to issue general wage orders. Yet, at the same time, the new arrangements did not involve a shift to a highly decentralized and voluntaristic pattern of wage determination as practised, for example, in Britain and the United States. For one thing, a basic component of the existing system, namely, national awards with blanket coverage, was retained. For another, the new provisions required that tripartite consultations occur before each wage round. The main purpose of such consultations, at least from the perspective of the Government, was to provide a regular forum through which the central organizations of labour and capital could be informed about the state of the economy, the nature of the Government's economic strategy and the overall level of nominal wage growth consistent with this strategy. In other words, it supplied an opportunity for sharing information, shaping expectations and attempting to build a consensus.

There was also provision for the parties to negotiate a wage guideline, if this were deemed to be mutually desirable. Hence, the new system could readily accommodate a formal bilateral or tripartite wage accord — perhaps along the lines of the British Social Contract of the mid 1970s — should there be sufficient support for such a concept. On the other hand, it was consistent with the new arrangements for a Government to reject the idea of pay guidelines, managed wage rounds and central co-ordination and pursue a very different economic strategy — regardless of union and employer views. Thus, the new wage fixing system was open-ended. What kind of policy emerged in any particular year would depend on the attitudes and objectives of the various parties.

Transitional Arrangements

Whilst agreement on the character of the post-freeze wage fixing system was achieved relatively quickly, the same was not the case with respect to the question of appropriate transitional arrangements. For its part, the FOL favoured a package of proposals including: an immediate general wage order of NZ$15 a week (about five per cent for those on the average wage); a six-month period during which wages would be indexed to the consumer price index; a special "anomalies round" to resolve some of the serious problems caused by the freeze; and a delay in the resumption of normal wage negotiations until mid-1985. The aim of this package was to preserve real wages in the aftermath of the devaluation, and overcome the principal areas of tension in the bargaining arena before the new wage fixing system was put to the test.

Neither the Government nor the Employers Federation accepted this approach. The Government opposed the idea of a general wage order on the grounds that it would do little to ease the transition process, it would do nothing to reduce the rigidity of relative wages, and it would lead to an unacceptable rise in nominal wages, particularly if granted in the context of an anomalies round. Similarly, the principle of wage indexation was rejected because of its potentially inflationary consequences. Finally, the idea of an anomalies round found little favour because of the difficulties of determining what constituted a special case or a serious anomaly. Instead, the Government argued that an early return to wage bargaining would be best. To avoid a free-for-all, however, Ministers acknowledged the need for continued restraints, and hence favoured a "managed" wage round preferably achieved by means of a negotiated wage guideline.

In order to facilitate such an agreement lengthy consultations took place, including a series of formal tripartite meetings in November. Some progress was made at these talks. For example, the parties agreed upon a set of rules to govern the conduct of the wage round. These provided that:

(a) All existing awards and collective agreements would have their term extended to 38 months, subject to the condition that no document expired before 1 December 1984 or after 1 March 1985;

(b) Award negotiations would be compressed into a four-month period between 3 December and 31 March, with the period for conciliation restricted to three days for major awards, and one or two days for less important negotiations. (This provision, it was hoped, would limit the scope of negotiations and reduce the likelihood of unions taking industrial action in pursuit of their claims.);

(c) The major trend-setting documents, such as the Metal Trades Award, the Electrical Contractors Award and the General Drivers Award, would be negotiated, as usual, at the beginning of the wage round; and

(d) The minimum term of new wage agreements would be nine months rather than the normal 12 months. This would enable negotiations for the 1985/86 wage round, and all subsequent wage rounds, to commence early in the spring as had become customary during the 1970s (New Zealand Employers Federation, 1986, pp.85-87).

But on the vital question of a wage guideline, there was no consensus. Initially, the Employers Federation wanted a two per cent guideline, the Government one of four per cent, and the FOL/Combined State Unions one of 11.2 per cent. By the end of November, just prior to the start of the wage round, there was still a substantial gap. The Government, with the tacit support of the employers, had moved its position to 4.75 per cent, while the FOL/Combined State Unions were seeking 9.6 per cent. The FOL/Combined State Unions indicated a willingness to accept a lower figure than this, but only in return for various concessions. Since these were unacceptable to the Government, Ministers declared a unilateral guideline of four to five per cent and wage negotiations commenced for the first time in almost three years.

The 1984/85 Wage Round

Conciliation talks involving the main trend-setting bargaining groups such as the engineers, drivers, electricians, printers and freezing workers began on 3 December 1984 as scheduled. Towards the end of the three days allocated for these negotiations the parties were still some distance apart: the unions involved were demanding at least seven per cent while the employers were offering no more than 5.5 per cent. At this stage a series of high level discussions took place involving a number of senior Ministers, Government officials and key union and employer advocates. As a result, an agreement was reached late in the evening of 5 December with respect to the Metal Trades and General Drivers Awards. This provided for:

(a) The incorporation of the NZ$8.00 per week general wage order of 1 April 1984 into hourly rates;

(b) An increase in hourly rates and allowances for the 1984/85 round of 6.5 per cent at the mid point of the wage scale and a restoration of previous relativities. (This meant, for example, that the lowest rates in the Metal Trades Award were raised by 6.1 per cent while tradesmen received 7.02 percent.); and

(c) A term of ten months, rather than the nine-month term previously agreed upon during the tripartite discussions (New Zealand Employers Federation, 1986, pp.90-91).

As expected, pay increases of a similar amount were agreed upon soon afterwards by the parties to the Electrical Contractors Award and the 6.5 per cent figure became the unofficial guideline for the remainder of the wage round. As table 9.4 shows, of the 115 non-state linked awards settled up to 22 February 1985, 100 (or roughly 87 per cent) involved increases in basic rates of between 6.0 per cent and 7.5 per cent. This tendency for subsequent pay settlements to mirror closely the increases negotiated in the lead awards followed the pattern established between 1977 and 1982.

It would be wrong, however, to over-emphasize the degree of uniformity which occurred during the 1984/85 round. First, most workers received pay increases marginally higher than those negotiated in the key awards, particularly those groups settling towards the end of the round. Second, a number of important bargaining groups, largely through the exercise of industrial action, secured rises well above the going rate. For example, hotel workers won an increase of 8.4 per cent together with improved allowances, and brewery maintenance tradesmen (after a lengthy stoppage) gained increases totalling about 16 per cent. Third, with the lifting of the wage freeze there was a substantial rise in the remuneration of top executives, senior managers, accountants and many other groups whose skills were in short supply.[3]

Finally, despite efforts by the Employers Federation, there was a significant increase in second-tier bargaining, especially in the Auckland region where labour shortages were severe in a number of trades (Kirk, 1985, pp.1-2; New Zealand Employers Federation, 1986, pp.92-97). This meant that many workers received wage increases well in excess of the going rate. Among such groups were those involved in the forestry industry, food processing, car assembly, carpet manufacturing, and the steel industry (New Zealand Employers Federation, 1986, pp.92-97).

Table 9.4
Award settlements in 1984/85 wage round[a]

Percentage movement	No of settlements	%
Under 6	1	0.7
6.01-6.5	45	33.1
6.51-7.0	14	10.3
7.01-7.5	41	30.1
7.51-8.0	4	2.9
8.01-8.5	2	1.5
8.51-9.0	1	0.7
9.01-9.5	2	1.5
9.51-10.0	4	2.9
Over 10.0	1	0.7
State linked	21	15.4
Total	136	100.0

Notes: a Award settlements up to 22 February 1985.
Source: Hansard, Vol. 462, 22 March 1985, p.3973.

Partly as a result of these developments, average earnings rose more rapidly than basic award rates. For example, whereas award rates moved on average by 7.9 per cent in the year to September 1985, average total weekly earnings rose by 9.9 per cent and average ordinary time hourly earnings by 10.3 per cent. This was higher than the Government had hoped, but it was not surprising given the economic circumstances: skill shortages; rapid economic growth (gross domestic product grew by 6.3 per cent in the year to 31 March 1985; an accelerating rate of inflation; a large Budget deficit; and an unexpectedly loose monetary policy. Moreover, despite the increase in earnings of roughly ten per cent, both real wages and real disposable incomes continued to decline (see tables 9.2 and 9.3) This fall in living standards undoubtedly contributed to the rise in rank-and-file militancy experienced during 1985/86.

The Background to the 1985/86 Wage Round

In formulating a suitable policy stance for the 1985/86 wage round the Government was influenced by various considerations. Firstly, for economic and political reasons

Ministers wanted to reduce the inflation rate quickly to a level comparable with that of New Zealand's main trading partners (i.e. less than five per cent). To achieve this wage settlements would have to be well below the 16.6 per cent rate of inflation in the year to June 1985, preferably in the vicinity of ten per cent. Second, if the process of structural change initiated in mid-1984 was to be effective and if the adjustment costs — in terms of higher unemployment and lost output — were to be minimized, then it was desirable for relative wages to respond to changing market conditions. This meant that the dispersion of award settlements and second-tier agreements would need to be greater than had been the pattern during the previous wage round. And this implied that a wage guideline would be undesirable. In any case, the Government was mindful, given the experiences of the 1984/85 wage round, that a guideline would be difficult to negotiate and probably even harder to enforce. Lange has emphasized this point on several occasions:

> We discovered very early on in the piece that you can't do trades there — because the parties have to impose the outcome on their members ... I tell you the Government could honour a trade, but I am certain the union movement and Employers Federation would not *(National Business Review,* 11 July 1986, p.20).

For these reasons, the concept of a guideline found little favour amongst Ministers and their advisers.

But how, then, did the Government believe that the average level of settlements during the 1985/86 wage round could be kept significantly below the prevailing rate of inflation? It appears that senior Ministers were influenced by a number of arguments (Boston, 1985a, pp.76-77). First, the economic downturn which had begun to take hold in the rural sector was thought likely to alter the relative bargaining strength of unions and employers and hence reduce the possibility of a wage explosion. Second, the Government's policies to deregulate the economy, encourage competition and liberalize trade were expected to increase the resistance of employers to large wage claims. Third, it was thought that the reforms to the wage fixing system in late 1984, in particular the introduction of voluntary arbitration, would have a moderating influence on the average level of award settlements. Fourth, Ministers doubted predictions that there would be a rise in rank-and-file militancy as had occurred in roughly similar circumstances in Britain (1978/79) and Australia (1981/82). Fifth, it was hoped that union leaders out of loyalty to the Government would use their discretionary power to ensure restraint. Finally, it appears that the Cabinet was persuaded by Treasury arguments to the effect that as long as the Government pursued a firm, non-accommodating monetary policy and as long as this policy was deemed to be credible by pay negotiators, then wage inflation would be restrained. In other words, it was assumed that if the unions and employers believed that high wage settlements would result in greater unemployment and lower real output growth, they would modify their settlements accordingly. This line of reasoning — sometimes referred to as the "credibility hypothesis" — had much in common with the economic strategy adopted by the Thatcher Government (see Buiter and Miller, 1983). It was somewhat strange, therefore, that despite the evidence available from the British experiment and the manifold theoretical flaws in the credibility hypothesis (Llewellyn, 1980; Perry, 1983; Schelling, 1982; Taylor, 1982) a Labour Government in New Zealand should have resurrected these arguments and employed them with such vigour. The puzzle grows further when one remembers the difficulties which Ministers experienced during 1985 in gaining control over the various monetary aggregates (see Keenan, 1986).

The Tripartite Wage Conference which met between 20 May and 18 August 1985 achieved little. The sessions began with the Government indicating that its macroeconomic policies would be "consistent with nominal growth in national income of the order of 10-3 percent in 1985/86, falling to around 7-9 per cent in 1986/87" (Treasury, 1985, p.13). It further assumed that award rates during the 1985/86 wage round would increase by ten per cent, with wage drift on top of this of about two per cent. Although it was emphasized that these figures were predictive, rather than prescriptive, it was evident that wage increases of about this magnitude were expected and desired by Ministers and their advisers. Both the FOL/Combined State Unions and the Employers Federation responded negatively to the Government's approach. The FOL/Combined State Unions rejected the proposition that inflation could be controlled in the short run solely through monetary instruments and claimed that wage negotiators would be little influenced by the Government's threats not to accommodate a high wage round. Instead they argued for a "broadly-based incomes policy" involving restraints on prices, profits, rents, dividends, and the incomes of the self-employed (Federation of Labour/Combined State Unions, 1985, p.3). They also dismissed the Government's indicative guideline of ten to 12 per cent as too low, called on Ministers to "manage" the exchange rate, and demanded a large increase in the statutory minimum wage (from $100 to $208 a week).

But in terms of a specific strategy for the 1985/86 wage round the union movement was divided. Initially, there was some support for a general wage order prior to the round to reduce the likely pressures on negotiators and maintain living standards. However, as in late 1984 this suggestion was rejected by the Government on the grounds that it would exacerbate, rather than reduce, bargaining pressures and the overall movement of wages. On the vital question of a guideline there was no agreement amongst union leaders. Some favoured a guideline, assuming it was sufficiently high, in the belief that it would ensure a reasonable uniformity of settlements and thereby assist low-paid groups lacking bargaining power. Others, however, thought that a guideline would be unduly restrictive. Because of this division of opinion, the FOL/Combined State Unions did not press for a guideline during the tripartite talks.

The Employers Federation shared the union movement's assessment that the pursuit of a tight, non-accommodating monetary policy would be insufficient to prevent higher wage and price inflation in the short term (New Zealand Employers Federation, 1985, p.10). Indeed, employers were fearful that without Government intervention or an agreed guideline there would be a pay explosion. Hence, when it became apparent that no guideline would be forthcoming, the Federation called for a postponement of the wage round until major reforms had been made to the industrial relations framework. This proposal was firmly rejected by the Government. At the end of the Tripartite Wage Conference in mid-August, therefore, the views of the parties remained widely divergent. The Government and the Employers Federation wanted a moderate wage round in the ten to 12 per cent range and much greater wage flexibility. By contrast, the union movement wanted to preserve the national award system, improve the relative position of the lower paid, and halt the fall in real wages. In the event, the only gain made by the unions during the Tripartite Wage Conference was an increase in the legal minimum wage. This was raised $70 to $170 a week, the first significant increase for a decade. Five awards were affected by the move.

The 1985/86 Wage Round

Any hopes that the Government had of securing a moderate wage round were dashed in early September 1985 when the Higher Salaries Commission announced massive pay increases for those under its jurisdiction. The Commission's Report, the first in four years, gave rises of 30 to 37 per cent, backdated to 1 April 1985 (Higher Salaries Commission, 1985). For example, the Prime Minister's basic salary was increased by 37 per cent to NZ$117,500 per annum (or NZ$142,000 including allowances). Such increases, which were based largely on movements in the remuneration of senior executives within the private sector since 1981, had a significant effect on pay expectations and as a direct result many unions revised their wage claims upwards. Although the Government criticized the Commission and complained about the timing of the Report, it rejected advice to pass retrospective legislation altering the Commission's determinations. From this point onwards, it was plain that pay settlements would be well above the Government's target range of ten to 12 per cent.

The main features of the 1985/86 wage round can be summarized as follows. To begin with, there was a major escalation in industrial unrest in both the public and private sectors with a substantial increase in the number of stoppages, the number of workers involved, and the duration of strike action (see table 9.5).[4] As a result, the number of working days lost from industrial stoppages reached the highest level since the waterfront strike in 1951. This put New Zealand in the unenviable position, albeit temporarily, of being one of the most strike prone countries in the

Western world. An interesting feature was the extent to which normally passive groups either threatened to, or actually took, industrial action. In addition to traditionally more militant groups, such as engineers, drivers, carpenters, labourers, meat workers and timber workers, there were strikes by bank officers, clerical workers, journalists, cleaners, teachers, traffic officers and laboratory workers, to name but a few. Another notable feature was the protracted nature of some of the disputes. For those familiar with the British scene, such events were reminiscent of the "winter of discontent" in 1978/79. On that occasion the union movement, by means of widespread industrial action, broke the Labour Government's five per cent pay guideline and achieved settlements averaging three times this figure (Dorfman, 1983, pp.59-91). Significant in both situations was the lack of restraint exercised by the union leadership and the unwillingness of the Government to stand firm in the face of threatened industrial action by its own employees.

Table 9.5
Industrial stoppages in New Zealand 1960-86

Calendar year	Stoppages[a]	Workers involved ('000)[b]	Working days lost ('000)[b]
1960-1970 av.	130	37	106
1970-1980 av.	412	121	303
1979[c]	523	158	382
1980[d]	360	128	373
1981	291	135	388
1982	333	156	330
1983	333	141	372
1984	364	160	425
1985	384	183	759
1986[e]	90	56	1021

Notes: a The number of stoppages includes both partial and complete stoppages and lock-outs. The number of lockouts were: 1979 (2); 1981 (2); 1982 (4); 1983 (1); 1985 (2).

b Excludes workers indirectly involved.

c Excludes the General Strike on 20 September 1979.

d Since 1980 work stoppages involving a demand on a third party (rather than an employer) or which did not involve terms or conditions of employment have been included in the statistics.

e Five months to the end of May 1986.

Source: Monthly Abstract of Statistics (May 1986)

The pattern of settlements in the private sector during 1985/86 was broadly similar to the previous round: the main trend-setting awards were amongst the first to be negotiated giving increases in basic rates of at least 15.5 per cent; over 70 per cent of subsequent awards settled within one per cent of this figure (see table 9.6); and, as in 1984/5, there was a tendency for settlement levels to creep up slightly as the round progressed. Yet there were also some important differences. Whereas in

1984 the going rate had been established by the Metal Trades Award and the General Drivers Award, in 1985 it was the Electrical Contractors Award which set the pace. The initial settlement of 15.5 per cent, which was reached on 27 September, could have been even higher had it not been for threats from senior Ministers to impose wage controls if employers granted rises of 16 per cent or more.

Table 9.6
Award settlements in the 1985/86 wage round[a]

Percentage movement	No of settlements	%
14.0–14.49	1	0.4
14.5–14.99	1	0.4
15.0–15.49	4	1.7
15.5–15.99	131	55.7
16.0–16.49	30	12.8
16.5–17.50	26	11.1
Over 17.5	30	12.8
State linked	12	5.1
Total	235	100.0

Notes: a Award settlements up to 7 May 1986.
Source: Employers Federation Wage Settlement Report Summary for 1985-86 Wage Round.

Another difference from 1984/85 was the extra importance attached to allowances by union negotiators. For example, carpenters secured a new industry allowance of $1 an hour on top of their general rise of 15.5 per cent. Large pay increases were also secured by various low-paid groups. Among notable settlements were: general cleaners (30.1 per cent – arbitrated), private hospital domestics (22 per cent), school cleaners (21.5 per cent), and tearoom and restaurant employees (19 per cent). Not all lower paid workers fared as well, and no significant narrowing of skill differentials occurred.

In contrast to 1984/85, second-tier bargaining was less marked during the 1985/86 round. There were a number of reasons for this (New Zealand Employers Federation, 1986, p.102). Given the high level of most award increases few employers were in a position to make additional concessions. Further, several key awards, such as the Metal Trades Award, included "pass-on" memoranda forbidding second-tier bargaining as long as employers moved paid rates in line with award rate increases. Finally, one of the important objectives of the union movement during the 1985/86 round was to preserve the integrity of the national award system. For this to be realized, second-tier bargaining had to be restrained.

The other major difference from 1984/85 related to developments in the public sector. As often happens during a lengthy period of wage controls, public sector pay rates fell behind corresponding rates in the private sector during the freeze (see Fallick and Elliott, 1981, pp.100-127). This situation was exacerbated in 1984/85 when most public sector rates were increased by seven per cent, somewhat less than the average movement in private sector earnings. The relative fall in public sector pay, together with the rapid economic growth during 1983-85, led to a substantial loss of personnel from the state sector.[5] Thus, by the start of the 1985/86 wage round serious staff shortages had emerged throughout the public sector and it was evident that large pay increases would be necessary to stem the flow. As matters transpired, most public servants obtained rises of at least 20 per cent, with some groups gaining substantially more: nurses (31 to 38.5 per cent), police (about 30 per cent), teachers (about 23 to 35 per cent) and the armed forces (22.7 percent on average). Overall, it is estimated that public sector pay rates rose on average by almost 25 per cent during the 1985/86 round, one of the largest annual movements in New Zealand's history. For the Government, seeking to cut the Budget deficit and curb State spending, it was a most unfortunate outcome.

To sum up, the 1985/86 round represented a major short-term victory for the union movement. The national award system remained intact. The relative position of some low-paid groups was enhanced. Employer attempts to remove work-related restrictions and encourage greater bargaining flexibility were defeated. And most workers gained a significant improvement in their living standards. For example, as table 9.3 shows, wage and salary earners in full-time employment secured an average increase in their real disposable incomes of 4.3 per cent in the year to June 1986. Against this, the large pay increases, coupled with the strengthening of the exchange rate during 1985/86, adversely affected the competitiveness of the exposed sector of the economy. This contributed to the downturn in economic activity and brought a large increase in unemployment during the middle of 1986, particularly in secondary centres.

The 1986/87 Wage Round

One of the unexpected consequences of the 1985/86 wage round was that it encouraged many employers and union leaders to give more serious consideration to the possibility of a wage accord or managed wage round in 1986/87. On the one hand, union leaders recognized that with economic activity contracting and the rural sector in a financial crisis they would not be able to secure a similarly high level of settlements; nor were the gains in real wages and real disposable incomes likely to be repeated. Moreover, there was the possibility that employers would seek to exploit the economic downturn and make a determined bid to break the national award system. Such a move, it was feared, would have a deleterious effect on the wages of poorly organized groups of workers, particularly the low paid. In these circumstances, the idea of a managed round offered the prospect of greater stability of incomes, together with the preservation of traditional relativities and bargaining structures.

On the other hand, employers were keen to avoid another wage round characterized by a high level of industrial disruption. They were also concerned that, notwithstanding the economic situation, wage settlements might be both substantial (i.e. over ten per cent) and relatively uniform. Added to this, both parties feared that the major tax reforms to be introduced on 1 October 1986 would have a destabilizing effect on wage negotiations. For example, it was estimated that the new Goods and Services Tax would raise consumer prices by at least five per cent — and this at a time when inflation remained in double digits (see Chapter 10).

The case for a managed wage round was advanced in the union movement by senior members of the FOL including Ken Douglas, Rex Jones and Rob Campbell. Although not universally supported, the concept received the broad endorsement of the FOL annual conference in May and was pursued during the Tripartite Wage Conference by the union representatives. For various reasons, however, the parties were unable to reach agreement on an acceptable formula. The FOL argued for a package of proposals including: the negotiation of a wage guideline to be applied uniformly across all industries and regions; the right for unions to engage in direct bargaining with employers over conditions of work and in order to resolve various anomalies; and the implementation of a mid-term review during the first half of 1987 (see Technical Working Party, 1986). The aim of this would be to assess the impact of GST on prices and then adjust wages so as to preserve real disposable incomes at a level comparable to that applying at the time of the election in July 1984.

By contrast, the Employers Federation rejected the idea of a single, uniform, across-the-board wage increase, arguing instead that account needed to be taken of those industries in severe economic difficulties, such as the meat industry and the rural servicing sector. Likewise, the Federation dismissed the idea of trying to maintain living standards at some arbitrary level and, although in principle not opposed to a two-stage wage increase, contended that the size of the second step would have to be determined well in advance; otherwise businesses would face additional uncertainty over their future wage costs. Finally, the Federation claimed that if a central deal was struck on an overall level of wage increases for the round, there should be no direct bargaining over conditions and non-wage matters. This meant, in effect, that normal wage bargaining would be suspended for a year.

As in previous years, therefore, the Tripartite Wage Conference broke up in August 1986 without having made much progress on the major issues under discussion. There were, however, some important differences. Although the parties remained divided on the details and application of a wage accord, unlike the situation in 1985 many employers and union leaders were still attracted to the idea. As a result, further initiatives were taken during the first week of the wage round in mid-September to find a formula satisfactory to both parties. It appears that significant progress was made during these talks. Yet at the very moment when an agreement was in sight the Government intervened and declared that the round would continue as normal. The main reason given by the Prime Minister was that the parties had failed to meet a pre-arranged deadline of 9.00am, 22 September. However, the FOL and the Employers Federation claimed that there had been no such agreed deadline and it appears that Ministers had other reasons for scuttling a wages deal. In particular, it was felt that a managed or regulated round would inhibit wage flexibility, that it would not produce a significantly lower overall level of wage increases, and that the use of regulations to enforce any central deal between the parties would put New Zealand back on the slippery path towards comprehensive economic controls. It also appears that Ministers were influenced by lobbying against a managed round by members of the Business Roundtable, Federated Farmers and a number of trade unionists, including Rob Campbell, previously an advocate of a wage accord.

The other major difference from 1985 was that expectations of the probable level of wage settlements in the forthcoming round fell substantially during the course of the 1986 Tripartite Wage Conference. Whereas in April it was expected that settlements would be in the vicinity of the rate of inflation (ten to 11 per cent), by August expectations had virtually halved. The reasons for this included: the economic downturn in the non-metropolitan centres with many plant closures and rapidly rising unemployment; the desire of the union movement to preserve the national award system and prevent greater bargaining fragmentation; the recognition that the October tax changes and the introduction of a guaranteed minimum family income would give a substantial boost to the real disposable incomes of many wage and salary earners; doubts over the willingness of workers to take strike action in pursuit of big wage claims; and evidence of growing management "militancy". In the weeks leading up to the wage round there were lockouts by employers at three large plants – the Tasman pulp and paper mill at Kawerau, the New Zealand steel expansion site at Glenbrook, and the Ford car assembly plant at Wiri. In each case the lockouts were sparked by management efforts to overcome restrictive work practices or reduce manning levels. Interestingly, this trend for employers to adopt a more confrontational industrial relations strategy is in line with developments elsewhere during the 1980s, such as Australia, Britain and the United States (Crouch, 1986, pp.8-10; Hince, 1986, pp.9-11).

The first major settlement in the 1986/87 wage round was on 7 October when the parties to the General Drivers Award agreed on a six per cent increase in wages and conditions. Significantly this settlement was well below the prevailing inflation rate of 11 per cent and less than half the expected rate (of approximately 13 to 14 per cent) in the year to September 1987. This implied an acceptance by the union of a big cut in real wages, though real disposable incomes were not anticipated to fall much because of the October tax cuts. The settlement was also notable for being the smallest increase negotiated in a major award under conditions of free wage bargaining since 1969.

At the time of writing (October 1986) it seemed likely that the 1986/87 wage round would produce average settlements in the six to eight per cent range, thereby bringing New Zealand's rate of wage inflation more into line with that of its major trading partners. One possible implication of this is that the implicit indexation of wages to prices which has characterized pay determination in New Zealand for several decades has been broken, albeit temporarily. It also suggests that real wages are not as inflexible downwards in a recession as has been generally believed. If so, then the behaviour of the New Zealand labour market in the less rigidly controlled economic environment inaugurated in 1984 may have more in common with that of the United States than often supposed, and correspondingly less in common with European countries. Further evidence will be needed, however, before definitive conclusions can be reached.

Industrial Relations Reform: A Brief Comment

Not long after the reform of the *Industrial Relations Act* in late 1984 the Government announced that it would undertake a comprehensive review of the industrial relations system in the private sector, the first such review since the early 1970s. After many months of hard work by Labour Department staff a Green Paper was published in December 1985 (New Zealand Government, 1985). This provided a detailed analysis of the existing system, and included a series of questions concerning possible future directions. Interested parties were invited to make submissions by 30 April 1986.

Altogether 188 submissions were received, the most widely publicized being those of the FOL, the Employers Federation and the Business Roundtable. The submissions revealed a wide divergence of views on the part of the union movement and the main employer groups on issues such as the role of the State in industrial relations, the appropriate framework of legal rights and privileges, the future of the national award system, the place of second-tier bargaining and the rules for union membership. For example, whereas the FOL defended the existing system of industrial conciliation and arbitration and called for only minor modifications, both the Employers Federation and the Business Roundtable argued for radical changes. In particular, they wanted the abolition of the national award system and the blanket coverage provision, more flexible, enterprise-based bargaining structures, an end to the virtual State monopoly in the provision of conciliation, mediation and arbitration services, and the restoration of voluntary unionism. Only through such reforms, it was contended, would there be the change in employee attitudes and performance incentives necessary to enhance the industrial relations environment and improve productivity.

Once all the submissions had been received a small committee of Ministers (Palmer, Rodger and Prebble) and Labour MPs (Gerbic, Isbey and Wilde) was established to prepare policy recommendations for consideration by the Cabinet. In undertaking this task the Committee was influenced by various conflicting pressures. For instance, it needed to avoid policy changes of a kind that would generate undue uncertainty, provoke widespread and intense union resistance, or permanently damage the relationship between the political and industrial wings of the labour movement. At the same time, the reforms needed to be sufficiently radical so as to undercut the National Party's campaign for labour market deregulation and to ensure that the integrity of the Government's economic strategy was not compromised by any undesirable or unjustifiable rigidities in the existing industrial relations framework. The Committee was also keen to initiate legislative changes that would assist unions to respond creatively to the new economic environment and provide more and better services to their members.

After lengthy deliberations a White Paper setting out the Government's planned reforms was published in late September (*Government Policy Statement*, 1986). A Labour Relations Bill giving effect to these changes is expected to be introduced in late 1986 and enacted in time for the 1987/88 wage round.

The main reforms outlined in the White Paper can be summarized as follows:

1. The Arbitration Court will be divided into two separate bodies, an Arbitration Commission to deal with matters connected with disputes over the fixing of wages and conditions of employment (so-called disputes of interest), and a Labour Court with sole jurisdiction over all legal matters arising out of the implementation of the new Labour Relations Act (so-called disputes of rights). The jurisdictional split is similar to that between 1973 and 1977 when there was an Industrial Commission and an Industrial Court.

2. Registration procedures, whereby a union secures the exclusive right to represent a particular category of workers, are to be retained, but in order to qualify for registration a union must have at least 1000 members. This minimum membership size is in line with the recommendations of the Hancock Committee in Australia and will effectively do away with about 150 of New Zealand's 233 unions. Another important change is the removal of one of the requirements for union amalgamation, namely that the unions in question be in "related industries". These reforms will have profound implications for the character of unions in New Zealand.

3. Another significant and also highly contentious innovation is a procedure whereby a group of workers will have the right, by means of a secret ballot, to alter their union coverage. Such a procedure, referred to as union "contestability", was rejected by the Labour Party Conference in August 1986 and the Labour Caucus. The main objection is that it will generate undesirable competition between unions for members, thereby diverting union resources away from the provision of membership services.

4. The restriction on the scope of negotiations to "industrial matters" will be removed. This means that unions and employers will be able to make their own

decisions about the proper matters for negotiation, be it the provision of child care facilities, the introduction of superannuation schemes, the term of the award, or whatever. In addition, the question of compulsory union membership will become a subject of negotiation, as was the case between 1961 and 1976. Hence, unions and employers will have the opportunity to decide whether an award or agreement requires voluntary or compulsory membership provisions. Where the parties are unable to agree the matter will be determined by a secret ballot of the workers concerned.

5. Another important change relates to the relationship between national awards and second-tier settlements. Under the new arrangements each worker will be covered by only one enforceable award or agreement. Thus, unions will be required to elect, for each group of workers covered by an award, whether their wages will be determined by the provisions of the award or by a separate agreement. At the same time the blanket coverage provision will be retained.

6. In accordance with the Government's proposals, both the costs associated with negotiations and the enforcement of awards and agreements will be the responsibility of the parties. In order to facilitate such enforcement, union representatives will be given the right to inspect wage and time records, to copy their contents, to enforce the keeping of wages and time records, and to interview any person on an employer's premises.

7. Other planned changes include the broadening of the grounds for union membership to include persons unemployed or seeking work, measures to encourage greater union democracy and the accountability of elected officials, modifications to personal grievance procedures, the amalgamation of the existing Conciliation and Mediation Services, and the removal of the power of the Minister of Labour to deregister unions.

Reactions to the White Paper were varied. Clearly many employers had hoped for even more radical changes. The Director of the Employers Federation, Jim Rowe, commented that "the Government has laboured mightily to produce a mouse" (*National Business Review*, 3 October 1986, p.14). Many union leaders also expressed serious reservations, especially with respect to the contestability provisions and the measures to dislodge second-tier arrangements from the national award system.

What implications will the proposals in the White Paper have for industrial relations in New Zealand? First, in order to fulfil the new membership requirement, and also finance the costs of negotiating and enforcing awards and agreements, the typical union will be much larger than has been the case hitherto. They will also be less regionally based and skill specific. Which unions will benefit most from the new arrangements, however, remains to be seen. Second, given the wider scope for negotiations and the contestability provisions, the character of unions will change: they will become more business-like and probably less ideologically oriented; they will provide a wider range of membership services; they will employ more legal and economic advisers; and they will become more open and democratic. Third, the radical restructuring of the Arbirtration Court is likely to reduce delays and improve access to the legal process for the resolution of disputes.

It is not clear what impact the reforms will have on the conduct of collective bargaining or the level at which bargaining occurs, be it national, regional, industry or enterprise based. Some union leaders have argued that the more powerful bargaining groups will contract out of the national award system. This will have the effect over time of reducing the relative wages of those groups left within the award system, thereby intensifying income inequalities. Moreover, it is asserted that any trend towards more decentralized bargaining arrangements is likely to be reinforced by the pressures on the labour market exerted by trade liberalization, product market deregulation and economic restructuring. Indeed, it may well be that the Government's general economic reforms will have more effect on the operation of the labour market than its specific changes to the industrial relations framework. Against this, some employers have suggested that there will be little incentive under the new procedures for bargaining groups to opt out of the national award system, partly because of the added risks associated with such a strategy. Consequently, no significant expansion of enterprise-based bargaining is probable. In fact, there is the possibility that the new arrangements will merely intensify the existing rigidities. Until the reforms outlined in the White Paper have been implemented there will be no way of determining which view is correct.

Conclusion

Since the early-to-mid 1970s New Zealand has experienced low productivity growth, low real-wage growth, relatively high rates of wage and price inflation, rising unemployment and historically high levels of industrial unrest. In July 1984 the Labour Government embarked on a comprehensive package of economic reforms designed to rectify these problems. As noted in this chapter, the strategy adopted has not been entirely consistent with that heralded in the party's election manifesto. In particular, the Government has abandoned any quest for an incomes policy or a system of centralized wage fixing, arguing instead for less State inter-vention in wage determination and greater flexibility in the operation of the labour market in both the private and public sectors.

Judging by the short-term consequences of this approach, there is little to commend it: as predicted there was a post-freeze wage explosion, albeit delayed by the willingness of the unions to exercise restraint during the 1984/85 wage round; there was a big increase in industrial unrest during 1985/86 with the number of working days lost due to strikes reaching virtually unprecedented levels; and as the long awaited economic downturn took hold in 1986, there was a spate of plant closures and a significant rise in unemployment — to rates in excess of ten per cent in some provincial towns and cities. Moreover, the policy changes led to serious rifts within the union leadership, and also brought a deterioration in the relationship between the political and industrial wings of the labour movement.

Yet transitional problems of this nature were widely expected, and it would be wrong to evaluate the merits of Labour's strategy solely on the basis of its short-term political and economic effects. The more important question is what happens in the medium-to-long term. For example, will the current strategy produce faster productivity growth and higher living standards? Will the rate of economic growth be sufficient to bring a steady fall in the rate of unemployment, especially in provincial areas? And will there be a return to a more tranquil industrial relations climate such as that which characterized New Zealand during the 1950s and 1960s?

The answers here will depend a good deal on the strategies adopted by capital and organized labour and the pattern of management-employee relations which develops. At least two scenarios can be identified. The first model is exemplified to some extent by the British experience under the Thatcher Government. The hallmarks of this include the reassertion of managerial prerogatives by employers, the resort to highly confrontational tactics when deemed necessary to achieve productivity gains, and the adoption of a hostile, defensive posture by many trade unions. The results of this approach, at least in the British case, have been mixed. On the one hand, productivity has improved, there has been moderate economic growth and real wages have risen. On the other hand, unemployment has reached record levels, industrial relations have been soured in a number of industries, the union movement weakened, fragmented and demoralized, and the workforce increasingly divided into two groups: a "core" component enjoying favourable employment packages and job security, and a "peripheral" component with inferior employment conditions and limited job security.

An alternative scenario would involve a much more collaborative relationship between capital and organized labour. Here the main features would include employee-participative organizational structures, a greater reliance on gains sharing and profit-related bonus schemes, more flexible working conditions and employment packages, a greater acceptance of technological innovation, a wider range of union services, and better on-the-job, company-specific training and retraining. Such an approach, it can be argued, would best enable New Zealand to survive the rigours of international competition and prosper in the era of "flexible specialization" into which the world economy is moving (Sabel, 1984). Whether New Zealand follows this path will ultimately depend on the attitudes of the labour market parties. In this the Government cannot dictate. It can, however, ensure that the framework of industrial relations legislation facilitates, rather than hinders, the development of co-operative employee-management relations. It can also provide appropriate active labour market policies to assist the process of economic restructuring.

Notes

1 With the decision of the FOL in May 1986 to join with the Combined State Unions to form the Council of Trade Unions the union movement in New Zealand will be better able to speak with a single voice. At the same time, it should be noted that the FOL's decision has prompted the formation of yet another union federation. In mid-1986 this represented seven unions including the watersiders, seamen, cooks and stewards, and railway workers.

2 For a variety of reasons, including geographic proximity, limited migration restrictions and cultural similarities, there is significant integration of the New Zealand and Australian labour markets (see Economic Monitoring Group, 1986, pp.25-31).

3 For example, according to a survey conducted by PA Management Consultants, the salaries of senior executives and highly skilled workers rose significantly in the 12 months to September 1985: chief executives, 19.8 per cent; marketing managers, 20.4 per cent; financial controllers, 18.3 per cent; chief accountants, 14.6 per cent; and computer programmers, 18 per cent (see *The Dominion*, 16 October 1985).

4 There is some doubt concerning the reliability of New Zealand statistics on industrial stoppages. According to a study by Raymond Harbridge of the Industrial Relations Centre at Victoria University, the number of stoppages reported by the Department of Labour during the union movement's right to bargain campaign in 1984 were understated by 40 to 50 per cent. If this understating is common, then New Zealand's industrial relations record is even worse than generally believed (see *The Press*, 10 April 1986).

5 For instance, the turnover rate in the public service rose from 8.9 per cent in the year to March 1984 to 12.6 per cent in the year to March 1985. In the first six months of 1985 the public service lost about 5000 staff, roughly eight per cent of its total.

References

Boston, J. (1984) *Incomes Policy in New Zealand 1968-1984* Wellington, Victoria University Press.

Boston, J. (1985a) Incomes Policy and the 1985-86 Wage Round: From Non-Market Failure to Market Failure? *New Zealand Journal of Industrial Relations* 10: 65-82.

Boston, J. (1985b) Corporatist Incomes Policies, The Free-Rider Problem and the British Labour Government's Social Contract. In Cawson, A. (Ed.) *Organized Interests and the State* London, Sage.

Boston, J. (1986) Is Corporatism a Viable Model for New Zealand? Paper presented to a seminar at the Industrial Relations Centre, Victoria University of Wellington.

Brittan, S. and Lilley, P. (1977) *The Delusion of Incomes Policy* London, Temple Smith.

Brosnan, P. (1983) Tripartite Wage Agreement: A Feasible Objective? In Buckle, R. (Ed.) *Inflation and Economic Adjustment: Proceedings of a Seminar* Department of Economics, Victoria University of Wellington.

Buiter, W. and Miller, M. (1983) Changing the Rules: Economic Consequences of the Thatcher Regime *Brookings Papers on Economic Activity* 2: 305-365.

Burch, M. (1985) Coping with Stagflation: Some Policy Lessons from Australia *Political Quarterly* 56: 409-418.

Campbell, R. and Kirk, A. (1983) *After the Freeze: New Zealand Unions in the Economy* Wellington, The Port Nicholson Press.

Crouch, C. (1977) *Class Conflict and the Industrial Relations Crisis* London, Humanities Press.
Crouch, C. (1985) Conditions for Trade Union Wage Restraint. In Lindberg, L. and Maier,
    C. (Eds) *The Politics of Inflation and Economic Stagnation* Washington D.C., The Brook-
    ings Institution.
Crouch, C. (1986) The Future Prospects for Trade Unions in Western Europe *The Political
    Quarterly* 57: 5-17.
Dorfman, G. (1983) *British Trade Unionism Against The Trades Union Congress* London,
    Macmillan.
Douglas, R. (1985) *Budget 1985* Wellington, Government Printer.
Economic Monitoring Group (1986) *Labour Market Flexibility* Wellington, New Zealand
    Planning Council.
Fallick, J. and Elliott, R. (Eds) (1981) *Incomes Policies, Inflation and Relative Pay* London,
    Allen and Unwin.
Federation of Labour/Combined State Unions (1985) *Outlook on the Economy* Paper for the
    Tripartite Wage Conference, Wellington.
Federation of Labour (1986) *Looking Ahead: A More Just Industrial Relations System*
    Wellington.
Flanagan, R., Soskice, D. and Ulman, L. (1983) *Unionism, Stabilisation and Incomes Policy*
    Washington D.C., The Brookings Institution.
Gerritsen, R. (1986) The Necessity of "Corporatism": The Case of the Hawke Labor
    Government *Politics* 21: 45-54.
Government Policy Statement on Labour Relations (1986) Wellington, Government Printer.
Grant, W. (Ed.) (1985) *The Political Economy of Corporatism* London, Macmillan.
Harbridge, R. and Edwards, D. (1985) The Federation of Labour's Right to Bargain
    Campaign: Its Background, Impact and Effectiveness *New Zealand Journal of Industrial
    Relations* 10: 129-139.
Hawke, G. (1982) Incomes Policy in New Zealand. In Walsh, P. (Ed.) *National Incomes
    Policy* Industrial Relations Centre, Victoria University of Wellington.
Hayek, F. (1980) *Unemployment and the Unions: The Distortion of Relative Prices by Monopoly
    in the Labour Market* Hobart Paper 87, London, Institute of Economic Affairs.
Higher Salaries Commission (1985) *General Review As At 1 April 1985* Wellington,
    Government Printer.
Hince, K. (1986) The Management of Industrial Relations: Inaugural Address, Victoria
    University of Wellington.
Hodge, W. (1985a) Industrial Relations Legislation in 1984 *New Zealand Journal of Industrial
    Relations* 10: 29-34.
Hodge, W. (1985b) Industrial Relations Legislation in 1985 *New Zealand Journal of Industrial
    Relations* 10: 157-161.
Keenan, P. (1986) Review of Monetary Policy *Quarterly Predictions* June: 27-37.
Kirk, A. (1985) *Incomes Policy and the Wage Round* Paper for IPS/IRC Seminar on Incomes
    Policy and the 1985-86 Wage Round, Victoria University of Wellington.
Lange, D. (1986) The New Welfare State: Prestonpans, Mackintosh Memorial Lecture.
Lash, S. (1985) The End of Neo-corporatism? The Breakdown of Centralized Bargaining in
    Sweden *British Journal of Industrial Relations* 23: 215-239.
Layard, R. (1982) Is Incomes Policy the Answer to Unemployment? *Economica* 49: 219-239.
Llewellyn, D. (1980) Can Monetary Targets Influence Wage Bargaining? *The Banker* 130:
    49-53.
Long-Term Reform Committee (1983) *A Description of Wage Fixing and Industrial Relations
    in the Private Sector* Wellington, 8 September.

Long-Term Reform Committee (1984a) Progress Report to the Plenary Session, Wellington.

Long-Term Reform Committee (1984b) Final Statement of Understanding, Wellington.

Maital, S. and Benjamini, Y. (1980) Inflation as a Prisoner's Dilemma *Journal of Post Keynesian Economics* 2: 459-481.

Marks, G. (1986) Neocorporatism and Incomes Policy in Western Europe and North America *Comparative Politics* 18: 253-277.

Meade, J. (1982) *Stagflation: Volume 1: Wage Fixing* London, Allen and Unwin.

Minford, P. (1980) *Is Monetarism Enough?* London, Institute of Economic Affairs.

Mulvey, C. (1984) Wage Policy and Wage Determination in 1983 *Journal of Industrial Relations* 26: 112-119.

New Zealand Business Roundtable (1986) *New Zealand Labour Market Reform: A Submission in Response to the Green Paper, "Industrial Relations: A Framework for Review"* Wellington.

New Zealand Employers Federation (1985) *Statement to the Tripartite Wage Conference* 12 June.

New Zealand Employers Federation (1986) *The Industrial Relations Green Paper: An Employers Perspective* Wellington.

New Zealand Government (1985) *Industrial Relations: A Framework for Review* Vols I & II, Wellington, Government Printer.

New Zealand Labour Party (1984) *Policy Document* Wellington, Standard Press.

Okun, A. (1981) *Prices and Quantities: A Macroeconomic Analysis* Oxford, Basil Blackwell.

Perry, G. (1983) What Have We Learned About Disinflation? *Brookings Papers on Economic Activity* 2: 587-602.

Plowman, D. (1984) Full Circle: Australian Wage Determination 1982-1984 *New Zealand Journal of Industrial Relations* 9: 95-112.

Rawson, D. (1986) *Unions and Unionists in Australia* Sydney, Allen and Unwin.

Report of the Committee of Review (1985) *Australian Industrial Relations Law and Systems* Vols I-III Canberra, Australian Government Publishing Service.

Sabel, C. (1984) Industrial Reorganization and Social Democracy in Austria *Industrial Relations* 24: 62-89.

Schelling, T. (1982) Establishing Credibility: Strategic Considerations *American Economic Review: Papers and Proceedings*: 77-80.

Schmitter, P. and Lehmbruch, G. (Eds) (1979) *Trends Towards Corporatist Intermediation* London, Sage Publications.

Sutcliffe, C. (1982) Inflation and Prisoners' Dilemmas *Journal of Post Keynesian Economics* 4: 574-585.

Taylor, J. (1982) Establishing Credibility: A Rational Expectation's View Point *American Economic Review: Papers and Proceedings*: 81-85.

Technical Working Party (1986) *Report to the Tripartite Wage Conference 1986.*

Tobin, J. (1986) High Time to Restore the Employment Act of 1946 *Challenge* May-June: 4-12.

The Treasury (1984) *Economic Management* Wellington, Government Printer.

The Treasury (1985) *The State of the New Zealand Economy* Briefing Paper for the 1985 Tripartite Wage Conference.

The Treasury (1986) *The State of the New Zealand Economy* Briefing Paper for the 1986 Tripartite Wage Conference.

Walsh, P. (1982) Myth and Reality in Industrial Relations: Moderates, Militants and Social Contracts *New Zealand Journal of Industrial Relations* 7: 77-82.

10

The 1985 Tax Reform Package

Claudia D. Scott

This chapter examines the 1985 package of tax and benefit reforms, in particular the introduction of the Goods and Services Tax (GST). The case for GST is reviewed by considering its rationale and likely impact on efficiency, equity and administrative simplicity. Benefit reforms are discussed only briefly with attention directed to income support measures for families.

Taxation and Benefit Reform

In the 1984 Budget the Minister of Finance, Roger Douglas, announced the Government's intention to introduce a comprehensive broad-based consumption-type Value Added Tax (using credit offset mechanisms) called the Goods and Services Tax. Initially it was intended that this would take effect from 1 April 1986, but in June 1985 the Government announced that its introduction would be delayed for six months, largely for administrative reasons. On 26 March 1985 a White Paper was issued which provided draft legislation and proposals for the administration of GST. Submissions were called for (to be received by 17 May 1985) and these were referred to a private sector advisory panel for review. Revised draft legislation, incorporating many changes recommended by the panel, was then referred to a Parliamentary Select Committee and the legislation was passed in December. In the *Statement on Taxation and Benefit Reform* of August 1985, the Minister of Finance announced further details concerning the reform package including: ten per cent GST on all goods and services to replace the Wholesale Sales Tax on most items and certain selective taxes; simplification and flattening of income tax scales; reform of business taxes including introduction of a full imputation system for taxation of distributed company income from the 1988/89 financial year; introduction of a new package of family assistance for low and middle income families including a tax credit (Family Support), and provision for a guaranteed minimum family income for those in full-time paid employment. With the exception of imputation, the introduction of GST and associated tax and benefit reforms took place on 1 October 1986.

Figure 10.1 shows the effect of the introduction of GST on changing the tax mix — a shift between 1985/86 and 1986/87 (in full year financial terms) from 74.5 per cent total direct taxation to 64.6 per cent; and from 25.5 per cent indirect taxation (including highways) to 35.4 per cent. The forecast cost of the Taxation and Benefit

Reform Package was put at NZ$1057 million. In terms of its significance for fiscal policy, the annual ongoing cost was estimated to be NZ$737 million.

Figure 10.2 shows the proposed changes to the personal income tax scale and compares them with both pre- and post-1982 Budget levels. In this context, the reforms can be seen as part of a process which has flattened the overall scale and reduced the number of marginal rates in the tax schedule. (See Appendix II for a detailed chronology of tax reforms over the 1984-86 period.) The family income support measures have replaced the family rebate (introduced in 1982) and Family Care (1984). Family Support will provide tax credits to families and also a guaranteed minimum family income of NZ$250.00 (for one child) plus $22.00 per week for each additional child. (See Appendix I for a chronology of family income support measures during the 1982-86 period.)

The latest measures are consistent with the broad trend in reforms to the family income support package over recent years. The 1986 reforms have: (a) confirmed the emphasis on selective assistance to families with low income earnings as well as to social security beneficiaries; (b) made benefit levels bear a direct relation to family size; and (c) made additional progress toward a closer linking of the tax and benefit systems.

Figure 10.1
Change in composition of tax receipts (percentage of total tax revenue)

Tax system for financial year ending March 1986

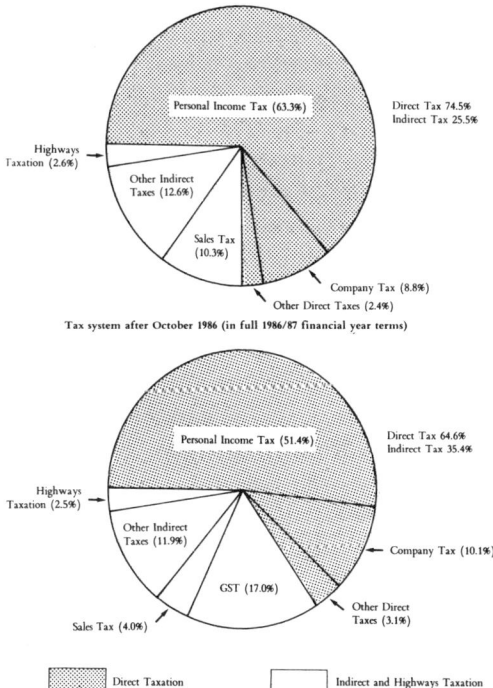

Personal Income Tax (63.3%)
Direct Tax 74.5%
Indirect Tax 25.5%
Highways Taxation (2.6%)
Other Indirect Taxes (12.6%)
Sales Tax (10.3%)
Company Tax (8.8%)
Other Direct Taxes (2.4%)

Tax system after October 1986 (in full 1986/87 financial year terms)

Personal Income Tax (51.4%)
Direct Tax 64.6%
Indirect Tax 35.4%
Highways Taxation (2.5%)
Other Indirect Taxes (11.9%)
Company Tax (10.1%)
GST (17.0%)
Sales Tax (4.0%)
Other Direct Taxes (3.1%)

Direct Taxation   Indirect and Highways Taxation

Figure10.2
Marginal tax rate schedules, 1982 and 1985

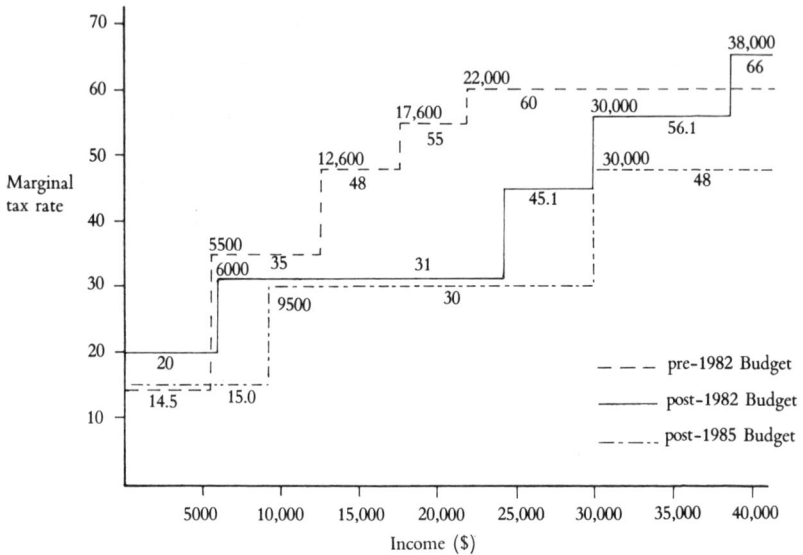

The revenue from a ten per cent GST has been estimated at NZ$2700 million in 1986/87 terms; however, about NZ$1300 million of this revenue will be used to reduce or eliminate a number of existing indirect taxes. Film Hire Tax, Lottery Duty, International Departure Tax and Domestic Air Travel Tax will be superseded by GST. Levies and special taxes — such as Road User Charges, the National Roads Fund portion of Motor Spirits Duty and equivalent taxes on Compressed Natural Gas and Liquefied Petroleum Gas — will be retained and GST applied as well. Customs Duty, Energy Resources Levy, and Motor Vehicle Fees and Charges will also remain as well as the Consolidated Account portion of Motor Spirits Duty and equivalent taxes on other petroleum fuels. Motor vehicles (the subject of a 30 per cent and 33 per cent tax under the Wholesale Sales Tax) will have a special tax imposed so as to hold the price of motor vehicles constant, though the Finance Minister accepts the principle that taxes on vehicles should be no higher than on other commodities. Some measures were stimulated by a desire to maintain revenue and the 1985 *Statement* records the Government's intention "to phase down the special tax on motor vehicles as and when revenue and economic conditions permit" (p.11). Racing duty will continue, but at a lower rate of duty to take account of GST. In addition to GST, selective taxes will continue to be levied on alcoholic beverages and tobacco products.

Evaluating GST

A well-established belief in the public finance literature is that a broad-based consumption tax is preferable to a narrowly based tax in terms of economic efficiency and horizontal equity. Consequently, as an approach to taxing consumption, the notion of a broadly based single-rate tax on the sale of goods and services is deemed superior to sales taxes with substantial base exemptions and the use of selective excise taxes. However, for some time the literature also showed a marked preference for direct taxes over indirect taxes and for income taxes over consumption taxes.

It is hard to find precise reasons for a more positive attitude in recent years towards indirect consumption taxes, though ample evidence exists of such a change of view. Earlier arguments which promoted the virtues of direct progressive personal income taxes (and, at best, tolerated indirect consumption taxes) have given way to more serious consideration of the merits of direct expenditure taxes, either on their own or in conjunction with a broadly based indirect consumption tax.

Greater interest in indirect taxes on consumption could, in part, reflect the failure of countries to implement a comprehensive income tax. Moreover, taxpayer opposition to direct taxes, particularly progressive income taxes, has led to a search for less visible forms of taxation and to a redesign of income taxes to reflect flatter marginal tax rate schedules in the name of controlling tax avoidance and evasion and promoting stronger work incentives and lower wage claims. Related to such developments is the issue of the tax mix and the relative merits of achieving some appropriate balance between direct taxes on income and indirect taxes on consumption over moves toward a single comprehensive tax base.

Many reasons have been given to support the introduction of GST in New Zealand. The GST Budget Booklet (1984, pp.12-13) suggested four urgent demands for GST revenues:

(a) to enhance income support measures for low income families and individuals;

(b) to halt the growth in average rates of personal tax and allow reductions in marginal rates of income tax;

(c) to reduce the scope of the existing wholesale sales tax; and

(d) to contribute to a permanent reduction in the government deficit before borrowing.

The possibility of using GST to make reductions in the deficit was not mentioned in a discussion paper released on 17 March 1985, suggesting most GST revenue would be spent on reforms to the benefit and tax systems. The statement suggested that a primary motivation for the reform was the objective of altering the "tax mix" — the share of taxes on income as opposed to taxes on consumption — rather than a change in the total tax take. It was seen as a means of reducing the system's heavy reliance on personal income taxes and lowering average and marginal tax rates.

Many discussions concerning the merits of a particular tax proposal proceed via reference to well-established criteria for a good tax. Listings of the criteria show some variations but are fundamentally concerned with efficiency/neutrality, equity and administrative simplicity.

Efficiency/neutrality considerations examine the impact of the tax on economic outcomes with an emphasis on incentive effects (e.g. to save, invest, work). Closely associated with efficiency concerns are notions of a neutral tax which has the attractive feature of eliminating distortions between the relative prices of goods and/or services which affect resource allocation and the behaviour of producers and consumers.

Equity considerations concern the overall fairness of the tax. To be useful, the procedural requirements for horizontal equity (equal treatment of equals) and vertical equity (unequal treatment of unequals) require explicit specification of distributional goals including appropriate concepts of income and the tax unit. Despite the tendency of certain parts of the tax policy literature to associate the achievement of vertical equity with progressivity, there is little in the way of a firm theoretical basis to such analysis. Increasingly, Governments have been making use of expenditures and tax-expenditures as well as taxes to achieve particular distributional goals (and for some Governments to have substantial influence over the returns to factors of production). Hence, there seems little basis in linking given distributional goals with prescriptions concerning the schedule of marginal tax rates on personal income.

The concept of *administrative simplicity* concerns the more practical aspects of a tax, and assesses total administrative and compliance costs in relation to revenues received. This involves estimating the associated administrative costs (to the revenue authority) and compliance costs (to taxpayers).

The objective of revenue neutrality suggests that the reform proposals have, as their prime concern, some change to the manner in which the burden of the tax system is spread among individuals and families. The impact of the reform package is difficult to measure. The changes in the personal tax scales will confer considerable benefits to those on higher incomes; however, adjustments to the benefit and tax systems have been introduced which are designed to give some protection to lower income groups. Major changes to the tax system will provide different incentives for people to work, consume, save, and invest. Accurate estimates of the impact of such a reform package must await more detailed information about the responses of various groups.

The merits of GST relative to a Retail Sales Tax or an extended Wholesale Sales Tax (broadened base plus a stand-alone tax on services) are discussed with regard to the criteria of efficiency, equity and administrative simplicity by Scott and Davis (1985, p.29). Though there is a tendency to overstate, it is accepted that GST may have greater potential to hold tax avoidance in check owing to the audit trail which

results from a credit offset consumption-type tax relative to a Retail Sales Tax —
where tax is collected at the final stage rather than in instalments throughout the
production and distribution chain. Retail Sales Tax has some potential for tax-
on-tax effects when, in the absence of a credit system, items sold at retail level
become inputs to the production of other goods or services. Administrative and
compliance costs of the GST are higher than a Retail Sales Tax, though the
magnitude of this difference is keenly debated and is sensitive to the administrative
features of the tax.

Given the trade-off between higher administrative and compliance costs of the
GST over the Retail Sales Tax and the slightly improved efficiency associated with
it, the choice of Retail Sales Tax *versus* GST has centred on the issue of the tax rate.
The support of international tax advisers for the use of GST increases the higher the
tax rate to be imposed. Although there is no percentage that is universally accepted,
tax rates in excess of seven to eight per cent have been often discussed by the New
Zealand Treasury as points where serious attention should be given to a value added
tax, though Australian counterparts have suggested rates of about 12 per cent. The
comments of Kay are interesting in this regard; he suggests that:

> ... it is simply not worth introducing VAT at a low rate, unless with the clear
> intention of increasing it when tax payers and consumers grow used to it. VAT makes
> sense only if a substantial substitution of VAT for income tax is envisaged — not
> necessarily immediately. Only at European rates of 15 per cent to 20 per cent is it likely
> that the total costs of VAT per £ of revenue collected will be significantly less than the
> costs of income tax (1984, p.20).

International trends reveal a strong move from wholesale sales taxes and retail
sales taxes to value added taxes in both developed and developing countries. In 1985
15 out of 22 OECD countries with major consumption taxes had a value added tax
in operation or firm plans for its implementation. Relative to value added taxes in
other countries the GST is a model of simplicity with its broad base and limited
exemptions. The proposals survived pressures for exemption for a variety of reasons.
One advantage was that the GST was being introduced as part of a tax switch and
compensation could be achieved more efficiently through tax credits (or deduc-
tions), benefit adjustments or reforms to income tax than through the use of
exemption and zero rating. Some estimates of the incidence of GST were made using
data from the Department of Statistics *Household Expenditure and Incomes Survey of
1983-84* based on the assumption of full-forward shifting in a partial equilibrium
framework (i.e. that the full burden of the tax is borne by consumers). The results
are reported in Scott, Goss and Davis (1985) but are not directly comparable with
other published work because estimates do not reflect the impact of the tax reform
on income and expenditure patterns. The results of the studies do not support a case
for the introduction of exemptions particularly since the experiments are conducted
on the assumption that revenue remains constant. Selective exemptions have only a

minor impact on the overall incidence of sales taxes since the distribution of consumption expenditure on any particular item is not sufficiently different from the distribution of consumption expenditure overall to have a marked impact on the incidence of taxes. These results are reassuring given the losses in administrative simplicity associated with exemption.

In both New Zealand and Australia the reform of indirect taxes has been linked to a concern with the tax mix and some underlying notion of correct balance in the share of taxes derived from taxes on income and from taxes on consumption. In New Zealand the Minister of Finance has suggested that the level of taxation is appropriate but that the share of taxes raised from personal incomes is too large. Crude measures of the level of taxation, such as total taxes in relation to gross domestic product, suggest that New Zealand is not a high tax country by OECD standards. In 1982, 14 out of 23 OECD countries collected more tax revenue in relation to gross domestic product than New Zealand. However, if one considers appropriate levels of taxation should be assessed in terms of giving value for money at the margin, then evidence of avoidance and evasion may reveal a preference for private over public goods. Given the trend toward an increase in the share of revenues raised from personal income taxes, proposals for reform suggest that undue strain on the income tax base should be relieved by making greater use of the consumption base. In a country without a comprehensive capital gains tax and top marginal tax rates of 66 per cent, it is suggested that those who evade taxes on income will not be so successful in avoiding taxes on consumption.

A good discussion of the two bases is provided by Bradford (in Walker and Bloomfield, 1983). However, an assessment of the merits of altering the tax mix requires some judgement as to the virtues of using multiple bases over a single comprehensive base. It has been suggested, particularly in the Australian debate, that proposals for altering the tax mix have facilitated the broadening of the income tax base (e.g. introduction of capital gains and fringe benefit tax) which would otherwise have been impossible.

Challenges to the appropriateness of a particular tax mix call for some specification of a benchmark. In New Zealand's case this is not defined as some specific share, but sometimes as a matter of returning to an earlier tax mix. Yet another is the average OECD experience. However, close scrutiny of the trends does not yield a watertight case for the Labour Government's reforms.

Table 10.1 shows the share of total taxation raised from different broad categories of taxes in 1982 for OECD countries and reveals New Zealand to be top (at 69.1 per cent) and Australia fourth (at 55.2 per cent) in terms of the share of revenues raised from taxes on income and profits. However, one also notes an inverse relation between the share of taxes raised on income and profits and the share raised from social security taxes — with Australia and New Zealand distinguishing themselves as the only two OECD countries without a separate social security tax. Ten OECD

Table 10.1
Share of total taxation raised from different broad categories of taxes: 1982

	1000 Income & profits	2000 Social security	3000 Payroll	4000 Property	5000 Goods & services	6000 Other
Australia	55.20	—	5.20	7.94	31.66	—
Austria	26.51	31.93	6.44	2.64	31.30	1.17
Belgium	42.47	29.77	—	1.74	25.95	0.07
Canada	43.79	11.27	—	9.02	34.60	1.32
Denmark	55.75	2.82	—	4.47	36.82	0.13
Finland	49.33	8.40	—	2.36	39.68	0.23
France	18.03	43.17	2.21	3.69	29.66	3.24
Germany	34.00	36.18	—	3.28	26.52	0.02
Greece	19.13	32.36	0.17	4.78	42.08	0.02
Ireland	34.54	15.03	0.78	3.70	45.95	1.47
Italy	31.99	47.23	—	2.97	16.47	—
Japan	45.01	30.37	—	8.94	15.42	1.35
Luxembourg	43.14	28.03	0.67	5.87	22.29	0.27
Netherlands	30.71	41.62	—	3.60	23.79	0.27
New Zealand	69.08	—	—	7.23	23.70	—
Norway	41.63	21.52	—	1.72	34.55	0.59
Portugal	22.90	28.53	2.22	1.49	43.23	1.64
Spain	25.95	46.46	0.61	4.03	22.07	0.89
Sweden	44.14	27.91	2.57	1.01	24.21	0.16
Switzerland	41.93	31.01	—	7.48	19.59	—
Turkey	59.33	5.00	—	5.81	29.86	—
United Kingdom	37.96	16.94	3.32	12.72	28.97	0.09
United States	44.76	27.71	—	10.07	17.45	—
Unweighted ave age						
OECD total	39.88	24.49	1.05	5.07	28.95	0.56
OECD (Europe only)	36.63	27.44	1.06	4.07	30.17	0.63
EEC	34.77	29.32	0.72	4.68	29.85	0.66

Source: Revenu= Statistics of OECD Member Countries 1965–1983

Table 10.2
Share of New Zealand and OECD tax revenues from different tax categories (all figures percentages)

	1965		1972		1977		1982	
	NZ	OECD[a]	NZ	OECD[a]	NZ	OECD[a]	NZ	OECD[a]
Total income and profits (1000)	60.53	35.23	62.67	36.90	69.99	38.86	69.07	39.88
(a) Corporate[b]	20.66	9.20	14.03	7.94	11.02	7.53	7.90	7.75
(b) Personal[b]	39.39	26.32	48.19	29.49	58.53	31.91	60.69	32.65
Social security (2000)	–	18.18	–	20.95	–	23.72	–	24.49
Payroll (3000)	–	1.05	2.21	1.15	–	1.33	–	1.05
Property (4000)	11.54	7.97	9.50	7.16	8.07	5.99	7.23	5.07
Goods & services (5000)	27.93	37.14	25.62	33.44	21.94	29.66	23.70	28.95
(a) General consumption[b]	7.65	11.70	8.16	13.34	7.47	12.99	11.26	13.96
(b) Specified goods[b]	18.53	23.24	15.71	18.17	13.09	14.82	11.34	13.40
Other (6000)	–	0.43	–	0.40	–	0.44	–	0.56

Notes: a Average unweighted share of OECD countries.
b Excludes taxes unallocatable between (a) and (b).
Source: Compiled from data provided in Revenue Statistics of OECD Member Countries 1965–1983

countries, including Australia, have payroll taxes as well. By aggregating all taxes on profits and income, whether paid by employer or employee, New Zealand's ranking alters. For example, after combining the taxes on income and profits with social security contributions, New Zealand ranks eleventh of the OECD countries; this position is unaltered if payroll taxes are also included.

Table 10.2 looks at the share of New Zealand and average (unweighted) OECD revenue from different categories in four different periods. Having regard for its lack of a payroll tax and a social security tax, the New Zealand experience does not appear to be vastly different from the average OECD experience. New Zealand's somewhat greater share of income taxes and lower share of consumption taxes holds for the periods shown. The share of taxes on personal income has risen and that on corporate income has fallen, although the decline in the corporate share in New Zealand has been more rapid than the average OECD experience. The OECD average was 9.2 per cent in 1965 and 7.75 per cent in 1982, while the New Zealand average was 20.66 per cent in 1965, but only 7.9 per cent in 1982.

An interesting problem related to the introduction and/or extension of broad-based consumption taxes concerns the appropriate role for customs and excise taxes, other indirect taxes, and taxes on selective goods and services, as part of a major reform of indirect taxes. Since selective taxes are often a prominent feature of indirect tax systems, it is important to consider the nature and timing of appropriate adjustments to selective taxes which should accompany the introduction of a value added tax. For countries at an early stage of development, selective taxes provide a simple and certain source of revenue, particularly in the case of excise taxes levied on the basis of value rather than quantity. While there are exceptions, in many countries the range of excise goods narrows as development progresses. The trend away from selective taxation is often associated with the increased use of broadly-based consumption tax systems and the expanded use of direct taxes.

When considering the appropriate role of excise taxes within a GST regime it appears that there is a conflict between introducing a flat rate broad-based consumption tax and maintaining specific excises on commodities with relatively inelastic demand on the grounds that they are good "revenue raisers". Selective taxes, however, can still be justified on the grounds that consumption of the good involves an external cost to third parties and, in principle, higher taxes on alcohol, tobacco and motor fuels could be continued on this basis. However, certain conditions should be fulfilled, including some relationship between the level of tax and the external cost involved. When such revenues are imposed on the grounds of external costs but this condition is not met, the case for applying GST on top of specific excises becomes weakened and compromises the principle of neutrality which suggests a uniform rate.

GST at a uniform ten per cent rate on a broad base was estimated by the Treasury to have a one-off Consumer Price Index impact of five per cent after allowing for remission of certain existing indirect taxes, though other research on this question suggested a higher rate of 6.6 per cent (Wells, 1986). Compensatory measures, such as the five per cent adjustment of social security benefits, will serve to soften the impact of GST on particular groups, including beneficiaries and low income families.

As a reform of the existing wholesale sales tax, GST has much to commend it. The Wholesale Sales Tax is noted for its narrow base (estimated Treasury (1984, p.255) as only 37 per cent of the potential Wholesale Sales Tax base) which excludes services and value added by retailers. Thus, the Wholesale Sales Tax manages to tax less than one-quarter of total consumption. GST at ten per cent will reduce the six *ad valorem* rates which operate under the Wholesale Sales Tax (from ten to 50 per cent, with a 20 per cent standard rate) to one single rate. It will apply comprehensively to goods and services and these are defined widely under the Act to include all kinds of personal and real property. The tax applies to supplies made for a consideration in the furtherance of a taxable activity and includes rates, levies and charges of public authorities, which are deemed to be consideration for services received. Exports are zero rated and rental accommodation, financial services and goods supplied by donation to a non-profit organization are exempt.

One interesting aspect of tax reform proposals in New Zealand was that they had a striking resemblance to proposals in Australia. Both Australia and New Zealand designed reforms which placed emphasis on changing the tax mix, on the need to reduce tax avoidance and evasion and offered compensation to particular groups for the effects of the consumption tax on prices. The main difference, however, was that the broad-based consumption tax did not even survive one day at the Tax Summit in Australia. Once the broad-based consumption tax was rejected, indirect tax reform proposals centred on a combination of modifications to the wholesale sales tax plus a stand-alone retail tax on services. This means that the change in tax mix in Australia will be much less than originally planned. (See Kesselman (1985) and Morgan (1985) for a discussion of the Australian reforms.)

To some extent the different experiences reflect variations in the policy making process. In the case of Australia, there were pressures arising from a need for a tripartite adoption of the proposals at the Tax Summit. Analysis of the effects of the proposals was substantial and enabled an informed debate to take place. In contrast, the New Zealand experience was more one of "selling" GST to the public and, while compensation to particular groups was part of the package, there were no efforts formally to negotiate the policy with unions or business groups. Attempts by certain New Zealand unionists to oppose the tax at regional Labour Party conferences were thwarted by the Government and its supporters. Such challenges occurred before the rate of GST and the specifics of tax reform and benefit reforms were known, blunting the policy debate and assisting the process of selling GST.

Since the announcement of GST, the Inland Revenue Department has worked hard on a programme of education for taxpayers and their advisers. Public education concerning GST has been promoted by the establishment of a GST Coordinating Office with a June 1985 to October 1986 Budget of NZ$2.66 million. Located across from Parliament Buildings, headed by a prominent accountant seconded from the private sector and drawing on the services of communication specialists, the office has produced an impressive array of resource material. Special brochures have been prepared to explain the effects of GST on particular groups such as farmers, retailers and local authorities. The GST Coordinating Office works closely with the Inland Revenue Department though some of its creations — such as the great, greedy, kiwi income tax machine and the video *Working with GST*, starring Barry Crump as a possum trapper and Peter Bland as proprietor of a shop specializing in possum skin bikinis — stand somewhat apart from the more traditional material prepared by Inland Revenue.

Despite the introduction of GST in October 1986, its long-term future is still in some doubt as a commitment has been given by the National Party to remove GST when next elected. The National Party accepts the need to alter the tax mix and put greater reliance on consumption taxes, but promises to replace GST with a type of indirect tax which can be administered more efficiently. In the absence of information on the administrative and compliance costs of alternative forms of indirect consumption taxes, debates concerning the future of the GST are likely to be dominated largely by political rather than economic issues.

Tax Reform: Bridging Theory and Practice

The public debate in New Zealand over the past few years has revealed some major gaps between the theory and practice of tax reform. Uncertainties regarding the merits of a mixed over a single comprehensive base, whether or not a flat tax achieves neutrality, whether or not a change in tax mix will improve work incentives and whether the burden of GST will be fully shifted forward to consumers, were largely ignored in public discussions. An interesting recent contribution to the list of theoretical doubts is a paper by Sieper (1986) who challenges the assumption that adoption of the broad-based consumption tax in the context of a tax switch in Australia would inevitably cause a one-off rise in the consumer price index. This view is shared by Schuyler (1984, p.iv) who suggests that the Government could, through proper conduct of monetary policy, avoid such an impact on inflation.

The ten per cent rate of GST has now been enshrined in legislation. However, the new income tax scales are not indexed and therefore limit the ability of the tax system to maintain a particular mix of income and consumption taxes. The notion that New Zealand's tax structure should be kept in line with average OECD experience seems simplistic, if not vacuous. However, if accepted as a goal for tax reform, it is hard to resist suggestions for greater "alignment" through the reintroduction of a social security tax or a comprehensive capital gains tax.

Whether the introduction of GST is, as the television commercial suggests, "the key to lower income tax and a better future" is of course open to debate. GST has been portrayed as the key to other desirable changes, including improvements in benefit reforms (particularly assistance to families) and in work incentives. It has also been seen as a way of stemming avoidance and evasion of the income tax system by those on higher incomes, though base-broadening measures may bring about even greater improvements. The list of achievements is too substantial to credit to GST alone and, to some extent, gives insufficient weight to the role which overall tax reductions have played in creating conditions in which "most people are better off".

Mention has been made of the dual role of the New Zealand reforms in reforming the indirect tax base and changing the tax mix. Of the two objectives, one can be more certain of the merits of GST as a reform of the tax base than as a required change to the tax mix. There is some risk that greater reliance on GST and indirect taxes could serve to postpone efforts to broaden the income tax base (to include capital gains and comprehensive treatment of fringe benefits) and provide what Kesselman has termed "a politically expedient diversion from thornier problems of tax reform" (1985, p.22).

References

Advisory Panel on Goods and Services Tax (1985) *Report to the Minister of Finance,* Wellington.

Ashton, T. and St John, S. (1985) *Insights into Excises: A Focus on Alcohol, Tobacco and Motor Fuels Taxation* Wellington, Institute of Policy Studies.

Bird, R. and Oldman, O. (1974) *Readings on Taxation in Developing Countries* Baltimore, Johns Hopkins University Press.

Cnossen, S. (1985) Sales Taxation: An International Perspective. In *Taxation Issues of the 1980s* Sydney, Australian Tax Research Foundation.

Due, J. (1970) *Indirect Taxation in Developing Economies* Baltimore, Johns Hopkins Press.

GST Coordinating Office (1986) *Understanding GST — A Guide to the Legislation* Wellington, Government Printer.

GST Coordinating Office (1985) *A Fairer Deal* Wellington, Government Printer.

GST Coordinating Office (1985) *Working with GST* Wellington, Government Printer.

Head, J. and Bird, R. (1983) Tax Policy Options in the 1980s. In Cnossen, S. (Ed.) *Comparative Tax Studies in Honor of R. Goode* Amsterdam, North Holland.

Kay, J. (1984) VAT — Report from the U.K. paper presented to the Canadian Tax Foundation Conference, mimeo.

Kesselman, J. (1985) Assessing Australian Tax Reform Proposals *Economic Papers* 4: 18-41.

Kesselman, J. (1986) Role of the Tax Mix in Tax Reform. In Head, J. (Ed.) *Changing the Tax Mix* Sydney, Australian Tax Research Foundation.

Koopman-Boyden, P. and Scott, C. (1984) *The Family and Government Policy in New Zealand* Sydney, George Allen and Unwin.

McLure, C. (1972) *Value Added Taxes: Two Views* Washington D.C., American Enterprise Institute.

Morgan, D. (1986) An Agenda for Tax Reform. In Head, J. (Ed.) *Changing the Tax Mix* Sydney, Australian Tax Research Foundation.

New Zealand Government (1985) *Statement on Taxation and Benefit Reform* Wellington, Government Printer.

New Zealand Government (1985) *Goods and Services Tax Act 1985* Wellington, Government Printer.

OECD, (1984) *Revenue Statistics of OECD Member Countries 1965-83* Paris, OECD.

Pechman, J. (Ed.) (1980) *What Should be Taxed — Income or Expenditure?* Washington D.C., Brookings Institution.

Schuyler, M. (1984) *Consumption Taxes: Promises and Problems* Washington D.C., Institute for Research on the Economics of Taxation.

Scott, C. and Davis, H. (1985) *The Gist of GST* Wellington, Institute of Policy Studies.

Scott, C., Goss, P. and Davis, H. (1985) *The Incidence of Indirect Taxes Vol. 1* Wellington, Institute of Policy Studies.

Sieper, E. (1986) Macroeconomic Implications of a Switch to Consumption Taxation, paper presented to the New Zealand Association of Economists, mimeo.

St John, S. (1983) *Financial Assistance for Families and the 1983 Budget* Report prepared for the New Zealand Committee for Children.

St John, S. (1984) *Interim Report on the Financial Position of Families Incorporating the Effects of the 1984 Budget* Report prepared for the New Zealand Committee for Children.

St John, S. (1985) *The Impact of the 1985 Budget Changes on Families* Report prepared for the New Zealand Committee for Children.

Tait, A. (1972) *Value Added Tax* New York, McGraw-Hill.

Task Force on Tax Reform (1982) *Report of the Task Force on Tax Reform* Wellington, Government Printer.

Walker, C. and Bloomfield, M. (1983) *New Directions in Federal Tax Policy for the 1980s* American Council for Capital Formation, Washington D.C., Center for Policy Research Cambridge, Ballinger.

Wells, G. (1986) *The Impact of GST on the CPI* Wellington, Institute of Policy Studies.

11

ANZUS and the Nuclear Issue

Roderic Alley

The decision taken in February 1985, to ban from New Zealand's ports and harbours the entry of naval vessels deemed nuclear armed or nuclear propelled, was easily the most significant and contentious foreign policy event of the fourth Labour Government. This precipitated a major internal debate and reassessment of New Zealand's international security policies. It resulted in American responses that degraded and atrophied the ANZUS arrangement as both a diplomatic and military entity, generated and sustained political tensions between New Zealand and countries normally regarded as close allies, and yet also evoked wider international responses that ranged from castigation of the ship ban as naive to its endorsement as an act of moral integrity. Whether in support or condemnation, the response beyond New Zealand was often one of surprise that the ban had been imposed at all. Within New Zealand, however, even the Government's opponents would have conceded such developments were hardly unexpected. In the preceding years of the 1981-84 Parliament, protest over nuclear ship visits intensified as did a wider public awareness regarding nuclear weaponry. At the 1984 General Election the incumbent National Party was the only party to favour a continuation of the then existing arrangements regarding the entry of nuclear ships.

This chapter describes the background to the 1985 nuclear ship ban dispute. In addition, it explores the political dynamics that shaped the early 1985 decision, the public dimensions of the dispute, and the wider foreign policy implications involved. Why the dispute elicited markedly contrasting interpretations as to its causes and its consequences will also be considered. Whether construed as a mistake or an inception, few disagreed that the ship ban represented a distinctive climacteric in the evolution of New Zealand's contemporary foreign relations.

The Anti-Nuclear Intensification

When the Labour Party was elected to office in July 1984, a variety of strands comprising different interests, values and priorities were intertwining, compelling New Zealand to adopt a more independent role in its foreign relations. From a generational perspective, Lange's new administration was dominated by individuals who had been socialized into public life during the formative experiences of the Vietnam War. For them, that episode represented not just a failure of nerve on the part of New Zealand to say no to the United States; but, equally, it violated deeply entrenched Labour Party principles emphasizing the peaceful settlement of disputes, and the imperatives of social and economic amelioration ahead of physical coercion as the most appropriate response to Third World conflicts. To some degree, this stance was seen as vindicated by the Guam Doctrine enunciated by the United States during the final phase of the Vietnam War, which urged greater security self-reliance among America's allies and their consequential need to strengthen appropriate forms of regional co-operation. This impetus was not just heeded, but acted upon by the third Labour Government of 1972-75.

Such direction towards stronger regional co-operation and responsibility – particularly in the South Pacific – was thus legitimized by the United States, facilitated by decolonization and accorded bipartisan support within New Zealand. It was also consolidated by a powerful, if negative, force in the form of continued atmospheric testing of nuclear weapons by France at Muroroa Atoll in French Polynesia. Although that programme switched to underground operations in 1974, the actual volume of tests increased as did French obduracy in the face of legal, public and diplomatic efforts by New Zealand and other states to prevent it.

A further factor involved the increasing willingness of the United States from 1976 to emphasize that the freedom of port access for its vessels was a necessary condition for the maintenance of ANZUS. This arrangement, it was argued, had its part to play in the total global security of the West which, in turn, was underpinned by the doctrine of nuclear deterrence. This posture, unlike the earlier Guam Doctrine, was now seen as justified in the light of developments such as the 1979 intervention by the Soviet Union in Afghanistan. However, the more this global dimension was emphasized by the United States in attempted vindication of port visits to New Zealand, the greater the local opposition to such visits became.

The sources of this opposition, in what was loosely described as "the Peace Movement", were as varied as the tactics employed by the interests concerned to promote it. Defining the precise nature, workings, or effects of this activity proved difficult. Consequently political authorities within, as well as beyond New Zealand, encountered problems in gauging its true strength. A persistent characteristic was the lack of any one dominant central organization: a wide spectrum of bodies, supporting personnel, foci of interest, regional or local identification, attitude to public visibility or affiliation, and access to more established institutions such as political parties, all had to be considered. Some interests, while according high priority to the anti-nuclear cause, believed it was only explicable, and therefore amenable to action, through an understanding of linking factors – be that environmental degradation, the inferior treatment of women, the imposition of threatening and non-accountable technologies, corporate profits, or violated human integrity and moral principles.

Some of the cause groups concerned commanded support through their professional standing. Here the best example would be the New Zealand branch of the International Physicians for the Prevention of Nuclear War. From 1983 this organization brought increasing publicity and attention to bear in a field where it could claim authority and expertise: the actual medical consequences of a nuclear conflict. Thus the Parliamentary Disarmament and Arms Control Committee, established in 1982 in response to growing public concern over the nuclear issue, regarded the 1983 submission of the International Physicians for the Prevention of Nuclear War as sufficiently authoritative for inclusion as an appendix to its final report. According to one analyst, that Committee, when considering disarmament, paid "greatest heed to those considered to have special expertise, professional standing, and a measure of objectivity, particularly doctors, scientists, and engineers" (Candy, 1986, p.140).

Other groups were oriented more directly to the threat of nuclear weapons and the arms race as a political phenomenon requiring direct action and protest, including the obstruction of ship visits when they occurred. One such body was the Campaign Against Nuclear War (CANWAR); another focus involved the designation of local "nuclear-free zones" by local authorities, the aim of this being to signify legitimacy, build cumulative pressure, and enhance the symbolic impact of anti-nuclear public postures. Much of this voluntary activity was decentralized, scantily funded, and supported because it offered an alternative to working through established systems such as political parties. Crothers and Murray argue:

> This organisational proliferation places considerable strain on the collective capacity of the movement, especially as there is the further cross-cutting difficulty of regional groupings and a lack of a nation-wide framework. The only consensus of the goals of these groups would seem to focus upon influencing government policy on the exclusion of nuclear arms or more generally nuclear propelled warships and other means of transport, from not only New Zealand ports but also the territorial limits (Crothers and Murray, 1983, p.33).

Prior to 1985, the main objective uniting these various groups within the Peace Movement was their support for a nuclear-free New Zealand and South Pacific. Following the 1985 ship ban to New Zealand, and in particular the American response to it, the movement's activities were probably better co-ordinated than at any time previously. Had the nuclear ship ban initiative been reversed, these groups in combination with other disaffected elements possessed the potential to harm Labour's electoral prospects. Nevertheless, the same broad anti-nuclear movement also contained groups that deliberately avoided partisan identification on this issue, maintaining that in doing so their strength, independence, and credibility was enhanced not weakened in the eyes of politicians and public alike. Few groups though, notwithstanding a distinctive local flavour to their activities, divorced their attempts from a wider international apprehension about nuclear weaponry – be that its escalating deployment in Europe, the major military build-up instigated by the Reagan Administration from 1981, or the worsening political relations between the superpowers.

The Position of the New Zealand Labour Party

The New Zealand Labour Party's stance on the anti-nuclear question is the product of a long history of attitudes and motivations, in comparison to the more immediate catalyst of the recently established peace movement. Despite the changes of emphasis sustained by the party since its formation in 1916, whether in ideology, style of leadership, economic policy, or response to change within New Zealand itself, the evidence indicates persistent determination to achieve a greater independence in the conduct of foreign relations. Under conditions where the older symbols of unity and appeal were ageing and degenerating, a determination for greater international independence remained a fixed star to sail by. McIntyre suggests "remarkable consistency" in the ideology of Labour towards international questions and identifies anti-militarism, anti-imperialism and internationalism as significant (1985, p.25). Brown has described early and continuing Labour attitudes on international issues as comprising "a blend of socialist idealism, sometimes pacifism, together with a suspicion of the designs and ramifications of international capitalism and a scepticism of official explanations" (1962, p.108). These themes were more recently highlighted in the Labour Party's submission to the 1986 Public Enquiry on the Future of New Zealand's Strategic and Security Policies. In respect of defence and security, the submission emphasized independence, disarmament and the peaceful settlement of disputes; the role of social and economic development as a key means to enduring security; collective security as originally conceived through the United Nations; and greater self-reliance in defence (New Zealand Labour Party, 1986, p.3).

Yet for these principles to have any real impact, it was increasingly appreciated within the Labour Party after its 1975 defeat that the organization had to reform what was then regarded as a dilapidated system of internal policy formulation. This began to occur, and as it gathered momentum it coincided and interacted with a growing anti-nuclear focus, not just against French testing but also against ANZUS. For one analyst, the changes in policy formulation involved "substantially increased participation in policy formulation and made the parliamentary party more accountable in this vital area, at least while the party was in opposition" (Strachan, 1985, p.161). Labour parliamentarians could now only ignore at their peril the demands for greater access to policy making which were emanating from the grassroots of the party.

Nevertheless, conscious that any unadorned demand for a complete withdrawal from ANZUS could be electorally damaging, Labour's senior politicians insisted that a compromise be struck on the issue prior to facing the electorate. Thus, at the 1983 Annual Conference, under the guidance of Sir Wallace Rowling, a posture of "qualified alignment" was approved, if somewhat grudgingly by some within the party. While New Zealand's "unconditional anti-nuclear stance" was endorsed along with support for a nuclear-free South Pacific, this position was deemed possible within what was termed a "renegotiated ANZUS". As Sir Wallace explained to the Conference: "If of course our allies are not prepared to accept our anti-nuclear position as the bottom line, it will be they who have to do the withdrawing from existing arrangements" (New Zealand Labour Party, 1986, p.12).

It is of considerable interest that the doubts, existing within the Labour Party as to whether its 1983 Conference compromise really went far enough, surfaced so soon and so volubly after the party won office a year later. Hence in September 1984, after barely eight weeks in office, the new Prime Minister, David Lange, faced a party again demanding the full withdrawal of New Zealand from ANZUS. That the Conference surprised itself with this decision revealed as much about the cooling climate of New Zealand-United States relations as it did about the willingness of the Labour Party to trust its newly elected Government to remain faithful to the compromise carefully constructed in 1983.

The Political Dynamics of the Buchanan Cancellation

On the day following Labour's July 1984 electoral victory American Secretary of State, George Shultz, speaking in Canberra just prior to departing for New Zealand to attend a scheduled ANZUS Council meeting, said he hoped the recent electoral outcome would pose no greater threat for ANZUS than had the Australian Labor Party's (ALP) 1983 win in Australia. Indirectly, this acknowledged that the review of ANZUS conducted by the Hawke Government, while disappointing to critics within the ALP, was greeted with satisfaction by the Reagan Administration. It also implied an assumption by the Americans — subsequently demonstrated to be unfounded — that as far as ANZUS matters were concerned, "Australia-New Zealand" shared similar characteristics; if a Labor Government in Canberra could resolve its local ANZUS difficulties, why not a similar Government in Wellington? Upon meeting Lange, Shultz allowed his host, then in the midst of a financial and constitutional crisis, a breathing space on the ship visit question. The latter believed that he took from the former an undertaking that a compromise was possible so that, after six months, the United States could "request" a ship visit the acceptance of which was deemed essential for any continuation of ANZUS as far as the Americans were concerned.

This six months was significant for what it revealed about how both sides of the growing dispute utilized the time to strengthen their respective positions. For the United States, the issue was relatively uncomplicated. Provided certain assumptions were accepted, a ship ban by New Zealand was indefensible. These assumptions included: (a) the United States and New Zealand, by an evolved treaty arrangement in ANZUS, comprised part of the overall fabric of Western security, which for its effectiveness had to remain united; (b) that security was underpinned by the deterrence provided by nuclear weapons; and, (c) while of no great strategic moment, any decision by New Zealand to ban the entry of ships would be a demonstrable failure to bear a fair share of the total burden, weaken the credibility of the Western alliance system, and encourage other states within it to relax their obligations.

In a word, the American position spelled indivisibility. Exceptions could not be made for any ally, no matter how small, loyal, geographically inconsequential, or credible regarding its previous willingness to bear arms in conflicts on behalf of alliance solidarity — all of which applied to New Zealand. From a direct military perspective, a key consideration was the increasing operational indivisibility of the United States Navy between its conventional and nuclear-capable functions: for example, under way since 1984 and involving an ongoing programme of substantial modification, was the conversion of United States ships to permit their delivery of Sea Launched Cruise Missiles (i.e. Tomahawk). Such systems are capable of delivering either nuclear or conventional high explosive warheads from forward-based positions in the Northern Pacific. And if indivisibility was a way of reminding the New Zealanders that the Australian ANZUS review had caused no real problems for Hawke, and that the two trans-Tasman partners should not jeopardize their own ANZAC tradition over a matter such as ship visits, then it was also made clear that the weight of America's other allies, once brought to bear upon a recalcitrant Lange, could prove far from politically cost free for his Government. By various methods, some more subtle than others, these messages were conveyed by Washington to Wellington after July 1984.

For the New Zealand Labour Party, an effective ship ban excluding nuclear-armed and propelled vessels was irreducible as a minimum condition. To a substantial number in the party, including some Members of Parliament, that position was in itself a dilution of previous party conference resolutions calling for a complete withdrawal from ANZUS. That withdrawal was again endorsed by the Party Conference in September 1984, reflecting an attempt to neutralize the pressure being applied to the new Government from various quarters to accept a compromise. An October ANZUS exercise held in New Zealand, forcing detours for civilian aircraft flying the Auckland-Wellington route, was construed by those in the Labour Party keen to mount an effective ship ban, as an attempt to influence public opinion towards a favourable view of ANZUS.

Intensifying the manoeuvering of both sides in the growing dispute was a shared belief that, within Labour's 1984 election policy, there was scope to advance significantly contrasting policies. Thus for the United States, if the new Government accepted the continuation of ANZUS, it must also accept nuclear ship visits. For the anti-nuclear majority in the Labour Party, there was nothing in ANZUS precluding a ship ban. Under such circumstances, it was not surprising that the distinctions between vessels deemed nuclear *armed*, nuclear *propelled* and nuclear *capable* were placed under growing public scrutiny. Without doubt, the anti-nuclear cause in New Zealand wanted an effective ban on all three categories. In contrast, it was evident that Lange, certainly prior to the July 1984 election, was more concerned about nuclear-armed than nuclear-propelled vessels. Within the Reagan Administration, it seems, there was a grudging readiness to try and work out some *modus vivendi* between these positions.

After several months of diligent effort by officials in Washington and Wellington, it was believed that a compromise over ship visits was feasible. Although there was no movement from the public position of the United States concerning its "neither confirm nor deny" policy regarding the presence of nuclear weapons aboard visiting vessels, to the extent possible, it was conveyed that a proposed visit by *USS Buchanan*, a conventionally powered guided missile destroyer, would not upset the New Zealand Government. That the vessel was neither nuclear propelled, nor armed with a weapons system exclusively designed to deliver nuclear weapons, could be ascertained without great difficulty. But it was less clear whether or not the vessel's inventory was dual capable, or suitable for the delivery of conventional high explosive and nuclear warheads. It was this third element which aroused serious misgivings in the Labour Caucus of 31 January 1985, when the proposed visit of the *Buchanan* was discussed.

Handling the matter at short notice while the Prime Minister was absent in the Tokelau Islands (to which communications were poor) the Deputy Prime Minister, Geoffrey Palmer, had said that if a vessel was found to be capable of carrying nuclear weapons, this would not *necessarily* be a basis for its exclusion from a New Zealand port. But it was not just this statement that aroused suspicion that the New Zealand Government was on a slippery slope to compromise, so much as its proximity in timing to the leaking of a letter written by Hawke to Lange. This stated firmly that, so far as the Australian Government was concerned, any notion that ANZUS had more than one meaning and entailed different obligations for its members was unacceptable. Although Palmer regretted the publication of the Hawke letter, he claimed "some in New Zealand fear that the New Zealand Government will buckle. I assure them that it will not" (*The Dominion*, 26 January 1985). In saying that though, Palmer needed look no further than his own Caucus, a growing number of whom were expressing resentment at what they construed, rightly or wrongly, as a gross and unwarranted intrusion in local affairs by Canberra at the behest of Washington. Further it was also likely that rumours, then circulating in ALP circles, that the New Zealand Government was on the verge of announcing that a ship visit was acceptable would have soon crossed the Tasman. Accordingly, when Lange returned from the Tokelau Islands, he was soon aware of the gathering pressure for non-compromise that had escalated within his party.

The key Caucus meeting proved yet another illustration as to how this body and its deliberations imparts to the New Zealand political system a function distinctive within the Westminster tradition (see Jackson, 1978, pp.159-164). While the Government knew that on this particular matter it would have incurred grave risks by not allowing deliberation within Caucus, equally, nobody within the parliamentary party was entirely sure what the outcome of such deliberations would produce. Any notions the Government might have entertained about an acceptance of the *Buchanan* being simply approved by Caucus were unrealistic, even though there were Labour MPs worried by the likely political costs of such a ban through its perceived damage to ANZUS. Unlike the progressive degradation of ANZUS as an operational entity that followed the ship ban, it has to be recalled that early in 1985 the arrangement was still in being.

Shaping the position of the majority in Caucus (those favouring a veto on the *Buchanan* visit) were the following considerations. First, there were suspicions that once the *Buchanan* was accepted, the Government would be set on a course of continuing compromise which, eventually, would whittle away Labour's anti-nuclear policy. Unless a stand was made, and made decisively, there was no certainty that Lange would not at some stage find the increasingly dual capability of the United States Navy and its ship visits such a negation of his party's anti-nuclear policy as to make it untenable and therefore not worth persevering with. Second, the majority in Caucus claimed that without the compliance of the party at large in what it was attempting, the Government would founder on the reef of suspect compromise, alienate many of its most loyal, active and informed supporters, defy a majority in the community opposed to nuclear weapons entering New Zealand, and thus risk electoral defeat. By emphasizing that the ship ban would be *party* as much as *Government* policy, the Caucus acknowledged that the political risk of not sustaining an effective and comprehensive ban would result in damage wider than just a policy reversal. Third, the situational conditions of early 1985 favoured an effective ban. Resentment existed towards what was regarded as external interference in New Zealand affairs, while public protest (especially in Auckland), lobbying of the Government by anti-nuclear groups, and considerable news media attention, heightened the "either-or" situation facing the Government.

A final factor involved the information available to the Caucus. Notwithstanding public American strictures as to the importance of consistently adhering to a "neither confirm nor deny" policy regarding the presence of nuclear weapons aboard visiting vessels, the Labour Caucus was satisfied that this had not prevented it from gaining the information necessary for making a decision. For a majority of Labour Members of Parliament a vessel that was nuclear capable might well be armed, if not for the proposed visit, then almost certainly later. This interpretation mystified and angered the Americans and led to swift accusations, following the imposition of the ban on port access, of being misled by New Zealand into believing that the *Buchanan* was acceptable. Another equally valid interpretation of American resentment was the naked fact of being seen to be refused by a small country over a matter touching the core of superpower status: credibility as a nuclear weapons power of the first rank.

In the event, the Caucus resolved that the New Zealand Government should go back to the United States with the suggestion that a revised request for port access include only a vessel that was neither nuclear armed, propelled nor capable. This alternative proved unacceptable to the United States; consequently, New Zealand formally refused to agree to the original *USS Buchanan* request. From that point the die was cast and the dispute hardened into impasse. Although far from unexpected, the swiftness and seeming severity of the American response, against what by any standards could only be described as a loyal ally, took many New Zealanders by surprise. For the American State Department, the ship ban could not go "cost free". A series of initial measures were announced, including an effective cancellation of planned naval exercises, a progressive scaling down of intelligence flows to New Zealand, and the "postponement" of the scheduled July ANZUS Council meeting. The American Secretary of Defence, Caspar Weinberger, said New Zealand was following a course that could do itself great harm, a statement described as "most regrettable" by Lange. Meanwhile, Hawke described ANZUS as a treaty in name only; Margaret Thatcher expressed disappointment in Lange's stance, while a United States Senator called for a removal of trade advantages enjoyed by New Zealand in the American market.

The Public Dimension

Unlike most disputes involving foreign relations, even in democracies, the ship ban dispute was unusual for its range and depth of public involvement. While it is too early to make definite judgements, three features deserve preliminary attention. Firstly, the dispute encouraged the contending sides to actively contest a presumed middle ground in order to gain greater public support for their respective positions. Secondly, there is the data provided by the public opinion polls. Thirdly, there was the interaction of the dispute with attitudes within the New Zealand community, whether shaped by gender, generation, region or social background, and focusing upon matters such as security, nuclear deterrence, and notions about New Zealand's role in the world.

One of the most commonly identified and remarked upon features of the public's view of the nuclear ship ban was the conflicting evidence of support. The public opinion polls consistently showed a sizeable majority of New Zealanders opposed to the entry of nuclear weapons into New Zealand, and yet the same polls consistently showed a comfortable majority favouring a retention of ANZUS and New Zealand's membership within it. Even allowing for some shifts of opinion over time, that basic finding never sustained effective challenge. This was significant since it allowed opposing sides in the dispute to claim they already had majority support for the essence of their case. Hence for those supporting the ship ban, a majority wanted just that — meaning ANZUS should adjust accordingly. For those opposed to the ban, a majority supported ANZUS — meaning that the anti-nuclear groups should adjust to that reality. Thus among the many letters written to the newspapers, the statements of position published by involved groups, the petitions organized by activists, or in the joint declarations issued by concerned individuals, a common theme involved the necessity for the opposing side to adjust to the wishes of the majority.

Once the ship ban was in place, and following Lange's widely publicized Oxford Union debate with the Reverend Jerry Falwell in March 1985, the international dimension of the domestic New Zealand debate widened considerably. Whether spontaneous or solicited, contrasting views from abroad were often voiced, and these opinions were regarded by local protagonists as adding weight to their arguments. As the dispute hardened into an impasse, the contest by opposing sides revolved more around the most appropriate defence and foreign policy options now before the country.

When the ban was instituted, the Government found that it had an increase in support for its policy, although it is difficult to divorce that increase from public resentment at the somewhat overbearing official American response. Thus, in late August of 1984, a New Zealand Herald-National Research Bureau Poll found that 58 per cent of its respondents opposed visits by nuclear-armed vessels *(New Zealand Herald, 6 October 1984)*. With the ban in place, a February 1985 Heylen-Eye Witness Poll found that 73 per cent approved of banning the entry of nuclear weapons into New Zealand *(Evening Post, 19 January 1985)*. As indicated, the polls also revealed consistent majorities favouring a retention of New Zealand membership in ANZUS.

Of greater volatility was opinion regarding the actual salience of the dispute in comparison to other issues confronting New Zealanders. After the dispute erupted, in February 1985 a New Zealand Herald-National Research Bureau Poll indicated ten per cent of the sample ranked nuclear ships as their major area of concern, this trailing the 22 per cent most concerned about unemployment, and the 21 per cent most concerned about the economy in general *(New Zealand Herald, 7 March 1985)*. A further six per cent of the same poll listed defence-ANZUS issues as their major field of concern. Barely four months later, the same polling organization indicated that less than one per cent of their sample cited either nuclear ships or defence-ANZUS issues as matters of major concern to them *(New Zealand Herald, 26 June 1985)*. By October, however, those two issues were attracting five per cent and three per cent salience respectively, undoubtedly influenced by some vigorous public exchanges and publicity between the United States and New Zealand surrounding

Palmer's abortive visit to Washington in September 1985 to reconcile differences. By early 1986, the salience of the issue was again receding with no more than four per cent of a total poll sample concerned with nuclear ships and defence-ANZUS issues *(Otago Daily Times,* 22 March 1986). By July, the corresponding figure was three per cent *(New Zealand Herald,* 12 August 1986). Understandably, such trends warrant cautious interpretation as it is unclear for whom these issues are salient.

As far as the attitudinal dimension of the dispute was concerned, the public was afforded ample opportunity to reflect and respond on a number of wider implications. In December 1985, the Government published for public comment and response a discussion paper one aim of which was to "attempt an analysis of the more central propositions" *(The Defence Question,* 1985, p.2). The focus for these deliberations was an independent Committee of Enquiry on the Future of New Zealand Strategic and Security Policies (see Chapter 12 of this volume). It is indeed difficult to envisage either the publication of the discussion paper, or the establishment of the Committee of Enquiry, had the open rupture with the United States not occurred in the wake of the nuclear ship ban. Although these measures were dismissed in some quarters as a cosmetic attempt by the Government to have the public respond with what it wanted to hear anyway, others were less sure. Numerous anti-nuclear groups welcomed the opportunity as a dual shoring up of both their own and the Government's positions. They saw the Enquiry as providing a catalyst for tangible definitions of position, circulation of information, and actual submission of findings. For other groups, less confident as public activists, the convening of the Enquiry was a recognition of their legitimacy and self worth. Opponents of the Government's ship ban saw the exercise as an opportunity to rally opinion in order to influence the outcome of the polling exercise conducted on behalf of the Enquiry.

For the Government, the public review bought valuable time: fortuitously, the Enquiry's gestation during the first half of 1986 witnessed international events that hardly damaged the Government's position, including the United States bombing raid on Libya, the Chernobyl nuclear plant disaster and small, but real signs of a thaw emerging in superpower relations over arms control. The Enquiry also encouraged a reconsideration of New Zealand's defence needs before the planned official review commenced its deliberations.

The longer this debate was sustained, the more evident it became that the polarizations involved were as much about contrasting attitudes as about specifics of policy. For those favouring an undisturbed ANZUS, the key symbols and images involved themes such as trust, solidarity, commitment, deterrence, guarantee, hostility, strength, the Soviet threat, reliability, cost, vulnerability, Communism, World War II, and protection. For those favouring the ship ban the key symbols and images employed terms such as independence, self-reliance, nuclear risk, internationalism, morality, sovereignty, choice, region, disarmament, communication, indigenous, constructive, legal, and legitimate. Obviously wider matters of national identification were thought to be at stake. And although the ship ban dispute was distinct and unprecedented, nevertheless it fed directly from an unresolved agenda of nationhood thoroughly aroused by still recent events such as the Springbok Rugby Tour of 1981. In total these activities, including the proposed 'nuclear free' legislation, involved less a definitive expression of attitudes to security so much as a direct incentive to shape and develop them. Previous official Defence Reviews, including those issued in 1978 and 1983, had indicated the need for more self-reliant, regionally based policies. With the nuclear ship ban in place, and a vacuum apparent as the operative credibility of ANZUS faded by the month, it was necessity as much as choice that urged a fundamental public reassessment of previously accepted doctrines guiding New Zealand's security.

The 'Nuclear Free' Legislation

In December 1985, the Government tabled for relevant parliamentary scrutiny its proposed legislation designed to give statutory endorsement to New Zealand as a nuclear-free state. That move represented a further step which, like the ship ban itself, structured the impasse in ways that further narrowed the ground for compromise. As well as giving statutory endorsement to a number of international arms control agreements to which New Zealand was already a party (such as the Nuclear Non Proliferation Treaty), the proposed legislation designated the territorial scope of the New Zealand Nuclear Free Zone. The Bill then outlined various prohibitions regarding the manufacture, acquisition, possession, or "having any control over" nuclear explosive devices. This applied to New Zealand nationals or servants of the Crown, either within or beyond New Zealand. Other prohibitions directly relating to New Zealand included the storage, stockpiling, transporting, deployment or testing of nuclear explosive devices as well as similar prohibitions on biological weapons.

Clause 9 of the Bill attracted the greatest attention by far; it was subject to much comment, recommended amendment, and attention by the parliamentary committee considering public submissions to the legislation. In Clause 9, responsibility is exclusively designated to the Prime Minister (a rare procedure in New Zealand statutes) for the purpose of considering any request for the entry of a foreign warship into the internal waters of New Zealand. In doing so, the Prime Minister is to "have regard to all relevant information and advice concerning the strategic and security interests of New Zealand". Presumably having done so, the Prime Minister would only then grant approval for entry if "satisfied that the warships will not be carrying any nuclear explosive device upon their entry into the internal waters of New Zealand". Far less equivocally, the Bill simply bans the entry of any ship that is nuclear propelled into the internal waters of New Zealand.

Critics of the proposed legislation claimed the operative Clause 9 was too weak; the word "satisfied", it was believed, placed far too much on trust with the Prime

Minister. Accordingly, some argued that a further section of the Bill, concerning the establishment of a Committee on Disarmament and Arms Control to advise the Government on these matters and the implementation of the legislation, be strengthened so that it could act as the body to whom the Prime Minister would be accountable for any decision regarding the entry of foreign warships. Critics maintained that wording such as "nuclear explosive device" is too narrow under conditions where the accoutrements of nuclear weapons capability, including delivery systems, command, control and communications functions, are just as important to ban and prohibit from New Zealand as the nuclear warheads themselves.

From a quite different perspective, Clause 9 also had its critics — in particular the United Kingdom and United States Governments. Whether through visits such as that conducted by Baroness Young, a British Minister of State in April 1986, or by numerous statements from senior American officials, it was made plain that the legislation represented a clear breach of "neither confirm nor deny" precepts concerning the disclosure of nuclear weaponry aboard visiting ships. The legislation also raised difficulties for these Governments in the event of New Zealand services personnel being involved, at some future date, in military exercises where they could well be collaborating with their counterparts from nuclear weapons states "having control over nuclear explosive devices".

Faced with these countervailing pressures, it grew increasingly obvious throughout 1986 that the Government would not amend the legislation to any major degree. By mid-year, after Lange had met with Thatcher in London and with Shultz in Manila, it was clear a parting of the ways had been reached. As it had already indicated, the United States confirmed that the passage of the legislation meant that Washington would no longer regard itself obligated to provide a security guarantee to New Zealand through ANZUS. In turn, such a withdrawal was greeted sceptically by the New Zealand Government on the grounds that there was nothing in the ANZUS Treaty providing for such a guarantee anyway. The New Zealand Government was also aware of the tightly drawn and circumscribed conditions outlining the criteria concerning the foreign commitment of United States combat forces. These were detailed clearly in November 1984 and quoted by Australian Defence Minister, Kim Beazley, the following May (Beazley, 1985, p.398).

The Wider Dimension

For the New Zealand Government, the tabling of its proposed 'nuclear free' legislation was important less for what was in it than for the way it forced the United Kingdom and the United States, *as nuclear weapons powers*, to declare their hand. The perception that solidified in New Zealand was that nuclear weapons powers were indeed different when it came to promoting their security interests.

Could it really be maintained that a "neither confirm nor deny" policy was intended to reassure the public of New Zealand that their security was being enhanced by an absence of nuclear weapons? And was it not apparent that neither the British nor the Americans had been forthcoming in their condemnation of the French outrage against the *Rainbow Warrior*, an act ostensibly perpetrated in the name of Western nuclear deterrence? These questions underlined the claims consistently made by the Government that its stance on the entire issue was one of opposition to all nuclear weapons, in itself nothing new when the record of New Zealand support for a Comprehensive Test Ban Treaty is considered.

In this respect the New Zealand Government had Australian support. Both countries had co-operated closely over recent years in jointly sponsoring United Nations General Assembly resolutions favouring a comprehensive test ban. In September 1985, the Australian Ambassador to the United States said that on the question of continued French testing the United States was "being less than helpful" and that if it wanted to, it could "exert strong influence on France to cease testing ... So far the United States has not only refrained from any such persuasion but has tended to give a good deal of credence to French arguments that the testing does no particular harm". Furthermore, the Ambassador added, it is "precisely that French testing which has been a major influence in the formation of the climate of opinion in New Zealand and which is now causing such anxiety to both the United States and the Australian governments in relation to the future of ANZUS" (Dalrymple, 1985, pp.822-23).

A further external dimension involved the comparisons that were drawn between New Zealand and the positions of other aligned states regarding nuclear weapons. This was, in part, motivated by attempts from various sources to see whether such comparisons might encourage a compromise in the continuing impasse between New Zealand and the United States. Most attention was devoted to countries that, although formally aligned to the United States, placed various qualifications, if only declaratory, on their willingness to accept nuclear weapons on visits to their territories, be it land, air or sea. But of the examples cited, whether Japan, Denmark, Spain, Norway or even France, no evidence was forthcoming that the United States was prepared to acknowledge any divergence from its "neither confirm or deny" policy. Some cases illustrated a degree of trust (critics claimed connivance) by host states concerned, when they maintained that the United States respected their wishes not to accept nuclear weapons in either transit or deployment. For those in New Zealand supporting an unambiguous nuclear ban, this was more a case of placing telescopes to blind eyes. These countries, including NATO members such as Norway and Denmark, have claimed that they do not have nuclear weapons either stored or deployed on their territories and that they do not host strategic nuclear delivery systems such as *Trident* submarines. These positions were not unlike that recommended for New Zealand by the opposition National Party throughout the ship ban dispute.

More intriguing was the Chinese case where, for at least part of 1985, it seemed the Americans acknowledged they had agreed that their ships visiting that country would not be nuclear armed. This was modified with suitable sinuosity to a position where the United States said they would not be sending such vessels and the Chinese said they would not be hosting them, thus obviating the necessity for any formal breach of the "neither confirm nor deny" principle. If anything, the New Zealand public was left more confused than enlightened by such comparisons.

What made the New Zealand position distinctive, making the rupture with the United States over ANZUS increasingly inevitable, was the Lange Government's continuing adherence to the principle that nuclear weapons entry into New Zealand was an issue that could not be fudged. Like pregnancy, it was a condition that either did or did not exist; a matter that, given consistently stated military demands of the United States, was not amenable to compromise.

Advantageously for the Lange Government, the longer the impasse continued and the more tenaciously it clung limpet-like to the ship ban, the greater the supporting unity of the Labour Party on the issue. Had the ship ban buckled under American pressure, many in the Labour Party already dismayed by the brisk "more market" economic restructuring of Finance Minister, Roger Douglas, could well have voted with their feet and departed the organization.

Ironically, the Australian position which helped precipitate the dispute in early January 1985, underwent its own modification towards New Zealand. While far from pleased with the turn of events, the Hawke Government soon appreciated that its own interests in the region would not be helped by a protracted dispute between New Zealand and the United States. Just such an example was the 1985 South Pacific Nuclear Weapons Free Zone Treaty, promoted by the Australians through the South Pacific Forum, and regarded as an initiative designed to further isolate France over its nuclear testing in the region. Moreover, because ANZUS has remained a triangular structure, there was at least some support to the claim that an Australian-New Zealand connection was as much part of a now inevitably refurbished ANZUS for those countries as the United States-Australian link. That said there was no denying that the ship ban hastened an arrival at a fork in the road pointing to an eventual formalization of both sets of bilateral links. This occurred at San Francisco in August 1986 when Australia and the United States confirmed their continuing military ties, and expressed joint opposition to New Zealand's port and air access policies that had "caused the disruption of the alliance relationship between the United States and New Zealand". Accordingly the United States suspended "its security obligations to New Zealand under the ANZUS treaty" (*The Dominion*, 13 August 1986). However, it was also clear from this meeting that Australian-New Zealand military and political co-operation would continue unimpaired. This was a recognition that ANZUS had never accomplished such uneasily residing goals as effective antipodean security and integration into doctrines of global containment. These differing objectives were never remote from the unresolved New Zealand–United States nuclear ship dispute that dominated so much of the time and attention of the fourth Labour Government.

References

Beazley, K. (1985) ANZUS: Regional Defence Implications *Australian Foreign Affairs Record* 56: 397–402.

Brown, B. (1962) *The Rise of Labour* Wellington, Price Milburn.

Candy, G. (1986) *Parliamentary Scrutiny of Foreign Policy in New Zealand* Unpublished MCA Thesis, Victoria University of Wellington.

Crothers, C. and Murray, G. (1985) Auckland Attitudes on International and Peace Issues New Zealand Political Studies Association Conference Paper, Auckland.

Dalrymple, R. (1985) Partners, Friends and Allies: Australia and the Pacific *Australian Foreign Affairs Record* 56: 818–25.

The Defence Question: A Discussion Paper (1985) Wellington, Government Printer.

Jackson, W.K. (1978) Caucus: The Anti-Parliament System? *The Parliamentarian*59: 159–164.

McIntyre, W. (1985) Labour Experience in Foreign Policy. In Gold, H. (Ed.) *in New Zealand Foreign Policy* Auckland, Benton Ross.

The New Zealand Labour Party (1986) *Submissions of the New Zealand Labour Party to the Committee of Enquiry on the Future of New Zealand's Strategic and Security Policies* Wellington, Mimeo 1–34.

New Zealand Parliament (1985) New Zealand Nuclear Free Zone, Disarmament and Arms Control Bill, Wellington, Government Printer.

Strachan, D. (1985) A Party Transformed: Organisational Change in the New Zealand Labour Party 1974-82. In Gold, H. (Ed.) *New Zealand Politics in Perspective* Auckland, Longman Paul.

12

The Defence Committee of Enquiry
A Unique Opportunity for Public Participation

Kevin Clements

> The Colonials, moreover, are generally men of mingled strength and simplicity. Their strength makes them unconscious of obstacles, and they attack the most delicate questions much as one opens a path through a virgin forest with an axe. Their outlook, not too carefully reasoned, and no doubt rather scornful of scientific thought, makes them incapable of self distrust. They have, like almost all men of action, a contempt for theories; yet they are often captured by the first theory which turns up if it is demonstrated to them with an appearance of logic sufficient to impose upon them. In most cases they do not seem to see difficulties, and they propose simple solutions for the most complex problems with an astonishing audacity. At heart they are probably convinced that politics are not as complicated as they have been made out to be, and that a little courage and decision are all that is required to accomplish the reforms of which Europe is so afraid (Siegfried, 1982, p.53).

Siegfried's 1904 comments about the innovative and reforming zeal of Richard Seddon's Liberal Government and the desire of many New Zealanders to lead the world in social and political reform seem eminently applicable to the fourth Labour Government and the current wishes of the New Zealand people. In the economic field, Rogernomics has imposed itself upon every sector of the economy and in the areas of Foreign Affairs and Defence the 1984 campaign slogan of "no nuclear powered or armed ships in New Zealand ports" has had a remarkable effect on alliance relationships and traditional views of defence.

In 1904, however, New Zealand could afford to be radical internally because it was externally secure and firmly part of the British Imperial system.

> ... Their autonomy may be as complete as possible, but they feel vaguely, without admitting it to themselves, that behind them stands watching a powerful protector, who will be there at the moment of danger, and who, if necessary, will be ready to repair their blunders (pp.53-54).

In the 1980s, however, the same external assurances in the fields of finance and foreign affairs do not apply. Since the run down of British military power in the Pacific in the 1960s and British entry into the European Economic Community in 1973, successive New Zealand Governments have had to live with the consequences of their economic and foreign policy decisions. The 1975-84 National Administration tended to adopt a rather cautious attitude to defence and foreign affairs. The fourth Labour Government, however, campaigned for a foreign policy that placed principle above pragmatism. The Labour Party has always had an idealistic approach to international relations. The first Labour Government, for example, promoted a "moral" foreign policy and campaigned for global collective security through the League of Nations (Bennett,1986). During the 1940s Peter Fraser promoted the United Nations, and the third Labour Government of Norman Kirk protested against French nuclear testing, recognized the People's Republic of China, and encouraged New Zealanders to start thinking of themselves as an independent Pacific nation rather than a West European outpost. Successive Labour Party conferences have always provided a venue for vigorous debate on foreign policy and defence issues.

In recent times the foreign policy debates at such conferences have focused on New Zealand's membership of ANZUS. The left wing of the party has argued that withdrawal would allow Labour to assert a moral position, reduce the risk of New Zealand becoming a nuclear target, separate New Zealand from all nuclear associations and facilitate the pursuit of a truly independent foreign policy. The centre-right of the party has argued for the retention of ANZUS on the grounds that it is in line with public opinion, constitutes New Zealand's ultimate security guarantee, keeps defence costs to a minimum, provides New Zealand with access to Washington and assists trade. It is also argued that the option of armed neutrality is too expensive, while unarmed neutrality would leave New Zealand too vulnerable.

On 13 May 1983 Bill Rowling, the then Labour spokesperson for Foreign Affairs, sent a memo to members of the party's Policy Council which canvassed the ANZUS options. It summarized them as follows: (a) to maintain, (b) to withdraw, and (c) to review. The arguments in favour of the *status quo* and withdrawal were as outlined above. The argument for review was as follows:

1. It would put New Zealand in line with the stand taken by the new Australian Labour Government;

2. The Treaty in its present form is clearly out of time;

3. There is a need for a vital economic association to replace a sterile military obligation;

4. It could work for effective economic stability in the region rather than be preoccupied with defence arrangements;

5. It could ensure that the association was compatible with New Zealand's promotion of a nuclear weapon free South Pacific;

6. It could allow the promotion of a truly equal partnership with any action requiring unanimous approval from all three partners; and,

7. It could ensure there was absolutely no surrender of national sovereignty (Rowling, 1983, p.2).

Rowling recommended the review option for a variety of reasons. He thought it possible to establish a joint Australian and New Zealand initiative that the United States could not ignore. He did not wish to close off options for a new Labour Government, and thought that it might be possible to revitalize the New Zealand-United States relationship. He also wanted to promote procedures that ensured equality and unanimity between the parties, allowed a right of veto, and would indicate whether the promotion of the South Pacific Nuclear Weapon Free Zone (NWFZ) was compatible with continued membership of the ANZUS alliance. He also underlined the party's desire to impose a ban on nuclear-armed and nuclear-propelled ships, although in relation to the latter he acknowledged that there was room for debate. In relation to the "neither confirm nor deny" policy of the United States and the intimation that a nuclear ship ban would mean the end of ship visits, Rowling's memo stated:

> A Labour Government could respond that if the United States did end all visits, then it would be Washington and not Wellington that had rendered ANZUS ineffective. In the unlikely event that the United States makes it clear that the "price" of maintaining ANZUS is United States nuclear ship visits, then a Labour Government could argue that it is important to note that despite all the US warnings, they have not stated that Labour's NWFZ and nuclear ship policy will end ANZUS, although they have noted that it will affect the United States ability to carry out its treaty obligations in this part of the world. *It is most unlikely that the US would end ANZUS as a result of Labour implementing its anti-nuclear policies* . The United States would not want to be seen bullying a small ally on the sensitive nuclear issue ... In short it can be argued that a Labour Government could call the bluff of those who argue that promoting NWFZ and banning nuclear armed ships would end ANZUS ... The review option, it can be argued, has the advantage of leaving open the possibility that Labour will be able to obtain its NWFZ objects and remain in ANZUS (author's italics) (pp.6-7).

The review option was adopted by the Policy Council and the 1983 party conference, and after the 1984 election provided a mandate for the Labour Government to implement a ban on all nuclear-powered and armed ships. This eventually resulted in the specific refusal to approve the visit of the USS *Buchanan* (see Chapter 11).

The United States responded swiftly by drastically reducing intelligence sharing and defence co-operation, cancelling joint military exercises and reciprocal visits by senior military personnel, and excluding New Zealand from certain intelligence conferences. The flow of much classified information which hitherto had automatically been given to New Zealand was also cancelled. Despite the fact that the Australian Prime Minister contemplated calling an emergency meeting of the

ANZUS Council to discuss these sanctions and to work out a way of preserving the trilateral relationship, no trilateral ANZUS discussions have taken place since the Labour Government assumed office. Thus the desire of Bill Rowling and the Labour Government to review and renegotiate ANZUS did not materialize. On the contrary, New Zealand found itself in the difficult position of promoting a policy of a nuclear-free New Zealand in ANZUS on a bilateral basis alone.

The Minister of Defence, Frank O'Flynn, put a brave face on the American sanctions by stating that:

> ... New Zealand stands at the threshold of a new era in its defence and security policies. The announcement of the US response to the Government's policies on nuclear weapons has cleared the air of uncertainty of recent months. Now we know where we stand, we intend to hold to our principles and we are ready to accept the consequences. The Government wants to continue and was prepared to continue to co-operate with all New Zealand's alliance partners as before. It was as committed as ever to the broad Western alliance and had no intention of withdrawing from ANZUS. Because of the unfortunate US attitude, New Zealand had to learn to stand on its own two feet ... In New Zealand's changed circumstances the Government has to do more about security and defence not less ... (O'Flynn, 1985).

The Minister of Defence indicated also that New Zealand's forces would be oriented primarily to the South Pacific with a capacity to contribute to wider interests in South East Asia when, and as, occasion demanded. He also indicated that there would be an expansion of trans-Tasman links. He committed the Government to expanding its own supplies of intelligence and maintaining a presence in Singapore while looking for further ways in which New Zealand could contribute to international peace-keeping operations.

The Minister's statement was designed for both an internal and an external audience. Internally it was intended as a morale boost for the armed services who were faced with quite serious personnel retention problems. Externally, it was intended to signal to the United States that New Zealand was prepared to go it alone if necessary. The statement preceded a discussion in the United States Foreign Affairs Sub-Committee on Asia and the Pacific which was set up on 19 March 1985 to discuss New Zealand's ship ban. From this point on, however, it was clear that the Government had to develop a coherent defence policy to meet three contingencies: first, a United States accommodation of New Zealand's anti-nuclear stance and the resumption of a trilateral ANZUS on conventional terms alone; second, a continuation of the stand-off with the result that New Zealand would have to forge closer links with Australia in some bilateral defence arrangement; and third, in the event of bilateral trans-Tasman relationships proving difficult, the development of policies that would provide for armed neutrality or non-alignment. This last strategy had been rejected by Labour's Policy Council in response to Rowling's 1983 memo.

Establishing the Committee of Enquiry

The Government could have updated the 1983 Defence Review to take account of the United States reaction to its nuclear weapons ban but it decided to conduct its own review in order that a truly Labour defence policy could be formulated. It could have done this by consultations within Cabinet, Caucus and the New Zealand Defence Council, but decided that it wished to take into account the interests and preferences of New Zealand citizens as well. This was innovative because defence and security issues are normally the sacred preserve of defence and foreign affairs professionals in consultation with the Government of the day. Cynics might say that the decision to consult the public was another attempt to postpone difficult defence investment decisions, or alternatively, to buy the Government time to generate greater public support for its foreign and defence policies. Idealists and those concerned about facilitating public participation in political decision-making, on the other hand, approved of this exposure of defence and security issues to public debate.

Irrespective of which interpretation is correct, it is clear that the incorporation of a public component into a defence review process is unique within Western democratic systems. Sweden and Australia, for example, have just completed reviews of their defence and security needs. Sweden, which has a long tradition of open and consultative Government, appointed a committee of seven consisting of current and former Members of Parliament to prepare a report on the orientation of Sweden's security policy and the future development of its defence after 1986/87. This report is almost entirely based on the views of defence and security experts (SOU: Swedish Official Reports Series, 1985). Similarly in Australia, the Australian Minister of Defence entrusted one person, Paul Dibb, to conduct a review of Australia's defence and security interests (Dibb, 1986). Whatever else history might decide about the value of the 1986 Defence Enquiry process, it will merit a footnote as a rather bold attempt to provide a public input into areas which normally pass unchallenged, where information remains classified, threat assessments are sometimes based on faulty intelligence, and there is considerable secrecy about why key strategic decisions are made.

In September and October 1985 there were preliminary discussions about how best to incorporate the views of the public into the defence review process. Initially a Royal Commission on Defence was mooted: it was decided, however, that this would be unnecessarily formal and legalistic. The solution proposed and accepted by Cabinet and Caucus was that a Defence Committee of Enquiry would be established independent of the Government and empowered to explore public opinion and attitudes on defence. This Committee would then submit its report to the Prime Minister who would pass it on to the Defence Council for the final determination of the 1986 Defence Review.

On 10 October while the composition of such a committee was being discussed, 17 retired senior officers, from the New Zealand armed services issued a public statement arguing that the Government should modify its inflexible anti-nuclear stance. This statement appeared some ten days after the United States Ambassador to New Zealand, H. Monroe Browne, had stated that the Reagan Administration felt "kicked in the teeth" by New Zealand's ban on nuclear warships and only one day after David Lange had met United States officials to discuss the ship ban. The former service chiefs argued for a reassertion of New Zealand's traditional approach to nuclear deterrence and the maintenance of a fully operational ANZUS. They argued that if the ANZUS rift was not repaired quickly it might have an adverse impact on other Western allies, and that while New Zealanders desired to be nuclear free there was a bigger majority in support of the preservation of the ANZUS relationship. They concluded that "the current policy should be abandoned" (*The Press*, 9 October 1985, p.25).

The Government was clearly displeased at the statement as shown by the Prime Minister's initial reaction:

> Those geriatric generals can carry on like this for as long as they like ... To prejudge the ANZUS standoff in such an alarmist manner would not help bring about a resolution. Labour would hold fast to its determination not to allow nuclear weapons in New Zealand and would fulfil its treaty obligations in conventional terms (*The Press*, 9 October 1985).

What was most distressing to the Prime Minister, however, was that he had advised the former chiefs by letter that they would be welcome to participate in the Defence Review process and indeed the Prime Minister's Department was actively considering a number as candidates for appointment to the Defence Enquiry Committee. Highly placed Government officials and Members of Parliament believed that this particular statement was deliberately timed to make it difficult to incorporate former military professionals onto the Committee, thereby reducing its credibility and effectiveness.

Throughout October and November 1985 the search continued for suitable members of the Defence Enquiry Committee. The search was co-ordinated by the Advisory Group in the Prime Minister's Department. While there were consultations with the Minister of Defence's office it was not directly involved. At the end of November specific offers were made to four people. The chairmanship of the Committee was offered to Frank Corner. He had impeccable foreign affairs credentials having been a former permanent head of the Ministry of Foreign Affairs, New Zealand Permanent Representative to the United Nations (1962-67) and Ambassador to the United States (1967-72). He had also been a close personal advisor to eight former Prime Ministers and had a particularly good working relationship with Norman Kirk. Indeed, Corner was instrumental in the development of Kirk's consciousness of New Zealand as a Pacific nation. The military position was offered to Major General Brian Poananga. He had been Chief of General Staff from 1978 to 1981 and had been appointed as New Zealand's first High Commissioner to Papua New Guinea at the time of independence. I was appointed to the Committee because of my work on disarmament issues in Geneva and my known anti-nuclear stance, and because I had been a non-governmental representative on the New Zealand delegation to the 1984 Non-Proliferation Treaty Review in Geneva. The fourth person selected for the committee was Diane Hunt, a scientist on leave from the Policy Research Unit of the Department of Scientific and Industrial Research (DSIR), who had been previously involved with the Commission for the Future.

The Prime Minister announced the composition of the Committee on 5 December 1985. He made great play of the fact that the Committee represented very diverse interests and embodied people who were supportive of, as well as opposed to, Government policy. When asked how such a committee could be expected to agree, the Prime Minister commented:

> Prime Minister: Well that is the point you see. This is a committee which is not there to form an agreement. It is there to make recommendations and to alert Government to particular strands of view, to different perspectives. We do not expect to have Dr Clements, Major General Poananga, Mr Frank Corner and Diane Hunt sing in unison.
>
> Question: So will they make different recommendations?
>
> Prime Minister: They will certainly. I could not imagine, in fact it would have to be a report of such stupefying blandness that they could all agree on it (Lange, 5 December 1985, pp.2-3).

The Prime Minister was also asked whether or not it would be possible for serving military personnel to make submissions; he indicated that they would be encouraged to do so. This was later qualified by the Chief of Defence Staff who informed the Committee that he did not wish to appear before it in public and did not consider it appropriate for other serving personnel to do so since they would have an opportunity to make their views known through the Defence Council deliberations on the Defence Review. He insisted that any Defence personnel who wished to make submissions to the Defence Committee of Enquiry should do so through the line of command. This was confirmed in a formal statement from the Minister of Defence on 20 December 1985.

Setting the Agenda

The terms of reference of the Committee were as follows: (a) to receive and hear public submissions on the Government's Green Paper (*The Defence Question*) on the future of New Zealand's defence policy; (b) to question groups and individuals making submissions; (c) to commission polling to provide objective data on public attitudes to defence and security questions; and (d) to prepare for Government a report, based on the public hearings and poll data, which would be taken into account in the preparation of the Defence Review.

In *The Defence Question* it was noted that:

> The Committee's report on public attitudes towards strategic and security issues will be published after completion of its hearings and investigations. It is envisaged that the Committee will wish to *comment on the practicability or otherwise of the main viewpoints and proposals it receives, and it may make specific recommendations on key issues.* This report and its recommendations will be taken into account by the Government in the preparation of the 1986 Defence Review (author's emphasis) (*Defence Question,* 1985 p.3).

The Defence Question provided a very useful framework for discussing defence and security issues. It mapped out four key elements of Government policy, namely: (a) how to secure New Zealand against external threat, terrorism or other challenges to vital interests; (b) how to ensure the stability of the South Pacific and maintain a close relationship with Australia; (c) how to promote greater self reliance in New Zealand's defence; and (d) how to maintain the anti-nuclear policy as "a basic starting point in defining the future New Zealand defence stance" (*Defence Question,* 1985, p.4). It then surveyed proposals for unarmed defence, isolationism, armed neutrality, and outlined areas of specific responsibility in the South Pacific, Antarctica, and with Australia. Attention was devoted to ANZUS and whether or not New Zealand armed forces should play a role in South East Asia. Ways in which New Zealand could contribute to a more peaceful world through peace-keeping, disarmament negotiations and other non-military efforts were also discussed. The Green Paper considered various threat scenarios and the defence capabilities required to deal with them, and concluded by addressing the cost of defence. In essence, it provided a series of defence and security dilemmas which it was hoped New Zealanders would comment on. It was released on 20 December 1985 and favourably received by the media. Peace groups and Service groups ensured its rapid circulation to their respective constituencies.

During the preliminary discussions of the Committee about the issues raised by *The Defence Question* it was argued that international as well as national reactions should be elicited. As a result, copies of the document were sent to various overseas experts; positive responses were received from senior advisors to the Stockholm Institute of Peace Research, the World Policy Institute in New York, the Institute of Strategic Studies in London and the Geneva Institute of Peace Research. These experts considered *The Defence Question* a refreshingly new approach to old problems and that the New Zealand Government was adventurous in stimulating a public debate about defence and security issues in the light of its anti-nuclear stance.

The initial meetings of the Committee were co-ordinated by the Prime Minister's Advisory Group, rather than by the office of the Minister of Defence. Indeed, the Committee did not meet formally with the Minister of Defence at any time during the entire review process. While the preliminary discussions were largely procedural the Committee agreed to work towards a consensus in the final document. Although it was acknowledged that any member of the Committee had the right to dissent and write a minority report, it was felt important to try and reconcile the divergent views within the Committee as an example to the community.

At the second meeting a series of questions on defence and security that needed clarification were tabled. These became the basis for the informal and off-the-record briefings the Committee received from officials in Foreign Affairs, Defence, Civil Defence, the DSIR and the Prime Minister's Department during January 1986. These discussions were wide ranging and provided the Committee with information on the threats facing New Zealand, defence capabilities, alliance relationships, and the disruption to United States–New Zealand military intelligence contacts. The briefing sessions were substantively useful; more importantly, they enabled the Committee members to get to know one another better and discover areas of agreement and disagreement on defence and security. After several briefings it became very clear that there was a generational divide and that the views of Corner and Poananga had been shaped by experiences very different from those that had conditioned Diane Hunt and myself. Corner, for example, had gained his early diplomatic experience during the Cold War and viewed the Soviet Union with scepticism. For Diane Hunt and myself the Vietnam War was a much more critical conditioning experience in determining our perception of United States foreign policy. In relation to the nuclear deterrent there was a greater willingness on the part of Corner and Poananga to acknowledge its success in the post-war years and see it as an essential component of a global collective security framework. These early discussions were always frank and vigorous and while there were profound disagreements about the ways in which members viewed the world, these were always amicable and a positive appreciation of the views and attitudes of each other developed.

In addition to having a series of private briefings throughout January, the Committee started to receive public submissions in response to *The Defence Question*. These submissions were logged by the secretariat, summarized and recorded. Each member of the Committee received a copy of every submission. After two or three hundred submissions had been read the Committee started work preparing the public opinion poll. It was decided the questionnaire should reflect the concerns raised by those who had taken the time and effort to write submissions to the Committee and which covered the areas that had been outlined in the Green Paper. A group of experts in public opinion polling were assembled to help design the questionnaire and work out a suitable sample frame for the survey. By the second meeting with these experts a preliminary questionnaire had been formulated which the Committee considered addressed most of the concerns raised in submissions and the Green Paper. At this point the Committee called for tenders from professional polling agencies. From these tenders and subsequent interviews the National Research Bureau was selected. The questionnaire was modified slightly by the National Research Bureau. A series of group discussions were conducted with young urban adults, older urban adults, adults living in a rural environment and adults of Pacific Island descent. These groups were asked if they had any problems in understanding any of the questions, whether they were biased and whether there were additional questions that ought to have been asked. The National Research Bureau altered specific parts of the questionnaire as a result of these qualitative interviews. The Committee accepted the changes and the questionnaire was tested in a pilot survey of 100 respondents. The National Research Bureau and the Department of Statistics then worked out a suitable sampling frame that would ensure the final sample was representative of the entire population. In particular, the Committee insisted that the poll be representative in terms of age, sex, urban and rural areas, and ethnicity.[1]

The Submissions

Public submissions to the Committee officially ended on 28 April 1986; by this stage over 4000 submissions had been received. A good proportion of the last thousand were from persons who responded to a pro-nuclear ANZUS advertisement in the major metropolitan dailies. These particular submissions were logged but not given as much weight as the more carefully considered and often very lengthy submissions written either from a non-nuclear perspective or from a more traditional approach to defence and security. There were a large number of more reflective submissions and these had a profound impact on Committee members because of their insights into the implications of an unconditional anti-nuclear policy.

Nine public hearings were held between 6 March and 24 April 1986 at which it was decided the proponents of anti-nuclear or alternative approaches to defence as well as those arguing for a more traditional often pro-deterrent approach should appear.[2] The Committee did this partly for political reasons, since it believed it important that the hearings be credible to all sides of the defence debate, and partly because it was considered important to encourage a dialogue among contending positions. These public hearings provided opportunities for the Committee to explore particular public concerns about defence and security, as well as facilitating a debate among the Committee members themselves.

The final hearing was an opportunity to hear the views of New Zealand's political parties. The Socialist Unity Party, the New Zealand Democratic Party and the New Zealand Values Party all advocated policies of neutrality or non-align-

ment; all called for a more independent foreign defence policy and all suggested
New Zealand should withdraw from military alliances and nuclear-related systems.
The Values Party, for example, argued that New Zealand's perception of the world
was greatly distorted by a past reliance on United States intelligence and that New
Zealand should vigorously separate itself from all United States military activities.
The New Zealand Democratic Party also advocated withdrawal from ANZUS, a
policy of neutrality, and a diplomatic campaign to encourage other South Pacific
nations to follow New Zealand's lead in creating a South Pacific zone of peace.
These suggestions were made in the context of the Democrats' overall foreign policy
stance of self reliance — self sufficiency in energy, import substitution and counter
trade. The Democrats believed that a policy of neutrality would lessen the chance of
New Zealand becoming involved in a nuclear conflict and wanted New Zealand to
work towards making Antarctica a world wildlife park. The Socialist Unity Party,
a Soviet-aligned communist party, advocated a more vigorous anti-nuclear stance,
withdrawal from ANZUS and other aggressive pacts, a policy of non-alignment,
opposition to arms manufacturing and the media (which they believed served the
interests of the armaments industry), the creation of a Ministry of Peace and the
incorporation of peace studies in the school curriculum.

The National Party argued that New Zealand's defence and security policies
followed from an appreciation of New Zealand's place in the Pacific. Their
spokespersons argued that the Pacific was becoming a zone for superpower contention, and since New Zealand is an attractive country in terms of natural resources
and sparse population, the National Party suggested it might some day be subject to
threat of invasion. National rejected any idea of pursuing policies of neutrality
because New Zealand is isolated and strategically expendable. The Opposition
emphasized that New Zealand shared democratic traditions with the Western
community; consequently non-alignment was not an option for National — on the
contrary, full participation in the Western alliance was New Zealand's only effective
defence policy. Were the Labour Government to choose any other option, the next
National Government would return New Zealand to full membership of the
Western alliance. They reiterated the suggestion of the 1983 Defence Review that
defence forces must be capable of independent operation in the South Pacific region
and that the South Pacific was New Zealand's appropriate sphere of interest.
National concluded by saying that ANZUS had preserved New Zealand's security
for 33 years and continued membership was absolutely essential for maintaining
stability in the region.

The Labour Party's submission outlined why the bipartisan consensus on foreign
policy that had prevailed until 1966 had broken down. The first explanation was the
National Government's commitment of New Zealand troops to Vietnam; the
second was the high profile of nuclear weapons issues in New Zealand in the 1960s,
in particular the commencement of French nuclear testing in 1966 which strained

the loyalty of the Labour Party to the nuclear nations in the Western alliance. During the 1970s Labour pursued a nuclear-free policy; it was only by the end of the 1970s that support developed for a withdrawal from ANZUS. The major reason for taking a more independent stance and proposing withdrawal from the alliance was the limited progress made by the United States in response to the anti-nuclear desires of large sections of the global community. Labour's spokespersons argued that Labour had always been internationalist never isolationist, so that even outside an alliance Labour would support strong internationalist policies at the United Nations and within the South West Pacific. The starting point for the Labour Party submission was greater self-reliance and an unconditional anti-nuclear stance. These were coupled with a reaffirmation of the special responsibility for promoting development in the South Pacific and a close defence relationship with Australia.

Considerable time was spent delineating the difference between the Labour Government's position and that of the Labour Party conference on the future of ANZUS. Although the Government has been arguing for a nuclear-free New Zealand within ANZUS, Labour conferences over the years have been saying very clearly that they see no future for ANZUS. The conferences believe that ANZUS is irrelevant to the question of strategic balance in the Pacific and that the military technology and training that flowed from ANZUS membership often had little to do with New Zealand's defence needs. Labour's spokespersons argued that ANZUS was not a necessary ingredient for a friendly relationship with the United States, even if it were an important ingredient for a close relationship. They argued that, separated from a military alliance, New Zealand could develop other kinds of relationships with the United States which would help maintain the shared interests between the two countries. In relation to the specific question of the nuclear ship policy, Labour's spokespersons argued that:

> ... the 1984 ANZUS policy was promoted in good faith and on the assumption that the Treaty was loose and flexible enough to accommodate our unconditional non-nuclear stance. The present United States Administration has disagreed with that assumption. The New Zealand Labour Party has asserted that the non-nuclear stance is non-negotiable. Resumption of the former level of military co-operation under ANZUS cannot be conditional on New Zealand's acceptance of nuclear weaponry. In the context of the impasse which has been reached we submit that it is now appropriate to develop post-ANZUS arrangements for New Zealand's defence based on ANZAC-South Pacific relationships and on promoting greater security arrangements in the framework of the United Nations (New Zealand Labour Party, 1986, pp.22-23).

It was assumed that the nuclear-free stance the Government had adopted provided the only credible platform from which to promote disarmament regionally and internationally. In terms of threat perception there was an assumption by Labour that there was a need to have a capacity to respond to low level threat, but that

higher level threats such as invasion were unlikely to occur. Finally, and in line with
the policy to withdraw from ANZUS and opt for a more self-reliant policy,
Labour's spokespersons suggested that New Zealand's defence capabilities should
reflect a more limited orientation and not be arranged to suit wider alliance forward
defence strategies. The submission provoked a very interesting debate and was
widely reported in the media. Subsequently, the Prime Minister issued a press release
indicating that while the submission may have reflected party opinion it was not
representative of Government policy.

The diverse submissions received and the public hearings of 107 of them gave the
Committee a good appreciation of the range of opinion on defence and security
issues that existed within the community at large. These submissions fell into three
major categories.

Category One
Firstly, there were those who endorsed the conventional view of collective security
and an acceptance of nuclear deterrence with all that this implied in terms of a
reversal of New Zealand's ban on ship visits by nuclear-armed and powered
warships (*Defence and Security*, part II, chapters 4-6). Proponents of this policy felt
that New Zealand's interests and sympathies were clearly linked to the Western
nations; a threat to any one of those nations constituted a threat to New Zealand,
and therefore it was necessary to contribute to the defence of Western values
globally. Those who held this view argued for peace through strength and believed
that the Soviet Union constituted the largest single threat to New Zealand and its
wider Western interests. Those who proposed nuclear collective security believed
very strongly that New Zealand's isolation did not confer any guarantee against
potential threats and that New Zealand was far too small to stand alone. They
believed that the ANZUS Treaty provided protection from external aggression; had
served New Zealand well in the past; was indispensable to the efficiency and the
professionalism of New Zealand's armed forces, and enabled the Government to
pursue other interests more effectively. There was a strong concern, however, that
New Zealand should not be free riders and that alliance obligations should be
fulfilled in whatever ways seemed appropriate. New Zealand's strategic perimeter
was the whole world, and there was a commitment to forward defence, even though
most submissions arguing this position acknowledged that New Zealand's primary
responsibility lay with Australia and the South Pacific. While the abhorrence of
nuclear weapons was acknowledged, by and large proponents of nuclear collective
security argued that the nuclear deterrent had prevented global war. In relation to
arms control there was concern that New Zealand could do more for disarmament
from within an alliance framework than from outside. People making submissions
along these lines gave greater prominence and priority to ANZUS than to arms

control and rejected the nuclear ship ban. In terms of cost, they argued that as much as was necessary should be spent to safeguard adequately New Zealand's global interests.

Category Two

By far the largest proportion of written submissions received argued for non-nuclear defensive systems. Anti-nuclear protagonists started from the assumption that nuclear weapons were morally abhorrent and that nuclear war constituted the greatest single threat to the world including New Zealand. Consequently, any sane defence and security policy had to address what most people considered the biggest threat. For some this meant a nuclear-free New Zealand in ANZUS. People who proposed this solution argued being nuclear free did not necessarily rule out conventional alliances. A second group, however, claimed that a nuclear-free New Zealand in ANZUS, given that the dominant partner in the relationship had nuclear weapons, was a sham and because of this New Zealand must withdraw from all alliances with nuclear powers. Many submissions called for a withdrawal from ANZUS on grounds that it tied New Zealand into a web of relationships over which it had no control, made New Zealand a nuclear target, compromised national sovereignty and that ANZUS, intentionally or not, linked New Zealand by association to objectionable United States foreign policies. Critics of ANZUS also argued that it had led New Zealand into other nations' wars, did not guarantee effective security, that its benefits both in terms of military technology and intelligence were grossly overrated, and that it did not provide New Zealand with any real influence in Washington.

While most non-nuclear submissions emphasized the overwhelmingly negative effect of nuclear war, they also acknowledged that there were various other threats which New Zealand should address. Anti-nuclear proponents tended to have a much more benign view of the strategic environment than nuclear collective security proponents and believed it possible to secure the South West Pacific region by developing closer relationships with Australia, extending relationships within the South Pacific, withdrawing forces from Singapore and by pursuing co-operation with all countries in the immediate region. In terms of arms control and disarmament, those who opted for non-nuclear policies felt that this gave New Zealand credibility to argue for effective arms control at the United Nations and in bilateral discussions. In terms of force structure many of the individuals and groups that promoted non-nuclear armed defence also had very clear ideas about the specific types of forces they wished to see developed in New Zealand. There was a strong preference for New Zealand defence forces to have an exclusively defensive capacity. There were a variety of suggestions for developing coast guard forces, a regionally focused Air Force capability, and self-reliant nationally based defence. Some advocates of this position also developed proposals for guerilla defence and some variants on the Swiss Citizen Army.

Category Three

Another group of New Zealanders adopting an anti-nuclear stance argued very strongly that there was no particular need for New Zealand to have any armed forces at all. Advocates of such unarmed defence systems firmly believed that New Zealanders should begin thinking of non-violent ways for ensuring their security and defence. Most submissions along these lines were *strongly* anti-nuclear and antagonistic towards all weapons of mass destruction. Protagonists of unarmed defence had a conscientious objection to all armed forces. Persons associated with this pacifist position could not see any immediate or long-term threat to New Zealand.

In addition to the orthodox pacifist position a large number of submissions focused on the need for more active non-violent defence and proposed an idea, originated by Professor Gene Sharp from Harvard University, called civilian-based defence. The major assumption of civilian-based defence is that the whole population and all its institutions become the fighting force against the would-be invader; instead of resisting aggression with armed force, civilian defenders utilize psychological, economic, social and political non-violent resistance. There was a recognition on the part of the advocates of civilian-based defence that it was a long-term strategy, but most felt that there was sufficient merit in the proposals for New Zealand to embark upon a process of transarmament. Proponents of this position tended to argue for the disbanding of the armed forces, withdrawal from all military alliances, the withdrawal of New Zealand troops from Singapore, a complete ban on all warships (whether nuclear or not) and all military aircraft, and the modification of existing defence forces into civil defence forces.

The Public Opinion Poll

The poll results revealed some very interesting data.[3] First, it became clear that New Zealanders had an instinctive empathy with traditional allies – Australia and Britain. Almost five out of every ten respondents claimed that they would "get on very well" with people from these countries; the United States ranked third, followed by the Netherlands, South Pacific Island countries and Japan. France, not surprisingly in the light of the *Rainbow Warrior* affair, elicited the strongest negative response with 26 per cent indicating that either they would "not get on very well", or "poorly", with the French, a figure twice the number who thought they would "get on very well" with the French. The poll also indicated some generational differences. Those in the over 35 year age bracket felt considerably stronger empathy with traditional allies than did the under 35 generation, although even this younger group displayed strong sentiments in favour of traditional allies.

In terms of threat perception the Committee decided there were three components: the likelihood of a particular threat; the seriousness of that threat if it eventuated; and the country posing the threat. The responses to questions on threat revealed an interesting pattern: 91 per cent identified the poaching of fisheries within New Zealand's 200 mile economic zone as the most likely threat, though only 23 per cent regarded this as a worry. The second most likely threat was the occurrence of terrorist acts in New Zealand: 74 per cent identified this as something that was probable, with 39 per cent worried about the issue. Nuclear and conventional war worried 44 per cent and 43 per cent respectively, but the prospect of a nuclear war worried twice as many people as the prospect of a conventional war: in fact, 48 per cent of the population ranked nuclear war as the greatest worry amongst the list of possible threats.

The countries that were thought to pose a specific military threat to New Zealand were the Soviet Union (31 per cent), the United States (14 per cent) and France (13 per cent). More Labour Party supporters identified the United States as a threat than did National supporters. *Thus the concern about nuclear war and the nuclear superpowers was reflected not only in the submissions but in the public opinion poll as well.*

There was very widespread support for alliances with other countries: 82 per cent felt that New Zealand should form alliances, while only 14 per cent thought the contrary. In relation to ANZUS specifically, seven out of ten respondents supported New Zealand's membership, while only one in ten opposed membership of ANZUS. The strength of support for ANZUS varied quite considerably according to party identification; for example, 93 per cent of National supporters favoured continuing membership (the majority strongly so) while only 58 per cent of Labour supporters did so (and generally with less enthusiasm). The poll also asked people to explain their view of ANZUS. The main reasons given for supporting ANZUS were that New Zealand needs the general support of major powers (25 per cent); the country is too small to defend itself (25 per cent); historical friendship and trading relations (13 per cent); the military aspect of ANZUS (14 per cent); improved security for New Zealand (13 per cent); and that common interests should continue (13 per cent). The main reasons for opposition to ANZUS were: United States nuclear policies (26 per cent); that ANZUS would not protect New Zealand (16 per cent); would involve New Zealand in war (15 per cent); a preference for neutrality and have alliances only in wartime (18 per cent); United States domination of ANZUS (11 per cent); anxiety over threats by the United States on the nuclear ship question (nine per cent); a general mistrust of the United States (eight per cent); and a positive preference for a New Zealand-Australian alliance (five per cent) (*Defence and Security*, p.41).

After asking respondents whether they wished to form alliances, they were then asked to identify the countries which should be New Zealand's alliance partners. The three most mentioned countries were Australia (68 per cent), the United States (52 per cent) and Great Britain (35 per cent): only 14 per cent of the population

230

favoured alliances with South Pacific countries; 68 per cent identified Australia as New Zealand's natural alliance partner. This affiliation was reinforced by the answers given concerning the importance of Australia to New Zealand defence and security interests; 64 per cent considered Australia "very important" and 28 per cent "important" to New Zealand defence and security. Furthermore, 70 per cent supported defence co-operation with Australia under all circumstances, 25 per cent supported in some circumstances, and only three per cent argued that there should be no defence co-operation with Australia under any circumstances. If there were an attack on Australia 81 per cent argued that New Zealand should assist Australia in all or most circumstances (p.41.)

   While there was strong support for alliances in the poll data there was equal, if not stronger, opposition expressed to nuclear weapons and anxiety about the risk of nuclear war. The stationing in New Zealand of land-based nuclear weapons was overwhelmingly opposed (92 per cent) as was the stationing of biological and chemical weapons. There was a similarly strong rejection of nuclear testing, especially in overseas territories of nuclear weapons states or in other people's territory, and 75 per cent of all respondents opposed the testing of unarmed missiles in the South Pacific. In relation to the specific question of ship visits, three per cent were in favour of just banning nuclear powered ships, 28 per cent favoured banning only nuclear armed ships, while 38 per cent favoured banning both. In other words *69 per cent of the population were in favour of maintaining a ship ban of some sort* and only 28 per cent of the population favoured lifting that ban. The reasons cited for maintaining the ban were varied — the risk of accidents; the presence of such ships made New Zealand a potential target in the event of nuclear war; a broad opposition to nuclear arms; a general support for disarmament; and a feeling that the ban was a suitable disarmament initiative for New Zealand to adopt. The 28 per cent who favoured access for nuclear-powered or armed ships believed that visits by allied vessels should be allowed, considered that it improved security and was a condition of ANZUS membership, and in any case felt that nuclear power was safe. Not surprisingly, given the numbers of people that supported alliances, when questioned whether they would allow visits by non-nuclear ships, 86 per cent supported such visits.

   The salience of the nuclear issue for New Zealanders was reflected in a series of questions on voting behaviour at the 1984 election and for projected voting behaviour at the time of the poll. Nuclear issues have become a more important electoral determinant. At the previous election, 41 per cent of those surveyed indicated that the parties' nuclear policies were "very important" or "important" in determining their electoral choice. The 1986 poll showed that this percentage had climbed to 58 per cent, with foreign and defence policies and the anti-nuclear question of greater importance to Labour than National voters (p.106).

   The questionnaire asked respondents to indicate their preferred defence option.

The results produced seven broad categories:
1. Allied to the United States and Australia, including the nuclear capability (24 per cent);
2. Allied to the United States and Australia, but New Zealand being separated from all nuclear aspects (42 per cent);
3. No alliances, but friendly relationships with the United States and Australia in a conventional defence capacity (13 per cent);
4. Armed neutrality (eight per cent);
5. Allied to Australia only (four per cent);
6. Unarmed neutrality, no armed forces (four per cent); and
7. Allied to some other country (two per cent).

Interestingly, only 25 per cent of the sample rejected an alliance framework, while 72 per cent considered New Zealand should remain in alliances: of this number, however, only 24 per cent wanted a nuclear alliance. *The overwhelming preference, representing 73 per cent of the poll, was for a nuclear-free defence policy.*

In relation to the specific question of ANZUS and ship visits, respondents were asked whether they wished to be in ANZUS and allow visits by nuclear ships (37 per cent opted for this); New Zealand in ANZUS and no visits by nuclear ships (44 per cent); and New Zealand out of ANZUS and no nuclear ships (16 per cent) (see table 12.1). *The most preferred option and indeed the first preference of New Zealanders in this question was for New Zealand to be a member of ANZUS without allowing nuclear ship visits.* This of course was also Government policy.

Those who supported ANZUS without nuclear ship visits were asked a further question: "If staying in ANZUS without nuclear ship visits proves impossible, what is your next choice?" This produced the following distribution: New Zealand in ANZUS allowing nuclear ships (33 per cent); New Zealand out of ANZUS and no nuclear ship visits (62 per cent). These responses were then added back into the initial two groups producing the following aggregate figures. If a nuclear-free New Zealand in ANZUS is impossible a small majority, 52 per cent, would favour being in ANZUS and allow nuclear ship visits, 44 per cent were in favour of New Zealand being out of ANZUS with no visits by nuclear ships, with four per cent don't knows. Clearly the margin of error in this figure is rather high, but it does indicate the division that existed in April and May in relation to the dilemma of maintaining alliance membership while pursuing an unconditional anti-nuclear policy.

This particular crunch question assumed greater significance for the Committee of Enquiry after the Manila meeting between David Lange and George Shultz, in which the American Secretary of State indicated that New Zealand and the United States had parted company albeit as friends (see Chapter 11). Until this time there seemed a reasonable possibility that New Zealand might have been able to achieve what the now Ambassador to Washington, Bill Rowling, thought could be achieved in 1983 — namely a nuclear-free New Zealand within the framework of ANZUS.

Figure 12.1
Preferred ANZUS/ship visit option (first choice)

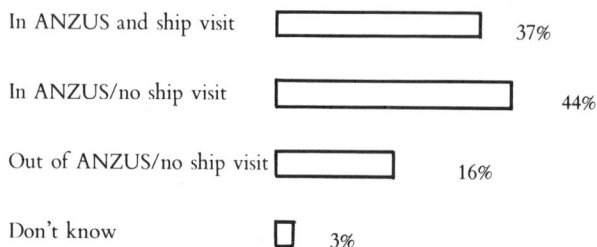

In ANZUS and ship visit ⬜ 37%

In ANZUS/no ship visit ⬜ 44%

Out of ANZUS/no ship visit ⬜ 16%

Don't know ⬜ 3%

Preferred ANZUS/ship visit option if nuclear ships necessary for ANZUS

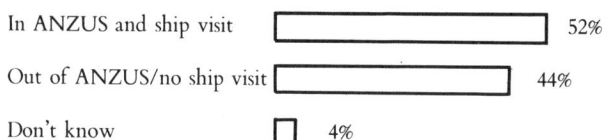

In ANZUS and ship visit ⬜ 52%

Out of ANZUS/no ship visit ⬜ 44%

Don't know ⬜ 4%

Source: Defence and Security: What New Zealanders Want (1986) annex, p.76a.

Prior to the Manila meeting with Shultz the Committee prepared a background brief for Lange giving the poll results and endeavouring to analyze the major parameters of the conflict between New Zealand and the United States. While preparing this, the Committee thought it useful to try and work out exactly what a nuclear-free New Zealand meant. Eight levels of nuclear "freedom" were defined:

Level 1. No stationing of nuclear weapons or nuclear power generators in New Zealand. (This has always been New Zealand's position.)

Level 2. No joint facilities that play a direct part in the nuclear strategy. (This has always been New Zealand's position.)

Level 3. No transit of nuclear-powered or armed vessels or aircraft through or over New Zealand sea or land, and no stopping in New Zealand harbours or airports.

Level 4. No training or exercising of our armed forces with a nuclear weapon state.

Level 5. No installations in New Zealand which have any connection with the military operations of a nuclear country.

Level 6. No alliances with a nuclear state.

Level 7. No alliance or military relationship with a country (e.g. Australia) which has an alliance with a nuclear state or provides facilities which assist a nuclear strategy.

Level 8. No equipment or units in New Zealand armed forces which could in any circumstances assist a nuclear state (pp.62-63).

Many people making submissions to the Committee argued that the Government should move to level eight and completely dissociate New Zealand from any nuclear weapons state. Others, especially those promoting nuclear collective security, preferred New Zealand remaining at level one. *It is clear from the poll data that most New Zealanders want the Government to remain at level three.* This has proved unacceptable to the current United States Administration and, as a consequence, although ANZUS still exists as a legal treaty it has ceased to exist as an operational trilateral alliance.

In the course of preparing the brief for Lange, the Committee worked hard to try and reconcile the competing principles of anti-nuclearism supported by 73 per cent of the population, and alliance membership supported by 72 per cent. Throughout deliberations a defence policy was sought that would command a higher level of consensus than the 52 per cent in favour of ANZUS with an unfettered ship visit policy. It was concluded that it might be possible to develop a theoretical consensus as high as 80 per cent around the policy of a nuclear-free New Zealand in ANZUS if it were possible to reach an agreement with the United States which respected New Zealand's nuclear-free status. The United States was unable to make this concession to New Zealand and the domestic policy option which would satisfy the majority ceased to be a possibility.

Within the Committee there was a division of opinion about what to do next. Two members wished to maintain an operational ANZUS, with a "tactful" ship visit policy that would not breach the "neither confirm nor deny" policy. The other two members, myself included, had an unconditional anti-nuclear policy as the bottom line and opted for a bilateral ANZUS relationship with Australia while leaving the door open for the possibility that a different United States Administration might be able to acknowledge New Zealand's anti-nuclear stance. It was hoped that a future American Administration would place friendship and the alliance above global nuclear containment, that it would not impose unacceptable requests on the New Zealand Government, and that it would begin to see defence, in this part of the world at least, in conventional terms alone. Leaving the door open offered the possibility of maintaining some anti nuclear leverage over the one nuclear power to whom New Zealand was allied. By moving in a direction of neutrality (which was supported at the most by only 25 per cent in the poll) New Zealand would forgo any opportunity of constraining, even marginally, the nuclear policies of the United States. To remain open to a continuing allied status, however, is a rather controversial position since the United States has shown few signs that it is interested in any multilateral arms control or disarmament initiative, and has not shown any noticeable willingness to allow itself to be disciplined by its allies. Nevertheless, since an allied relationship with the United States exists, albeit attenuated, New Zealand has more responsibility for its actions than for the actions of the Soviet Union, and the anti-nuclear position imposes an obligation to press the Americans, as well as the Soviets, to ensure progress on arms control and disarmament.

What the United States must understand is that if it values New Zealand as an ally as well as a friend it needs to accept the anti-nuclear sentiments of New Zealanders. If there were any prospect of American recognition of New Zealand's anti-nuclear stance this would be very heartening to other alliance partners who wish to be non-nuclear and Western: hopefully the Warsaw Pact too could begin the difficult process of diminishing reliance on nuclear weapons as its ultimate security guarantee.

The Report and Government's Response

Given the poll preferences outlined above, the Committee was faced with the difficult task of reconciling these results with the submissions in order to develop a report that would fulfil the terms of reference. Moreover, given the diverse and varied nature of the written submissions, it was impossible to quantify them and add their results to the poll findings. Therefore, it was decided that the best way to deal with the submissions was to draw selected quotations from them and allow the persons writing them to speak in their own words in relation to the three general policy options outlined above. The poll data was utilized to give an indication of the representativeness of these submissions in the community as a whole. The Committee's report, therefore, tried to do justice to both the submissions and the poll results.

Another difficulty concerned how much interpretive comment or opinion should be added by the Committee to the straightforward reporting of the sub-missions and poll data. It was decided to demarcate clearly such comments and the Committee built on the briefing paper prepared for the Prime Minister to do this. The Committee endeavoured to do justice to the principles of anti-nuclearism, as well as the principles of collective security, and also looked at the alternatives confronting New Zealand if the preferred option of a nuclear free New Zealand in ANZUS proved impossible. In particular, the nature of the relationship with Australia was emphasized.

Towards the end of the deliberations the chairman introduced a draft conclusion based on the poll result giving a small majority (52 per cent) in favour of return to operational ANZUS and acceptance of ship visits. The Committee, however, was unwilling to allow any policy recommendation to be based on this figure of 52 per cent because it did not provide sufficient popular basis for developing a consensual or bipartisan foreign policy to take New Zealand into the 1990s and beyond. Moreover, it would undermine the Government's anti-nuclear policy. It was equally clear, however, that there was only minority support in both the submissions and the poll for New Zealand pursuing a policy of neutrality, non-alignment or semi-alignment. This meant the Committee was left with only one choice, namely the enhancement of a bilateral conventional ANZUS relationship with Australia. This would satisfy some although not most of those who wanted to retain collective security arrangements, and most but not all of those who wanted a nuclear-free defence.

As outlined in the report there are many challenges to be confronted in the development of such a relationship. The Committee gave very serious consideration to Paul Dibb's *Review of Australia's Defence Capabilities* and had extensive discussions with Dibb when he visited Wellington towards the end of July 1986. There are very real differences between the Australian view of alliances and that of New Zealand; Australia, for example, believes that its best protection against the risk of nuclear war was and is Government support for global deterrence coupled with policies aimed at effective arms control. The Australian Government has firmly committed itself to maintaining a close relationship with the United States through ANZUS in order to assure continued supplies of American intelligence, logistic support arrangements, weapons acquisition, and technology transfers. While they acknowledge that there is no requirement for Australia to become involved in United States contingency planning for global nuclear war, they are committed to making a tangible contribution to the ANZUS alliance by acting as willing hosts for the joint United States-Australian facilities at Pine Gap and Nurrangar and by allowing B52 bombers passage through Australia. In so far as New Zealand's anti-nuclear policy conflicts with Australia's commitment to nuclear deterrence and a close relationship with the United States it is fair to expect that there will be areas of significant disagreement in New Zealand-Australia relations. This will probably mean that New Zealand will have to work out a defence relationship suitable for the Australasian/South West Pacific region alone, and agree to disagree with Australia in terms of global nuclear containment strategies.

The Committee was very concerned, however, that the New Zealand Government and the New Zealand people have a realistic assessment of the difficulties involved in negotiating an equal relationship between Australia and New Zealand, given the far higher commitment of the Australian Government to defence expenditure and the different global and regional perceptions of security. It is clear both from the New Zealand poll, and others conducted in Australia, that New Zealanders feel more secure and confident about their strategic environment than do their trans-Tasman counterparts. Australians have a greater degree of anxiety about potential military threats and do not feel the South East Asian region, contiguous to Northern Australia, is a tranquil region of the world. New Zealanders, on the other hand, generally feel that the South West Pacific region is very benign and non-threatening. Despite these caveats the Committee accepted a compromise conclusion which, among other recommendations, urged an enhancement of the bilateral ANZUS relationship with Australia as the major component of New Zealand's future defence policy (pp.73-74).

Having agreed to such a compromise, the Committee sent its report to the Prime Minister for consideration before publication. The final report was submitted on Friday 1 August 1986; over the weekend it was shown to Helen Clark MP, the Chairperson of the Foreign Affairs and Defence Select Committee. The Prime Minister's Advisory Group and Helen Clark apparently felt that the report was not as balanced as the Committee assumed it to be; they believed it to be embarrassing to the G |vernment, and thought it was a reassertion of the *status quo* rather than a report that would establish new defence policy directions for New Zealand. At this stage the peace movement attempted to encourage the publication of a dissenting minority report; they did so for the reasons mentioned above and because they believed that the contents of the report fundamentally undermined the Government's anti-nuclear stance. Conversely, the Committee believed the report to be a substantial legitimation of Government policy. Furthermore, there was an obligation on all Committee members, having worked out a report in good faith and agreeing to a set of recommendations which reflected public opinion and indicated some new directions, that the report remain unanimous.

There were three reasons why we did this:

1. We had committed ourselves to a consensus document at the beginning of our discussions in order to indicate possible ways in which the defence dilemma might be resolved.

2. From an anti-nuclear perspective I considered it important to associate myself with more "traditional" approaches to defence so that people espousing these views could not dismiss anti-nuclearism as an impracticable "fringe" position and therefore not to be taken seriously.

3. If I had been forced into writing a minority position there is little doubt that the majority position would have urged a resumption of ship visits on terms acceptable to the United States.

On Sunday 3 August, I received a series of telephone calls from sections of the peace movement urging me to write a dissenting report. The following day I received a telegram on behalf of the Wellington Peace Committee urging me to dissociate myself from the report. I then indicated to the Director of the Prime Minister's Advisory Group that this pressure was inappropriate. He concurred that it was, but argued that the report, as a whole, was embarrassing to the Government and that it read far too much like a personal memo from the chairman of the Committee. It was suggested to him that the report was fair, objective and balanced, reflected the diversity of opinion and that the best strategy would be for the Government to accept it, highlight those parts which were sympathetic to current policy and allow the community to debate the other conclusions.

My powers of persuasion were not very effective and later in the afternoon of 4 August when the Committee met the Prime Minister he thanked us for the report, accepted most of the recommendations and then raised a series of questions about technical aspects of presentation in the report and interpretation of the survey data. In particular, he was worried about why we had not quantified the submissions as most of these were anti-nuclear. Secondly, he raised questions of bias in the historical introduction (written by the chairman, with the section since 1970 written by myself). Thirdly, a number of issues were raised concerning the crucial question relating to ship visits which gave a small majority in favour of remaining in ANZUS and allowing access by nuclear ships. Fourthly, he raised a series of questions about the assessment chapter and whether or not ANZUS provided a security guarantee. He was also angered by the fact that on page 12 of the report we had indicated that "in retrospect it is easy to see negotiating mistakes" in relation to the ship visit policy. The report was returned to the Committee. The parliamentary press gallery was conscious of the fact that the report had been handed back and there was considerable speculation in both the New Zealand and international media concerning the contents of the report and why the Prime Minister had returned it for clarification.

The Defence Committee of Enquiry met to consider the Prime Minister's questions on the weekend of 9 and 10 August. The mood was one of annoyance that the Prime Minister had asked for clarification of what was considered to be a clear report. It was thought essential that, as we were an independent committee, the draft that had been handed to the Prime Minister should not be changed. Consequently, the response to the questions was prepared as an addendum to the original report. Prime Ministerial opposition to the report, combined with the pressures for a minority report, had a unifying effect on the Committee. The answers to the Prime Minister's questions (pp.82-90) and the Prime Minister's response (pp.91-94) were stronger than the original formulations. The Committee elaborated on why submissions were not quantified (other than those that were simple to quantify such as newspaper coupons); it provided a detailed background to the historical context chapter and, in particular, the circumstances surrounding the ANZUS treaty (in which the chairman of the Defence Committee of Enquiry was involved as First Secretary in Washington at that time); it provided a detailed response to the questions relating to survey methodology (drawing on the National Research Bureau, the Department of Statistics and independent experts); it responded to the questions raised in relation to the logic of anti-nuclearism and collective security and the "neither confirm nor deny" policy; it reiterated why ANZUS did constitute an effective security guarantee; and finally, it addressed the question of "negotiating mistakes".

The Prime Minister indicated that he wished to discuss the report and the response to his questions with Cabinet before he would agree to publication and came under increasing media pressure to explain the continued delay. The report was finally sent to the Government Printer on 18 August and was launched at a press conference 21 August 1986.

The report was well received by the media, most of whom thought it a fair and objective evaluation of New Zealand public opinion on defence and security issues. It was considered to be a reasonable statement of New Zealand's clear anti-nuclearism and the defence dilemma this precipitates. The Prime Minister held a press conference at which the anti-nuclear sentiments of New Zealanders and their commitment to maintaining an anti-nuclear stance were highlighted.[4] The Leader of the Opposition made a public statement highlighting the collective security sentiments of the report. To some extent, both drew what they wanted from the report for their own different political purposes, and both did an injustice to the report as a whole because throughout it had attempted assiduously to combine anti-nuclear sentiments with the desire for alliances. The Committee struggled hard to find ways in which contradictory opinions could be combined in order to develop a new bipartisan consensus about defence and security issues and ensure a smooth transition from an old to a new foreign affairs and defence paradigm.

In retrospect it seems that the Government made a tactical blunder in not accepting the report and it will be interesting to see what direction the Government will take in the second phase of the review process and, in particular, which parts of the Enquiry will be incorporated into the 1986 Defence Review.[5]

As a general point, it must be acknowledged that defence and security issues raise fundamental questions about New Zealand society and national identity. The Committee was reminded by some Maori groups, for instance, that it should not assume that Pakeha, Western conceptions of defence are applicable to the Maori and Polynesian members of New Zealand/Aotearoa. Similarly, young people informed us that the experiences of the older generation, conditioned as they were by perceived Soviet expansionism and the Cold War mentality, should not be automatically extended to the generation of the 1960s and beyond.

A New Agenda

New Zealand exists in one of the most secure strategic environments in the world. It is difficult to imagine any regional power that would have the desire or capability to attack Australia or New Zealand. Most strategic analysts agree that it would take five to ten years for any regional power with hostile tendencies to generate the capability required to mount a successful invasion. Indeed, the only two countries that have any immediate capability are the Soviet Union and the United States, neither of which has any reason for or intention of launching invasions.

This benign strategic environment means that the New Zealand Government and people need not feel pressured into making precipitate defence decisions. It is to be hoped, therefore, that the final stages of the 1986 Defence Review are not rushed. It seems clear that the morale and professionalism of the defence forces will be enhanced most of all by a reflective Review that establishes clear directions to take New Zealand into the twenty-first century. The following five proposals are offered as guidelines for establishing new defence and foreign policy initiatives.

1. At this critical transition period it would be desirable for the National Party to join Labour in acknowledging New Zealand's desire to be unconditionally nuclear-free at level 3 of the previously mentioned scale. A bipartisan declaration to this effect would signal to the United States and other nuclear powers that all New Zealand political parties are serious in their determination to dissociate themselves from global nuclearism. Nuclear powers wishing to deal with New Zealand will, therefore, have to acknowledge that being absolutely nuclear free is a non-negotiable minimum requirement. Such an affirmation would reduce the possibility of external interference in New Zealand domestic politics and expand the area of bipartisan agreement.

2. In relation to enhancing the bilateral defence relationship with Australia, the New Zealand Government should indicate that defence co-operation does not extend to tacit or explicit support for Australian contributions to global nuclear deterrence through the bases at Pine Gap and Nurrangar. While both of these bases contribute towards arms control verification, they also have a critical role to play in providing damage and strike assessment information before and during a nuclear war. New Zealand's commitment to an anti-nuclear strategy conflicts with Australian support for this aspect of United States nuclear war fighting plans. The enhanced bilateral relationship, therefore, should concentrate on regional conventional defence alone and there must be an agreement to disagree with the Australians on global nuclear strategy.

3. It is eminently desirable that ANZUS — whether viewed in terms of two bilateral relationships or as trilateral relationships on conventional terms alone — be transformed, renamed and enlarged into a regional alliance by incorporating South Pacific Forum countries and possibly ASEAN. This would be consistent with the original ANZUS spirit. An enhanced arrangement would ensure a more regional, defensive, non-aggressive focus based on conventional arms alone. Furthermore, it would provide a more appropriate vehicle for promoting a global collective security system under the aegis of the United Nations as ANZUS was originally intended to do. This might have the desirable effect of making South East Asia and the South West Pacific less dependent on the United States. It would also be consistent with the Guam doctrine and hopefully provide a means of ensuring the achievement of genuine nuclear weapon-free zones in Asia and the Pacific.

4. A more regional orientation for New Zealand's defence forces and foreign policy should be accompanied by accelerated efforts to promote confidence building and trust between East and West in the Pacific area. The recently completed

Stockholm Conference on Security and Disarmament in Europe provides a suitable model for such initiatives. A key priority for the region is to remove the possibility of superpower contention and impose strategic denial on all nuclear powers. Special efforts should be made to try and resolve tensions in the conflict areas of Korea and Indo-China.

5. If regional denuclearization, stability and security become goals for New Zealand and other countries in South East Asia and the South West Pacific it ought to be possible for the most secure parts of the region to contemplate alternatives to military security such as civilian-based defence and the process of transarmament. While this remains a Utopian vision at the moment it should not be lost sight of, since eventually there has to be a universal recognition that no disputes are solved by war and that non-violent strategies and negotiations are infinitely preferable. New Zealand's benign strategic position means that it can afford to be innovative and experiment with a combination of military and civilian means of achieving security.

The 1986 Defence Committee of Enquiry established that it would be difficult to return to a defence strategy based on nuclear deterrence, and it is possible that New Zealand might be leading the world towards a non-nuclear future, thus confirming Siegfried's conclusion that: "a little courage and decision are all that is required to accomplish the reforms of which Europe [and North America] is so afraid" (p.53).

Notes

1 The detailed methodology is contained in the annex to the report of the Defence Committee of Enquiry. A survey of 1600 was taken and the sample coincided very closely with the demographic profiles reported in national statistics. At a 95 per cent confidence level the maximum margin of error due to sampling variations is plus or minus 2.5 per cent. All interviews in the final survey were carried out during the period 26 April to 19 May 1986.

2 These were in Auckland, Wellington, Christchurch, Dunedin, Nelson and Rotorua.

3 It should be stressed that these poll results provide a snapshot of opinion at one point in time. It is conceivable a repeat of the same poll would produce different results. The Committee was conscious of this and tried not to reify the results. Some criticism of the report fails to grasp this fact. Nevertheless, until another poll is conducted these results are the best guide we have as to New Zealanders' opinions on defence.

4 When questioned Lange argued "... the recommendations were sound as I said some time ago. I think we have had a problem in that the purpose of the Committee has been misunderstood. It is there to filter public attitudes towards defence and security and to report to the Government on that so that the Government might take that into account in formulating the Defence Review. It was never the function of this Committee to actually do a Defence Review. I was able to talk to the Cabinet about some of the polling data and Cabinet was very easy about that report. It is in fact a substantial endorsement of the Government position ... its judgement of public opinion is very perceptive indeed" (Transcript, post-Cabinet press conference, 18 August 1986).

5 Malcolm Templeton, the Director of the Institute for Policy Studies at Victoria
   University, has produced a transitional report (10 October 1986) entitled *Defence and
   Security: What New Zealand Needs*, which starts where the Defence Committee on
   Enquiry finished. This will also be incorporated into the final Defence Review.

References

Bennett, B.S. (1986) *New Zealand's Moral Foreign Policy 1935-1939: The Promotion of Collective
   Security through the League of Nations*, unpublished MA Thesis, University of Canterbury.
The Defence Question (1985) Wellington, Government Printer.
Defence and Security: What New Zealanders Want: & Annex (1986) Wellington, Government
   Printer.
Dibb, P. (1986) *Review of Australia's Defence Capabilities* Canberra, Australian Government
   Publishing Service.
O'Flynn, F. *The Press* 1 March 1985, p. 1.
Lange, D. "Transcript, Post-Caucus Press Conference", 5 December 1985.
New Zealand Labour Party (1986) Submission to the Defence Committee of Enquiry on the
   Future of New Zealand's Strategic and Security Policies.
Rowling, W.E. (1983) Memo to members of the Labour Party Policy Council on ANZUS
   options.
Rowling, W.E. (1984) New Zealand Foreign Policy: Time for a Change? *New Zealand
   International Review* 9: 8.
Siegfried, A. (1982) *Democracy in New Zealand* Wellington, Victoria University Press.
Sweden's Security Policy: Entering the 90s (1985) Report by 1984 Defence Committee Stock-
   holm SOU Swedish Official Reports Series 23: Stockholm.

13

Labour and Africa

Martin Holland

The question of direct New Zealand diplomatic representation with Africa has been raised intermittently over the past two decades, but the economic and trade requirements of contemporary New Zealand foreign policy have traditionally condemned African relations to the lowest of priorities: even Central Asia and Latin America have taken preference, despite New Zealand's Commonwealth heritage. Why did New Zealand abandon this foreign policy of African isolation, having adhered to it for most of the twentieth century, in 1985?

Just as with the other policy areas examined in this book, the desire to change both the image and substance of New Zealand policy by eradicating the legacy of the Muldoon premiership and National Party dominance has been the momentum behind this innovative phase of foreign relations. More precisely, this change was indicative of a series of related factors: (a) a concerted political and moral opposition to apartheid; (b) the extension of foreign relations from its purely trade-oriented base to include internationalism and global responsibility; and, (c) a general change in New Zealand's foreign policy modifying its status as a small state.

The "international trader" phase typical of the 1960s and 1970s began to give way to that of "international actor" in the 1980s (Jackson, 1980, p.224). This theme has been the dominant criterion behind the conduct of foreign affairs throughout the Lange Administration. There is clearly a belief, whether realistic or not, that New Zealand is no longer a small state and can join the other established (if not major) actors on the world stage, particularly through multilateral organizations such as the United Nations. The extension of New Zealand's external relations into Africa was the logical manifestation of this perception.

David Lange personifies this emerging national self-confidence. However, while innovative, it would be incorrect to regard Labour's current approach to foreign policy as particularly new. It constitutes an elaboration and restatement of previous policy, the origins of which can be found in the Kirk leadership of the previous Labour Government of 1972-75. One commentary on the Kirk premiership illustrates this derivation admirably. Writing in 1975 Alley described Kirk's new direction in foreign policy as a:

> ... readiness to probe accepted assumptions about the nature of international political relations and especially New Zealand's place in them ... Why should good ideas about feasible forms of international co-operation be any less practicable on account of their

originating from small states of modest capabilities? And may not such states actively promote their objectives in ways of their choosing rather than just reacting derivatively to the initiatives of others? (Alley, 1975, p.5)

Before the history of past relations and the content and possible consequences of the new approach can be examined, New Zealand's foreign policy needs to be located within a suitable analytical framework. New Zealand's international role has traditionally been defined as that of a small state. The six pertinent characteristics of this classification are: (a) low participation in world affairs; (b) a narrow scope of foreign policy; (c) the dominance of the trade criterion in foreign policy-making; (d) a predilection for multilateral associations; (e) a moral emphasis; and, (f) a tendency towards unintentional conflict with major allies. What evidence is there that New Zealand's foreign policy has conformed to these conditions?

Writing in 1980, Henderson, Jackson and Kennaway argued that the form and substance of New Zealand's past international relations have generally fitted this classification. They concluded that during the post-war period, New Zealand had successively distanced itself from a colonial and American focus (unwillingly so in the case of Britain's membership of the European Community), foregoing global commitments in preference to more regional or parochial policy issues. This was reflected in the 1978 Defence Review's concern with Pacific security and in former National Foreign Minister Talboy's recognition that New Zealanders were primarily "*Homosapiens pacificus australis* – South Pacific Man" (Henderson et al., 1980, p.4). The colonial myopia had finally been adjusted, resulting in a reduced international role and scope of activity for New Zealand. To fill this vacuum, New Zealand embraced a series of multilateral and bilateral associations as the chief mechanism for influencing and monitoring foreign affairs. Paradoxically, the United Nations was not regarded as the appropriate vehicle for the expression of this small state personality; rather, regional organizations and arrangements predominated, e.g. ASEAN, South Pacific Forum, CER, and SPARTECA. Although the direction of New Zealand's international relations up until the end of the 1960s had been somewhat erratic, subsequently there was a clear emphasis placed on trade and economic priorities over those of a political or ideological nature in dictating foreign policy objectives. While this has led New Zealand to seek diverse markets (thus in a limited sense expanding the incipient regionalism), the central point is that recent foreign policy has been the servant of the export needs of the country. Clearly, New Zealand confirmed the commonly held assumption that a small state's foreign policy will reflect primarily economic issues, even to the extent of determining the location of Foreign Affairs overseas postings (Henderson et al., 1980, p.5).

The two remaining small state criteria are only partially applicable to the New Zealand post-1945 experience. Firstly, as a small state New Zealand is clearly the minor partner in both formal and informal relationships with other advanced Western democracies, notably the United States and United Kingdom. However, this disequilibrium has not implied compliance or a compromise of national interest. Secondly, the propensity for small states to adopt moral postures and leadership, unrestrained by the inhibitions of *realpolitik* and global responsibilities shouldered by major powers, is the least applicable of the six foreign policy characteristics. Contemporary New Zealand foreign policy (primarily under National governments) has been characterized by "realism rather than idealism" (Henderson et al., 1980, p.7). The exceptions to this tendency have been rare: lobbying in favour of a Pacific nuclear weapons-free zone and former Prime Minister Norman Kirk's explicit, if generally unimplemented, "firm moral basis" of foreign policy (Kirk, 1973, p.3).

Given these two qualifications, prior to 1984 New Zealand's foreign policy generally conformed to the classical view of small state behaviour. That comforting, if somewhat debilitating situation, has changed as a result of the foreign policy initiatives undertaken by the Lange Government. In particular, the development of relations with black Africa are indicative of a significant general shift in the emphasis and the purpose of New Zealand's foreign affairs. It would appear that, under Lange, New Zealand wishes to graduate from the lowly status of a small state and is striving for a wider recognition of its potential for an enhanced contribution to world affairs. Before an assessment of this new perspective is possible, Labour's policy must be considered in the context of New Zealand's recent history of relations with Africa.

Absence Makes the Heart Grow Fonder?
New Zealand-African Relations 1945-84

An important distinction to be established is the difference between New Zealand's relations with South Africa and those with black Africa. Although the policy implications of the two unavoidably overlap, as will be shown later, it is necessary initially to distinguish between them. Under previous Governments, these two issues have been fused, leading to policy intransigence and stagnation: one of the key features of Lange's African excursion has been to separate these *conceptually* and *pragmatically*.

South Africa

Three distinct phases in post-war New Zealand-South African relations can be identified: the policy vacuum prior to 1972; the 1972 to 1984 period of conflicting intentions; and the policy of concerted opposition to apartheid since 1984.

Despite increasing pressures for anti-South African resolutions to be adopted by the United Nations throughout the 1960s, the New Zealand position on apartheid remained conspicuously silent. During this period New Zealand only rarely supported an anti- South African resolution, preferring abstention to outright opposition (Sorrenson, 1976, pp.39-42). This absence of antipathy was also reflected in New Zealand's early endeavours to secure South Africa's readmittance to the

Commonwealth after Prime Minister Verwoerd withdrew in 1961. New Zealand's general refusal to treat South Africa as the pariah demanded by the majority of United Nations and Commonwealth members, was regarded widely as indicative of tacit acquiescence to South African policy by these two predominantly African and Asian bodies.[1]

The 1972-84 period was characterized by a familiar rhetorical condemnation of apartheid, a vacillating attitude towards continued sporting ties, and an aversion on the part of New Zealand Governments (irrespective of party) to infringe the right of freedom of association. The return of the Labour Government in 1972 prompted this change: almost immediately New Zealand began to vote in favour of United Nations apartheid resolutions, display vocal public criticism of the South African Government, culminating in the refusal to grant entrance visas for the proposed 1973 Springbok tour of New Zealand (despite Labour's pre-election assurance that it would not do so). However, this politicization of sport was not unique to New Zealand foreign policy: the typical Western approach to South Africa throughout the 1970s and early 1980s was an asymmetrical amalgam of rhetorical condemnation of apartheid with the firm conviction that any form of direct action (other than a sports isolation) would be undesirable, a conclusion bolstered principally by the commonly held misconception that sanctions do not work (Holland, 1985, p.414). Even under a Labour Administration, and despite the removal of all remaining preferential tariffs for South African goods, during the 1972-75 period exports to South Africa increased from NZ$6.6 million to NZ$10.7 million, and imports from NZ$4.4 million to NZ$9.7 million.

With the election of National in 1975, the international community's perception of New Zealand's opposition to apartheid was again undermined. In contrast to the anti-South African sports policy of the third Labour Government the new Prime Minister, Robert Muldoon, gave official blessing to the 1976 All Black tour of the Republic. The resulting retaliatory African boycott of the 1976 Montreal Olympics meant that within just three years New Zealand-African relations had declined from their zenith to an all time nadir. The 1977 Gleneagles interregnum, at least superficially, patched the Commonwealth divisions and restored a degree of credibility to New Zealand's continuing claim to be opposed to apartheid (Trainor, 1979, p.2). The text committed Commonwealth governments to take "*every prac-tical step to discourage* contact or competition by their nationals with sporting organizations, teams or sportsmen from South Africa". However, two additional clauses diluted this already malleable policy even further. Firstly, "it was for *each Government to determine in accordance with its laws* the methods by which it might best discharge these commitments"; and secondly, the indeterminate phrase "there were *unlikely* to be future sporting contacts of any significance" was preferred to a more explicit mandatory prohibition (Gleneagles Agreement, 1977; author's emphasis). The equivocal language of the compromise was sufficient to accommodate the appearance of a policy volte-face by Muldoon, whilst in reality this flexibility enabled New Zealand to maintain a contradictory, if non-explicit, policy culminating in the ill-fated 1981 Springbok tour of New Zealand.

Table 13.1
New Zealand-South Africa bilateral trade 1975-85 (NZ$ million, June years)

Year	NZ exports	NZ imports	Balance (visible)
1975/76	7.1	11.5	-4.4
1976/77	5.1	8.7	-3.6
1977/78	6.5	12.5	-6.0
1978/79	6.3	10.1	-3.8
1979/80	10.2	18.1	-7.9
1980/81	21.0	13.4	+7.6
1981/82	23.9	16.7	+7.2
1982/83	24.0	15.9	+8.1
1983/84	26.1	14.4	+11.7
1984/85	29.2	48.2	-19.0

While trade with South Africa remained modest (accounting for less than 0.2 per cent of New Zealand's trade in June 1984), the pre-1980 pattern of a negative balance was reversed during the last four Muldoon years (see table 13.1).

On assuming office in July 1984, the Ministry of Foreign Affairs provided Lange with background Briefing Papers on foreign policy issues requiring early attention (Ministry of Foreign Affairs, 1984): two concerned South Africa – the closure of the South African consulate and sporting contacts.[2] The Consulate had been established immediately after South Africa's withdrawal from the Commonwealth. The third Labour Government had been the first to take minor steps at reducing, if not cutting, diplomatic ties with South Africa. Kirk refused to confer ambassadorial privileges on the South African Consul, thereby restricting his access to civil servants rather than members of the Government. Lange's approach was more forthright. One of the new Government's first statements was to announce its intention to close the Wellington-based South African Consulate in accordance with the party's manifesto.[3] After a series of acrimonious public statements, but no official contact, the South African Government pre-empted the promised expulsion by closing the Consulate on 1 August 1984, an outcome which Lange found "very satisfactory". The closure saved the Government from the dilemma of choosing between merely closing the post or taking the more serious step of severing all consular relations. Either alternative would have required that the Consulate be given up to three months to terminate its affairs.

Given the divisive nature of the 1981 Springbok tour of New Zealand, it was somewhat surprising that the planned return All Black tour to South Africa arguably was only the third most important international crisis faced by the Lange Government in 1985, after the ANZUS and *Rainbow Warrior* issues. The tour question was more complex than that faced by the previous Labour Government. On this occasion attention was focused on the right (and power) of the Government to restrict the freedom of New Zealanders to travel, not the somewhat simpler question of withholding entry visas from South African sportsmen. As was to transpire, ineffective moral coercion proved the extent of the Government's authority.[4] The available legal sanction of revoking passports was not politically acceptable although, just as had been the case in 1975, special leave provisions for State Service employees were suspended.

After a drawn-out and often bitter dialogue with the Rugby Football Union, and despite clarification of the precise meaning of the Government's all too clear request of 30 March 1985 that "the tour must not proceed", the power of moral persuasion proved insufficient. On 18 April the Rugby Football Union Council announced that the tour was to go ahead. This outcome reflected the reluctance of all liberal democratic states to transgress certain individual rights, and the consequential inability of Governments then to do very much about their abuse. Only by imposing coercive restrictions on the free movement of individuals could the Government have ensured the implementation of its wishes. It was hardly credible to restrict this freedom for New Zealand rugby players, yet to denounce Pretoria for its Draconian pass laws and denying passports to anti-apartheid critics such as Tutu and Boesak. The tour was aborted only at the eleventh hour. An interim court injunction was granted by Mr Justice Casey on 13 July which prevented the All Blacks' departing while the case brought against the Rugby Football Union by two Auckland lawyers was still being heard. Faced with this delay and the threat of prosecution for contempt of court if the tour proceeded, the Rugby Football Union reluctantly and resentfully abandoned the proposed tour before the Court decided on the original case.[5]

It was ironic that independent individual legal action was required to secure the Government's policy objective. Despite this impotence, or perhaps because of it, the "spirit" of Gleneagles was maintained at least outwardly, as the Government argued it had taken "every practical step to discourage" the tour "in accordance with its (the Government's) laws". These steps constituted unanimous Parliamentary opposition to the tour, an almost unseemly and frank pleading with the Rugby Football Union Council and individual players, but precluded any direct financial retribution on the part of the Government, recourse to a referendum or any form of legislative compulsion. Even the subsequent rebel Cavaliers tour of South Africa in May 1986 did not result in the New Zealand Government being accused of impropriety by its Commonwealth partners.

In comparison to the other South African political events of 1985, the question of sports contacts was of relatively minor significance. The familiar rehearsal of empty anti-apartheid incantations gave way to accelerating international criticism and the introduction of moderate sanctions. Between May and October 1985 the United

States, Japan, Australia, Canada, Austria, the Nordic countries and the European Community (as well as individual European Governments) all adopted various economic measures in response to the rising level of repression being exerted by the South African Government (Holland, 1986a, pp.3-4). The Commonwealth Heads of Government Meeting of 22 to 24 October, brought the Commonwealth and New Zealand in particular in line with this global approach. The resultant Commonwealth Accord followed the precedents set by the European Community one month previously, calling for the immediate ban on oil sales, new contracts relating to nuclear technology, military co-operation, the import of arms and para-military equipment, and the cessation of cultural and scientific contacts except those designed to erode apartheid. Four additional measures were adopted, at least in principle: (a) a ban on all new Government loans to South Africa; (b) a "readiness" to unilaterally prohibit the import of Krugerrands; (c) an end of government funded trade missions to South Africa; and, (d) a ban on sales of computers for military/security use.[6] New Zealand's role at the Commonwealth Heads of Government Meeting was, as Lange commented, that of "bit players ... extras in the chorus" (*The Press*, 22 October 1985).

Despite Labour's sympathetic black Africa policy, there remains a degree of antipathy amongst a number of African Commonwealth countries towards New Zealand over former rugby contacts with South Africa. Clearly, New Zealand is required to establish its credentials as a sincere anti-apartheid ally. The first indication of this process emerged on 12 November 1985 with the announcement of a further set of restrictions in accordance with the Commonwealth initiative.[7] While compliance with these measures is relatively painless for New Zealand, the assurance was given that the Labour Government would adopt whatever further sanctions the Commonwealth deemed necessary. Somewhat inauspiciously, and with perverse historical timing, New Zealand-South African bilateral trade during Labour's first year in office swung dramatically in South Africa's favour. This aberration was caused by a single purchase of petroleum without which the balance of trade would have remained in New Zealand's favour and typical of the 1980-84 period.[8] With the ending of export credit guarantees for New Zealand exports to the Republic on 28 February 1986, the overall volume of trade should decline substantially.

A Commonwealth mini-summit was convened in August 1986 to discuss the Eminent Persons Group report on South Africa. The resultant communique called for the implementation of the measures agreed to in the Commonwealth Heads of Government Meeting Accord with the following additions: (a) a ban on all new bank loans to South Africa; (b) a ban on the imports of uranium, coal, iron and steel; and, (c) the withdrawal of consular facilities. In contrast to the United Kingdom's well publicized opposition to any mandatory action against South Africa, on 25 August 1986 the New Zealand Cabinet agreed to implement all of these further measures.

From being perceived as a silent supporter of white South Africa in the 1950s, 1960s and early 1970s, Government policy under Lange has realigned itself to such an extent that the likelihood of New Zealand playing some future mediating role in South Africa is an increasing possibility. This change in the conduct of foreign policy, in particular the successful separation of black Africa from South Africa as policy issues, may well serve as the foundation on which New Zealand's future African foreign policy will be built.

Seeds of a Black Africa Policy

New Zealand-African relations have a sparse history. It was as late as 1974 before President Nyerere of Tanzania became the first African head of state to visit New Zealand; a further two years elapsed before New Zealand reciprocated with the visit of the then Deputy Prime Minister, Talboys, to East Africa. Since then there has been a trickle of bilateral diplomatic contacts bolstered by more regular Commonwealth and international organization exchanges. The absence from one another's affairs has been mutual. The creation of a permanent New Zealand post in Africa has appeared on the political agenda intermittently, without success, since the early 1970s. Despite operating 47 overseas posts in 1985, prior to the establishment of the Harare High Commission New Zealand's African representation consisted only of cross-accreditation: the London High Commission was accredited to Nigeria and the New Zealand Ambassador resident in Athens also acted as the High Commissioner for Tanzania and Kenya. African representation in New Zealand has been equally distant: the Zambian High Commissioner and Nigerian Ambassador to Canberra are both cross-accredited to Wellington. Apart from these detached intermediaries, avenues for dialogue have been restricted to multilateral agencies. Why have New Zealand-African affairs assumed this obscure relationship?

The absence of diplomatic missions reflects a correspondingly negligible trading relationship. As suggested by Jackson, a direct correlation between New Zealand's overseas representation and bilateral trading patterns can easily be substantiated prior to 1985 (Jackson, 1980, p.225). Only economic markets significant to New Zealand's export capacity have traditionally warranted direct representation. African trade has been minimal, never exceeding more than 1.0 per cent of New Zealand's total trade: given this rider, there are a number of striking features. Firstly, as shown by table 13.2, since 1980 in excess of 90 per cent of New Zealand exports to Africa have gone to just ten of the 47 African states, with approximately 80 per cent concentrated in just three markets, none of which share any geographical affinity: South Africa, Mauritius and Nigeria. Secondly, New Zealand imports from African countries other than the top ten are negligible, never accounting for more than 4.8 per cent in the 1980s, with three-quarters of all African imports originating in just two countries in opposite hemispheres – Ghana and South Africa. Thirdly, although trade has been small, the balance of trade has been in New Zealand's favour except in 1984/85 when there was a deficit of NZ$17 million. (As already noted, this reversal was due to a single purchase of South African petroleum rather than an increase in

Table 13.2
New Zealand–Africa bilateral trade 1980–85

	1980/81	1981/82	1982/83	1983/84	1984/85
NZ exports (NZ000s)	53,436	72,156	64,969	50,393	62,517
NZ imports (NZ000s)	35,222	35,390	39,530	36,948	80,648
Balance of trade	+18,214	+36,766	+25,439	+13,448	-18,131
NZ exports to	%	%	%	%	%
South Africa	39.4	33.2	37.1	51.9	46.7
Mauritius	24.8	22.2	23.8	27.9	37.1
Nigeria	20.1	27.4	23.5	11.0	4.7
Ghana	b	b	b	.5	b
Malawi	1.6	2.1	4.0	a	2.6
Uganda	b	b	b	b	b
Tanzania	4.9	1.6	1.5	2.2	a
Kenya	2.7	2.0	1.0	1.3	1.7
Mozambique	2.2	1.7	3.6	1.7	1.3
Zimbabwe	a	a	1.4	a	a
Remaining countries[c]	4.3	9.8	4.1	3.5	5.9
NZ imports from	%	%	%	%	%
South Africa	38.0	47.2	40.1	39.0	60.1
Mauritius	a	a	.6	a	a
Nigeria	a	b	b	a	a
Ghana	42.8	31.5	32.0	29.3	21.5
Malawi	4.8	2.5	2.6	3.8	2.0
Uganda	2.2	.9	2.2	2.3	1.4
Tanzania	4.2	7.1	4.6	8.8	3.1
Kenya	3.4	3.7	5.4	3.7	2.7
Mozambique	a	a	b	b	b
Zimbabwe	1.7	5.5	8.2	8.3	6.0
Remaining countries[c]	2.9	1.6	4.3	4.8	3.2

Notes: a = less than .5 per cent
b = none
c = includes countries showing less than .5 per cent.

African trade in general.) Lastly, in addition to this export-import concentration, there is a peculiar asymmetry to New Zealand–African trade. Excluding South Africa, Ghana is the major African exporter to New Zealand, yet it has virtually no reciprocal market for New Zealand goods; conversely, Nigeria has traditionally been the third best market for New Zealand products, but has never captured more than 0.5 per cent of African exports to this country. Clearly, the notion of an "African" market is difficult to sustain.

Both the volume and skewness of trade can be partially explained by product imbalance. The complementary trade patterns typical of developed nations are absent: even if a positive desire to trade existed, it would be inhibited by a lack of markets, foreign currency, transport costs and of goods available for exchange. Excluding South African refined petroleum, the only significant imports from Africa in 1984/85 were all primary products: cocoa from Ghana (worth NZ$16.7 million) and the Ivory Coast (NZ$1 million), Kenyan and Ugandan coffee (NZ$1.1 million each), tobacco from Malawi (NZ$1.6 million) and Zimbabwe (NZ$4.8 million), vegetable fibres from Tanzania (NZ$2.4 million) and South African fruit produce (NZ$1.2 million). In return, New Zealand principally exported wool/textiles to Mauritius and South Africa (worth NZ$20.5 million), dairy produce to Mauritius, Malawi, Niger and Nigeria (NZ$5.7 million), fish and vegetables to South Africa (NZ$5.7 million), tallow to South Africa, Mozambique and Malawi (NZ$11.8 million) and lastly, machinery worth NZ$2.3 million to South Africa and Kenya. Given these structural limitations, trade will remain limited, if generally in New Zealand's favour.

Two further limitations on New Zealand's former relationship with Africa must be noted: external competition and infrastructural restrictions. Traditionally, francophone Africa has tended to shun trade relations beyond those with France. This cultural barrier was extended in 1975 with the signing of the first Lome Convention which gave 37 African states (now 45) preferential non-reciprocal tariff access to European Community markets. Faced with such competition, it was hardly surprising that New Zealand put greater emphasis elsewhere. Secondly, the map of Africa still reflects colonial political apportionment, not economic needs (Calvocoressi, 1985, p.32). Contiguous states often have only the most primitive links, some none at all, with port access restricted. A single African economic centre does not exist. For third parties to operate effectively either a network of posts or a specific regional focus is required. The substantial costs of such policies make them an unattractive proposition for small states.

Policy Substance

As in all policy formation, the Government's African policy was an amalgam of different, often competing, ideas. Four basic strands can be delineated: (a) political motivations, (b) aid and trade considerations, (c) international role aspirations, and (d) the problem of South Africa. Collectively they undermine New Zealand's classification as a small state.

The central feature of the policy has been the Government's inherited guilt complex (generated by sporting contacts with South Africa) and a conscious desire to improve primarily *political* relations with black Africa through the mechanism of *economic* relations. The dominance of the political over the economic can be seen in both the internal policy-making process and in the Government's public statements.

In June 1984, the Ministry of Foreign Affairs in a confidential report advised the Government that an African post was neither needed nor justified. However, the

Ministry was obliged to formulate policy options in the light of Labour's election pledge to establish such a post. Against this background, Foreign Affairs counselled a cautious dual approach. Noting that "more basic research was required", they concluded that the best approach:

> ... would be to open first in Commonwealth East Africa and to look to West Africa in a longer time-frame. Our closest African contacts in recent years have been with East African countries and these relationships provide a solid foundation on which to build effective resident representation (Briefing Papers, 1984, p.17).

Normally, overseas posts are opened on the suggestion and favourable report of the Ministry of Foreign Affairs: the Harare post was a clear exception to this procedure. Lange rejected this low profile advice preferring to highlight Africa as a major foreign policy excursion of his Government. Consequently, the Ministry was presented with a political *fait accompli* that an African post would be established, contrary to their recommendation. However, with Treasury support the Ministry did manage to dissuade the Government from opening two posts simultaneously (because of staffing constraints), delaying the decision on a second mission until after the next election. The development of relations with Africa should not have come as a complete surprise to Foreign Affairs. As early as 1978 the Labour Party had been considering the question of direct representation and such a possibility had been discussed quite extensively, albeit without strong advocacy, within Foreign Affairs prior to Labour's election. Nonetheless, the Government's policy initiation has led to renewed vigour in this area. While it might be unjustly cynical to describe this as "policy making by the seat of the pants", policy positions for a range of African, including specifically southern African, issues which previously had gone unaddressed have subsequently been established.

The political aspect of the policy was also demonstrated publicly. On 30 March 1985, Lange became the first New Zealand Prime Minister to tour Africa, visiting the Commonwealth nations of Botswana, Zimbabwe, Tanzania, Kenya and Zambia. Noting the neglected and often misunderstood relations with Africa, Lange advocated change by participating in, rather than reacting to, African situations. More precisely, the tour served three functions: firstly, it acted to counter adverse African reactions to the proposed 1985 South African rugby tour and redress former misconceptions; secondly, it presented Lange with a firsthand experience and assessment of probable post sitings; and lastly, it sought to raise the New Zealand public's awareness and, hopefully, acceptance of a black African policy. Sadly, the media's rather superficial and idiosyncratic reporting did little to enhance this third objective. One commentator who accompanied the tour noted "that as a result of the trip New Zealand's negative impressions of Africa have been confirmed, rather than dispelled or clarified; our stereotypes reinforced" (Watson, 1985, p.15).

In 1980 it was still commonly held that "earning the export dollar is the greatest single concern of our foreign relations [sic]" (Henderson et al., 1980, p.214). On taking office, Lange confirmed that "trade must be the first objective of diplomacy" (Lange, 1984, p.2). It is difficult to understand New Zealand's African policy in such terms unless trade is broadly defined to include aid, assistance·and reverse trade. In this sense, trade can be construed as a secondary component that activated the African policy. Despite the limited existing market, an African investment, though a costly and slow exercise (and thus not an incentive for supposedly small states), need not be economically irrational. The economic benefits to New Zealand have been left loosely defined intentionally; electorally, the policy has little advantage. In keeping with overall Government policy special export incentives or subsidies have not been established: a "return" is not anticipated at least during this decade. Thus, while an immediate increase in New Zealand exports is not the main purpose of the policy, Africa offers a potentially huge market. It is sensible to engage in short-term costs (e.g. the gradual erosion of the South African market) for the greater long-term benefits of relations with black Africa. In terms of pragmatic politics, the question is an even simpler one. Would a future black majority South African Government view with favour those countries who had extended regional assistance, or those who had shown a reluctance to disassociate themselves from Pretoria? This combination of the "political" with the "economic" further emphasizes the maturing of New Zealand's international actor phase and the erosion of a small state mentality.

Unlike the normal objective of maximizing export access, the moral tone of the North-South dialogue (if geographically inverted in this case) constitutes the dominant component of the trade relationship, the mechanisms being aid, technical assistance and reverse trade. In line with the gradual liberalization of import licensing, New Zealand's Generalized System of Preferences accorded to developing countries was revised. As of 1 July 1985, it was extended to give 36 Less Developed Countries (including 25 in Africa) duty-free access to New Zealand.[9] The moral imperative was emphasized by David Caygill, Minister of Trade and Industry, who acknowledged "a responsibility to assist developing countries to expand their trade, but the emphasis in future must be directed more towards the least developed nations which are in the greatest need of assistance" (Caygill, 1984, p.3). The opening of the Harare High Commission in 1986 has underlined this commitment. The post performs three main functions: (a) to identify projects suitable for New Zealand technical assistance and aid; (b) to encourage reverse trade (i.e. African exports to New Zealand); and, (c) as the lowest priority, to examine reciprocal access for New Zealand exports.

Turning to aid and assistance first, the extension, if nominal, of regional aid beyond the South Pacific and ASEAN is both a break from recent practice and a return to the more global commitments of the early post-war period. The preference for multilateral rather than bilateral agreements has not changed, however. An immediate example of this was a US$100,000 donation to the Southern African Development Coordination Conference in 1985 (*Foreign Affairs Review*, 1985, p.7). An exploratory visit by an Official Development Assistance-trade mission in October 1985 identified broad areas to be pursued by the High Commission with respect to aid and assistance. Despite a modest aid budget of NZ$200,000 for 1985/86 (out of a total bilateral aid budget of NZ$82.2 million), New Zealand commitment was initiated. Funds were provided (through the Southern African Development Coordination Conference) for the recruitment of a veterinarian for Botswana; two officials were brought to New Zealand to examine agricultural training; a grant for essential dairy machinery parts was provided for Tanzania; annual academic study awards for four students from each of the five accredited nations were created; and Volunteer Service Abroad was extended to cover Africa with increased Government funding. In all cases New Zealand responded to African defined needs and the exchange was primarily qualitative (drawing on New Zealand expertise) rather than monetary. Beyond the NZ$200,000 bilateral aid in 1985/86, New Zealand made further multilateral contributions totalling NZ$2 million: for 1986/87, aid to Africa was increased to NZ$1 million (out of an overseas aid budget of NZ$119.7 million). This new-found enthusiasm for an African programme, while modest by financial standards, was an interesting contrast to the lower priority placed on African affairs by the Hawke Government in Australia (Goldsworthy, 1985, p.456).

The Harare High Commission will be responsible for implementing assistance within broad categories: for example, New Zealand forestry expertise may be of use in Zambia, Kenya and Tanzania, whereas educational guidance, agricultural training and irrigation schemes are required throughout the region. However, all expertise is not automatically transferable to the African environment: New Zealand's experience in the dairy industry is of little value given the ecological problems faced by Botswana and Zambia. These developing countries' characteristics are compounded by financial instability and poor foreign reserves. Although the African aid budget was increased for 1986/87, financing and staffing constraints will limit the development of policy.

Six characteristics have been associated previously with the aid programmes of small states. In contrast to larger international actors, small states have a narrow geographic spread of aid recipients; are more generous donors; are more likely to achieve international aid targets (0.7 per cent of gross national product); tend not to assist their allies' "enemy" states; use moral criteria rather than self-interest to determine aid; and, lastly, prefer multilateral to bilateral programmes. Writing in 1980, Hoadley suggested that New Zealand's behaviour closely mirrored these characteristics (Hoadley, 1980, p.127). With the exceptions of multilateralism and moral criteria, these categories no longer describe New Zealand behaviour under Labour. Aid has again been extended beyond the Pacific Basin; the level of aid is now similar to that of larger countries (0.28 per cent for 1986/87) and probably less likely to reach international targets; and the denotation of friendly and enemy states requires revision in the light of African politics. New Zealand's current role as an international aid donor offers further evidence in support of the assertion that the emphasis in foreign policy in general has altered under Lange's premiership.

Aid, however, is not the only aspect of policy: New Zealand, along with the majority of developed nations, has had a shrinking aid budget over the past decade. In these circumstances reverse trade is seen as the better mechanism for assisting the developing world in the 1990s. The Developing Countries Liaison Unit (an adjunct of the Department of Trade and Industry) acts as a promotion organization for imports from developing countries. In 1985 the Unit was asked to identify those African products with New Zealand import potential and to facilitate initial contacts between exporters and importers. An analysis of possible reverse trade indicated that the relatively greater range of manufactured goods produced by Zimbabwe and Kenya placed them in the best position to benefit. The dependency of Botswana, Zambia and Tanzania on traditional primary products (e.g. tobacco, coffee, tea and minerals) is generally unattractive for New Zealand importers, and while these countries do offer a certain export potential, the overall contribution would be minimal.[10] In addition, all five countries share a common feature: an inability to compete. Despite the tariffs of the Generalized System of Preferences, in comparison with similar goods available from China, Korea and Taiwan, the extra freight charges accrued make African exports essentially non-competitive in the New Zealand market. The fact that there is no direct shipping between Africa and New Zealand, necessitating trans-shipment via Singapore or Australia, is indicative. It is more rational for an African exporter to compete in the friendlier European Community, Lome or regional markets, rather than in a geographically remote one of just three million people.

The third component of the African policy is a further refutation of New Zealand's small state classification and relates to the Government's wider international ambitions. Lack of African support has cost New Zealand the possibility of representation in multilateral organizations, in particular a seat on the United Nations' Security Council in the mid 1970s.[11] As already noted, the misunderstood view of sporting contacts with South Africa was the cause of this antipathy.

The final aspect shaping the African policy also related to South Africa. While the other strands were more influential, the creation of a new post was also an anti-apartheid gesture, though a consciously restrained one.

Why Harare?

The verdict of Christopher Laidlaw, New Zealand's first High Commissioner to Zimbabwe, that "Harare is the natural, logical choice" can be justified politically, geographically and economically. Firstly, it would be wrong to suggest that the choice of location was not without political contention. There was an intra-governmental struggle between those who viewed the post as essentially an anti-apartheid response and those who advocated that it should not be interpreted specifically as such an open attack. Had the policy been based exclusively on opposition to apartheid, the Zambian capital of Lusaka (headquarters of the African National Congress) would have been the appropriate location. As a frontline state, the choice of Zimbabwe served to restore New Zealand's tarnished image and offered better long-term prospects, rather than the immediate moral panacea and cathartic exercise provided by Lusaka.

Secondly, given the infrastructural constraints of the continent, New Zealand's approach was designed as "a regionally orientated operation" (Laidlaw, 1986, p.8). Harare will be cross-accredited to Botswana, Zambia, Tanzania and Kenya, provides the best logistical access to eastern and southern Africa and is serviced by a direct air link to Australasia. An additional attraction is that the comforts of pre-UDI Salisbury have not evaporated with independence: for Westerners, Harare is still undoubtedly the most pleasant of black African capitals. Thirdly, the meagreness of New Zealand-African trade meant that the unimpressive bilateral record with Zimbabwe was not of sufficient importance to disqualify Harare. Indeed, its agricultural, manufacturing and mineral base suggests that Zimbabwe will regain its pre-1965 position as a dominant regional economic force. Fourthly, it is not unrealistic to envisage Zimbabwe under Mugabe as a leading political force in black Africa by the end of the century. Harare is already Africa's second most important diplomatic centre (currently with more than 70 resident overseas posts), and in 1986 Zimbabwe took over the leadership of the 101 nation Non-Aligned Movement. Fifthly, despite civil unrest in Matebeleland and Mugabe's aspirations for a one party state, Zimbabwe holds the rare status of being an African multi-party parliamentary democracy: to date, the Lancaster House Constitution has been honoured.[12] Lastly, while not inevitable, Harare was the best of a limited range of alternatives; for various economic, political and infrastructural reasons, Nairobi, Gaborone, Lusaka and Dar-es-Salaam were even less attractive. The Prime Minister's safari in March 1985 served to confirm these departmental assessments at first hand.

The post's objectives reflect the broad economic and political needs already discussed. In the short term a working relationship with the Zanu Government has to be formed and contact with the other regional Commonwealth nations established. The High Commission will be responsible for conveying New Zealand's formal position on vital regional issues, such as human rights, irrespective of whether the offenders are north or south of the Limpopo. Informal contacts with the next generation of African élites will also encourage an awareness of New Zealand. In the long term the development of trade, multilateral and bilateral aid and assistance projects will become the main functions of the post: as already noted, a future South African mediating role is also a distinct possibility.

In terms of staffing Harare ranks as a middle order post comparable to those in Mexico or New Delhi. It became operational in May 1986 and consists of a staff complement of five seconded from Wellington plus local clerical staff.[13] Personnel from the Department of Trade and Industry may be added in due course: initially, local consultants will be engaged to explore local market potential. An unintended consequence of a higher foreign policy profile has been a change in the relationship between government and bureaucracy under Labour. On becoming the Government, Labour was advised that the Ministry of Foreign Affairs was "not well placed, in terms of its present staff numbers, to embark on a programme of expansion abroad" (Ministry of Foreign Affairs, 1984, p.14). Despite this recommendation, within the first 18 months of Labour's term the Ministry had to implement two political decisions, opening posts in New Delhi and Harare. Understaffing and financial constraints have led to an over reliance on administrative pragmatism at the expense of long-term resource planning. The recent development of New Zealand foreign policy, while laudable and politically enticing, demands greater bureaucratic support than has been available in the past. It is not simply a matter of finance: expertise in foreign affairs, particularly in relation to Africa, is a scarce commodity amongst New Zealanders.

Conclusion

In answer to the question "Why Africa?", a combination of personal and political factors are pertinent. There can be no doubt as to Lange's strong moral commitment to African development: this personal direction in foreign policy was complemented by political content, opposition to apartheid and Labour's growing concern for global responsibility. Collectively, these factors constitute the origins of the African policy. Like parsimonious parents who buy clothes two sizes too big for their child to grow into, New Zealand under Lange has created the potential for greater participation in foreign affairs: the expectation is that the child will not turn out to be undernourished. Arguably, the opening of relations with Zimbabwe was not so much about an African policy *per se*, but rather about New Zealand's aspirations as an independent international actor. The available evidence supports the notion of a maturing global role. Clearly the designation of small state is no longer valid. Four of the six characteristics associated with this classification cannot be applied to the African policy. Earlier inhibitions restricting participation in world affairs have been exorcised: the scope of Labour's foreign relations have become increasingly global; the trade-post correlation is no longer sustainable; and the criterion of unintentional conflict with allies inapplicable, unless South Africa is understood to represent the latter. Only two small state characteristics remain, multilateralism and morality. Paradoxically, with the exception of Kirk's earlier "firm moral basis" for foreign policy, the moral content of the African policy constitutes a clear departure from New Zealand's traditional

pattern of international behaviour. Additionally, examination of New Zealand's
African aid programme further underlines this small state misnomer.

The party political change towards the conduct of international affairs has been
significant. From the Labour perspective, Lange's goodwill tours of Africa, India,
Indonesia, the Philippines, China and Europe are indicative of New Zealand's
developing global conscience, combining realism with Western, Commonwealth and
Pacific considerations. The last vestiges of colonial myopia seem to have disappeared.
Conversely, the National Party still perceives New Zealand as a small state and rejects
any expansion in a global role not tied firmly to trade. Harare was viewed as an
expensive and unsound investment, further evidence of Labour disassociating New
Zealand from the Western Alliance, and as a symbolic action designed to highlight
National's apparent disdain for black Africa, thereby tainting them as sympathetic to
apartheid. National are not committed to closing the post, only to a review of its
financial viability by Foreign Affairs. However, National's decision to close the Indian
High Commission in 1982 sets an ominous precedent.

What might be the probable consequences of this new approach? Domestically, the
African policy does not seem to be an electoral factor of any importance. The
announcement of the Harare post drew only muted and short-lived criticism (to the
surprise and relief of the Prime Minister's Department). Only one question was raised
in Parliament and the media displayed a general lack of interest. The impact on
bilateral trade, while difficult to quantify, is likely to be marginal, at least in the short
term. In general, Africa does not produce the type of goods with which competitively
to flood the New Zealand market: given the stringent agricultural quarantine
requirements access may be short-lived. The greatest probable domestic consequence
is a bureaucratic one, namely, the staffing strains imposed on the Ministry of Foreign
Affairs and the Department of Trade and Industry. Clearly, all of these domestic
consequences are relatively cost free and more than compensated for by the international kudos accrued.

An assessment of the international consequences, while optimistic, is less clear-cut.
Given the image of a higher global responsibility, New Zealand's position within
international fora should be enhanced. The future seat on the United Nations'
Security Council may even be attained thanks to African support. The greatest danger
lies in the geo-politics of southern Africa. While an intensification of the South
African conflict may present New Zealand with a Commonwealth linked mediating
role the alternative scenario, that of becoming embroiled in an extended state of civil
war, is less than appealing. Similarly, a deterioration in Zimbabwe's domestic political
situation could prove diplomatically embarrassing for New Zealand.

The consequences for Africa are less contentious. Expertise, assistance, aid and the
lowering of import barriers are all necessary, if not sufficient, prerequisites for African
development. The reliance on multilateralism (primarily Commonwealth, United

Nations and Southern African Development Coordination Conference programmes) has engendered a favourable African perception of New Zealand's emerging global role.

The African policy can be viewed as consistent with the traditional Labour Party theme of idealism and is symbolic of an overall restatement and development of foreign policy. This somewhat unheralded change in the direction of New Zealand policy may prove to be the most significant and enduring feature of the fourth Labour Government. As one Government representative has suggested, Africa is just one aspect of this wider change:

> The opening up of new relationships in Africa is part of the Government's determination to extend the international reach of New Zealand contacts and cooperation, to have our voice heard more clearly and more distinctly in parts of the world where our interests are at stake (Laidlaw, 1986, p.9).

Such a transformation will not occur overnight. In the interim, the international community may continue to regard New Zealand as a small state, or as Lange ruefully commented "bit players ... extras in the chorus". Despite this, the Labour Government is clearly impatient to play a greater part.

Notes

1 The only positive action taken by New Zealand against South Africa was the withdrawal of certain trade preferences in 1961.
2 These were made publicly available subsequently, though with certain deletions.
3 The announcement made by Party President, Jim Anderton, on 17 July did, however, cause some policy confusion with David Lange subsequently asserting that such decisions were the preserve of the Prime Minister.
4 The success of Sir Robert Muldoon's appeal to New Zealand athletes not to attend the 1980 Moscow Olympics was an interesting contrast.
5 The actual case (which was only resolved on 20 March 1986 when the Privy Council denied the Rugby Football Union leave to appeal) charged the Rugby Football Union Council of not acting in the game's interests, thereby contravening the Rugby Football Union's own constitutional provisions.
6 Provision was made for the application of further sanctions if, after six months, South Africa had not made adequate progress towards reform. These included bans on: air links and promotion of tourism; all investment profits earned in South Africa; agricultural imports and taxation agreements; Government assistance for investment and trade with South Africa; all Government procurement in South Africa; and, on contracts with majority-owned South African companies.
7 These were an embargo on the sale/re-export of computer equipment to South Africa; a ban on the import of military hardware from South Africa; and the removal of export guarantees and Export-Import Corporation assistance for trade with South Africa.
8 This purchase (required when the Marsden Point refinery was closed) cost NZ$27.7 million and accounted for 58 per cent of all South African imports to New Zealand.

9   Some exceptions to this concession do exist (e.g. on trade policy and domestic industry protection grounds). Also a second change in the Generalized System of Preferences was to raise the threshold to exclude countries with more than 70 per cent of New Zealand's per capital Gross National Product.

10 The Unit identified the following potential areas for reverse trade: Zimbabwe — textiles, tea, steel products, parquet flooring; Botswana — textiles, woven products, handicrafts; Zambia — cotton textiles, copper wire and tubes, zinc and manganese for batteries, mineral talc, timber products; Tanzania — cotton textiles, car radiators, timber and handicrafts; Kenya — dried fruit, handicrafts, textiles, garments, cashew nuts, fishing flies, pyrethrum, timber, tea and coffee.

11 New Zealand's willingness to allow the United Nations Secretary-General to arbitrate over the *Rainbow Warrior* affair can be seen as further evidence of New Zealand wishing to improve its image as a responsible international actor, as well as promoting its case for a larger role within the United Nations.

12 The other African multi-party democracies are Botswana, Gambia, Lesotho, Mauritius and Senegal; Namibia's annexation and South Africa's racially restricted franchise exclude them from this category.

13 New Zealand representation consists of the High Commissioner, Deputy High Commissioner, First Secretary, Second Secretary (Administration) and a Senior Stenographer.

References

Alley, R.(1975) Introduction. In *New Zealand Foreign Policy: Occasional Papers 1973-74* Wellington, New Zealand Institute of International Affairs.

Calvocoressi, P. (1985) *Independent Africa and the World* London, Longman.

Caygill, D. (1984) Press Statement, 24 December, *Department of Trade and Industry*.

Goldsworthy, D. (1985) The Hawke Government and Africa: Hands Across the Ocean. *Australian Outlook* 39: 139-146.

Henderson, J., Jackson, W.K. and Kennaway, R. (1980) *Beyond New Zealand: the Foreign Policy of a Small State* Auckland, Methuen.

Hoadley, J.S.(1980) New Zealand, Small States and Foreign Aid. In Henderson, J, et al. *Beyond New Zealand: The Foreign Policy of a Small State* Auckland, Methuen.

Holland, M. (1985) The European Community and South Africa: Economic Reality or Political Rhetoric? *Political Studies* 33: 399-417.

Holland, M. (1986a) The Sanctions Dilemma: What Can Governments Really Do About South Africa? *New Zealand International Review* 9-2: 2-5.

Holland, M. (1986b) The African Initiative. *New Zealand International Review* 9-4: 7-11.

Jackson, W.K. (1980) New Zealand Foreign Service. In Henderson, J. et al. *Beyond New Zealand: the Foreign Policy of a Small State* Auckland, Methuen.

Kirk, N. (1973) New Zealand: a New Foreign Policy. *New Zealand Foreign Affairs Review* 23-6: 3-17.

Laidlaw, C. (1986) Stepping Across the Last Great Frontier. *New Zealand International Review* 9-2: 6-9.

Lange, D. (1984) Trade and Foreign Policy: a Labour Perspective. *New Zealand International Review* 9-4: 2-4.

Ministry of Foreign Affairs (1984) *Briefing Papers* Wellington, Government Printer.

Ministry of Foreign Affairs (1985) Strengthening Bonds. *New Zealand Foreign Affairs Review* 35-2: 3-9.

Sorrenson, M.P.K (1976) Uneasy Bedfellows: a Survey of New Zealand's Relations with South Africa. In *New Zealand, South Africa and Sport: Background Papers* Wellington, New Zealand Institute of International Affairs.

The Commonwealth Group of Eminent Persons (1986) *Mission to South Africa: the Commonwealth Report* Harmondsworth, Penguin/Commonwealth Secretariat.

Trainor, L. (1979) Has Gleneagles Worked? *New Zealand International Review* 4-4: 2-4.

Watson, R. (1985) Lange in Africa: the Media's Message. *New Zealand International Review* 10-4: 15-16.

Appendix I

Chronology of Family Income Support Measures 1982-86

1982 Introduction of new income tax scales (together with "temporary" ten per cent surcharge on the higher rates). These had little impact on the total tax paid by lower income families, but had the effect of reducing the difference in tax paid by one and two income families with equal aggregate income.

Amalgamation of the spouse, low income and young family rebates into the family rebate. This abated against *family* income in excess of NZ$9800 at 15 cents in the dollar, had a maximum value of NZ$1404, and was independent of the number of children (in excess of one) in the family. St John (1983) notes, however, that because recipients of the family rebate were excluded from receiving the principal income earners rebate, also introduced in 1982, the effective maximum value of the family rebate was only NZ$1092.

1983 Family rebate increased to NZ$1924 (NZ$1404 after excluding the Principal Income Earner Rebate) and the abatement rate increased to 20 cents in the dollar for income in excess of NZ$14000. Tax rate on incomes between NZ$6000 and NZ$24000 increased from 31 per cent to 31.5 per cent.

1984 Introduction of Family Care, a benefit of NZ$10 per child per week paid through the Social Welfare Department to families with one or more children eligible for the Family Benefit. The benefit abated at 25 cents in the dollar for family income in excess of NZ$20470. The definition of income employed was wider than that used in assessing eligibility for tax rebates. Social Welfare beneficiaries were excluded from Family Care, but were given an extra NZ$2 per week per child, in addition to the NZ$6 per week per child supplement they had received previously.

Additional assistance was made available to families with particularly low incomes to bring total earnings, plus family care, up to a minimum of NZ$180 per week. Increase in the marginal tax rate payable on incomes between NZ$6000 and NZ$25000 from 31.5 per cent to 33 per cent.

1986 Replacement of Family Rebate and Family Care with Family Support, a tax credit (distinct from rebates in that families with a negative tax liability will receive refund payments from the Inland Revenue Department) of NZ$36 per week for the first dependent child and NZ$16 per additional child. The credit abates at 18 cents in the dollar for family income in excess of NZ$14000. Payment is to be divided equally between parents. (Family Care was paid to the parent receiving the Family Benefit, and the Family Rebate to the principal income earner.)

Introduction of a guaranteed minimum family income. Full time earners with one child will have their weekly income topped up to NZ$250, inclusive of the Family Benefit and Family Support, plus NZ$22 per week for each additional child.

Family Support will be paid to all beneficiaries with children and replace child supplements. Beneficiaries with children will be subject to a modified income test, whereby they can earn up to NZ$60 per week before their benefit begins to reduce. As a major move toward better integration of the tax and benefit systems, all basic income-tested benefits which are not already taxable will become taxable.

Appendix II
Chronology of Events

Section A: Economic Events

1984

July 14   Labour wins snap election, and forms new Government.

July 15   Reserve Bank closes the Foreign Exchange Market for the NZ$ (as a result of a strong outflow of foreign exchange in the previous four weeks).

July 18   NZ$ devalued 20 per cent. All controls on interest rates revoked; prices, and professional fees and services frozen for three months.

August 15   Reserve Bank begins selling, trading and discounting of Government securities.

August 17   Douglas announces that total public debt has risen by NZ$5.2 billion during the period 1 April to 17 July 1984.

August 31   Government withdraws the one per cent monthly lending growth restriction as applied to financial institutions since 1983.

September 12 Three-day Economic Summit Conference opens.

September 13 Stan Rodger, Minister of Labour, announces new wage fixing procedures, and states that a new wage round will commence in November 1984.

October 4   Government rejects Federation of Labour claim for an immediate NZ$15 a week wage increase.

October 9   Lange announces that the original expiry date of the price freeze on 18 October will be extended to Budget day on 8 November 1984.

October 17   Lange announces that 1984/85 wage round will start on 1 December 1984 and finish on 1 March 1985, with tripartite discussions to begin immediately.

November 8 The fourth Labour Government's first Budget is presented to Parliament. It includes a surcharge on income earned by some National Superannuitants, and raises the price of petrol, fertilizer, irrigation, liquor, cigarettes, electricity, milk, road-user charges, motor vehicle licensing and prescription charges. In addition, a new family assistance programme – Family Care – is introduced, and major tax changes are announced.

December 6   Metal Trades and General Drivers Awards settle with wage increases of about 6.5 per cent.

December 21 The Minister of Finance announces that the liquidity management practices conducted by the Reserve Bank will be focused primarily on short-term financial flows.

1985

February 14 Government removes ratios requiring institutions to invest in Government and other public sector securities.

March 4   NZ$ floated.

March 5   Trading Banks forced to put up wholesale call rates to between 300 and 400 per cent to cover the large money outflow in the week before the dollar float.

March 6   Government abolishes limits on foreign ownership in New Zealand financial institutions, advertising agencies and fish processors.

March 12	Reserve Bank announces a new interest rate on Trading Bank compensatory depositions at 19.5 per cent, and the cancellation of the Government Stock Tender due to be released on 21 March.
March 13	Reserve Bank stabilizes short-term money market by buying NZ$250 million of short-term securities.
March 26	Government White Paper on new indirect taxation (GST) to be introduced on 1 April 1985 tabled in Parliament.
April 2	Mike Moore, Minister of Trade and Industry, announces that the allocation of licensed imports for 1985/86 has been set at 100 per cent of 1984/85 licences.
June 3	*The Economist* (London) praises the New Zealand Government for its "intelligent free market policies in socialist clothing".
June 13	1985 Budget presented in Parliament. Main features include a forecast Budget deficit of NZ$1.3 billion (or 2.8 per cent of Gross Domestic Product) and an increase in education spending.
June 17	Government defers the introduction of GST for six months from 1 April 1986 to 1 October 1986.
June 19	Registered unemployment drops 32.5 per cent over the previous 12 months.
June 23	The Labour Government receives strong international endorsement for its economic policies from the Organization for Economic Co-operation and Development.
June 26	Government announces a NZ$2.7 billion deficit on its overseas trade and financial transactions in the year to 31 March 1985.
August 20	Government delivers its statement on Taxation and Benefit reforms which include big cuts in personal income tax rates, a new Family Support scheme and a slight rise in company taxation to accompany the ten per cent GST package from 1 October 1986.
August 26	Government boosts the minimum adult wage by NZ$70 a week to NZ$170 affecting the bottom rates in a handful of awards.
August 31	The Reserve Bank denies that it has lost control of the growth in the money and credit markets.
September 3	The Combined State Unions accept a Government pay and conditions package including an interim eight per cent pay increase.
September 6	Higher Salaries Commission announces huge pay increases for Members of Parliament, senior public servants and academics.
September 10	The Minister of Trade and Industry, David Caygill, announces a two-stage reduction in tariffs.
September 18	The Government threatens to use the *Economic Stabilization Act* should the 1985/86 wage round be too high.
September 27	Trend-setting Electrical Contractors Award settled giving increases in basic award rates of 15.5 per cent. This becomes the "going rate" in subsequent settlements.
November 3	The Minister of Finance forecasts a "rough landing" for the New Zealand economy, including business failures and rising unemployment.
November 10	Government announces the removal of restrictions on the number of banks operating in New Zealand.

1986

January 22	The Reserve Bank announces it will review procedures for Government Stock tenders to prevent further defaults.
February 1	The Government launches a major programme to restructure its overseas debt.

February 3	The economy contracted by 0.3 per cent in the September quarter, according to the Statistics Department.
February 8	The size of the Government's February stock tender is set at NZ$400 million. The Government discloses a Budget deficit of NZ$3.6 billion for the first three-quarters of the 1985/86 financial year.
February 15	The Government sets up a committee of four senior Ministers to examine public sector expenditure cuts to hold down the Budget deficit.
March 17	New Zealand's total overseas debt rises to NZ$24.75 billion.
March 27	Government announces a new programme to cut public spending.
April 2	The Minister of Finance announces that the Government will hold three NZ$500 million tenders during the June quarter.
April 23	Government announces the 1985/86 Budget deficit figure of NZ$1.87 billion, NZ$500 million higher than expected.
April 30	Tripartite talks begin on 1986/87 wage round.
May 7	Lange calls for radical reform of the industrial relations system. Federation of Labour Conference votes in favour of an incomes accord for 1986/87 wage round.
May 19	Government announces expenditure reform plans.
May 31	The Minister of Trade and Industry announces the lifting of controls on the production and packaging of milk.
June 12	New Zealand's terms of trade slump to a ten-year low.
July 2	Government announces long awaited farm assistance package.
July 16	Government sets up a new Economic Development Commission to give advice to the Government on the costs and benefits of various policy options.
July 18	New Zealand's balance of payments deficit on current account reaches a record in the year to March 1986 of NZ$2.87 billion.
July 26	Douglas announces cuts in Government spending of NZ$1574 million for the 1986/87 financial year.
July 31	The Minister of Finance presents the 1986 Budget. Included are: price increases on cigarettes and cars; a decrease in the superannuitants surtax and petrol prices; tax loopholes to be plugged; Government to take over NZ$7.2 billion of "Think Big" and Producer Board debts.

Section B: Tax Changes

1984

November 8   The Minister of Finance presents his Budget for the 1984/85 financial year. The main tax reforms are:

(a) a comprehensive Goods and Services Tax (GST), accompanied by reform of existing indirect taxes (including the wholesale sales tax, which would be retained in a reduced form on a limited range of goods) and compensatory changes to the personal income tax and social welfare systems, to be introduced from 1 April 1986. It is also announced that the tax would be administered by the Inland Revenue Department and that the Government would release a White Paper early in 1985 containing proposals for the administration of GST and inviting public submissions;

(b) a fringe benefit tax on employer-provided cars, low-interest loans and free, subsidized or discounted goods and services, to be implemented from 1 April

1985, and payable quarterly by the employer at a flat rate of 45 per cent. (The revenue yield of the fringe benefit tax was forecast in the 1985 Budget to be NZ$200 million for the 1985/86 financial year, covering the first three-quarters collections from the tax, though the out-turn fell far short of the original forecast.);

(c) the personal tax exemption for life insurance premiums and superannuation contributions is abolished from Budget night for new life insurance contracts, personal lump sum superannuation and non-subsidized employee lump sum superannuation. In addition, a review of all aspects of the taxation of life insurance, superannuation and related areas is announced;

(d) the income tax rebate (maximum value of NZ$1,000 per annum for five years) for interest payments on first-home mortgages is removed for houses purchased after Budget night and the rebate of up to NZ$25 per annum for local body rates is terminated with effect from the income year commencing 1 April 1985;

(e) a surcharge on the taxable "other income" of each national superannuitant in excess of NZ$5200 per annum at the rate of 25 cents per dollar of this excess with the maximum surcharge equal to the national superannuation payment, is to be effective from the income year commencing 1 April 1985;

(f) the maximum value of the principal income earner rebate is increased from NZ$312 to NZ$520 per annum as part of the "low-income assistance package" (the major component of which is the Family Care programme) and the standard marginal tax rate on personal income is increased from 31.5 to 33 per cent across a slightly expanded income bracket to help reduce the overall cost of the reforms. Both measures take effect from 1 December 1984;

(g) wholesale sales tax rates on a variety of goods – e.g. computer equipment, records, recorded tapes, blank magnetic tapes, cosmetics, caravans and boats – are reduced (to either ten or 20 per cent);

(h) taxes on beer, wine and spirits are increased, in part as a move towards a more uniform approach to the taxation of alcoholic beverages.

December 6   Budget 1985 Task Force established – comprising Treasury, Department of Social Welfare and Inland Revenue Department officials – with the aim of facilitating preparation for personal income tax and social security benefit reforms in the light of GST.

December 18   Draft legislation to implement the fringe benefit tax is introduced and referred to the Commerce and Energy Select Committee. (Submissions were sought, and 312 received by 1 February 1985. The Select Committee reported back to the House with recommended amendments to the original draft legislation on 15 March 1985.)

1985

February 14   The Minister of Finance announces an increase in the exemption level of taxable "other-income" for the national superannuitant surcharge, in the case of single superannuitants, from NZ$5200 to NZ$6240 per annum. He also announces that married superannuitants would be able to split their other income up to a combined total of $10,400 per annum for the purpose of the surcharge with both changes to take effect from 1 April 1985.

March 18   The Ministers of Finance and Social Welfare release a Budget 85 Task Force document on the personal income tax and social security benefit systems and invite public submissions by 31 May 1985 relating to the reform of these systems.

March 23	The fringe benefit tax is enacted with effect from 1 April 1985.
March 26	White paper on GST, incorporating draft legislation, released by the Minister of Finance inviting public submissions by 17 May 1985. (These were later considered by an Advisory Panel.)
June 4	The GST Advisory Panel, after receiving 1459 submissions, present their first report suggesting, *inter alia*, a number of simplifications to the tax. Many of these recommendations are accepted by the Minister of Finance. Apart from the Panel's discussion of transitional issues (which were of a sensitive nature), the report – with the Minister's decisions incorporated – is released on 21 June. The GST treatment of financial services, land and residential accommodation is left aside for a second report.
June 6	The Minister of Finance releases proposals for the treatment of financial services under GST and invites public submissions to the Advisory Panel by 20 June. (This was later extended to 27 June.)
June 13	The Minister of Finance presents his Budget for the 1985/86 financial year. Given the intention to table a "tax and benefit Budget" later in 1985, few tax measures are announced. Those that are include: (a) an increase from 1 April 1986 in the exempt levels of taxable "other income" of national superannuitants to NZ\$12,000 per annum for married couples and NZ\$7200 per annum for single persons; (b) a reduction in sales tax on cash registers from 40 to ten per cent from Budget night, to assist businesses preparing for the introduction of GST.
June 15	In light of changes to GST agreed as a result of the first Advisory Panel report, and the need to allow adequate time for reference of the GST Bill to a select committee, the Deputy Prime Minister and Minister of Finance announce a delay in the introduction of GST from 1 April 1986 to 1 October 1986.
August 20	The Minister of Finance presents his Statement of Taxation and Benefit Reform. This announces: (a) GST rate to be a uniform ten per cent with an estimated one-off impact on the Consumer Price Index of no more than five per cent after allowing for remission of certain existing indirect taxes; (b) a review of remaining indirect taxes; (c) transitional measures relating to GST on long-term contracts. (d) an increase in the company and fringe benefit tax rates from 45 to 48 per cent from the income year commencing 1 April 1986, to coincide from 1 October 1986 with the new top marginal income tax rate; (e) the Government's intention to introduce a full imputation system for taxation of distributed company income from the 1988/89 financial year; (f) the taxation from 21 August 1985 of income derived from overseas by New Zealand companies by way of dividends on redeemable preference shares or interest on convertible notes where the related payment is deductible to the offshore firm; (g) the Government's intention to introduce an intermediate withholding tax on domestic interest payments from 1 April 1987; (h) a new three-rate personal income tax scale, featuring a reduction in the top rate from 66 to 48 per cent, and a transitional tax allowance for low-income full-time earners without children, to take effect from 1 October 1986, along with abolition of the principal income earner rebate;

(i) a new package of family assistance (Family Support) available to low- and middle-income families, including income earners, income-tested beneficiaries and national superannuitants. Where practical, Family Support will be delivered through the personal income tax system, allowing for tax credits if entitlement to assistance exceeds income tax liability. In addition, a guaranteed minimum family income of NZ$250 per week (including family benefit) for full-time earners with one dependent child, augmented on this basis by NZ$22 per week for each additional child, will form part of the new family assistance programme. These measures will become effective from 1 October 1986; and (j) all income-tested benefits not already taxed to become taxable on an end-of-year basis from 1 October 1986.

August 22   The Minister of Finance releases the second report of the GST Advisory Panel along with reports by the Treasury, concerning the application of GST to financial services, residential accommodation and property.

The GST Bill is also introduced into the House of Representatives and referred to the Finance and Expenditure Select Committee. Submissions are sought. Few exceptions are proposed to a very comprehensive consumption expenditure base.

December   GST legislation passed.
1986
October 1   GST introduced.

Section C: Foreign Affairs and Defence

1984
July 16   Lange meets United States Secretary of State, George Shultz, in Wellington.
July 20   Lange states that no South African sports team will play in New Zealand.
August 1   South African Consulate closes.
September 25   Sir Wallace Rowling appointed Ambassador to the United States.
October 18   The Police Association urges the Rugby Union to consider the political and social costs of any All Black tour to South Africa.

1985
January 29   The Government suggests a new proposal about the type of ship acceptable for New Zealand port visits.

January 30   Lange and the United States Ambassador to New Zealand, H. Monroe Browne, announce they are confident of solving the nuclear ships issue.

February 1   Lange replies to a United States request for a port visit, announcing that nuclear-capable vessels are not acceptable.

February 6   The United States Secretary of Defence, Casper Weinberger, and a senior State Department official threaten unspecified retaliation against New Zealand for refusing to accept a visit by a nuclear capable naval vessel.

February 8   The United States cancels a New Zealand Parliament defence select committee visit to the United States military headquarters in Hawaii.

February 27   At a meeting between Lange and the United States Deputy Assistant Secretary of State, William Brown, the United States announces it will drastically reduce its co-operation with New Zealand in intelligence sharing and defence fields.

February 28   The Deputy Prime Minister, Geoffrey Palmer, claims the United States no longer trusts New Zealand, because of the banning of United States nuclear ship visits to New Zealand ports.

March 3   Both Lange and Political Scientist, Dr Rod Alley, claim that the American Embassy is working to oust the New Zealand Government.

March 9   Lange assures Malaysia that New Zealand remains committed to regional security under the Five-Power-Defence Arrangement established in 1971.

March 19   New Zealand's ban on nuclear warships goes before the United States House of Representatives Foreign Affairs sub-committee on Asia and the Pacific.

March 28   Parliament opposes the New Zealand Rugby Union's proposed tour to South Africa.

April 18   The New Zealand Rugby Union approves the tour to South Africa.

             Hu-Yaobang, General Secretary of the Communist Party of China, visits New Zealand.

May 11   Palmer announces that French nuclear tests in the Pacific are unacceptable to the New Zealand Government and should cease.

May 23   The President of Ireland, Dr Patrick Hillery, visits New Zealand.

July 10   The Greenpeace protest ship, *Rainbow Warrior*, sinks after bomb blast.

July 11   The Minister of Defence, Frank O'Flynn, meets for talks with the United States Secretary of State, George Shultz.

July 13   The High Court issues an interim injunction stopping the rugby tour to South Africa.

July 15   The Rugby Union officially cancels the South African tour.

July 16   At the opening of talks with Australian Ministers, the United States Secretary of State accuses New Zealand of opting out of responsibilities essential to peace and security of the West.

August 5   Palmer outlines three scenarios for the New Zealand - United States nuclear ship issue: "The standoff can continue; there can be some resolution of the difficulties, or there will be a further deterioration in our relations".

August 7   The New Zealand Government signs the South Pacific Nuclear Free Zone Treaty with seven other South Pacific nations.

August 19   Lange says New Zealand will sue the French Government if their involvement in the *Rainbow Warrior* incident is proven.

August 28   In response to the Tricot Report, Lange says New Zealand would be restrained in taking any actions due to trade considerations and that the Tricot report was "too transparent to be a white-wash".

September 1 Lange announces that during Palmer's visit to Washington a suggestion will be made to the United States to send another warship to New Zealand.

September 5 The Minister of Defence announces the withdrawal of New Zealand forces from the multi-national force and observers in the Sinai.

September 6 New Zealand and Oman establish formal diplomatic relations at ambassadorial level.

September 13 The New Zealand Ambassador to Washington, Sir Wallace Rowling, announces that the misunderstandings between the United States and New Zealand over the nuclear ship ban are now over.

September 16 First state visit to New Zealand by an Arab Head of State, the Amir of Bahrain.

September 17 Lange discounts reports from Washington that New Zealand has dropped the judicial review provision from its proposed anti-nuclear Bill.

             In a speech to the National Press Club in Ottawa, Palmer asserts that the New

Zealand Government could not modify or abandon its anti-nuclear policies and survive politically.

September 19 The Kenyan Minister of Energy, K.N.K. Bivott, arrives in New Zealand for a five-day visit.

September 23 The French Prime Minister, Laurent Fabius, announces that they are "truly sorry" for the effect that the *Rainbow Warrior* affair has had on relations between New Zealand and France. He admits that French agents sank the ship acting on orders, and that this fact was hidden from Tricot investigations. As a result of the *Rainbow Warrior* affair, Lange says New Zealand compensation claims will run into millions of dollars.

September 24 Lange announces that British naval vessels would be welcome in New Zealand provided they were not nuclear armed or propelled.

Talks begin between New Zealand and France over the fate of the two French agents held in custody.

September 26 France agrees to compensate New Zealand for the bombing of the *Rainbow Warrior*.

September 27 Lange states that ANZUS may have to be scrapped.

October 1 The United States Ambassador to New Zealand, H. Monroe Browne, claims that the Reagan Administration felt "kicked in the teeth" by New Zealand's ban on nuclear warships.

October 7 The French Government cancels Palmer's visit to Paris to talk with French officials.

October 9 United States officials meet Lange to discuss ANZUS and the effect of New Zealand's nuclear ship ban.

October 10 A group of retired senior military personnel (the "geriatric generals") make public statements criticizing the Government's anti-nuclear policy.

October 13 Palmer claims that New Zealand's high non-nuclear profile overseas will benefit trade.

October 16 Palmer will neither confirm nor deny that New Zealand has equipment designed to detect the presence of nuclear weapons.

October 25 Lange addresses the United Nations General Assembly.

October 29 New Zealand establishes diplomatic relations at ambassadorial level with Algeria.

November 1 Retiring United States Ambassador to New Zealand, H. Monroe Browne, claims that shortly after the snap election in July 1984 Lange gave assurances that nuclear warships would be allowed into New Zealand ports.

November 6 Lange acknowledges French officials had raised the prospect of an early release of the agents from jail in New Zealand, although he says they were "not for sale".

November 8 Lange announces that compensation negotiations with France would resume after the *Rainbow Warrior* case had been dealt with by the Courts.

November 13 The New Zealand Government bans the import of gold Krugerrands from South Africa.

November 22 The two French agents, Mafart and Prieur, are each sentenced to ten years for their part in the *Rainbow Warrior* bombing.

December 2 The Nicaraguan Minister of Foreign Affairs, Revd Miguel D'Escoto, arrives in New Zealand on a goodwill visit.

December 4 Palmer has talks with Australian Government officials on New Zealand's anti-nuclear legislation.

December 5   Lange announces the appointment of the Defence Committee of Enquiry.
December 6   At a press conference in Canberra, Palmer claims that New Zealand's anti-nuclear legislation was watered down due to American pressure.
December 10   Anti-nuclear legislation introduced into New Zealand Parliament.
December 20   The Government's Green Paper *The Defence Question* is published.

1986

January 15   The new United States Ambassador to New Zealand, Paul Cleveland, arrives.
January 30   Talks between French and New Zealand officials over compensation for the *Rainbow Warrior* bombing reach a stalemate.
February 20   The French Government puts a partial ban on New Zealand's NZ$8.5 million lamb brain exports.
April 5   Lange makes representation to the former Canadian Prime Minister, Pierre Trudeau, to help mediate the dispute between France and New Zealand.
April 11   In an interview on Australian television, Lange suggests New Zealand could be prepared to deport the two agents to one of France's overseas territories.
April 14   Lange discounts reports of the release of the two French agents before the French Presidential election in March 1988.
May 5   Lange states there is no possibility of a marine enquiry into the sinking of the *Rainbow Warrior*.
June 1   The Dutch Prime Minister, Jan Lubbers, offers a mediation proposal to Lange and the new French Prime Minister, Jacques Chirac.
June 6   Lange announces that New Zealand would not enter into any arbitration of the *Rainbow Warrior* dispute by a third party until France lifts all sanctions on New Zealand imports.
June 19   The New Zealand and French Governments agree to take the *Rainbow Warrior* dispute to the United Nations Secretary-General, Javier Perez de Cuellar, for arbitration.
June 26   Lange meets with the United States Secretary of State, Shultz, for further talks over New Zealand's ban on nuclear ships.
June 27   Lange announces that the United States has withdrawn its security pledge to New Zealand.
July 3   Lange says the nuclear ship row is finally over.
July 7   The United Nations Secretary General announces that the two French agents will be transferred to the French Military base on Hao Island, where they will remain for three years. France will also pay New Zealand US$7 million in compensation.
July 11   The two French agents leave New Zealand.
August 1   The report of the Defence Committee of Enquiry is submitted to the Prime Minister.
August 4   Lange asks Defence Committee of Enquiry to clarify sections of the report.
August 21   The original report of the Defence Committee of Enquiry, the Prime Minister's questions and the Committee's responses are published.

Contributors

Dr **Roderic Alley** is a Senior Lecturer in Political Science at Victoria University and Chairman of the Research and Publications Committee of the New Zealand Institute of International Affairs. His most recent publications are *New Zealand and the Pacific* (Ed.) (1984), and The Emergence of Party Politics, in B. Lal (Ed.) *Politics in Fiji* (1986). Dr Alley's area of expertise covers international politics and the Pacific, arms control and disarmament, and politics in New Zealand and the Pacific.

Dr **Jonathan Boston** is a Lecturer in Political Science at the University of Canterbury. Prior to this he was an Investigating Officer with the New Zealand Treasury and a Research Fellow at the Institute of Policy Studies at Victoria University. His main research interests lie in the fields of public policy and political economy and recent publications include *Incomes Policy in New Zealand* (1984) and articles in *Political Science* and the *New Zealand Journal of Industrial Relations*.

Dr **Kevin Clements** is a Senior Lecturer in Sociology at the University of Canterbury and served on the 1985/86 Defence Committee of Enquiry. He was also Deputy Chairperson of the International Year of Peace Committee, and a consultant to the UNESCO Advisory Committee on Communications. Dr Clements' most recent publications include (with F. Corner, D. Hunt and B. Poananga) *Defence and Security: What New Zealanders Want* (1986); The Quest for Peace: Review of the NPT Review Conference *New Zealand International Review* (1986); and New Zealand's Relations with the UK, the US and the Pacific, *Alternatives: A Journal of World Policy* (1986).

Brian Easton until recently was the Director of the Institute of Economic Research. His most significant publications include *Social Policy and the Welfare State in New Zealand* (1980); *Income Distribution in New Zealand* (1983); and *Wages and the Poor* (1986).

Dr **Jerome Elkind** is a Senior Lecturer in Law at the University of Auckland. He is the author of several books and many articles on aspects of international and constitutional law, his latest book being *A Standard for Justice: A Critical Commentary on the Proposed Bill of Rights* (1986).

Dr **Robert Gregory** is a Senior Lecturer in the School of Political Science and Public Administration at Victoria University, specializing in public policy and public administration. His most recent publications include *Politics and Broadcasting: Before and Beyond the NZBC* (1985); *The Official Information Act: A Beginning* (Ed.) (1984); and Understanding Public Bureaucracy *Public Sector* (1982).

Dr **Martin Holland** is a Senior Lecturer in Political Science at the University of Canterbury and a Jean Monnet Visiting Fellow at the European University Institute for 1987. His research interests include political recruitment, South Africa and the European Economic Community. His most recent publications include *An Introduction to the European Community* (1983), *Candidates for Europe* (1986) and articles in *The British Journal of Political Science*, *Political Studies*, *The World Today* and the *New Zealand International Review*.

John Roberts is Professor of Public Administration at Victoria University, specializing in the structure and process of New Zealand Government Administration. He has contributed chapters to *Right Out* (1972) and *Promise and Performance* (1975) and written various articles and reviews in *Public Sector* and the *New Zealand Journal of Public Administration*.

Nigel Roberts is the Director of Continuing Education at Victoria University. His research interests include political sociology and comparative politics. He is the author of *New Zealand and Nuclear Testing in the Pacific* (1972), *Election '78* (1978) (with McRobie) and *Political Tolerance in Context* (1985) (with Sullivan, Shamir and Walsh).

Dr **Claudia Scott** is a Reader in Economics at Victoria University, leader of the Indirect Tax Project at the Institute of Policy Studies and chairperson of the Ministerial Review of Health Benefits. She has researched widely in the areas of public finance, public policy and social policy. Among her most recent publications are: *Inside G.S.T.* (1986) (with Teixeira and Devlin); *Choices for Health Care* (1986) (with Fougere and Marwick); *The Gist of G.S.T.* (1985) (with Davis); and *The Family and Government Policy in New Zealand* (1984) (with Koopman-Boyden).

Geoffrey Skene was awarded an Australian Parliament Political Science Fellowship for 1984-85 and is currently a Ph.D. student at the Australian National University working on legislative behaviour. He has recently had articles published in *Public Sector* (1985), *The Australian Journal of Public Administration* (1985) and contributed to *New Zealand Politics in Perspective* (1985).

Dr **Jack Vowles** is a Lecturer in the Department of Political Studies at Auckland University. His main research interests are New Zealand politics, public policy and socialist thought. His recent publications include: Delegates Compared: A Sociology of the National, Labour and Social Credit Conferences 1983 *Political Science* (1985); Business and Labour: Major Organized Interests in the Political Economy of New Zealand, in *New Zealand Politics in Perspective* (1985); and Ideology and the Formation of the NZLP *New Zealand Journal of History* (1982).

Index